THE WITCHCRAFT
SOURCEBOOK

This collection of documents illustrates the development of ideas about witchcraft from ancient times to the twentieth century. Most of the sources come from the period between 1400 and 1750, when more than 100,000 people – mainly women – were prosecuted for witchcraft in Europe and colonial America. During these years the prominent stereotype of the witch as an evil magician and servant of Satan emerged. Catholics and Protestants alike feared that the Devil and his human confederates were destroying Christian society.

The sources include trial records, demonological treatises and sermons, literary texts, narratives of demonic possession, and artistic depiction of witches. The documents reveal how contemporaries from various periods have perceived alleged witches and their activities. Brian Levack shows how notions of witchcraft changed over time. He looks at the connection between gender and witchcraft and the nature of the witch's perceived power.

This anthology provides students of the history of witchcraft with a broad range of sources, many of which have been translated into English for the first time, with commentary and background by one of the leading scholars in the field.

Brian P. Levack is the John Green Regents Professor of History at the University of Texas, Austin. His publications on the history of witchcraft include *The Witch-Hunt in Early Modern Europe* (1995) and *Witchcraft and Magic in Europe: The eighteenth and nineteenth centuries* (1999).

THE WITCHCRAFT SOURCEBOOK

Edited by
Brian P. Levack

Routledge
Taylor & Francis Group

NEW YORK AND LONDON

First published 2004 in the USA and Canada
by Routledge
711 Third Avenue, New York, NY 10017

Simultaneously published in London
by Routledge
2 Park Square, Milton Park, Abingdon, Oxon OX14 4RN

Routledge is an imprint of the Taylor & Francis Group, an informa business

Selection and editorial matter © 2004 Brian Levack; individual
chapters and extracts © the original copyright holders

Typeset in Garamond and Helvetica by
Florence Production Ltd, Stoodleigh, Devon

Printed and bound in Great Britain by
CPI Antony Rowe, Chippenham, Wiltshire

Library of Congress Cataloging in Publication Data
Levack, Brian P.
The witchcraft sourcebook/Brian Levack.
p. cm.
Includes bibliographical references and index.
1. Witchcraft – History – Sources.
2. Magic – History – Sources.   I. Title.
BF1566.L475 2003
133.4′3′09–dc21   2003008535

British Library Cataloguing in Publication Data
A catalogue record for this book is available from the British Library

ISBN 10: 0–415–19505–5 (hbk)
ISBN 10: 0–415–19506–3 (pbk)
ISBN 13: 978–0–415–19505–8 (hbk)
ISBN 13: 978–0–415–19506–5 (pbk)

CONTENTS

ILLUSTRATIONS

PREFACE

I have compiled this sourcebook to make available a wide selection of primary source documents regarding the history of European witchcraft, especially during the period when thousands of individuals were prosecuted for witchcraft in secular and ecclesiastical courts. I have included a variety of literary and legal sources, but the large majority of them are treatises about witchcraft and records of witchcraft trials. A close relationship existed between those two types of sources: the treatises were often intended to promote or discourage the prosecution of witches, and they often cited legal cases to support their arguments.

Most of the documents run between 750 and 3,500 words in length. I have observed the lower limit to prevent the authors' views from being misrepresented by isolated quotations. I have observed the upper limit to allow for the inclusion of a sufficiently large number of documents in the volume. Even selections of more than 3,000 words, however, can fail to capture the essence of the author's views. I have tried to minimize this risk by reproducing what are in my opinion the most significant and representative passages of these texts, as well as those most commonly cited by contemporaries.

In editing documents that appeared originally in English, I have modernized spelling, capitalization, and punctuation. I have translated most foreign words and phrases or included the translation in brackets. I have also used brackets to identify unfamiliar terms and to add words that make the original text more comprehensible. In most cases I have omitted marginal notes or footnotes that appeared in the original texts, and in the few cases where I have included them, they appear within parentheses.

In compiling this sourcebook I have benefited from the generosity of many scholars. Valerie Kivelson supplied me with the entire translated text of the trial at Lukh, Muscovy, in 1652. Robin Briggs made available to me his transcript of the trial of Françatte Camont in Lorraine in 1598. Gustav Henningsen provided me with the transcript of Alonso de Salazar Frias's

Second Report in advance of its publication. Stuart Clark advised me regarding the selection of particular documents. In translating texts from Latin, German, and French I received much valuable assistance from my colleagues Ernest Kaulbach, Leslie Holland, Susan Boettcher, Alison Frazier, and Julie Hardwick. All errors of translation that remain, however, are my sole responsibility.

Austin, Texas
2003

ACKNOWLEDGMENTS

The following documents are reprinted with permission: Chapters 2, 6, and 58 from Georg Luck (ed.), *Arcana Mundi: Magic and the Occult in the Greek and Roman Worlds: A Collection of Ancient Texts*, copyright 1985, reprinted with permission of the Johns Hopkins University Press; Chapter 10 from *The Sorcery Trial of Alice Kyteler*, edited by L. S. Davidson and J. O. Ward, Binghamton, NY, by permission of Pegasus Press, copyright 1993, Medieval and Renaissance Texts and Studies; Chapter 11 from Edward Peters, *The Magician, the Witch and the Law*, copyright 1978 by Edward Peters, reprinted with permission of the University of Pennsylvania Press; Chapter 18 from Martín Del Rio, *Investigations into Magic*, edited by P. G. Maxwell-Stuart, 2000, Manchester University Press, Manchester, UK; Chapter 26 from Jean Bodin, *On the Demon-Mania of Witches*, translated by Randy A. Scott, Center for Reformation and Renaissance Studies, Toronto, 2001; Chapter 29 from *Cautio Criminalis* by Friedrich Spee von Langenfeld, edited by Marcus Hellyer, Charlottesville, Va., 2003, reprinted with permission of the University of Virginia Press; Chapter 53 from Gustav Henningsen (ed.), *The Salazar Documents: Inquisitor Alonso de Salazar Frias and Others on the Basque Witch-Persecution* (1609–1614), reprinted with permission of Brill Academic Publishers; Chapters 44 and 51 from *Witches, Devils and Doctors in the Renaissance*, edited by George Mora, Binghamton, NY, 1991, reprinted with permission of Medieval and Renaissance Texts and Studies; Chapter 55 (*Works*), from *The Collected Works of Spinoza*, edited by Edwin Curley, Volume I, copyright 1985, by Princeton University Press, reprinted by permission of Princeton University Press; Chapter 55 (*Letters*) from *Spinoza, The Letters*, translated by Samuel Shirley, copyright 1995 by Hackett Publishing Company, reprinted by permission of Hackett Publishing Company, Inc. All Rights Reserved; Chapter 60 from *Three Jacobean Witchcraft Plays*, edited by Peter Corbin and Douglas Sedge, 2001, Manchester University Press, Manchester UK.

Every effort has been made to obtain permission to reproduce copyright material. If any proper acknowledgment has not been made, we would invite copyright holders to inform us of the oversight.

INTRODUCTION

The documents included in this collection describe European beliefs regarding witchcraft and record the trials of individuals for allegedly engaging in this activity. Most of the texts were written between 1400 and 1750, when European secular and ecclesiastical courts tried and executed tens of thousands of people for the crime of witchcraft. This collection also includes several texts that were written in ancient and medieval times. The witch beliefs and magical practices of those earlier chronological periods deserve to be studied in their own right, but in this collection they are included mainly because of their relevance to the later prosecutions. The only document written after 1750 is a twentieth-century drama regarding a case of witchcraft that took place in the late sixteenth century.

The sources in this volume include biblical and classical literary texts, treatises by theologians and lawyers, manuals for inquisitors, trial records, sermons, narratives of cases of demonic possession, laws regarding the practice of magic and witchcraft, and dramas about witches. All these texts are primary sources in the sense that they are original documents, not accounts or interpretations written by modern scholars. The great majority of the documents reflect the views and the prejudices of ruling or educated elites; only the trial records allow the voices of illiterate villagers to be heard.

Even the trials do not always provide an accurate account of what uneducated villagers believed and what activities they engaged in. Many confessions of witches were made under torture or the threat of torture, and therefore they provide a better indication of what judges and inquisitors wanted the accused to say than what the accused had actually done. Only when the witches denied the charges against them at the beginning of a trial, such as Françatte Camont in Lorraine (Chapter 36) or Bridget Bishop at Salem (Chapter 43), can we have confidence that the voices we hear are those of the accused. The depositions of witnesses may be considered superior sources in that they at least give a better sense of how the witch was viewed by her neighbors, but even that testimony could be manipulated by court officials who recorded the depositions. Some witnesses, moreover, were themselves subjected to torture. As a record of popular beliefs and practices, therefore, these legal records have serious limitations and must be treated with appropriate caution.

Definitions of witchcraft

The English word "witchcraft," which is used to describe the subject of these texts, has been assigned many meanings and is the subject of endless scholarly debate. In the most general sense a witch is a person who possesses a supernatural, occult, or mysterious power to cause misfortune or injury to others. This definition has broad application, including evil figures like Medea depicted in classical literature as well as the targets of witch-hunts in many African societies today. Witches defined in this broad sense generally share a number of characteristics, including isolation from the community, an envious or malicious personality, and the inheritance or acquisition of power from another witch. This definition includes both men and women, even though the stereotype of the witch in most societies is female, and most of those individuals who have been identified as witches have been women. The definition excludes only those persons who were considered by contemporaries to be beneficent or "white" witches. It also excludes self-proclaimed witches or neo-pagans in contemporary Western societies, who insist that their powers are used only for religious and beneficent purposes.

During the early modern period of European history the words "witch" and "witchcraft" acquired more precise definition. The witch became a person who exercised maleficent magical power by virtue of having made a pact with the Devil. This definition was embellished in various ways so that witches in many European countries came to be viewed, as least among those who were educated, as people who worshipped the Devil collectively in nocturnal assemblies, where they sacrificed and ate infants, engaged in promiscuous sex, and mocked the rituals of Christianity. Witches were believed to be members of a new and dangerous sect of heretics who used magic to destroy human and animal life and who threatened the entire moral order. Defined in this way, witchcraft became the most serious crime imaginable, combining assorted felonies, such as murder and the destruction of property, with the spiritual crimes of heresy and fornication. Only a definition of the crime in this full sense was capable of inspiring the determined, sometimes frenzied campaigns to identify, prosecute, and execute witches that took place throughout Europe during the early modern period, especially between 1580 and 1630.

Not all Europeans accepted the stereotype of the witch as a person engaged in collective Devil-worship. Many educated clerics and laymen believed that witches made pacts with the Devil, but they did not always claim that they gathered in nocturnal assemblies. The number of witches charged with attending these "sabbaths" varied from place to place, but overall they formed a minority of all accused witches. The original suspicion and accusation of witches, moreover, which in most cases came from the witches' neighbors, were based primarily on the belief that the witches had harmed them by magical means. Charges of Devil-worship were usually introduced at a later stage of the judicial process, when legal officials interrogated accused witches and often forced them to confess. Belief in human commerce with demons was not absent in peasant communities, and during periods of witch-hunting successful efforts were made to educate villagers regarding the demonic menace. But the primary concern of villagers remained their neighbors' efforts to harm them by magical means, and that concern lay at the root of most witchcraft accusations.

During the early modern period, demonologists made distinctions between witchcraft and magic. The witch, to be sure, was a special type of magician, but she was not to be confused with the people who summoned up demons in order to achieve fame or power. In many European languages different words were often used to identify the two crimes. The crimes were related closely enough that ritual magicians might, on occasion, be prosecuted for witchcraft, but they were rarely executed. The practice of magic took many forms, but it usually involved the recitation of certain formulas and the invocation of spirits. It could be performed for either malevolent or benevolent purposes. Its practitioners were often educated men who insisted that they could order the Devil to produce magical effects. By contrast witches in the early modern period were usually women who were believed to have practised a very simple form of magic and who had become the servants of Satan. Their crime was considered more horrifying than that of ritual magicians.

Belief and skepticism

The majority of the sources included in this volume were written by men who condemned the practice of witchcraft in print or who participated in the trials of those who were suspected of this crime. These men believed in the reality of witchcraft and thought that they had a religious duty to identify and prosecute witches. A preponderance of credulous sources is to be expected in a volume illustrating the development of witch-beliefs and the means by which witches were brought to trial. It is important to note, however, that throughout the early modern period, beliefs in the reality of witchcraft were often contested. In two Parts the voices of skepticism and dissent receive special attention. Part IV, which reproduces a variety of texts regarding the methods for prosecuting witches, includes works by five men who objected to the trial of witches on the grounds that innocent people were being convicted of crimes they did not commit. Part VII presents texts of seven thinkers who doubted or rejected the reality of witchcraft, either in general or in specific instances. The literature of witchcraft not only details the evil of the witches' crime but gives expression to the doubts of those who thought their crime might be imaginary.

Part I

WITCHCRAFT
AND MAGIC IN THE
ANCIENT WORLD

This Part brings together a brief sample of the texts from the period of biblical and classical antiquity that contributed to the formation of witch beliefs in the Middle Ages and the early modern period. The subject of witch-craft and magic in the ancient world is a field in its own right, and this selection of documents can only represent some views of witchcraft that prevailed in those early cultures. The seven documents produced in this part have been selected either because they became important sources in their own right during the period of prosecution or because they describe beliefs or traditions that persisted in one way or another into the later period.

Two of the chapters in this Part fall clearly into the first category. Chapter 1, the account of the witch of Endor in the Old Testament, is one of many biblical sources that were quoted frequently during later periods of European history, especially during the period of witch-hunting. The account of Saul's consultation of a diviner from Endor to summon up the ghost of Samuel became the subject of many commentaries that sought to establish the extent to which the Devil was involved in this exercise of magical power. Chapter 7, which was even more frequently cited during subsequent periods of European history, was that of the greatest church father, St Augustine, who described the powers of the Devil on earth, identified him as the source of all magic, and condemned the practice of magic as idolatry, paganism, and heresy.

Classical texts, even those that took a skeptical view of witchcraft, also contributed to the construction of an enduring image of the witch figure. Horace's presentation of the character of Medea in one of his *Epodes* (Chapter 5), which draws on earlier representations of the same character in earlier classical literature, contributed to later representations of witchcraft by Roman and Renaissance dramatists (see Part VIII). Further representations of the witch figure and her powers appear in the literary work of the Latin writer Apuleius, whose fictional work *The Golden Ass* described the powers of witches to change men into beasts and alter the appearance of their faces. (Chapter 4).

Three documents describe magical practices in the Greco-Roman world. The curses cast on Roman charioteers serve as examples of the type of *maleficia* performed by witches during the period of prosecution (Chapter 3). The alleged practice of love magic to prevent sexual union between two parties, which is described in Chapter 6, also recurs frequently in the records of witchcraft trials in the sixteenth and seventeenth centuries. Finally the account of Apuleius's own trial for witchcraft in the northern African regions of the Roman Empire contains a defense of the practice of magic that many Neoplatonic magicians later made in the Middle Ages and the fifteenth and sixteenth centuries (Chapter 2).

1

THE WITCH OF ENDOR

Throughout the period of witch-hunting in the early modern period, demon-ologists and clerics cited texts from the Bible to endorse the actions they were taking against alleged witches. The two most common texts cited were the condemnation of witchcraft in Exodus 22:18, "Thou shalt not suffer a witch to live," and the narrative of the witch of Endor in the first book of Samuel. Although frequently cited, the relevance of these biblical texts to contemporary witchcraft had been a subject of considerable controversy. The controversy centered on whether witchcraft as discussed in the Bible was the same crime as witchcraft in the sixteenth and seventeenth centuries. Demonologists writing in the skep-tical tradition, such as Robert Filmer and Johann Weyer, argued that there was a difference between a Hebrew witch and the early modern European witch. The biblical passage regarding the witch of Endor was especially problematic. In this text Saul, faced with a Philistine enemy, consults with a medium from the town of Endor to help him summon up Samuel's ghost and thus obtain guidance as to how to defeat his foe. Early modern commentators debated a number of issues regarding this text. The main question concerned the guilt of Saul for practising necromacy, which according to early modern demonological theory involved the use of demonic power regardless of its intention. This discourse led to the further questions whether the apparition of Saul was real or the product of demonic illu-sion and whether the voice that Saul heard was that of Samuel or the Devil. These questions contributed in turn to a further debate concerning the reality of all dreams, visions, and apparitions. James VI of Scotland posed the further question in *Daemonologie* (1597) whether Samuel was a witch, since in James's view God would never have allowed the Devil to produce the specter unless the person who appeared in that form was in fact a witch (Chapter 28). One of the speakers in James's dialogue answered this last question by arguing that since Samuel was already dead, he could not be accused of witchcraft. The text of the witch of Endor is 1 Samuel 28: 1–25.

Source: *The Holy Bible Containing the Old Testament and the New* (1611).

And it came to pass in those days, that the Philistines gathered their armies together for warfare, to fight with Israel. And Achish said unto David, Know thou assuredly, that thou shalt go out with me to battle, thou and thy men. And David said to Achish, Surely thou shalt know what thy servant can do. And Achish said to David, Therefore will I make thee keeper of mine head for ever.

Now Samuel was dead, and all Israel had lamented him, and buried him in Ramah, even in his own city. And Saul had put away those that had familiar spirits, and the wizards, out of the land. And the Philistines gathered themselves together, and came and pitched in Shunem: and Saul gathered all Israel together, and they pitched in Gilboa. And when Saul saw the host of the Philistines, he was afraid, and his heart greatly trembled. And when Saul inquired of the Lord, the Lord answered him not, neither by dreams nor by Urim, nor by prophets. Then said Saul unto his servants, Seek me a woman that hath a familiar spirit, that I may go to her, and inquire of her. And his servants said to him, Behold, there is a woman that hath a familiar spirit at Endor.

And Saul disguised himself, and put on other raiment, and he went, and two men with him, and they came to the woman by night: and he said, I pray thee, divine unto me by the familiar spirit, and bring me him up, whom I shall name unto thee. And the woman said unto him, Behold, thou knowest what Saul hath done, how he hath cut off those that have familiar spirits, and the wizards, out of the land: wherefore then layest thou a snare for my life, to cause me to die? And Saul sware to her by the Lord, saying, As the Lord liveth, there shall no punishment happen to thee for this thing. Then said the woman, Whom shall I bring up unto thee? And he said, Bring me up Samuel. And when the woman saw Samuel, she cried with a loud voice: and the woman spake to Saul, saying, Why hast thou deceived me? for thou art Saul. And the king said unto her, Be not afraid: for what sawest thou? And the woman said unto Saul, I saw gods ascending out of the earth. And he said unto her, What form is he of? And she said, An old man cometh up; and he is covered with a mantle. And Saul perceived that it was Samuel, and he stooped with his face to the ground, and bowed himself.

And Samuel said to Saul, Why hast thou disquieted me, to bring me up? And Saul answered, I am sore distressed; for the Philistines make war against me, and God is departed from me, and answereth me no more, neither by prophets, nor by dreams: therefore I have called thee, that thou mayest make known unto me what I shall do. Then said Samuel, Wherefore then dost thou ask of me, seeing the Lord is departed from thee, and is become thine enemy? And the Lord hath done to him, as he spake by me: for the Lord hath rent the kingdom out of thine hand, and given it to thy neighbour, even to David: Because thou obeyedst not the voice of the Lord, nor executedst his fierce wrath upon Amalek, therefore hath the Lord done this thing unto thee this day. Moreover the Lord will also deliver Israel with thee into the hand of the Philistines: and tomorrow shalt thou and thy sons be with me: the Lord also shall deliver the host of Israel into the hand of the Philistines.

Then Saul fell straightway all along on the earth, and was sore afraid, because of the words of Samuel: and there was no strength in him; for he had eaten no bread all the day, nor all the night. And the woman came unto Saul, and saw that he was sore troubled, and said unto him, Behold, thine handmaid hath obeyed thy voice, and I have put my life in my hand, and have hearkened unto thy words which thou spakest unto me. Now therefore, I pray thee, hearken thou also unto the voice of thine handmaid, and let me set a morsel of bread before thee; and eat, that thou mayest have strength, when thou goest on thy way. But he refused, and said, I will not eat. But his servants, together with the woman, compelled him; and he hearkened unto their voice. So he arose from the earth, and sat upon the bed. And the woman had a fat calf in the house; and she hasted, and killed it, and took flour, and kneaded it, and did bake unleavened bread thereof: And she brought it before Saul, and before his servants; and they did eat. Then they rose up, and went away that night.

2

A SORCERY TRIAL
IN THE SECOND
CENTURY CE

———◦◦◦◦———

Lucius Apuleius of Madaura, a Latin writer and Platonist philosopher of the second century CE, had a deep interest in the occult sciences. In the northern African town of Oea he married a wealthy widow, Aemilia Pudentilla, who was a number of years his senior. Shortly after the marriage some of his wife's relatives accused him of having used sorcery to win her affections and thus acquire her property. The crime of sorcery in Roman law was punishable by death. His trial took place before Claudius Maximus, the proconsul in Sabratha. Apuleius presented a brilliant defense, not only of himself but of the practice of magic, which he compared to the work of priests and which he identified with philosophical inquiry. Apuleius also made the judge aware of the prejudices that inspired the accusations against him, especially those that dealt with his recent arrival in Odea and his marriage. Similar circumstances lay at the root of accusations of witchcraft in later periods of European history. In his defense Apuleius anticipated many of the arguments that learned magicians in the medieval and early modern periods, many of whom were learned in the Platonic tradition, justified the practice of their craft.

Source: From Apuleius, *Apology*, in Georg Luck (trans. and ed.), *Arcana Mundi* (Baltimore and London, 1985), pp. 110–113.

I will now deal with an actual charge of magic. He [the accuser] has spared no effort to light the flame of hatred against me, but he has falsely raised everyone's expectations by some old wives' tales he told. I ask you, Maximus [the judge]: have you ever seen a fire started from stubble, crackling sharply, shining far and wide, getting bigger fast, but without real fuel, with only a feeble blaze, leaving nothing behind? This is their accusation, kindled with abuse, built up with mere words, lacking proof, and, once you have given your verdict, leaving no trace of slander behind.

Aemilianus' slander was focused on one point: that I am a sorcerer. So let me ask his most learned advocates: What is a sorcerer? I have read in many books that *magus* is the same thing in Persian as *priest* in our language. What crime is there in being a priest and in having accurate knowledge, a science, a technique of traditional ritual, sacred rites and traditional law, if magic consists of what Plato interprets as the "cult of the gods" when he talks of the disciplines taught to the crown prince in Persia? I remember the very words of that divine man [Plato]. Let me recall them to you, Maximus: "When the young prince has reached the age of fourteen, he is handed over to the royal tutors. There are four of them, chosen as the most outstanding among the Persian elders. One is the wisest, one the most just, one the most restrained, one the bravest. One of them teaches [the crown prince] the 'magic' of Zoroaster, the son of Ormazd, which is the worship of the gods. He also teaches [him] the art of being king." Listen to this, you who rashly slander magic! It is an art acceptable to the immortal gods, an art which includes the knowledge of how to worship them and pay them homage. It is a religious tradition dealing with things divine, and it has been distinguished ever since it was founded by Zoroaster and Ormazd, the high priests of divinities. In fact, it is considered one of the chief elements of royal instruction, and in Persia no one is allowed lightly to be a "magus" any more than they would let him be king.

Plato also writes, in a different context, about a certain Zalmoxis, a Thracian, but an expert in the same art, that "there is a certain mental therapy in incantations, and that incantations consist of beautiful words." If this is so, why should I not be permitted to learn the "beautiful words" of Zalmoxis or the priestly traditions of Zoroaster? But if my accusers after the common fashion think of a "magus" primarily as a person who by verbal communications with the immortal gods and through the incredible power of his incantations can perform any miracles he wants, why are they not afraid to accuse a man who, as they admit themselves, has such powers? For there is no protection against such a mysterious, such a divine, power as there is against other things. If you summon a murderer before a judge, you come with a bodyguard; if you charge a poisoner, you take special precautions with your food; if you accuse a thief, you watch your possessions. But if you demand the death penalty for a magus, as they define him, what escort, what special precautions, what guards, can protect you against an unexpected, inevitable catastrophe? None, of course, and so this is not the kind of charge a man who believes in the truth of this sort of thing would make.

But it is a fairly common misunderstanding by which the uneducated accuse philosophers. Some of them think that those who investigate the simple causes and elements of matter are antireligious, and that they deny the very existence of gods, as for instance, Anaxagoras, Leuacippus, Democitus, Epicurus, and other leading scientists. Others, commonly called "magi," spend great care in the exploration of the workings of providence in the world and worship the gods with great devotion, as if they actually knew how to make the things happen that they know do happen. This was the case with Epimenides, Orpheus, Pythagoras, and Ostanes. Similarly, later on, the "Purifications" of Empedocles, the "Daemon" of Socrates, the "Good" of Plato, came under suspicion. I congratulate myself to be associated with so many great men.

I am afraid, however, that the court may take seriously the silly, childish, and naïve arguments brought forward by my accusers in order to substantiate their charges – for the simple reason that they have been made. My accuser asks: "Why have you tried to get specific kinds of fish?" Why should a scientist not be allowed to do for the sake of knowledge what a gourmand is allowed to do for the sake of his gluttony? He asks: "What made a free woman marry you after having been a widow for fourteen years?" Well, is it not more remarkable that she remained a widow for such a long time? "Why did she, before she married you, express certain opinions in a letter?" Well, is it reasonable to demand of someone the reasons for someone else's opinions? "She is older than you, but did not reject a younger man." But this alone is proof enough that no magic was needed; a woman wished to marry a man, a widow a bachelor, a mature lady a man her junior. And there are more charges just like that: "Apuleius has in his house an object which he secretly worships." Well, would it not be a worse offense to have nothing to worship? "A boy fell to the ground in Apuleius' presence." What if a young man, what if an old man, had fallen when I was there, perhaps stricken by illness, perhaps simply because the ground was slippery? Do you think you can prove your accusation of magic by such arguments, the fall of a little boy, my getting married to my wife, the purchase of fish?

[Apuleius deals with the subject of fish and argues that he was motivated only by scientific interest; then he turns to the incident of the boy who suddenly fell down in his presence.]

My accusers claim that I bewitched a boy by an incantation with no witness present and then took him to a secret place with a small altar and a lantern and only a few accomplices present, and there he was put under a spell and collapsed; he lost consciousness and was revived. They did not dare go any further with their lie. To complete their fairy tale they should have added that the boy uttered a lot of prophecies. For this, of course, is the prize of incantations. This miracle involving boys is not only a popular superstition but is confirmed by the authority of learned men. I remember reading in the philosopher Varro, a thoroughly learned and erudite man, stories of this kind, and especially this one. There was at Tralles an inquiry by means of magic about the outcome of the Mithridatic War: a boy was gazing at a reflection of Mercury in water, and then foretold the future in one hundred sixty lines of verse. Varro also tells that Fabius, having lost five hundred denarii, came to consult Nigidius, who inspired some boys by a spell to reveal where exactly a pot with part of the sum was buried and how the rest had been dispersed; one denarius actually found its way to the philosopher Marcus Cato, who acknowledged having received it from a servant as a contribution to the treasury of Apollo.

I have read these and many other stories about boys in magical rituals, and I cannot make up my mind whether to believe them or not. But I do believe Plato when he says that there are divine powers that rank both by their nature and location between gods and men and that all kinds of divination and magic miracles are controlled by them. It also occurs to me that the human soul, especially a boyish, unsophisticated soul, can be lulled to sleep by soft music and sweet smells and hypnotized into oblivion of reality, so that gradually all consciousness of the body fades from memory and the soul returns and retreats into its own true nature, which, of course, is immortal and divine, and thus, as if it were in a kind of slumber, can predict the future. Well, no matter whether this is true or not, if one were to believe this sort of thing, the boy with the gift of prophecy, whoever he is, from what I hear, must be handsome and healthy, also intellectually alert and articulate, to make sure that the divine power takes up lodgings in him, as if he were a respectable house – if it is really appropriate for such a power to squeeze itself into the body of a boy! It could also be that the boy's mind, when awakened, quickly applies itself to the business of divination, which may be his natural, spontaneous gift, which can easily be picked up without being dulled or damaged by any loss of memory. For, as Pythagoras used to say, you must not carve a statue of Hermes from just any piece of wood. If this is true, please tell me who that healthy, sound, gifted, handsome boy was whom I chose to initiate by my incantation. As a matter of fact, Thallus – you mentioned his name – needs a physician rather than a magician.

3

CURSE TABLETS AGAINST ROMAN CHARIOTEERS

In all societies there are individuals who perform harmful magic – the exercise of some preternatural or occult power to bring misfortune to another person. The most common form of such maleficent magic is the utterance of a curse or a hex on the intended victim. During the early modern period of European history maleficent magic, known in Latin as *maleficium*, was considered one of the main features of witchcraft. In Roman times one form that such curses took was their inscription on leaden tablets and the dedication of these curse tablets to pagan gods. To ensure their effectiveness, a nail or sharp object was sometimes driven into the tablet, often through the name of the intended victim. This practice gave the curse the added dimension of image magic, since the person's name was considered an image or extension of the person himself. The following curses, which come from the period of the Roman Empire, were used to bring about the defeat of drivers in chariot races. They stand therefore as early examples of magic used to achieve victory in sporting events.

Sources: The transcription of the first curse is recorded in *Inscriptiones Latinae Selectae*, ed. H. Dessau (Berlin, 1906), vol. 2, part 2, p. 999, no. 8753. The second and third curses are recorded in R. Wünsch, *Antike Fluchtafeln* (Bonn, 1912), nos 4 and 5.

1   This curse was written in Latin during the late Roman Empire. It was found at Hadrumetum in northern Africa:

I adjure you, demon, whoever you are, and I demand of you from this hour, from this day, from this moment that you torture and kill the horses of the Greens and Whites, and that you kill and smash their drivers Clarus, Felix, Primulus and Romanus, and leave not a breath in their bodies. I adjure you, demon, by him who has turned you loose in these times, the god of the sea and the air.

2　This curse from Carthage, inscribed on a lead tablet, was written in Greek during the third century CE. It begins with a fifty-line invocation of assorted divinities, including Hermes, and then proceeds:

Help me in the circus on 8 November. Bind every limb, every sinew, the shoulders, the ankles, and the elbows of Olympus, Olympianus, Scortius, and Juvencus, the charioteers of the Reds. Torment their minds, their intelligence, and their senses so that they may not see where they are going – neither they nor the horses they are going to drive, Aegyptus, Callidromus, and any other horses yoked with them, Valentinus and Lampadius . . . and Maurus, the offspring of Lampadius, and Chrysaspis, Iuba and Indus, Palmatus and Superbus. . . . Bubalus, the offspring of Censorapus, Ereis and any other horse of theirs likely to run . . . may none of them gain the victory.

3　The following spell, found near Carthage, was directed chiefly against a driver of the Blues, Victoricus, "son of Earth, the mother of every living thing." The curse was obviously accompanied by the sacrifice of a cock. The conclusion reveals that the writer knew something of the Hebrew scriptures.

As this cock is bound, legs, wings and head, so bind the legs, hands, head and heart of Victoricus, the charioteer of the Blues tomorrow, and the horses he is going to drive, Secundinus, Juvenis, Advocatus, Bubakus, and Laureaus, Pompeianus, Beanus, Victor and Eximius. . . . I adjure you by the God of Heaven above, who sits on the Cherubim, who divided the land and set apart the sea, by Iao, Abriao, Arbathiao, Adonai Sabao, that you bind Victoricus and Dominator, so that they may not come to victory tomorrow. Now. Now. Quick. Quick.

4

APULEIUS:
THE POWER OF WITCHES

The most famous work of fiction by Apuleius, the author of the Document in Chapter 2, is *The Golden Ass*. Also known as *Metamorphoses*, the story was based on a Greek tale, possibly written by his contemporary Lucian (*c.*115–200 CE). It contains many autobiographical elements. Like Apuleius himself, the hero of the novel, Lucius, dabbles in magic and is finally rescued by the goddess Isis and finds true knowledge in her religion. The work contains two narratives that illustrate the power of witches. In one of these a witch figure by the name of Photis, whose mistress is a more advanced sorceress, Pamphilia, transforms Lucius into an ass. Isis transforms him back into a human shape. In the second narrative, excerpted below, a character named Thelyphron tells a story regarding the ability of witches to gnaw off faces of their victims. Apuleius was almost certainly skeptical of the reality of metamorphosis and this type of maleficent power, but his stories were not always viewed in that skeptical way. Like many classical texts, *The Golden Ass* was used as evidence for the reality of witchcraft during the early modern period. Like Horace and Seneca, Apuleius also contributed to the depiction of the classical witch figure.

Source: Apuleius, *The Golden Ass*, translated by R. Graves (New York, 1951), pp. 42–50.

While I was still a university student at Miletus, I came over to attend the Olympian Games. Afterwards, feeling a strong desire to visit northern Greece, I travelled through most of Thessaly. One unlucky day I arrived at Larissa, having run through nearly all the money I had brought with me, and while I was wandering up and down the streets, wondering how to refill my purse, I saw a tall old man standing on a stone block in the middle of the market place. He was making a public announcement at the top of his voice, offering a large reward to anyone who would stand guard over a corpse that night.

I asked a bystander: "What is the meaning of this? Are the corpses of Larissa in the habit of running away?"

"Hush, my lad," he answered. "I can see that you are very much of a stranger here, else you would realize that you are in Thessaly where witches are in the habit of gnawing bits of flesh off dead men's faces for use in their magical concoctions."

"Oh, I see! And would you mind telling me what this guardianship of the dead involves?"

"Not at all. It means watching attentively the whole night, one's eyes fixed on the corpse without a single sideways glance. You see, these abominable women have the power of changing their shape at pleasure: they turn into birds or dogs or mice, or even flies – disguises that would pass scrutiny even in a Court of Law, and by daylight too – and then charm the guardians asleep. I won't try to tell you all the extraordinary ingenious tricks that they use when they want to indulge their beastly appetites; at any rate, the usual reward of from a hundred to a hundred and fifty drachmae for the night's job is hardly worth the risk. Oh – I was almost forgetting to tell you that if next morning the guardian fails to hand over the corpse to the undertakers in exactly the same condition as he found it, he is obliged by Law to have bits cut from his own face to supply whatever is missing."

That did not frighten me. I boldly told the crier that he need not repeat the announcement. "I'm ready to undertake the job," I said. "What fee do they offer?"

"A thousand drachmae, because this is a job that calls for more than usual alertness against those terrible harpies: the deceased was one of our first citizens."

"All this nonsense leaves me unmoved," I said. "I am a man of iron, I never trouble to go to sleep, and I have sharper eyesight than Lynceus, the *Argo*'s look-out man. In fact, I may say that I am all eyes, like the giant Argos whom Jupiter once put in charge of the nymph Io."

I had hardly finished recommending myself for the job before the old man hurried me along to a big house with its gates locked and barred. He took me through a small side door and along corridors until I reached a bedroom with closed shutters, where a woman in deep black sat wailing loudly in the half-light.

The crier went up to her and said: "This man undertakes to guard your husband's body tonight; and he agrees to the fee."

She pushed back the hair that shaded her beautiful grief-stricken face, and implored me to be vigilant at my post.

"You need have no anxiety, Madam, if you make it worth my while afterwards."

Nodding absently, she got up and led me into an adjoining room, where she showed me the corpse lying on a slab and wrapped in a pure white linen shroud. After another fit of weeping, she called in seven mourners as witnesses, also her secretary who had his writing materials with him. Then she said: "Gentlemen, I call you to witness that the nose is undamaged, so are both ears, the eyes are still in their sockets, the lips are whole, the chin the same." She touched each feature as she mentioned it, and the secretary wrote out the inventory, which the witness signed and sealed.

I asked her as she was going away: "Will you be good enough, Madam, to see that I have everything I need for my vigil tonight?"

"What sort of things?"

"A good large lamp with enough oil in it to last until day-break; pots of wine; warm water for tempering; a cup; and a plateful of cold meat and vegetables left over from your supper."

She shook her head angrily: "What an absurd request! Cooked meat and vegetables indeed in this house of mourning, where no fire has been lighted for days! Do you imagine that you have come here for a jolly supper party? You are expected to mourn and weep like the rest of us." Then, turning to her maid: "Myrrhina, fill the lamp, bring it back at once, shut the door, and leave the guardian to his task."

All alone with the corpse I fortified my eyes for their vigil by rubbing them hard and kept up my spirits by singing. Twilight shaded into night, and night grew deeper and deeper, blacker and blacker, until my usual bed time had passed and it was close on midnight. I had been only a little uncomfortable at first, but now I was beginning to feel thoroughly frightened when all of a sudden a weasel squeezed through a hole in the door, stopped close by me and fixed her eyes intently on mine. The boldness of the creature was most disconcerting, but I managed to shout out: "Get away from here, you filthy little beast, or I'll break your neck. Run off and play hide and seek with your friends the mice. Do you hear me? I mean it."

She turned tail and skipped out of the room, but as she did so, a sudden deep sleep stole over me and dragged me down into bottomless gulfs of dream. I fell on the floor and lay there so dead asleep that not even Delphic Apollo could have readily decided which of us two was the corpse: the body on the slab or the body on the floor. It was almost as though I had actually died and my corpse had been left without a guardian.

At last the darkness began to fade and

The sentries of the Crested Watch 'gan shout

– crowing so loud that I eventually awoke, picked up the lamp and eventually ran in terror to the slab. I pulled back the shroud and examined the corpse's face closely: to my huge relief I found it unmutilated. Almost at once the poor widow came running in, still weeping, with the seven witnesses behind her. She threw herself on the corpse and after kissing it again and again had the lamp brought close to make sure that all was well. Then she turned and called: "Philodespotus, come here!"

Her steward appeared. "Philodespotus, pay this young man his fee at once. He has kept watch very well."

As he counted me out the money she said: "Many thanks, young man for your loyal services; they have earned you the freedom of this house."

Delighted with my unexpected good luck, I gently tossed the bright gold coins up and down in my hand and answered: "I am much obliged to you, Madam. I shall be only too pleased to help you out again, whenever you may need my services."

These words were scarcely out of my mouth when the whole household rushed at me with blows and curses, in an attempt to cancel their dreadful ominousness. One punched me in the face with his fists, another dug his elbows into my shoulder, someone else kicked me, my ribs were pummelled, my hair pulled, my clothes torn and before they finally threw me out of the house I felt like Adonis mauled by the wild boar, or Orpheus torn in pieces by the Thracian women.

When I paused in the next street to collect my senses, and realized what I had said – it had certainly been a most tactless remark – I decided that I had got off lightly enough, all considered.

By and by, after the customary "last summons," the agonized calling of his name by the relatives in case he might be only in a coma, the dead man was brought out of the house; and since he had been a man of such importance he was honoured with a public procession. As the cortège turned into the market place, an old man came running up, the tears streaming down his face. In a frenzy of grief he tore out tufts of his fine white hair, grabbed hold of the open coffin with both hands and screamed for vengeance.

"Gentlemen of Hypata!" he cried, his voice choking with sobs, "I appeal to your honour, I appeal to your sense of justice and public duty! Stand by your fellow-citizen, this poor nephew of mine; see that his death is avenged in full on that evil woman, his widow. She, and she alone, is the murderess. To cover up a secret love-affair and to get possession of her husband's estate she killed him – she killed him with a slow poison." He continued to sob and scream, until the crowd was stirred to indignant sympathy, thinking that he probably had good ground for his accusations. Some shouted: "Burn her! Burn her!" and some: "Stone her to death!" and a gang of young hooligans was encouraged to lynch her.

However, she denied her guilt with oaths and tears (though these carried little conviction), and devout appeals to all their gods and goddesses in Heaven to witness that she was utterly incapable of doing anything so wicked.

"So be it then," said the old man, "I am willing to refer the case to divine arbitration. And here is Zatchlas the Egyptian, one of the leading necromancers of his country, who had undertaken, for a large fee, to recall my nephew's soul from the Underworld and persuade it to reanimate the corpse for a few brief moments."

The person whom he introduced to the crowd was dressed in white linen, with palm-leaf sandals on his feet and a tonsured head. The old man kissed his hands and clasped his knees in a formal act of supplication. "Your reverence," he cried, " take pity on me. I implore you by the stares of heaven, by the gods of the Underworld, by the five elements of nature, by the silence of night, by the dams that the swallows of Isis build about the Coptic island, by the flooding of the Nile, by the mysteries of Memphis, and by the sacred rattle of Pharos – I implore you by these holy things to grant my nephew's soul a brief return to the warmth of the sun, and so re-illumine his eyes that they may open and momentarily regain the sight that he has forfeited by his descent to the Land of the Dead. I do not argue with fate, I do not deny the grave what is her due; my plea is only for a brief leave of absence, during which the dead may assist me in avenging his own murder – the only possible consolation I can have in my overwhelming grief."

The necromancer, yielding to his entreaties, touched the corpse's mouth three times with a certain small herb and laid another on its breast. Then he turned to the east, with a silent prayer to the sacred disk of the rising sun. The whole market-place gasped expectantly at the sight of these solemn preparations, and stood prepared for a miracle. I pushed in among the crowd and climbed up on a stone just behind the coffin, from which I watched the whole scene with rising curiosity.

Presently the breasts of the corpse began to heave, blood began to pour again through its veins, breath returned to its nostrils. He sat up and spoke in a querulous voice: "Why do you call me back to the troubles of this transitory life, when I have already drunk of the stream of Lethe and floated on the marshy waters of the Styx? Leave me alone, I say, leave me alone! Let me sleep undisturbed."

The necromancer raised his voice excitedly "What? You refuse to address your fellow-citizens here and clear up the mystery of your death? Don't you realize that if you hold back a single detail I am prepared to call up the dreadful Furies and have your weary limbs tortured on the rack?"

At this the dead man roused himself again and groaned out to the crows: "the bed in which I lay only yesterday is no longer empty; my rival sleeps in it. My newly married wife has bewitched and poisoned me."

The widow showed remarkable courage in the circumstance. She denied everything with oaths, and began contradicting and arguing with her late husband as though there were no such thing as respect for the dead. The crowd took different sides. Some were for burying the wicked woman alive in the same grave as her victim: but others refused to admit the evidence of a senseless corpse – it was quite untrustworthy, they said.

The corpse soon settled the dispute. With another hollow groan it said: "I will give you incontrovertible proof that what I say is true, by disclosing something that is known to nobody but myself." Then he pointed up at me and said: "While that learned young student was keeping careful watch over my corpse, the ghoulish witches who were hovering near, waiting for a chance to rob it, did their best to deceive him by changing shape, but he saw through

20

all their tricks. Though the bedroom doors were carefully bolted, they had slipped in through a knot-hole disguised as weasels and mice. But they threw a fog of sleep over him, so that he fell insensible, and then they called me by name, over and over again, trying to make me obey their magical commands. My weakened joints and cold limbs, despite convulsive struggles, could not respond immediately, but this student who had been cast into a trance that was a sort of death, happened to have the same name as I. So when they called: 'Thelyphron, Thelyphron, come!' he answered mechanically. Rising up like a senseless ghost he offered his face for the mutilation that they intended for mine; and they nibbled off first his nose and then his ears. But to divert attention from what they had done, they cleverly fitted him with a wax nose exactly like his own, and a pair of wax ears. The poor fellow remains under the illusion that he has been well rewarded for his vigilance, not meanly compensated for a frightful injury."

Terrified by this story, I clapped my hand to my face to see if there were any truth to it, and my nose fell off; then I touched my ears, and they fell off too. A hundred fingers pointed at me from the crowd and a great roar of laughter went up. I burst into a cold sweat, leaped down from the stone, and slipped away between their legs like a frightened dog. Mutilated and ridiculous, I have never since cared to return to Miletus; and now I disguise the loss of my ears by growing my hair long and glue this canvas nose on my face for decency's sake.

5

HORACE:
CANIDIA AS A WITCH
FIGURE

———=◦◦◦=———

In his *Fifth Epode*, the Latin Poet Horace, or Quintus Horatius Flaccus (65–8 BCE), describes how Canidia, identified as a witch, has led a group of witches, which includes Sagana, Veia, and Folia, to kidnap a Roman boy of noble birth and bury him up to his chin. Their purpose was to obtain his liver so that they could make a love potion from it and regain the affection of Varus, Canidia's former lover. Canidia believes that Varus has not responded to her because one of her rivals has given her a counter-charm. The boy pleads for his life and then directs a terrible curse against the witches. In depicting Canidia, Horace contributes to the creation of the classical witch-figure, which Ovid and Seneca had already helped to form. That image was enduring, and it influenced early modern depictions of the witch, especially during the period of the Renaissance, when works of classical authors had great authority and influence. Horace's depiction of Canidia was not intended to instill fear of magic and witchcraft in his audience. His grotesque image of the witch, in this epode and in *Satire* 1.8, where he shows Canidia digging for human bones in the cemetery at night, is intended to mock and debunk witchcraft, not to give it credibility. He was skeptical of the powers of magic, and he opposed the payment of witches for their services. He apparently also supported legislation by the Roman Emperor Augustus to suppress the actual practice of magic.

Source: Horace, *Epode V, Canidia's Incantation* in C. E. Bennett (trans.)
Horace, the Odes and Epodes (Cambridge, Mass., 1914), pp. 375–381.

"But in the name of all the gods in heaven that rule the world and race of men, what means this tumult, and what the savage looks of all of you bent on me alone? By thy children, I implore thee, if Lucina, when invoked, came to help an honest birth, by this bauble of my purple dress, by Jupiter, sure

22

to disapprove these acts, why like a stepmother dost thou gaze at me, or like a wild beast brought to bay with hunting-spear?"

When after making these complaints with quivering lip, the lad stood still, stripped of boyhood's emblems, a youthful form, such as might soften the impious breasts of Thracians, Canidia, her locks and dishevelled head entwined with short vipers, orders wild fig-trees uprooted from the tombs, funereal cypresses, eggs and feathers of a night-roving screech-owl smeared with the blood of a hideous toad, herbs that Iolcos and Iberia, fertile in poisons, send, and bones snatched from the jaws of a starving bitch – all those to be burned in the magic flames. But high-girt Sagana, sprinkling through all the house water from Lake Avernus, bristles with streaming hair, like some sea-urchin or a racing oar; and Veia, by no sense of guilt restrained, groaning o'er her labours, with stout mattock was digging up the ground, that, buried there, the lad might perish gazing at food changed twice and thrice during the tedious day, his face protruding only so much as swimmers, when hanging in the water by the chin – and all for this, that his marrow and his liver, cut out and dried, might form a love-charm, when once his eye-balls, fixed on the forbidden food, had wasted all away. Gossiping Naples and every neighbouring town believed that Folia of Ariminum, the wanton hag, was also there – Folia, who with Thessalian incantation bewitches stars and moon and plucks them down from heaven. Then fierce Canidia, gnawing her uncut nail with malignant tooth – what did she say, or rather what did she leave unsaid!

"O faithful witnesses of my deeds, Night and Diana, thou art mistress of the silent hour when mystic rites are wrought, now, even now, lend me your help! Now against hostile homes turn your wrath and power! While in the awesome woods the wild beasts lie in hiding, wrapped in soft slumber, may Subura's dogs bark at the old rake, – a sight for all to laugh at – anointed with an essence such as my hands ne'er made more perfect! What has befallen? Why fail to work the dire philtres of the barbarian Medea, with which before her flight she took vengeance on the haughty paramour, mighty Creon's daughter, what time the robe, a gift steeped in poisoned gore, snatched away in fire the new-made bride. And yet no herb nor root, lurking in rough places, escaped me. He lies asleep on perfumed couch, forgetful of all mistresses. Aha! He walks at will, freed by the charm of some cleverer enchantress. By no wonted potions, Varus, thou creature doomed bitterly to weep, shalt thou return to me; and summoned by no Marsian spells, shall thy devotion be revived. A stronger draught pour out, to meet thy scorn; and sooner shall the heaven sink below the sea, with earth spread out above, than thou shouldst fail to burn with love for me, even as burns the pitch in smoky flame."

At this the lad no longer, as before, essayed to smooth the impious creatures with gentle speech, but, doubtful with what words to break the silence, hurled forth Thyestean curses: "Your magic spells have not the power to alter right and wrong, nor to avert human retribution. With curses I will hound you; by no sacrifice shall my awful execration be warded off. Nay, even when, doomed to die, I have breathed my last, at night I will meet you as a fury; and as a ghost I will tear your faces with crooked claws, as is the Manes' power; and seated on your restless bosoms, I will banish sleep with terror. The rabble, pelting you with stones on every side along the streets, shall crush you, filthy hags. Then by and by the wolves and birds that haunt the Esquiline shall scatter far and wide your unburied limbs, nor shall this sight escape my parents – surviving me, alas!"

6

LOVE MAGIC IN
ANTIQUITY

⎯⎯⎯⎯⎯◦◦◦◦⎯⎯⎯⎯⎯

One of the forms of magic that had a long association with witchcraft, not only in ancient times but during the the Middle Ages and the early modern period, was love magic. Witch-figures like Medea in classical literature were skilled in these arts, and the survival of recipes and the records of court cases against practitioners attest to their widespread use. Love magic could be considered positive, in the sense that it could be used to arouse sexual passion of one person for another, or negative in the sense that it was intended to prevent a person from engaging in sexual activity with another. During the Middle Ages and the early modern period the Church considered it evil regardless of its intentions, not only because it involved commerce with demons but also because it often abetted illicit sexual unions. Love magic, however, was often not prosecuted as severely as other forms of magic, unless it was intended to prevent conception by married couples. The following prescriptions from the fourth century CE provide evidence of the actual practice of love magic in antiquity.

Source: Georg Luck (trans. and ed.), *Arcana Mundi* (Baltimore and London, 1985), pp. 92–93.

Take wax or clay from a potter's wheel and shape it into two figures, one male and one female. Make the male look like Ares in arms. He should hold a sword in his left hand and point it at her right collarbone. Her arms must be tied behind her back, and she must kneel. Attach the magic substance to her head or neck. On the head of the figure representing the woman you wish to attract write: [magical words].

[list of the parts of her body, including the genitals, on which magical words must be written]

Take thirteen iron needles, stick one into her brain and say: "I prick your brain, X."

25

[list of other parts of the body to be pricked; each time the magician has to say: "I prick this part of the body of X, to make sure that she thinks of no one but me, Y."]

Take a lead plate and write the same formula on it and tie it to the figures in three hundred sixty-five knots with thread from a loom and recite the "Abrasax, hold tight" formula, which you know, and deposit this at sunset near the tomb of someone who died before his time or died a violent death, with flowers of the season. The spell that must be written and recited is this:

"I deposit this binding spell with you, gods of the underworld, [magical words] and the Korē Persephone Ereschigal and Adonis, the [magical words] Hermes of the underworld, Touth [magical words] and powerful Anubis, who holds the keys of those in Hades, the gods and daemons of the underworld, those who died before their time, male and female, youths and maidens, year after year, month after month, day after day, hour after hour. I conjure all the daemons at this place to assist this one daemon. Wake up for me, whoever you are, male or female and go to every place, to every street, into every house, and fetch and bind. Bring me X, the daughter of Z, whose magical substance you have, and make her love me, Y, the son of A. Let her not have intercourse, neither from front nor from behind, and let her not have pleasure with any other man except me, Y. Let her, X, not eat, not drink, not love, not be strong, not be healthy, not sleep, except with me, X, because I conjure you in the name of the terrifying one, the horrifying one. When the earth hears his name, it will open up. When the daemons hear his awful name, they will be afraid. When rivers and rocks hear his name, they will burst. I conjure you, daemon of the dead. . . .

"Yes, drag her by her hair, her entrails, her genitals, to me, Y, in every hour of time, day and night, until she comes to me, Y, and remains inseparable from me. Do this, bind [her] during my whole life [to me] and force her, X, to be my slave, the slave of Y, and let her not leave me for a single hour of time. If you fulfill this wish, I will let you rest at once.

"For I am Adônai [magical words], who hides the stars, the brightly radiating ruler of the sky, the lord of the world. . . .

"Fetch her, tie her, make her love and desire me, Y. . . . because I conjure you, daemon of the dead, by the terrible , the mighty one [magical words], to make you fetch X and make her join head to head, lips to lips, body to body, thighs to thighs, back to back, and do her job of making love with me forever and ever . . ."

7

ST AUGUSTINE:
DEMONIC POWER IN
EARLY CHRISTIANITY

━━━━━◦◇◦━━━━━

St Augustine (354–430), the Bishop of Hippo in northern Africa, is widely considered the founder of Christian theology. The greatest of the Church Fathers, his work acquired unassailable authority during the Middle Ages, and during the early modern period both Catholics and Protestants appealed to his writings. His most famous works were his autobiographical and mystical *Confessions,* his summary of Christian doctrine in *On the Trinity*, and his assault upon paganism in the *City of God*. He defended Christian doctrine against the early heresies of Pelagianism, Manichaeism, and Donatism. In several works, including *The City of God* (from which these excerpts are taken) and *The Divination of Demons*, Augustine condemns the practice of all magic, regardless whether it involved the invocation of demons (necromancy) or good angels (theurgy). Both forms of magic according to Augustine involved commerce with demons. He condemned the practitioners of these sacrilegious rites as pagans and heretics. Augustine's characterization of all magic, regardless of its intention, as demonic provided a doctrinal foundation for the late medieval condemnation of ritual magic (see Chapters 9, 11, and 12) against the claims of its clerical practitioners. Augustine's writings were also used to support the Protestant condemnation of both white and black witchcraft as equally wrong in the sixteenth and seventeenth centuries (see Chapter 19). Protestants followed Augustine in arguing that it was the process by which the magic was performed, not its intended effect, that made it sinful. In condemning theurgy Augustine claims that the Devil deceives the practitioners of these arts by presenting himself as an angel of light (a scriptural quote from St Paul) and of being able to turn himself into various shapes. Augustine characterizes all this as demonic deception, intended to entice Christians to worship false gods. This interpretation in no way undermines Augustine's condemnation of those who fall victim to such demonic deception;

they are still in error and guilty of idolatry. In the Middle Ages the ecclesiastical law known as the canon *Episcopi* (Chapter 8), often viewed as a skeptical document, takes the same position as Augustine.

From Saint Augustine [*The City of God*], trans. M. Dods (New York, 1950), pp. 312–316.

Book 10

Chapter 9. Of the illicit arts connected with demonolatry, and of which the Platonist Porphyry adopts some, and discards others.

These miracles, and many others of the same nature, which it were tedious to mention, were wrought for the purpose of commending the worship of the one true God, and prohibiting the worship of a multitude of false gods. Moreover, they were wrought by simple faith and godly confidence, not by the incantations and charms composed under the influence of a criminal tampering with the unseen world, of an art which they call either magic, or by the more abominable title necromancy, or the more honourable designation theurgy; for they wish to discriminate between those whom the people call magicians, who practice necromancy, and are addicted to illicit arts and condemned, and those others who seem to them to be worthy of praise for the pratice of theurgy – the truth, however, being that both classes are the slaves of the deceitful rites of the demons whom they invoke under the names of the angels. . . .

Chapter 10. Concerning theurgy, which promises a delusive purification of the soul by the invocation of demons.

But here we have another and a much more learned Platonist than Apuleius, Porphyry, to wit, asserting that, by I know not what theurgy, even the gods themselves are subjected to passions and perturbations; for by adjurations they were so bound and terrified that they could not confer purity of soul – were so terrified by him who imposed on them a wicked command, that they could not by the same theurgy be freed from that terror, and fulfil the righteous behest of him who prayed to them, or do the good he sought. Who does not see that all these things are fictions of deceiving demons, unless he be a wretched slave of theirs, and an alien from the grace of the true Liberator? . . . Rather let us abominate and avoid the deceit of such wicked spirits, and listen to sound doctrine. As to those who perform these filthy cleansings by sacrilegious rites, and see in their initiated state (as he further tells us, though we may question this vision) certain wonderfully lovely appearances of angels or gods, this is what the apostle refers to when he speaks of "Satan transforming himself into an angel of light." For these are the delusive appearances of that spirit who longs to entangle wretched souls in the deceptive worship of many and false gods and to turn them aside

28

from the true worship of the true God, by whom alone they are cleansed and healed, and who, as was said of Proteus, "turns himself into all shapes," equally hurtful, whether he assaults us as an enemy, or assumes the disguise of a friend.

Chapter 11. Of Porphyry's epistle to Anebo, in which he asks for information about the differences among demons.

It was a better tone which Porphry adopted in his letter to Anebo the Egyptian, in which, assuming the character of an inquirer consulting him, he unmasks and explodes these sacrilegious arts. In that letter, indeed, he repudiates all demons, whom he maintains to be so foolish as to be attracted by the sacrificial vapours, and therefore residing not in the ether, but in the air beneath the moon, and indeed in the moon itself. For, though he acknow-ledges that as a race demons are foolish, he so far accommodates himself to popular ideas as to call some of them benignant demons. . . . He inquires further, and still as one in doubt, whether diviners and wonderworkers are men of unusually powerful souls, or whether the power to do these things is communicated by spirits from without. He inclines to the latter opinion, on the ground that it is by the use of stones and herbs that they lay spells on people, and open closed doors, and do similar wonders. And on this account, he says, some suppose that there is a race of beings whose property is to listen to men – a race deceitful, full of contrivances, capable of assuming all forms, simulating gods, demons, and dead men – and that it is this race which brings about all these things which have the appearance of good or evil, but that what is really good they never help us in, and are indeed unac-quainted with, for they make wickedness easy, but throw obstacles in the path of those who eagerly follow virtue; and that they are filled with pride and rashness, delight in sacrificial odours, are taken with flattery. These and the other characteristics of this race of deceitful and malicious spirits, who come into the souls of men and delude their senses, both in sleep and waking, he describes not as things of which he is himself convinced, but only with so much suspicion and doubt as to cause him to speak of them as commonly received opinions. We should sympathize with this great philosopher in the difficulty he experienced in acquainting himself with and confidently assailing the whole fraternity of devils, which any Christian old woman would unhesitatingly describe and most unreservedly detest. . . .

Part II

THE MEDIEVAL
FOUNDATIONS OF
WITCH-HUNTING

During the Middle Ages the image of the witch that sustained the prosecutions of the early modern period gradually took shape. The image of a maleficent magician who concluded a pact with the Devil and worshipped him drew on many sources, including those deriving from the ancient world described in the previous Part. The image acquired many of its features in the medieval depictions and condemnations of ritual magicians as individuals who were guilty of idolatry and Devil-worship, and it also incorporated many beliefs regarding heretics who allegedly gathered secretly and performed all sorts of maleficent and obscene rites. The sources reproduced in this chapter reflect different stages in the development of this new and horrifying image of the witch. They cover the period from the promulgation of the canon *Episcopi*, which described certain women who were deceived by the Devil into thinking that they rode out at night to worship the pagan goddess Diana (Chapter 8), to the publication of the widely disseminated witchcraft manual, the *Malleus maleficarum*, in 1486 (Chapter 14).

Three of these documents deal in different ways with the practice of ritual magic and its condemnation in the thirteenth and fourteenth centuries. St Thomas Aquinas provided a foundation for this condemnation in the thirteenth century by arguing that all magic was caused by the exercise of demonic power. This position taken by Aquinas provided a theological foundation for the condemnation of certain forms of magic on the grounds that it involved making a pact with the Devil and was thus heretical (Chapter 9). The Spanish inquisitor Nicholas Eymeric presented the judicial case for prosecuting ritual magicians in the manual he compiled in the late thirteenth century (Chapter 11). An even more comprehensive statement of the Church's position on magic appears in a pronouncement by the theology faculty at the University of Paris in 1398. The faculty condemned as erroneous and in some cases idolatrous and blasphemous arguments magicians had been using to defend their practices (Chapter 12).

The image of the witch that took shape by the fifteenth century was much more horrifying than that of the ritual magician. By that time the witch's alleged activities involved collective Devil-worship, the murder and cannibalistic consumption of infants, copulation with demons, and the widespread destruction of life and property by occult means. Some of these charges had been levelled against heretics in the Middle Ages, and the prosecution of magic as heresy opened the possibility of integrating the invective against heretics with that against ritual magicians. An early indication of the emergence of this new image of the witch appears in the sorcery trial of Dame Alice Kyteler in Ireland in 1324. Kyteler and her associates were accused not only of having committed multiple murders by magical means and summoning up demons but also of having sexual intercourse with those demons and of rejecting their Christian faith (Chapter 10). The account of Kyteler's prosecution does not, however, depict the witches' sabbath in its full horror; that came only in the early fifteenth century with the writing of Johannes Nider's *Formicarius*, which drew upon the trials of lower-class heretical magicians during the early 1400s (Chapter 13). Even Nider's account, however, lacks a description of the witches' flight to the sabbath, which does not appear in many demonologies until the sixteenth century (see Chapter 21).

Somewhat surprisingly the latest document included in this chapter, the *Malleus maleficarum*, says little about the collective gatherings of witches. For that reason it does not deserve the reputation it has acquired as an encyclopedia of witchcraft. Some of the demonologies produced in the sixteenth century, especially those by Martín Del Rio and Nicolas Remy, could stake a better claim to encyclopedic description than that of the *Malleus*. Nevertheless, the *Malleus* does provide evidence of the transformation of the image of the educated, usually male ritual magician who commands demons into that of the predominantly female, illiterate practitioner of harmful magic who is accused of making a pact with the Devil and worshipping him collectively. By the end of the fifteenth century the magician had been turned into the witch.

8

CANON LAW AND
WITCHCRAFT

In the twelfth century the monk Gratian included this text in his *Decretum*, which formed one of the foundations of canon law – the law of the Catholic Church. Referred to as the canon *Episcopi* (the first Latin word of this particular text), the canon probably originated in the ninth century. It had been included in a guide to ecclesiastical discipline early in the tenth century. The canon *Episcopi* became one of the most famous and controversial texts in the history of witchcraft. The document acquired its fame and importance only after witch-hunting began in the fifteenth century. At that time it appeared to support a skeptical position regarding the reality of many witch beliefs, especially that of witches going out at night with Diana, a journey that was later interpreted as flight to the witches' sabbath. In the sixteenth century the skeptic Johann Weyer claimed that the canon was published "in order to refute the erroneous belief that they [witches] are transported bodily." More credulous authorities, such as Heinrich Kramer, the author of the *Malleus maleficarum* (1486), felt it was incumbent on them to explain away the skepticism to which this authoritative statement of church law apparently gave expression (Chapter 14). The work also laid the foundations for a demonological tradition that interpreted all sorcery as the result of God's providence. The canon is emphatic in affirming the sovereignty of God, who according to the text of the canon rules the universe and is able to change the substances of things. The canon *Episcopi* is also known for its leniency, because it does not consign sorcerers or witches to the flames. This claim to leniency must also be qualified. Drafted before the Church began to execute heretics, it instructs bishops to eject from their parishes the practitioners of the "pernicious art of sorcery," who are considered to be heretics, and to cleanse the church of this pest. It also labels the women who believe they go out at night with Diana as "wicked" and that by believing this to be true they too wander from the true faith. Both the sorcerers mentioned at the beginning of the text and the women deceived by Satan are therefore heretics.

Source: This translation of the canon *Episcopi* comes from H. C. Lea, *Materials Toward a History of Witchcraft* (Philadelphia, 1954), I, pp. 178–180.

Bishops and their officials must labor with all their strength to uproot thoroughly from their parishes the pernicious art of sorcery and malefice invented by the Devil, and if they find a man or woman follower of this wickedness to eject them foully disgraced from their parishes. For the Apostle says, "A man that is a heretic after the first and second admonition avoid." Those are held captive by the Devil who, leaving their creator, seek the aid of the Devil. And so Holy Church must be cleansed of this pest. It is also not to be admitted that some wicked women, perverted by the Devil, seduced by illusions and phantasms of demons, believe and profess themselves, in the hours of night, to ride upon certain beasts with Diana, the goddess of pagans, and an innumerable multitude of women, and in the silence of the dead of night to traverse great spaces of earth, and to obey her commands as of her mistress, and to be summoned to her service on certain nights. But I wish it were they alone who perished in their faithlessness and did not draw many with them into the destruction of infidelity. For an innumerable multitude, deceived by this false opinion, believe this to be true, and so believing, wander from the right faith and are involved in the error of the pagans when they think that there is anything of divinity or power except the one God. Wherefore the priests throughout their churches should preach with all insistence to the people that they may know this to be in every way false and that such phantasms are imposed on the minds of infidels and not by the divine but by the malignant spirit. Thus Satan himself, who transfigures himself into an angel of light, when he has captured the mind of a miserable woman and has subjugated her to himself by infidelity and incredulity, immediately transforms himself into the species and similitudes of different personages and deluding the mind which he holds captive and exhibiting things, joyful or mournful, and persons, known or unknown, leads it though devious ways, and while the spirit alone endures this, the faithless mind thinks these things happen not in the spirit but in the body. Who is there that is not led out of himself in dreams and nocturnal visions, and sees much when sleeping which he had never seen waking? Who is so stupid and foolish as to think that all these things which are only done in spirit happen in the body, when the prophet Ezekiel saw visions of the Lord in spirit and not in the body, and the Apostle John saw and heard the mysteries of the Apocalypse in the spirit and not in the body, as he himself says "I was in the spirit"? And Paul does not dare to say that he was rapt in the body. It is therefore to be proclaimed publicly to all that whoever believes such things or similar to these loses the faith, and he who has not the right faith in God is not of God but of him in whom he believes, that is, of the Devil. For of our Lord it is written, "All things were made by him." Whoever therefore believes

34

that anything can be made, or that any creature can be changed to better or to worse or be transformed into another species or similitude, except by the Creator himself who made everything and through whom all things were made, is beyond doubt an infidel.

9

ST THOMAS AQUINAS: SCHOLASTICISM AND MAGIC

St Thomas Aquinas (1225–1274), known as the Angelic Doctor, was a Dominican monk who taught at the University of Paris. He is widely considered the greatest theologian and philosopher of the High Middle Ages. The school of thought which he and his teacher, Albertus Magnus, defined and developed was scholasticism, a comprehensive intellectual system which drew extensively on the thought of the pagan Greek philosopher Aristotle. Scholastic theologians used Aristotle's metaphysical categories of form and matter, accidents and substances to explain the natural world and also provide a rational explanation of some theological truths. Scholasticism took a middle position on the relationship between faith and reason, claiming that reason could provide an explanation of some, but not all, doctrines of Christianity; the doctrine of the Trinity, for example, had to be accepted on faith alone. Aquinas gave formal definition to many doctrines of the Catholic Church, especially that of transubstantiation, which asserted that the bread and wine in the sacrifice of the Mass were transformed into the substance of the body and blood of Christ, while their accidents or appearances remained the same. Aquinas's two great comprehensive works, *Summa theologica* and *Summa contra Gentiles*, included discussions of the role of demons in the world and the practice of magic. These excerpts reveal how Aquinas used scholastic observation and logic to establish the demonic agency of all magic, a position already established in a very different way by St Augustine. The role of scholasticism in contributing to later ideas about witchcraft is highly debated. Aquinas said nothing about witchcraft as such, but his statements regarding magic and the power of the Devil were often cited by demonologists such as Heinrich Kramer (Chapter 14). In the most general sense, the scholastic tendency to attribute all activity that could not be explained by natural means to the supernatural realm encouraged a belief in witchcraft and demonic magic.

Source: St Thomas Aquinas, *The Summa Contra Gentiles* (London, 1928), III (2), pp. 70–75.

Whence the works of magicians derive their efficacy.

It remains for us to inquire whence the magic arts derive their efficacy: a question that will present no difficulty if we consider their mode of operation.

For in the practice of their art they make use of certain significative words in order to produce certain definite effects. Now, words, in so far as they signify something, have no power except as derived from some intellect, either of the speaker or of the person to whom they are spoken. From the intellect of the speaker, as when an intellect is of such great power that it can cause things by its mere thought, the voice serving to convey, as it were, this thought to the things that are produced. From the intellect of the person to whom the words are addressed, as when the hearer is induced to do some particular thing, through his intellect receiving the signification of those words. Now, it cannot be said that these significative words uttered by magicians derive efficacy from the intellect of the speaker. For since power follows essence, diversity of power indicates diversity of essential principles. Moreover, man's intellect is invariably of such a disposition that its knowledge is caused by things, rather than that it is able by its mere thought to cause things. Consequently, if there be any men that are able by their own power to transform things by words expressive of their thoughts, they will belong to another species, and it would be an equivocation to call them men.

Further. By learning we acquire, not the power to do a thing, but the knowledge of how to do it. Yet some, by learning, are rendered able to perform these magic works. Therefore they must have not only knowledge but also the power to produce those effects.

If someone say that these men, by the influence of the stars, are born with the aforesaid power, while others are excluded from it, so that however much the others, who are born without this power, may be instructed, they cannot succeed in performing these works; we reply, first that, as shown above, heavenly bodies cannot make an impression on the intellect. Therefore a man's intellect cannot, through the influence of the stars, receive a power whereby the vocal expression of its thoughts is productive of something.

And if it be said that the imagination produces an effect in the utterance of significative words, and that heavenly bodies can work on the imagination, since its operation is performed by a bodily organ: – this does not apply to all the results produced by this art. For we have shown . . . that these effects cannot all be produced by the power of the stars. Neither, therefore, can anyone by the power of the stars, receive the power to produce those effects. Consequently it follows that these effects are accomplished by an intellect to whom the discourse of the persons uttering these words is addressed. We have an indication of this in the fact that the significative words employed by the magician are *invocations, supplications, adjurations*, or even *commands* as though he were addressing another.

37

Again. Certain characters and definite figures are employed in the observances of this art. Now a figure cannot be the principle of either action or passion; else, mathematical bodies would be active and passive. Therefore matter cannot, by definite figures, be disposed to receive a certain natural effect. Therefore, magicians do not employ figures as dispositions. It remains, then, that they employ them only as signs, for there is no third solution. But we do make signs only to other intelligent beings. Therefore the magic arts derive their efficacy from another intelligent being, to whom the magician's words are addressed. . . .

That the intellectual substance which gives efficacy to the practices of magic is not good according to virtue.

We must further inquire what is this intellectual nature by whose power these works are done.

And in the first place it is plain that it is not good and praiseworthy, for it is the mark of an ill-disposed mind to countenance things contrary to virtue. Now this is done in these arts, for they are often employed in order to further adultery, theft, murder and like malefices, wherefore those who practise these arts are called *malefics*. Therefore the intellectual nature on whose assistance these arts depend is not well disposed according to virtue.

Again. It is not the mark of a mind well disposed according to virtue to befriend and assist men of evil life, rather than every upright man. Now those who practise these arts are often men of evil life. Therefore the intellectual nature from whose assistance these arts derive their efficacy is not well disposed according to virtue. . . .

Moreover. There is a certain deception and unreasonableness in the works of these arts, for they require a man indifferent to lustful pleasure, whereas they are frequently employed to further lustful intercourse. But there is nothing unreasonable or contradictory in the work of a well-disposed mind. Therefore these arts do not employ the assistance of an intellect that is well disposed as to virtue.

Besides, it is an ill-disposed mind that is incited by the commission of crime to lend his assistance to another. But this is done in these arts: for we read of innocent children being slain by those who practice them. Therefore the persons by whose assistance such things are done have an evil mind. . . .

10

THE TRIAL OF
DAME ALICE KYTELER,
1324

⸺◦◦◦⸺

The trial of Dame Alice Kyteler for sorcery by an ecclesiastical court in Ireland in 1324 marks one of the milestones in the development of the early modern stereotype of the witch. The trial conforms in its essential elements to that of ritual magicians prosecuted for performing *maleficium*. Dame Alice and her associates were accused of sacrificing animals to a demon and using powders, ointments, and lotions to commit murder and persuade young men whom she had infatuated by magical means to give their possessions to her. The accusation that she had had relations with an incubus demon also was a standard charge made against ritual magicians by the fourteenth century. The case did, however, possess a number of novel elements that are not found in the usual trials of ritual magicians in the early fourteenth century, and these elements anticipate many of the charges later brought against witches. The collective nature of the crime, the nocturnal meetings of Dame Alice and her associates, and their complete rejection of the Christian faith all were drawn from the stockpile of invective that monastic writers had written against heretics on the European continent during the previous two centuries. The official who prosecuted these sorcerers successfully integrated such claims made against heretics with the traditional charges made against ritual magicians, giving us an early glimpse of the fifteenth-century witch. The fact that these sorcerers were female, unlike most ritual magicians, makes the anticipation of charges against witches even more striking. The narrative of the case, which was written by Richard Ledrede, the bishop of Ossory, who prosecuted Dame Alice, makes it clear that these malefactors "practised all kinds of sorceries" as well as being "well-versed in all kinds of heresies." The end product is a more horrific view of ritual magicians than was available at this time. Nevertheless, the description of these activities does not yet contain all the elements of the witches' sabbath.

Source: *The Sorcery Trial of Alice Kyteler*, eds L. S. Davidson and
J. O. Ward. Medieval and Renaissance Texts and Studies (Binghamton, NY,
1993), pp. 26–30, 62–63, 70.

1.   While John XXII was pope, the following events took place in Ireland. During a visitation to his diocese, the venerable father, brother Richard, bishop of Ossory, held the customary inquest in which five knights and a large number of other nobles took part. The bishop discovered that in the town of Kilkenny there had been for a long time, and still were, very many heretical sorceresses who practised all kinds of sorceries and were well-versed in all kinds of heresies. Carrying the investigation of these witches as far as he was bound by the duties of his office, the bishop discovered that a certain rich lady, Dame Alice Kyteler, mother of William Outlaw, was involved in various heresies, along with several accomplices.

First it was claimed that, in order to get what they wanted by means of their foul sorceries, the sorceresses would deny faith in Christ and the church for a whole month or for a year, according to the extent of what they wished to obtain from the sorcery. During that time, they would believe in nothing that the church believed, they would not worship the body of Christ in any way, they would not go into a church, they would not hear mass, they would not eat the holy bread or drink the holy water.

Secondly, it was claimed that they were in the habit of making sacrifices to demons with living animals which they would cut into pieces and scatter around the crossroads as offerings to a certain demon who called himself the son of Art, from the humbler levels of the underworld.

Thirdly, that by means of their sorceries the witches would seek advice and answers from demons.

Fourth, that the witches were usurping authority and the keys of the church when they held their nocturnal meetings because by the light of waxen candles they would hurl the sentence of excommunication even at their own husbands, calling out, one by one, the names of each and every part of their body from the soles of their feet to the top of their head, and then at the end the witches would blow out the candles and say, "fi: fi: fi: amen."

Fifth, that in a skull from the head of a decapitated robber over a fire of oak wood, they would boil up the intestines and internal organs of the cocks which, as mentioned above, had been sacrificed to demons. They would mix in some horrible worms, add various herbs and countless other vile ingredients such as nails cut from dead bodies, hairs from the buttocks, and frequently clothes from boys who had died before being baptised.

From this mixture they would concoct various powders, ointments and lotions; they would even make candles from the fat left in the cooking pot; chanting different chants, they would incite people to love and to hate, to kill as well as to afflict the bodies of faithful Christians, and to do countless other things they desired.

Sixth, that the sons and daughters of the said lady's four husbands were publicly instituting litigation before the bishop, seeking remedy and assistance against the lady. Openly and in front of the people, they alleged that she had used sorceries of this kind to murder some of their fathers and to infatuate others, reducing their senses to such stupidity that they gave all their possessions to her and to her own son, thus impoverishing forever their sons and heirs. Moreover, the lady's present husband, the knight Sir John le Poer, had reached such a state through powders and lotions of this kind as well as through sorceries, that his whole body was emaciated, his nails were torn out and all hair removed from his body. This knight, however, with the help of one of the lady's servants, had forcibly grabbed from her hands the keys to the lady's chests. These he opened and found there a sack full of vile and horrible ingredients which he sent with all else that he had found to the aforesaid bishop in the hands of two trustworthy priests.

Seventh, that the said lady had a certain demon as *incubus* by whom she permitted herself to be known carnally, and that the demon called herself son of Art, or else Robin, Son of Art. Sometimes, it was claimed, he appeared to her in the shape of a cat, sometimes in the shape of a shaggy black dog, sometimes as a black man with two companions bigger and taller than himself, one of whom carried an iron rod in his hands. It was claimed that the lady entrusted herself and all her possessions to this demon from whom she admitted that she received her wealth and whatever she owned. . . .

36.   On this same day a heretic was burnt at the stake. She was Petronilla of Meath, an accomplice of the said Dame Alice. After being six times whipped on the order of the bishop for her sorceries, and finally found out to be a heretic, she admitted in front of all the clergy and people that under the influence of the said Dame Alice, she had totally rejected faith in Christ and the church, and three times on Alice's behalf she had sacrificed to demons. On one of these occasions, by the crossroads outside the city, she had made an offering of three cocks to a certain demon whom she called Robert, son of Art, from the depths of the underworld. She had poured out the cock's blood, cut the animals into pieces and mixed the intestines with spiders and other black worms like scorpions, with a herb called milfoil [common yarrow] as well as with other herbs and horrible worms. She had boiled this mixture in a pot with the brains and clothes of a boy who had died without baptism and with the head of a robber who had been decapitated. This was all done at Alice's instigation. Petronilla had also made many concoctions, lotions and powders which were to cause injury to the bodies of the faithful and arouse love and hate as well as to make the faces of certain women appear before certain people with horns like goats when particular incantations were added.

Petronilla said she had several times at Alice's instigation and once in her presence consulted demons and received answers. She had consented to a pact whereby he would be the medium between Alice and the said Robert, her friend. In public, she said that with her own eyes she had seen the aforesaid demon as three shapes, in the form of three black men, each carrying an iron rod in the hand. This apparition happened by daylight before the Dame Alice, and, while Petronilla herself was watching, the apparition had intercourse with Alice. After this disgraceful act, with her own hand she [Alice?] wiped clean the disgusting place with sheets from her own bed.

Among her other confessions she said that often she and Alice had put their own husbands under the sentence of excommunication, by lighting waxen candles and spitting various ways as the ritual required. And although in their unholy art she was mistress of the ritual, she was nothing, she said, in comparison with her mistress, from whom she had learnt all those things and many others. In fact there was no one in the kingdom of England more skilled nor did she think there was anyone in the world her equal in the art of witchcraft.

When the sacrament of penance was offered to her, Petronilla refused utterly in front of the whole people, and with her foul crimes publicly revealed, was duly burnt at the stake before a vast crowd of people with due formality. She was the first of so many heretic witches ever to be burnt at the stake in Ireland. . . .

43. The other heretics and soothsayers belonging to that pestiferous society of Robin Artisson were dealt with according to the law. Some were publicly burnt, some publicly revealed their crimes in front of the whole people and then, after abjuring heresy, had their outer clothes marked in front and behind with a cross, as is the custom. Others were solemnly whipped in town and in the market place; others were exiled outside the ciy and diocese; others, escaping the church's jurisdiction, were publicly excommunicated, while others were so terrified that they took to flight, hid, and have not yet been found.

11

NICHOLAS EYMERIC:
MAGIC AND HERESY,
1376

Nicholas Eymeric, an inquisitor in the Spanish kingdom of Aragon, wrote a manual for inquisitors, *Directorium Inquisitorium,* in 1376. The purpose of one section of the manual was to determine under what circumstances practitioners of magic would be guilty of blasphemy and heresy. Eymeric claimed that only when magicians summon up demons and make sacrifices to them should they be placed in that category and prosecuted by the Inquisition, the tribunal entrusted with the maintenance of Christian orthodoxy. His instruction in this matter includes a revealing summary of the various activities that ritual magicians engaged in during the fourteenth century. The people whom Eymeric is condemning in this context should be considered magicians, not witches. They conform even less than Dame Alice Kyteler and her associates did to the later, fifteenth-century stereotype of the witch. There is nothing in Eymeric, for example, about the performance of *maleficium.* Nevertheless, Eymeric's manual possesses immense importance for the development of that stereotype, since it provides clearly defined connections between the practice of demonic magic and heresy. As the crime of witchcraft became defined in the fifteenth and sixteenth centuries, demonological treatises and manuals served the function of informing the judicial authorities regarding the nature of the crime of witchcraft. Eymeric's manual, however, continued to be used in the Spanish and Roman inquisitions. There it had the effect of making the practice of relatively simple, non-maleficent magic both diabolical and heretical. Sometimes these cases were referred to as witchcraft, but like the fourteenth-century cases with which Eymeric was concerned, they should be labeled simply as magic.

Source: Edward Peters, *The Magician, the Witch and the Law* (Philadelphia, 1978), pp. 198–201.

The forty-second question asks whether magicians and diviners are to be considered heretics or as those suspected of heresy and whether they are to be subjected to the judgment of the Inquisitor of heretics. To this we answer that there are two things to be seen here, just as there are really two things asked in this question. The first is, whether magicians and diviners are subject to the judgment of the Inquisitor of heretics. The second, posed thusly, is whether they are to be considered as heretics or as those suspected of heresy.

1. The first thing to be considered . . . is that diviners and magicians must be distinguished; that is, there are two kinds of diviners and magicians.
2. Some are to be considered magicians and diviners just as are those who act purely according to the technique of chiromancy, who divine things from the lineaments of the hand and judge natural effects and the condition of men from this . . .
3. Some others, however, are magicians and diviners who are not pure chiromantics, but are contracted to heretics, as are those who show the honor of *latria* [adoration due to God alone] or *dulia* [reverence to be paid only to the saints] to the demons, who rebaptize children and do other similar things. And they do these things in order to foresee the future or penetrate to the innermost secrets of the heart. These people are guilty of manifest heresy. And such magicians and diviners do not evade the judgment of the Inquisitor, but are punished according to the laws pertaining to heretics.

The forty-third question asks whether those who invoke demons, either magicians or heretics or those suspected of heresy, are subject to the judgment of the Inquisitor of heretics. . . .

2. It appears to the Inquisitors from the above-mentioned books and from other books that certain invokers of demons manifestly show the honor of *latria* to the demons they invoke, inasmuch as they sacrifice to them, adore them, offer up horrible prayers to them, vow themselves to the service of the demons, promise them their obedience, and otherwise commit themselves to the demons, swearing by the name of some superior demon whom they invoke. They willingly celebrate the praises of the demon or sing songs in his honor, and genuflect and prostrate themselves before him. They observe chastity out of reverence for the demon or abstain upon his instructions or they lacerate their own flesh. Out of reverence for the demon or by his instructions they wear white or black vestments. They worship him by signs and characters and unknown names. They burn candles or incense to him or aromatic spices. They sacrifice animals and birds, catching their blood as a curative agent, or they burn them, throwing salt in the fire and making a holocaust in this manner. All of these things and many more evil things are found in consulting and desiring things from demons, in all of which and

in whichever the honor of *latria*, if the above things are considered intelligently, is clearly shown to the demons. If, note well, the sacrifices to God according to the old and the new law are considered, it is found that these acts are true sacrifices only when exhibited to God, and not to the demons. This, then, is the case with the first category of those who invoke or speak on behalf of demons. . . . And by this manner the priests used to invoke Baal, offering their own blood and that of animals, as one reads in 4 *Kings*, 18.

3.   Certain other invokers of demons show to the demons they invoke not the honor of *latria*, but that of *dulia*, in that they insert in their wicked prayers the names of demons along with those of the Blessed or the Saints, making them mediators in their prayers heard by God. They bow down before images of wax, worshipping God by their names or qualities. These things and many other wretched things are found described in the aforementioned books in which the honor of *dulia* is shown to demons. If, indeed, the means of praying to the Saints which the Church has diligently instituted and considered, it will clearly be seen that these prayers are to be said, not to demons, but only to the Saints and the Blessed. This, then, is the case of the second category of those who invoke demons. And in this manner the Saracens invoke Mohammed as well as God and the saints and certain Beghards invoke Petrus Johannis and others condemned by the Church.

4.   Yet certain other invokers of demons make a certain kind of invocation in which it does not appear clearly that the honor either of *latria* or *dulia* is shown to the demons invoked, as in tracing a circle on the ground, placing a child in the circle, setting a mirror, a sword, an amphora or something else in the way before the boy, holding their book of necromancy, reading it, and invoking the demon and other suchlike, as is taught by that art and proved by the confessions of many. This, then, is the third way of invoking demons. And by this means Saul invoked the spirit of the python through the Pythoness. In Saul's invocation, it is seen, no honor was done, neither *latria* nor *dulia*, as one reads in 1 *Kings*: 26. . . .

5.   . . . [T]he case or conclusion is that if the invokers of demons show to the demons they invoke the honor of *latria* by whatever means, and if they are clearly and judicially convicted of this, or if they confess, then they are to be held by the judgment of the Church not as magicians, but as heretics, and if they recant and abjure heresy they are to be perpetually immured as penitent heretics. If, however, they do not wish to desist, or if they say they wish to desist and repent but do not wish to abjure, or if they abjure and afterwards relapse, they are to be relinquished to the secular arm, punished by the ultimate torture according to all the canonical sanctions which judge other heretics.

This conclusion may be deduced in three ways: first, from the sayings of the saints and doctors of theology, second, from the sayings of the doctors of canon law, and third, from the decisions of the Church.

First, from the sayings of the theologians, Blessed Augustine in Book 10 of *The City of God*, speaking of sacrifices shown only to God and not to demons, says this: "We see that it is observed in each republic that men honor the highest leader by a singular sign which, if it is offered to someone else, would be the hateful crime of *lèse-majesté*. And thus it is written in the divine law under pain of death to those who offer divine honors to others. Exterior deeds are signs of interior deeds, just as spoken words are the signs of things. . . ."

By these words Augustine shows clearly that such sacrifice ought to be offered to God alone, and when it is offered to another than God, then by that deed one shows oneself to believe that that person is higher than God, which is heresy. Whoever, therefore, offers sacrifice to demons considers the demon as God and shows himself to believe the demon to be the true God by offering external signs. By which deeds they are to be considered heretics. . . .

[O]ur conclusion is also proved by the decisions of the Church. Indeed [the canon] *Episcopi* says this: "Bishops and their officials should abhor with all their strength . . ."And from this it appears that those who share and exercise the magical art are to be considered heretics and avoided . . . And from this it appears that the said evil women, persevering in their wickedness, have departed from the right way and the faith, and the devils delude them. If, therefore, these same women, concerning whom it is not contested that they offer sacrifices to the demons they invoke, are perfidious and faithless and deviate from the right way, as the said canon from the Council of Ancyra makes clear, then, as a consequence, if they have been baptized, they are to be considered heretics; since for a Christian to deviate from the right way and faith and to embrace infidelity is properly to hereticize. How much more, then, are Christians who show the honor of *latria* to demons and sacrifice to the demons they invoke to be said and considered to be perfidious deviants from the right way and faithless in the love of Christians, which is heresy — and by consequence to be considered heretics? . . .

12

THE UNIVERSITY OF PARIS: A CONDEMNATION OF MAGIC, 1398

In September 1398 the theology faculty at the University of Paris approved a set of twenty-eight articles condemning the practice of ritual magic. The articles determined that various arguments magicians had been using to defend their practices were erroneous and in some cases blasphemous. In making this pronouncement, the Parisian faculty presented the argument, developed by scholastic theologians during the fourteenth century, that the practice of summoning up demons and commanding them to perform deeds was heretical because it gave to demons what was due only to God. Jean Gerson, the theologian, political theorist, and devotional writer who was chancellor of the university at the time, appended the document in a somewhat altered form to his treatise condemning magic in 1402. The articles do not say anything about witchcraft as it came to be defined later in the fifteenth century. The faculty was concerned about the activities of literate magicians, many of whom were themselves clerics, not the practices of the women and men who were soon to be accused of practising simple *maleficia* and worshiping the Devil at the sabbath. Nevertheless, the theology faculty's condemnation of magical practices provided authoritative support for later condemnations of witchcraft, especially since the document included references to *maleficia* as well as the negotiation of pacts with the Devil. In the sixteenth century the condemnation was reprinted in the preface to Jean Bodin's *The Demon-Mania of Witches* (Chapter 26), while quotations from it appear in Lambert Daneau's *Dialogue of Witches* (Chapter 15) and Martín Del Rio's *Investigations into Magic* (Chapter 18). Johann Weyer, the sixteenth-century skeptic regarding witchcraft, also devoted the final chapter of his massive *De Praestigiis Daemonum* (Chapter 50) to this pronouncement, thereby providing support for his own condemnation of magic.

Source: This translation of the pronouncement is based on the Latin text
included in the preface to Jean Bodin, *Démonomanie des sorciers*
(Paris, 1580).

Determination made by the faculty of theology at Paris in the year of our lord 1398 regarding certain newly arisen superstitions

The first article is this: that to seek intimacy, friendship, and help from demons by means of magical arts, harmful magical acts [*maleficia*], and forbidden invocations is not idolatry. This is an error, because the demon is judged to be an undaunted and implacable adversary of God and man. He is incapable of ever receiving any truly divine honor or dominion by participation or by suitability, like other rational creatures that have not been condemned. Nor is God adored in these demons in a sign instituted at His pleasure, such as images and shrines.

The second article: that to give, or to offer, or to promise demons any sort of thing so that they fulfill the desire of man – even to bear something valued by them in their honor – is not idolatry. This is an error.

The third article: to enter an implicit or explicit pact with demons is neither idolatry nor a species of idolatry or apostasy. This is an error. And by "implicit pact" we mean every superstitious ritual, the effects of which cannot be reasonably traced to either God or nature.

The fourth: that it is not idolatrous to use magical arts to try to enclose, to force, to restrain demons in stones, rings or images consecrated – better, execrated – to their names, or even to make these objects come to life [by demons]. This is an error.

The fifth: that it is allowed to use magical arts or other kinds of superstition prohibited by God and the Church for any good moral purpose. This is an error because according to the Apostle, evil cannot be done that good may result from it.

The sixth: that it is allowed and even to be permitted to repel *maleficia* by other *maleficia*. This is an error.

The seventh: that someone can dispense with something in a particular situation in order to use such [arts] licitly. This is an error.

The eighth: the magical arts, similar superstitions, and their practice are unreasonably prohibited by the Church. This is an error.

The ninth: that the magical arts and *maleficia* lead God to compel demons to obey his precations. This is an error.

The tenth: that the offering of incense and smoke, performed in the exercise of such arts and *maleficia*, is in God's honor and pleases Him. This is an error and a blasphemy, since God would not otherwise punish or prohibit [it].

The eleventh: that to use such and do so is not to sacrifice or to make immolations to demons and, therefore, it is not damnable idolatry. This is an error.

The twelfth: that sacred words and certain kinds of devout prayers and fasts and cleansings and bodily self-control in boys and others [and] the celebration of Mass and other types of good works which are [all] performed in order to do these arts, that these [good] works exculpate the evil in the arts and do not, rather, indict it. This is an error, for by means of such sacred acts, an attempt is made to sacrifice something – even God Himself in the Eucharist – to demons. The demon makes these sacrifices either because he wishes to be honored like the Most High [Isaiah 14:14], or because he wishes to conceal his frauds, or to trap the simple-minded more easily and destroy them more damnably.

The thirteenth: that by such arts the holy prophets and other saints had the power of their prophecies and performed miracles or expelled demons. This is an error and blasphemy.

The fourteenth: that God by Himself and with no intermediary or with the good angels revealed such *maleficia* to holy persons. This is an error and blasphemy.

The fifteenth: that such arts can force the free will of a person to bend to the will or desire of another person. This is an error: and to try to do this is impious and nefarious.

The sixteenth: that for that reason the aforesaid arts are good and from God, and that it is permissible to practice them. For through their observance sometimes or often come about that which the observers seek or say, because good sometimes comes from them. This is an error.

The seventeenth: that such arts truly force and compel demons and not vice versa, i.e., that the demons pretend they are forced to seduce men. This is an error.

The eighteenth: that such arts and irreligious rites, lots, charms and conjurings of demons, mockeries, and other malefices in the service of demons never produce any effect. This is an error. For God does sometimes permit such things to happen: as was obvious in the magicians of Pharaoh and several other places, either because the practitioners or devotees have been given over to reprobate understanding for their bad faith and other terrible sins and deserve to be deceived.

The nineteenth: that good angels may be confined within stones and [that] they consecrate images or vestments or do other things included in these arts. This is an error.

The twentieth: that the blood of a little girl or of a goat or of another animal or a lamb's skin or pelt of a lion and other such things have the power to attract or repel demons by the exercise of such arts. This is an error.

The twenty-first: that images made of bronze, lead or gold, of white or red wax or other material, when baptized and exorcized and consecrated – rather, execrated! – as prescribed by these same arts, have tremendous powers on those days of the year described in the books of such arts. This is an error in the faith, in natural philosophy and in true astronomy.

The twenty-second: that it is not idolatry and infidelity to practice such arts and believe in them. This is an error.

The twenty-third: that some demons are good demons, others are omniscient, still others neither saved nor damned. This is an error.

The twenty-fourth: that the offerings of smoke, performed in such activities, turn into spirits or that the smoke offerings are due to the same spirits. This is an error.

The twenty-fifth: that one demon is King of the East and mainly by his merit, another of the West, another of the North, another of the South. This is an error.

The twenty-sixth: that the Sphere of Intelligence that moves the heavens flows into the rational soul in the same manner that the body of the heavens flows into the human body. This is an error.

The twenty-seventh: that the heavens, without any intermediary, produces our intellectual thoughts and our interior intentions, and that such [thoughts and intents] can be known through some magical tradition, and that it is permissible to certify the pronouncements made in this way. This is an error.

The twenty-eighth article: that such magical arts of any kind can lead us to a vision of the Divine Essence or to the spirit of the Saints. This is an error.

These determinations have been enacted by us and our deputies after prolonged and frequent examination; they have been agreed upon in our general congregation of Paris, called this morning and especially for this purpose at the church of St Mathurin, on the nineteenth day of the month of September in the year of our Lord 1398. We have witnessed the proceedings by the seal of the aforesaid faculty appended to these documents.

Figure 1 The Practice of Ritual Magic. A sixteenth-century depiction of a magician summoning up a demon. The magician is male, literate, and well attired. The magical circle was intended to protect the magician from the power of the demon whom he is summoning up. The practice of ritual or ceremonial magic became a major concern of the Church in the fourteenth century (see above, Chapters 9, 11, 12). Many ideas regarding the crime of witchcraft, especially the equation of magic with heresy, originated in the discourse regarding ritual magic in the Middle Ages. From the title-page of Christopher Marlowe, *Dr. Faustus* (London, 1636).

13

JOHANNES NIDER:
AN EARLY DESCRIPTION
OF THE WITCHES'
SABBATH, 1435

Between 1435 and 1437 Johannes Nider, a Dominican theologian who had become the head of the Dominican priory in Basel in 1431 and who had been named a lecturer at the University of Vienna in 1434, wrote a theological treatise titled *Formicarius* [The Ant-Heap]. Between 1431 and 1439 Nider also served as a prominent member of the ecumenical Council of Basel, having been appointed by that ecclesiastical synod to negotiate with the followers of the Bohemian heretic Jan Hus. *Formicarius* takes the form of a dialogue between a theologian, most certainly Nider himself, and a lazy student. In Book V, Nider describes the alleged activities of the new sect of heretics, known as *malefici* or witches, who combined the performance of harmful magic with ceremonies at which they allegedly rejected their Christian faith and performed various horrific acts. The examples Nider uses come primarily from Peter von Greyerz, a lay judge in the Swiss territory of Berne who had prosecuted a number of magicians in the Simme valley between 1392 and 1406. Nider also acknowledged two other sources: a Benedictine monk of noble blood who admitted to an earlier career as a necromancer and an inquisitor from the diocese of Autun. Nider's book appeared at the time when the first witchcraft trials referring to the witches' sabbath had taken place in Europe. It is unclear whether the individuals Peter von Greyerz convicted had actually described such activities at their trials or whether he had embellished his reports of the trials in light of later confessions. But by the time Nider wrote most of the elements of the witches' sabbath were already in place: cannibalistic infanticide, the renunciation of Christianity, the appearance of a demon in the shape of a human being, and instruction in the use of harmful magic. Other elements, such as flight to the sabbath, do not appear in Nider's account. Nider's purpose was to call attention to the danger of this new group of heretics, who were far more dangerous than any of the practitioners of demonic ritual magic who had been the major concern of the Church during the fourteenth century.

Source: The following excerpts from *Formicarius* have been translated
from the Latin text in *Quellen und Untersuchungen zur Geschichte
des Hexenwahns und der Hexenverfolgung im Mittelalter,*
ed. Joseph Hansen (Bonn, 1901), pp. 91–94.

Theologian: I will relate to you some examples, which I have gained in part from the teachers of our faculty, in part from the experience of a certain upright secular judge, worthy of all faith, who from the torturer and confession of witches and from his experience in public and private has learned many things of this sort – a man with whom I have often discussed this subject broadly and deeply – to wit, Peter, a citizen of Bern, in the diocese of Lausanne, who had burned many witches of both sexes, and has driven others out of the territory of the Bernese. I have moreover conferred with one Benedict, a monk of the Bendictine order, who, although now a very devout cleric in a reformed monastery at Vienna, was a decade ago, while still in the world, a necromancer, juggler, buffoon, and strolling player, well known as an expert among the secular nobility. I have likewise heard certain of the following things from the Inquisitor of Heretical Pravity at Autun, who was a devoted reformer of our order in the convent at Lyons, and has convicted many of witchcraft in the diocese of Autun.

And so there are now, or very recently have been, as the same inquisitor and master Peter have told me and rumour has it, some witches of both sexes in the area of Berne. These, against the tendency of human nature – indeed, against the manners of all species of animals with the exception of wolves – devour the babies of their own species and habitually consume them. In the town of Boltigen in the diocese of Lausanne, a certain chief witch named Stedelen was captured by the same Peter the judge. Stedelen confessed that in his practice over a period of time he had killed seven babies in the womb of the woman in the house where the woman and man lived, such that he aborted foetuses in the woman for many years. In the same house, he did the same to all the pregnant cows, none of which gave birth to any living thing for the same number of years, as the conclusion to this series of events proved. So when this vile person was questioned whether and how he was involved in all this, he revealed his crime by saying that he had placed a lizard under the front entrance to the house, which, if removed, would restore fertility to every animal living there. But when they searched for the lizard under the door and could not find it – perhaps because it had turned into dust – they carried away the dust as well as the dirt underneath it; and fertility returned to the woman and the animals that same year. Stedelen moreover, was forced to confess under torture, and the aforesaid judge finally consigned him to the flames.

Then the aforesaid inquisitor told me that in the duchy of Lausanne he had seen some witches cooking and eating their own children. The way that they would find out about this practice was, as he said, that the witches would come to a fixed meeting place, and would see the demon in the assumed likeness of a man. Their disciples had to promise to abjure Christianity, never to reverence the Eucharist and to stamp on the cross if they could do so without notice.

It was moreover widely known, the said judge Peter told me, that in the territory of Bern witches had devoured thirteen babies within a short period of time, with the result that public justice finally flared up sufficiently harshly against such murderers. When Peter had questioned one of the captured witches how they ate the babies, she said: "This is how. With unbaptized babies, even baptized ones if they are not protected by the sign of the cross and prayers, we kill them in our ceremonies, either in their cradles or by the sides of their parents, who afterwards are thought to have suffocated or to have died in some other way. We then quietly steal them from their graves and cook them in a cauldron until their bones can be separated from the boiled meat and the broth. From the more solid material we make an unguent suitable for our purposes and rites and transmutations. From the more liquid fluid, we fill up a flask or a bottle made out of skins, and he who drinks from this, with the addition of a few ceremonies, immediately becomes an accomplice and a master of our sect."

The same procedure was more clearly described by another young man, arrested and burned as a witch, although as I believe, truly penitent, who had earlier, together with his wife, a witch invincible to persuasion, escaped the clutches of the aforesaid judge Peter. The aforesaid youth, being again indicted at Bern with his wife, and placed in a different prison from hers, declared, "If I can obtain absolution for my sins, I will freely lay bare all I know about witchcraft, for I see that I have death to expect." And when he had been assured by the scholars that, if he should truly repent, he would certainly be able to gain absolution for his sins, then he gladly offered himself to death, and disclosed the methods of his youthful infection.

"The ceremony in which I was seduced," he said, "was as follows: First, on the Lord's day, before the holy water is consecrated, the future disciple must go with his masters into the church, and there in their presence must renounce Christ and his faith, baptism, and the Church universal. Then he must do homage to the *magisterulus*, that is, to the little master (for so, and not otherwise, they call the Devil). Afterward he drinks from the aforesaid flask, and this done, he forthwith feels himself to conceive and hold within himself an image of our art and the chief rites of this sect. After this fashion was I seduced; and my wife also, whom I believe of so great pertinacity that she will endure the flames rather than confess the least bit of the truth; but, alas, we are both guilty." What the young man had said was found in all respects to be the truth. For after confession, the young man was seen to die in great contrition. His wife, however, though convicted by the testimony of witnesses, would not confess the truth even under the torture or in death; but when the fire was prepared for her by the executioner, uttered in most evil words a curse upon him, and so was burned.

Figure 2 Demonic Temptation. The Devil was often described as first appearing to a woman in man's dress and tempting her into his service. This woodcut, taken from Ulrich Molitor's *De Lamis* (Cologne, 1489) reveals his true identity.

14

HEINRICH KRAMER:
MALLEUS MALEFICARUM,
1486

The witchcraft treatise *Malleus maleficarum* [the Hammer of Witches], first published in 1486, was primarily the work of Heinrich Kramer, a Dominican theologian and inquisitor known also by his Latin surname of Institoris. The book identifies another Dominican inquisitor, Jacob Sprenger, a member of the faculty of theology at the University of Cologne, as Kramer's co-author. It is unclear how much of a role, if any at all, Sprenger had in the production of the book; Kramer may have simply added his name to a document to which Sprenger had objected. In any event, Kramer was the principal author. The book was written at a time when the two inquisitors were encountering resistance in their efforts to prosecute witches in the area of upper Germany and the Rhineland. In 1484 they secured a bull from Pope Innocent VIII (Chapter 24) confirming their authority to proceed against witches in these areas. The bull was included as a preface to this work, which was intended to make authorities aware of the threat posed by witchcraft and to provide a manual for inquisitors who would try them. The treatise went into fifteen printings between 1486 and 1520 and another nineteen printings between 1569 and 1669, which was the most intense period of witch-hunting in Europe. The following excerpts from Part I illustrate three of the main themes of the book. The first is the determination to counteract the skeptical argument that witches do not exist, a position that Kramer argues is heretical. In this discussion Kramer contends that the canon *Episcopi* (Chapter 8), which asserted that witches claiming to go out at night with Diana were deceived by the Devil, was not a denial of the reality of witchcraft. The second theme is that the Devil needed witches as well as the permission of God to perform their destructive work. The third theme is the highly misogynistic argument that witchcraft was practised mainly by women whose intellectual feebleness, moral weakness, and sexual passion led them to become witches. The excerpts from Part II provide detailed descriptions of the various activities of witches, including copulation with demons (*incubi*), and the way in which the Devil prevented men from performing the sexual act. These latter sections provide further evidence of Kramer's preoccupation with the sexual aspects of witch-craft. Excerpts from Part III of the *Malleus*, which deal with the legal procedures used to try witches, appear in Chapter 25.

Source: *The Malleus Maleficarum of Heinrich Kramer and James Sprenger*, ed. Montague Summers (London, 1928), pp. 1–7, 11–12, 20–21, 41–44, 89, 94–98, 99–100, 111, 114–115, 117–118.

Part I

Question I. Whether the belief that there are such beings as witches is so essential a part of the Catholic faith that obstinacy to maintain the opposite opinion manifestly savours of heresy. . . .

Answer. Here are three heretical errors which must be met, and when they have been disproved the truth will be plain. For certain writers, pretending to base their opinion upon the words of St Thomas when he treats of impediments brought about by magic and charms, have tried to maintain that there is no such thing as magic, that it only exists in the imagination of those men who ascribe natural effects, the causes whereof are not known, to witchcraft and spells. There are others who acknowledge indeed that witches exist but they claim that the influence of magic and effects of charms are purely imaginary and phantasmical. A third class of writers maintain that the effects said to be wrought by magic spells are altogether illusory and fanciful, although it may be that the devil does really lend his aid to some witch.

The errors held by each one of these persons may thus be set forth and thus confuted. For in the very first place they are shown to be plainly heretical by many orthodox writers and especially by St Thomas, who lays down that such an opinion is altogether contrary to the authority of the saints and is founded upon absolute infidelity. Because the authority of the Holy Scripture says that devils have power over the bodies and the minds of men, when God allows them to exercise this power, as is plain from many passages in the Holy Scriptures. Therefore those err who say that there is no such thing as witchcraft but that it is purely imaginary, even although they do not believe that devils exist except in the imagination of the ignorant and the vulgar, and the natural accidents which happen to a man he wrongly attributes to some supposed devil. For the imagination of some men is so vivid that they think they see actual figures and appearances which are but the reflection of their thoughts, and then these are believed to be the apparitions of evil spirits or even the spectres of witches. But this is contrary to the true faith, which teaches us that certain angels fell from heaven and we are bound to acknowledge that by their very nature they can do many wonderful things which we cannot do. And those who try to induce others to perform such evil wonders are called witches. And because infidelity in a person who has been baptized is technically called heresy, therefore such persons are plainly heretics.

As regards those who hold the other two errors, those, that is to say, who do not deny that there are demons and that demons possess a natural power, but who differ among themselves concerning the possible effects of magic and the possible operations of witches: the one school holding that a witch can truly bring about certain effects, yet these effects are not real but phantastical, the other school allowing that some real harm does befall the person or persons injured, but that when a person imagines this damage is the effect of her arts she is grossly deceived. This error seems to be based upon two passages from the Canons where certain women who falsely imagine that during the night they rise abroad with Diana or Herodias. This may be read in the Canon. Yet because such things often happen by illusion and merely in the imagination, those who suppose that all the effects of witchcraft are mere illusion and imagination are very greatly deceived. Secondly, with regard to a man who believes or maintains that a creature can be made or changed for better or for worse, or transformed into some other kind or likeness by anyone save by God, the Creator of all things, alone, is an infidel and worse than a heathen. Wherefore on account of these words "changed for the worse" they say that such an effect if wrought by witchcraft cannot be real but must be purely phantastical.

But inasmuch as these errors savour of heresy and contradict the obvious meaning of the Canon, we will first prove our points by the divine law, as also by the ecclesiastical and civil law, and first in general. . . .

For the divine law in many places commands that witches are not only to be avoided, but also that they are to be put to death, and it would not impose the extreme penalty of this kind if witches did not really and truly make a compact with devils in order to bring about real and true hurts and harms. For the penalty of death is not inflicted except for some grave and notorious crime, but it is otherwise with death of the soul, which can be brought about by the power of a phantastical illusion or even by the stress of temptation. This is the opinion of St Thomas when he discusses whether it be evil to make use of the help of devils (11.7). For in the eighteenth chapter of *Deuteronomy* it is commanded that all wizards and charmers are to be destroyed. Also the nineteenth chapter of *Leviticus* says: "The soul which goeth to wizards and soothsayers to commit fornication with them I will set my face against that soul and destroy it out of the midst of my people." And again 20: "A man or woman in whom there is a pythonical divining spirit, let them die; they shall stone them." Those persons are said to be pythons in whom the devil works extraordinary things. . . .

That to deny the existence of witches is contrary to the obvious sense of the Canon is shown by the ecclesiastical law. For we have the opinions of the commentators on the Canon which commences: "If anyone by magic arts or witchcraft . . ." And again, there are those writers who speak of men impotent and bewitched, and therefore by this impediment brought about by witchcraft they are unable to copulate and so the contract of marriage is rendered void and matrimony in their cases has become impossible. For they say, and St Thomas agrees with them, that if witchcraft takes effect in the event of marriage before there has been carnal copulation, then if it is lasting it annuls and destroys the contract of marriage, and it is quite plain that such a condition cannot in any way be said to be illusory and the effect of imagination. . . .

It is most certain and most Catholic opinion that there are sorcerers and witches who by the help of the devil, on account of a compact which they have entered into with him, are able, since God allows this, to produce real and actual evils and harm, which does not render it unlikely that they can also bring about visionary and phantastical illusions by some extraordinary and peculiar means. The scope of the present inquiry, however, is witchcraft, and this very widely differs from these other arts, and therefore a consideration of them would be nothing to the purpose, since those who practise them may with greater accuracy be termed fortune-tellers and soothsayers rather than sorcerers. . . .

Wherefore since the Canon makes explicit mention of certain women, but does not in so many words speak of witches; therefore they are entirely wrong who understand the canon only to speak of imaginary voyages and goings to and from the body and who wish to reduce every kind of superstition to this illusion; for as those women are transported in their imagination, so are witches actually and bodily transported. And he who wishes to argue from this Canon that the effects of witchcraft, the infliction of disease or any sickness, are purely imaginary, utterly mistakes the tenor of the Canon, and errs most grossly.

Further it is to be observed that these who, whilst they allow the two extremes, that is to say, some operation of the devil and the effect, a sensible disease, to be actual and real, at the same time deny that any instrument is the means thereof; that is to say, they deny that any witch could have participated in such a cause and effect, these, I say, err most gravely: for, in philosophy, the means must always partake of the nature of the two extremes.

Moreover it is useless to argue that any result of witchcraft may be a phantasy and unreal, because such a phantasy cannot be procured without resort to the power of the devil, and it is necessary that there should be made a contract with the devil, by which contract the witch truly and actually binds herself to be the servant of the devil and devotes herself to the devil, and this is not done under any dream or under any illusion, but she herself bodily and truly co-operates with, and conjoins herself to, the devil. For this indeed is the end of all witchcraft; whether it be the means of casting spells by a look or by a formula or words or by some other charm, it is all of the Devil. . . .

This then is our proposition: devils by their art do bring about evil effects through witchcraft, yet it is true that without the assistance of some agent they cannot make any form, either substantial or accidental, and we do not maintain that they can inflict damage without the assistance of some agent, but with such an agent diseases, and any other human passions or ailments, can be brought about, and these are real and true. . . .

Question 2. If it be in accordance with the Catholic faith to maintain that in order to bring about some effect of magic the devil must intimately cooperate with the witch, or whether one without the other, that is, the devil without the witch, or conversely, could produce such an effect. . . .

Now with regard to the tenor of the Bull of our Most Holy Father the Pope, we will discuss the origin of witches and how it is that of recent years their works have so multiplied among us. And it must be borne in mind that for this to take place three things concur: the devil, the witch and the permission of God, who suffers such things to be. For St Augustine says, that the abomination of witchcraft arose from this foul connexion of mankind with the devil. Therefore it is plain that the origin and the increase of this heresy arises from this foul connection, a fact which many authors approve.

We must especially observe that this heresy, witchcraft, not only differs from all other heresy in this, that not merely by a tacit compact, but by a compact which is exactly defined and expressed it blasphemes the Creator and endeavours to the utmost to profane Him and to harm His creatures, for all other simple heresies have made no open compact with the devil, no compact that is, either tacit or exactly expressed, although their errors and misbelief are directly to be attributed to the Father of errors and lies. Moreover, witchcraft differs from all other harmful and mysterious arts in this point, that of all superstition it is essentially the vilest, the most evil and the worst, wherefore it derives its name from doing evil, and from blaspheming the true faith.

Let us especially note too that in the practice of this abominable evil, four points are required. First, most profanely to renounce the Catholic Faith, or at any rate to deny certain dogmas of the faith; secondly, to devote themselves body and soul to all evil; thirdly, to offer unbaptized children to Satan; fourthly, to indulge in every kind of carnal lust with incubi and succubi and all manner of filthy delights. . . .

Question 6. Concerning witches who copulate with devils. Why it is that women are chiefly addicted to evil superstitions.

As for the first question, why a greater number of witches is found in the fragile female sex than among men; it is indeed a fact that it were idle to contradict, since it is accredited by actual experience, apart from the testimony of credible witnesses. And without in any way detracting from a sex in which God has always taken great glory that His might should be spread abroad, let us say that various men have assigned various reasons for this fact, which nevertheless agree in principle. Wherefore it is good, for the admonition of women, to speak of this matter; and it has often been proved by experience that they are eager to hear of it, so long as it is set forth with discretion. . . .

Now the wickedness of women is spoken of in *Ecclesiasticus* xxv: There is no head above the head of a serpent, and there is no wrath above the wrath of a woman. I had rather dwell with a lion and a dragon than to keep house with a wicked woman. And among which in that place precedes and follows about a wicked woman, he concludes: All wickedness is but little to the wickedness of a woman. Wherefore St John Chrysostom says on the text, It is not good to marry (St Matthew xix): What else is woman but a foe to friendship, an inescapable punishment, a necessary evil, a natural tempta-tion, a desirable calamity, a domestic danger, a delectable detriment, an evil of nature, painted with fair colours! Therefore, if it be a danger to divorce her when she ought to be kept, it is indeed a necessary torture; for either we commit adultery by divorcing her, or we must endure daily strife. Cicero in his second book of *The Rhetorics* says: The many lusts of men lead them into one sin, but the one lust of women leads them into all sins; for the root of all woman's vices is avarice. And Seneca says in his *Tragedies*: A woman either loves or hates: there is no third grade. And the tears of a woman are a deception, for they may spring from true grief, or they may be a snare. When a woman thinks alone, she thinks evil.

But for good women there is so much praise that we read that they have brought beatitude to men, and have saved nations, lands and cities; as is clear in the case of Judith, Debbora, and Esther. See also 1 *Corinthians* vii: If a woman hath a husband that believeth not, and he be pleased to dwell with her, let her not leave him. For the unbelieving husband is sanctified by the believing wife. And *Ecclesiasticus* xxvi: Blessed is the man who has a virtuous wife, for the number of his days shall be doubled. And throughout the chapter much high praise is spoken of the excellence of good women; as also in the last chapter of proverbs concerning a virtuous woman. . . .

Others again have propounded other reasons why there are more super-stitious women found than men. And the first is, that they are more credulous; and since the chief aim of the devil is to corrupt faith, therefore he rather attacks them. See *Ecclesiasticus* xix: He that is quick to believe is light-minded and shall be diminished. The second reason is, that women are naturally more impressionable, and more ready to receive the influence of a disembodied spirit; and that when they use this quality well they are very good, but when they use it ill they are very evil.

The third reason is that they have slippery tongues and are unable to conceal from their fellow-women those things which by evil arts they know;

and, since they are weak they find an easy and secret manner of vindicating themselves by witchcraft. . . .

But because in these times this perfidy is more often found in women than in men, as we learn by actual experience, if anyone is curious as to the reason, we may add to what has already been said the following: that since they are feebler both in mind and body, it is not surprising that they should come more under the spell of witchcraft.

For as regards intellect, or the understanding of spiritual things, they seem to be of a different nature from men, a fact which is vouched for by the logic of authorities, backed by various examples from Scripture. Terrence says: Women are intellectually like children. And Lactantius: "No woman understood philosophy except Temeste. . . ."

But the natural reason is that she is more carnal than man, as is clear from her many carnal abominations. And it should be noted that there was a defect in the formation of the first woman, since she was formed from a bent rib, that is, a rib of the breast, which is bent as it were in a contrary direction to a man. And since through this defect she is an imperfect animal, she always deceives. For Cato says: When a woman weeps, she weaves snares. . . . And it is clear in the case of the first woman that she had little faith; for when the serpent asked why they did not eat of every tree in Paradise, she answered: Of every tree, etc. – lest perchance we die. Thereby she showed that she doubted and had little faith in the word of God. And all this is shown in the etymology of the word; for *Femina* comes from *Fe* and *Minus*, since she is ever weaker to hold and preserve the faith. And this as regards faith is of her very nature; although both by grace and nature faith never failed in the Blessed Virgin, even at the time of Christ's Passion, when it failed in all men.

Therefore a wicked woman is by her nature quicker to waver in her faith and consequently quicker to abjure the faith, which is the root of witchcraft. . . .

Part II

Question I

Chapter 1. Of the several methods by which devils through witches entice and allure the innocent to the increase of that horrid craft and company.

There are three methods above all by which devils, through the agency of witches, subvert the innocent and by which that perfidy is continually being increased. The first is through weariness, through inflicting grievous losses in their temporal possessions. For as St Gregory says: The devil often tempts us to give way from very weariness. And it is to be understood that it is within the power of a man to resist such temptation; but that God permits it as a warning to us not to give way to sloth. . . . Devils, therefore, through witches do afflict their innocent neighbors with temporal losses, that they are as it were compelled, first to beg the suffrages of witches, and at length to submit themselves to their counsels; as many experiences have taught us.

We know a stranger in the diocese of Augsburg, who before he was forty-four years old lost all his horses in succession through witchcraft. His wife, being afflicted with weariness by reason of this, consulted with witches, and after following their counsels, unwholesome as they were, all the horses which he bought after that (for he was a carrier) were preserved from witchcraft. . . .

Here it is to be noted that the devil is more eager and keen to tempt the good than the wicked, although in actual practice he tempts the wicked more than the good, because more aptitude for being tempted is found in the wicked than in the good. Therefore the devil tries all the harder to seduce all the more saintly virgins and girls. . . .

And here is an example. Two witches were burned in Ratisbon, as we shall tell later where we treat of their methods of raising tempests. And one of them, who was a bath-woman, had confessed among other things the following: that she had suffered much injury from the devil for this reason. There was a certain devout virgin, the daughter of a very rich man . . . and the witch was ordered to seduce her by inviting her to her house on some feast day, in order that the devil himself, in the form of a young man, might speak with her. And although she had tried very often to accomplish this, yet whenever she had spoken with the young girl, she had protected herself with the sign of the Holy Cross. And no one can doubt that she did this at the instigation of a holy angel, to repel the works of the devil . . .

It can be seen from this how craftily that old enemy labours in the seduction of souls. For it was in this way that the bath-woman whom we have mentioned, and who was burned, confessed that she had been seduced by some old woman. A different method, however, was used in the case of her companion witch, who had met the devil in human form on the road where she herself was going to visit her lover for the purpose of fornication. And when the incubus devil had seen her, and had asked whether she had recognized him, and she had said that she did not, he had answered: I am the devil, and if you wish, I will always be ready at your pleasure, and will not fail you in any necessity. And when she had consented, she continued for eighteen years, up to the end of her life, to practice diabolical filthiness with him, together with a total abnegation of the Faith as a necessary condition.

There is also a third method of temptation through the way of sadness and poverty. For when girls have been corrupted and have been scorned by their lovers after they have immodestly copulated with them in the hope and promise of marriage with them, and have found themselves disappointed in all their hopes and everywhere despised, they turn to the help and protection of devils; either for the sake of vengeance by bewitching those lovers or the wives they have married, or for the sake of giving themselves up to every sort of lechery. Alas! experience tells us that there is no number to such girls, and consequently the witches that spring from this class are innumerable. Let us give a few out of many examples.

There is a place in the diocese of Brixen where a young man deposed the following facts concerning the bewitchment of his wife.

In the time of my youth I loved girl who importuned me to marry her; but I refused her and married another girl from another country. But wishing for friendship's sake to please her, I invited her to the wedding. She came, and while the other honest women were wishing us luck and offering us gifts, she raised her hand and in the hearing of the other women who were standing round, said, You will have few days of health after today. My bride was frightened, since she did not know her (for, as I have said, I married her from another country) and asked the bystanders who she was who had threatened her in that way; and they said that she was a loose and vagrom woman. None the less, it happened just as she said. For after a few days my wife was so bewitched that she had lost the use of all her limbs, and even now, after ten years, the effects of witchcraft can be seen on her body. . . .

Chapter 2. Of the way by which a formal pact with evil is made.

The method by which they profess their sacrilege through an open pact of fidelity to devils varies according to the several practices to which witches are addicted. And to understand this it first must be noted that there are, as was shown in the First Part of this treatise, three kinds of witches; namely those who injure but cannot cure; those who cure, but through some strange pact with the devil, cannot injure; and those who both injure and cure. And among those who injure, one class in particular stands out, which can perform every kind of witchcraft and spell, comprehending all that all the others individually can do. Wherefore, if we describe the method of profession in their case, it will suffice for all the other kinds. And this class is made up of those who, against every instinct of human or animal nature, are in the habit of eating and devouring the children of their own species.

And this is the most powerful class of witches, who practice innumerable other harms also. For they raise hailstorms and hurtful tempests and lightnings; cause sterility in men and animals; offer to devils, or otherwise kill, the children whom they do not devour. But these are only the children who have not been reborn by baptism at the font, for they cannot devour those who have been baptized, nor any without God's permission. They can also, before the eyes of their parents, and when no one is in sight, throw into the water children walking by the water side; they make horses go mad under their riders; they can transport themselves from place to place through the air, either in body or in imagination; they can affect judges and magistrates so that they cannot hurt them; they can cause themselves and others to keep silence under torture; they can bring about a great trembling in the hands and horror in the minds of those who would arrest them; they can show to others occult things and certain future events, by the information of devils, though this may sometimes have a natural cause; . . . they can see absent things as if they were present; they can turn the minds of men to inordinate love or hatred; they can at times strike whom they will with lightning, and even kill some men and animals; they can make of no effect the generative desires, and even the power of copulation, cause abortion, kill infants in the mother's womb by a mere exterior touch; they can at times bewitch men and animals with a mere look, without touching them, and cause death; they dedicate their own children to devils; and in short, as has been said, they can cause all the plagues which other witches can only cause in part, that is, when the justice of God permits such things to be. All these things this most powerful of all classes of witches can do, but they cannot undo them.

But it is common to all of them to practice carnal copulation with devils; therefore, if we show the method used by this chief class in their profession of their sacrilege, anyone may easily understand the method of the other classes. . . .

Now the method of profession is twofold. One is a solemn ceremony, like a solemn vow. The other is private and can be made to the devil at any hour alone. The first method is when witches meet together in conclave on a set day, and the devil appears to them in the assumed body of a man, and urges them to keep faith with him, promising them worldly prosperity and length of life; and they recommend a novice to his acceptance. And the devil asks whether she will abjure the Faith, and forsake the holy Christian religion and the worship of the Anomalous Woman (for so they call the Most Blessed Virgin Mary), and never venerate the sacraments; and if he finds the novice or disciple willing, then the devil stretches out his hand, and so does the novice, and she swears with upraised hand to keep that covenant. And when this is done, the devil at once adds that this is not enough; and when the disciple asks what more must be done, the devil demands the following oath of homage to himself: that she give herself to him, body and soul, forever, and do her utmost to bring others of both sexes into his power. He adds finally that she is to make certain unguents from the bones and limbs of children, especially those who have been baptized; by all which means she will be able to fulfill all her wishes with his help. . . .

Chapter 4. Here follows the way whereby witches copulate with those devils known as incubi.

. . . But no difficulty arises out of what has been said, with regard to our principal subject, which is the carnal act which incubi in an assumed body perform with witches: unless perhaps anyone doubts whether modern witches practise such abominable coitus; and whether witches had their origin in this abomination. . . .

But the theory that modern witches are tainted with this sort of diabolical filthiness is not substantiated only in our opinion, since the expert testimony of witches themselves has made all these things credible; and that they do not now, as in times past, subject themselves unwillingly but willingly embrace this most foul and miserable servitude. For how many women have we left to be punished by secular law in various dioceses, especially in Constance and the town of Ratisbon, who have been for many years addicted to these abominations, some from their twentieth and some from their twelfth and thirteenth year, and always with a total or partial abnegation of the Faith? . . .

As to whether they commit these abominations together visibly or invisibly, it is to be said that in all the cases of which we have had knowledge, the devil has always operated in a form visible to the witch; for there is no need for him to approach her invisibly, because of the pact of federation with him that has been expressed. But with regard to any bystanders, the witches themselves have often been seen lying on their backs in the fields or in the woods, naked up to the very navel, and it has been apparent from the disposition of those limbs and members which pertain to the venereal act and orgasm, as also from the agitation of their legs and thighs, that, all invisibly to the bystanders, they have been copulating with Incubus devils. . . .

It is certain also that the following has happened. Husbands have actually seen Incubus devils swiving their wives, although they have thought that they were not devils but men. And when they have taken up a weapon and tried to run them through, the devil has suddenly disappeared, making himself invisible. And then their wives have thrown down their arms about them, although they have sometimes been hurt and railed at their husbands, mocking them, and asking them if they had eyes or whether they were possessed of devils. . . .

Chapter 6. How witches impede and prevent the power of procreation.

. . . Intrinsically they cause it in two ways. First, when they directly prevent the erection of the member which is accommodated to fructification. And this need not seem impossible, when it is considered that they are able to vitiate the natural use of any member, when they prevent the flow of the vital essences to the members in which resides the motive force, closing up the seminal ducts so that it does not reach the generative vessels, or so that it cannot be ejaculated, or is fruitlessly spilled.

Extrinsically they cause it at times by means of images, or by the eating of herbs; sometimes by other external means, such as cocks' testicles. But it must not be thought that it is by virtue of these things that a man is made impotent, but by the occult power of devils' illusions witches by this means procure such impotence, namely that they cause a man to be unable to copulate, or a woman to conceive.

And the reason for this is that God allows them more power over this act, by which the first sin was disseminated, than over other human actions.

Similarly they have more power over serpents, which are the most subject to the influence of incantations, than over other animals. Wherefore it has often been found by us and other Inquisitors that they have caused this obstruction by means of serpents or some such things.

For a certain wizard who had been arrested confessed that for many years he had by witchcraft brought sterility upon all the men and animals which inhabited a certain house. Moreover, Nider tells of a wizard named Stadlin who was taken in the diocese of Lausanne, and confessed that in a certain house where a man and his wife were living he had by his witchcraft successively killed in the woman's womb seven children, so that for many years the woman always miscarried. And that in the same way he had caused that all the pregnant cattle and animals of the house were during those years unable to give birth to any live issue. And when he was questioned as to how he had done this, and what manner of charge should be preferred against him, he discovered his crime, saying I put a serpent under the threshold of the outer door of the house, and if this is removed fecundity will be restored to the inhabitants. And it was as he said; for though the serpent was not found, having been reduced to dust, the whole piece of ground was removed, and in the same year fecundity was restored to the wife and to all the animals.

Part III

WITCH BELIEFS
IN THE SIXTEENTH
AND SEVENTEENTH
CENTURIES

By the mid sixteenth century the early modern European stereotype of witch-craft had been fully formed. This stereotype is often referred to as the composite notion of witchcraft, since it combined many different elements, or the cumulative concept of witchcraft, since those elements had been assimilated gradually over the course of many centuries. Ideas of maleficent magic performed through the power of the Devil, demonic temptation, the negotiation of a pact with the Devil, the collective worship of the Devil at the sabbath, the performance of amoral and anti-Christian activities at the sabbath, the nocturnal flight of witches, and their metamorphosis into beasts had all been integrated into a frightening depiction of the witch and her activities. This learned concept of witchcraft found expression in a number of demonological treatises written by educated theologians, inquisitors, and secular judges during the period between 1570 and 1700, which formed the most intense period of witch-hunting in Europe. The publication of these treatises, which usually went into multiple editions, helped to spread the belief in witchcraft among the educated and ruling elites of Europe. The frequent reference to the confessions of witches in these treatises gave them greater authority than they would otherwise have possessed as abstract theo-logical pronouncements. Like the earlier demonological treatises discussed in Part II, such as those by Heinrich Kramer and Johannes Nider, these treatises also encouraged the further prosecution of the crime.

These excerpts from nine different demonological works, drawn from among the many works that generally accepted the cumulative concept of witchcraft, are intended to illuminate the different features of that intellectual construct. Many of these works cover the same ground; reading demonological literature, just like reading witchcraft trials, can seem highly repetitive. But they all have different emphases, and often they disagree on particular points. Even the most credulous authors, moreover, harboured some doubts about the powers and activities of witches, and the assertive statements in their treatises were often intended more to resolve those doubts than to confirm their certainties. Some demonological writers, such as Johann Weyer and Reginald Scot went so far as to reject some of the basic components of the learned stereotype. The works of these men are excerpted in Part VI on the skeptical tradition.

Five of the documents in this Part were written by Catholic demonologists. Henri Boguet, the Burgundian judge, presents a graphic discussion of the threat posed by witches as well as a discussion of whether witches actually copulate with demons (Chapter 16). Nicolas Remy, a prosecutor from the duchy of Lorraine, gives considerable attention to the Devil's mark and the flight to the sabbath (Chapter 17). Martín Del Rio, a theologian in the Spanish Netherlands, presents a detailed discussion of the *maleficia* performed by witches and the role played by the Devil in those maleficent deeds (Chapter 18), while an Italian cleric, Francesco Maria Guazzo elaborates on the pact with the Devil (Chapter 20). Some of the most sensational activities of witches at the sabbath, especially their dancing and promiscuous sexual activities, find a commentator in the French secular judge, Pierre de Lancre (Chapter 21).

Protestants wrote the remaining four documents. Protestant demonologists generally accepted the same witch beliefs as their Catholic counterparts, but they had their own emphases. In his treatise of 1574 the French Calvinist Lambert Daneau presented some of the main themes in Protestant demonological thought (Chapter 15). William Perkins, an English theologian, typifies the work of many Protestant ministers who insisted that so-called white witches, such as healers, were just as culpable, and even more dangerous, than those performing maleficent deeds (Chapter 19). A Scottish cleric, James Hutchinson, used the Calvinist theology of the covenant to establish the guilt of children whose parents transported them to the sabbath (Chapter 23), while the most famous demonologist in New England, Cotton Mather, gives full expression to the Protestant connection between witchcraft and the expected Second Coming of Christ prophesied in the New Testament (Chapter 22).

15

LAMBERT DANEAU: PROTESTANTISM AND WITCHCRAFT, 1574

—————◦◦◦◦—————

Lambert Daneau, a French Calvinist theologian and minister, published a treatise on witches in 1574. The book took the form of a dialogue in which one speaker, Theophilus, responded to occasionally skeptical questions presented by the other speaker, Anthony. The treatise establishes some of the main themes of late sixteenth- and seventeenth-century Protestant demonology. One of the most salient of those features was a heavy reliance on Scripture. This biblicism is evident in Daneau's argument, in this selection, that to claim that witches were victims of melancholy was tantamount to the blasphemous denial of the biblical statement that the demoniacs whom Christ cured were also only melancholics and not possessed by demons. A second Protestant theme, echoed in many other Protestant treatises was that the increase in the number of witches was related to the prevalence of superstition and false religion that the Reformation was endeavoring to dispel. Daneau presents an interesting version of this interpretation by claiming that God consigned witches to Satan's service "in revenge for their contempt of his name." A third feature of Protestant demonological thought was an emphasis on God's sovereignty. In the Catholic tradition the Devil could do nothing without God's permission, but Protestants went further by establishing severe limitations on demonic power. Calvinists claimed that the age of miracles had ended in biblical times and that the magic performed by witches through the power of the Devil consisted of nothing more than wonders. Daneau makes this point in his treatise, and he also presents the argument, made by many other Protestant writers, that the Devil, despite his great power, could only work within the laws of nature. One of the effects of this line of thought was to make the crime of witchcraft primarily a spiritual offense, consisting in the pact with the Devil. This emphasis is clear in Daneau's treatise, and it was followed by most of the English demonologists of the late sixteenth and seventeenth centuries.

Source: Lambertus Danaeus, *A Dialogue of Witches, in Foretime Named Lot-tellers and Now Commonly Called Sorcerers* (London, 1575), chapters II, III, and IV.

Chapter II. Whether there be any sorcerers, that is to say, of this sort of witches.

. . . *Theophilus*. Moreover, these sorts of witches have always been well known in our country of France, which to be true, the innumerable acts of parliament against them do testify, which many learned men have gathered together of the matter. But chiefly a certain famous and solemn condemnation of articles and opinions, made by a Sorbonist of Paris, under Charles VI, king of France, in the year of our Lord 1398, maketh much of the proof of our opinion, which opinions the scholars of the university commonly possessed in Paris. Yea, hath not this our age seen many witches condemned of witchcraft?

Anthony. Can you show me the cause, Theophilus, why it should so be in our time?

Theophilus. Truly it is the terrible judgment of God against us, the cause whereof is unknown unto us. For the judgments of God, although they be hid from us, yet are they just and holy, as it appeareth in the xxv Psalm and x verse, most truly and godly, in the like argument, and as St Augustine sayeth, in his work *Of Denunciation of Devils*.

Anthony. Now, then, hath God any juster cause to punish men in this our age than he hath in former time, three hundred years ago?

Theophilus. Yea, surely, Anthony, greater than heretofore, how much more the world shamefully and obstinately reject the word of God and the revealed light thereof. For how much more do men nowadays show themselves unthankful towards God, the more just cause God taketh to forsake them and give them over to Satan, to revenge the contempt of his name. So that in these days, wherein is seen a most grievous and pitiful rebellion of men against God's true doctrine, Satan hath received the power from God to allure them unto him and to lift them, and there is given unto them the very effect and force of error to deceive, entrap, and lead away many, as the spirit of the Lord hath long since witnessed it should be, in the second of the Thessalonians, the second chapter, tenth verse, and that God would give him the power and gift to deceive that men should give credence unto Satan, and to lies and such should be damned as believed not the truth but have yielded to unrighteousness because they have not embraced the love of the truth that they might be saved.

Anthony. But some there be that hold the opinion that as these things which are reported of sorcerers are but devised and feigned, and if any such thing do chance, they come only by some sickness of the mind or by reason of some melancholic humour these appearances and fancies trouble them, not being any tokens or signs of the just judgment of God against men.

Theophilus. But truly they be very much deceived, friend Anthony, no less than those which supposed that the mad men possessed with devils, which lived in the time of our Lord and Saviour Jesus Christ, and were by him healed, were none other than men sick and troubled with melancholic, choleric diseases, whose opinion is altogether blasphemous, for they take away the certainty of the Christian faith and deny the divine nature of our Lord Jesus Christ, repugning and lying against the truth of the thing. For how could the devils have spoken within their bodies or with so great force have gone out of the possessed persons and have the members and parts of their bodies if these things were but mere dreams of troubled minds and fancies and only fits of melancholic diseases. So are sorcerers plainly miserable slaves unto Satan in subjection unto him; him do they worship, to him do they commit themselves, yea offer unto him candles of wax in token of honour. Yet some of them do seem more abject and filthily serviceable. For when Satan showeth himself unto them in the likeness of a man, the which is too shameful to speak, they kiss his buttocks, which thing certain of them afterward have frankly confessed themselves to have done. And therefore it happeneth unto them that they be delivered over into so reprobate sense of mind that God punisheth them most justly who, as I have declared, do most obstinately and thankfully either despise Christ's gospel which is offered unto them, or when they have received it and understand it, they take thereof very coldly and lightly. . . . So in this our age, wherein by his great and incomprehensible benefits towards mankind, as a special gift, he hath restored unto us the light of his holy gospel, of very justice he will have it, that more despisers of this revealed light, rather at this day than before, fall into the snares of Satan and become sorcerers, that is to say, addicted unto Satan, and that they which despise God may be the more terrified by example of these wretches, and the godly which with true faith embrace the gospel may more earnestly praise God, and in consideration of so great a benefit bestowed upon them, yield unto God the greater thanks, judging their own state to be blessed, since by the singular benefit of God they are delivered from so great a mischief and so great a power of the Devil . . .

Theophilus. I will yet add one thing that I may at length conclude this whole matter, namely, how men do become such kind of people upon divers and sundry causes. Some through great distrust in the promises and love of God towards them, others moved with exceeding and horrible vanity of mind and overmuch curiosity, do fall into the same vice, *toto* loftily despising the measure and degree of human nature. This, how true indeed it is, you may behold. For some are made sorcerers through hope of sufficiency to sustain their poverty, to whom Satan promiseth whole mountains of gold, as the proverb sayeth. Such of likelihood lacked money to supply the ordinary charges of their household, or else were far in debt, so that they gave themselves up willingly to the Devil in hope of money. Others seeing themselves oppressed by some of more power, and not having ability to defend themselves, and not able to abide or put up the injuries done unto them, have desired help of Satan (who is very ready to revenge and do murder), and with willing minds have submitted themselves unto him and become his slaves. Which two sorts of men have fallen only unto such wickedness through great distrust that God hath doth not love them, as though God had forsaken them and would not help them in their adversity. By these means many are carried away by Satan, especially country men, ignorant and poor people, and such as are injured, being willing to be made sorcerers. Other some there be, who being borne away with some vanity of a proud mind, while they are not able to contain themselves within the compass of man's understanding and capacity, do yield themselves vassals to Satan, being desirous to know things to come and foretell them to others, or else ambitiously desiring easily and with small travail to do those things which others cannot. By which means many of the honourable and learned sort are seduced by Satan, as certain noblemen and women of worship and honour, and many scholars. Whom all God justly hath punished for that they have refused him and wittingly vowed themselves to the Devil.

Chapter III. In what kinds of things sorcerers can cast their poisons to hurt them.
    . . . *Theophilus.* Forasmuch as these witches be devilish and very crafty, truly they are able to infect with their poison whatsoever is in the earth that is corruptible and mortal unless it be preserved by God. And there is nothing in this inferior world which is not of that sort, that is to wit, mortal and corruptible. Wherefore we must needs confess that their art hath power over all these inferior things.
    Anthony. Show me some examples of these things, gentle Theophilus.
    Theophilus. I will do so. And first is the most certain they have power over men, for that we daily behold, whilst some they kill with their poisons, and some they make sick and past recovery. I have seen them who, with only laying their hands upon a nurse's breasts, have drawn forth all the milk and dried them up. I have seen [them] that have caused unto some most grievous pain of the colic, wringings in the belly, gout, the palsy, the apoplexy, that have also made men lame and feeble, and cast them into other diseases, which neither themselves afterward neither yet most excellent learned physicians could know or cure. And these sorcerers do cruelly rage upon all men, of all genders, ages, and orders without choice or exception. What shall I say more? The servants and plowmen if they be angry will intoxicate their masters. And as for beasts and cattle, they poison them to death sundry ways, and if they be disposed, they will not kill them forthwith, but make them swell or make them lean and pine away, in such wise that there is nothing worse or more hurtful than their wickedness. Moreover, they will enchant wild beasts and make them stand still, that you may take them in your hand. . . . And as for herbs, trees, with all their berries and fruits and all such like things they may be by them intoxicated. . . . And corn fields into

other places I saw them remove. . . . And as touching air and water, what may be more easily corrupted than therefore that those elements shall neither be wholesome nor profitable to any, yea, rather pestiferous and hurtful. For sufficient proof whereof, may be that only some pestilent smell or vapour doth in such wise infect a whole region through which it breatheth, the most grievous and infectious diseases are thereby engendered . . . The water likewise running continually, which notwithstanding you will grant, may be corrupted. And look by what means the water may be corrupted, by the same also may be the air, because that filthy savour is dispersed and spread abroad through them both, which natural elements are thin and unable to resist. . . .

Anthony. Surely there are some that cannot believe that these can do such things, but rather that through great folly and ostentation of their art and ability they craftily make brags thereof, to make men afraid of them; or else that through madness they boast of it, for that some of them, being troubled with melancholic diseases, have sometimes imagined that they could do the like.

Theophilus. Indeed I confess, Anthony, that God first wrought the same, who by this means, and by these men as his instruments, punished the sins of men. But notwithstanding, I deny that which they affirm, that these things are always false dreams of diseased minds, when sorcerers say they infect the air, which indeed they do so often, and truly, which may thus be proved: First, that no cogitation or imagination of another man can be felt or perceived of us, neither can actually, as they say, hurt our body. Imagine that you had killed me, and suppose it in your mind as earnestly as you can, shall my good health therefore be altered, or in any point diminished? Surely not at all. For no man's false or vain imagination is able to infect or bring diseases upon any other man's body. But we feel how sorcerers effectively bring diseases. We see also how they have caused plagues, and those most grievous, with other such like effects, which cannot be denied. Moreover, in the midst of their pains and torments they confess they have done such things, specially when they be led to execution for their crimes. Finally, the consent and agreement which is found among them all confirmeth our opinion. For in vain cogitations and fancies of the mind there cannot be one selfsame voice, but one man may imagine a diverse thing from another. For every mind hath its own proper action, neither is it possible that among so many men, and dispersed abroad in so many places, one whole conformity of vain cogitations, not agreeing in place, time, nor manner of doing, could concord, agree or be correspondent unless these things chanced so and were indeed as they do report. Yea, moreover, I will tell a thing passing marvellous, they will tie a knot upon a point as our countrymen speak, that is to say, they can hinder and bind married couples that they shall not pay their due one to the other, or at leastwise that one of them shall not.

Chapter IV. After what sort and means sorcerers do intoxicate and poison things.

Anthony. Tell me the Theophilus, by what means worketh Satan in deed, whilst he would seem to work by enchantments or superstitions describing of characters, or certain forms of prayers.

Theophilus. I am about to do so. And to begin with all, I am certain and well assured of this, that Satan can do nothing but by natural means and causes. For whatsoever he doth either by himself or by his magicians and sorcerers, it is altogether either illusion of their minds and eyes, or only the true effect of natural causes. As for any other thing, or that is of more force, he cannot do it.

Anthony. Can he not also work miracles, as St Paul sayeth in the second to the Thessalonians, the second chapter, the ninth verse, and St John in the Revelation, the sixteenth chapter and fourteenth verse?

Theophilus. What call you a miracle, Anthony?

Anthony. I call a miracle a certain work which is done in a natural body contrary to the natural course and disposition thereof created by God. As for example, when iron swimmeth upon the water, as is reported in the second book of Kings, the sixth chapter and the sixth verse, when a stone sitteth upon the water, when water is truly turned into wine, when the dead are unfeignedly restored unto life.

Theophilus. Truly you have properly defined a miracle. For as Saint Augustine writeth, it must only be called a miracle which surmounteth the power of all things created, neither can be wrought by them. So that a miracle is only the work of God's power, being most worthily and properly to be termed by that name. But Saint Paul, and the Revelation in those places which you have commended, use not this word so strictly and precisely, but rather more at large for any kind of work which may seem strange and marvelous unto men, although it proceed from natural means and causes. So that this word miracle is oftentimes used for that which may more rightly be called a wonder. For as touching a miracle, Satan truly is able to work none, as you have most properly described a miracle.

16

HENRI BOGUET:
THE THREAT OF
WITCHCRAFT, 1602

In 1590 Henri Boguet, a judge in the county of Burgundy, published a demonological treatise, *Discours des Sorciers* [A Discourse on Witches], which presented
a comprehensive description of the dangerous sect of witches that he and many
other educated men in the sixteenth century believed was threatening Christian
civilization. A new edition of the *Discours*, beginning with a case of possession
and witchcraft tried in 1598, appeared in 1602, and there were a number of
further editions and printings between 1603 and 1611. Boguet based his treatise
on the cases of witchcraft he had adjudicated in the district of St Claude in
Burgundy. The treatise covers much of the same material as the other demonological works of the period, but two sections throw light on the outlook of lay
judges who were entrusted with the prosecution of witches. The first is the dedication of the work to the vicar-general of Besançon, which describes in alarming
terms the extent of the threat posed by witchcraft. The second is Boguet's
discussion of copulation of both female and male witches with the Devil, which
among other things reveals that concern with such matters was not limited to
celibate monks. The chapter on whether this copulation exists only in the imagination deals with a matter of some scholarly controversy, with Boguet using
testimony from witchcraft trials to prove that the Devil really did have intercourse
with witches. These excerpts are taken from the English translation of the second
edition of 1602.

Source: Henry Boguet, *An Examen of Witches*, trans. E. A. Ashwin, ed.
Montague Summers (London, 1929), pp. xxxi–xxxvi.

To Monsieur, Monsieur the Vicar-General of Besançon, Monsieur François de Rye, Abbot of Acey, Preseigne, etc.

Monsieur, I no longer marvel that there have formerly been witches who have said that if as many of them were men as there were women, and if they had a great lord as their leader, they would be strong enough to make war upon a king. For I have no doubt but that this would in such a case be easy for them, and that they would even overcome their enemies. I do not mean that they would do so by means of their spells and charms, although we read that this was done by Oddo, the great pirate and sea-rover, in Denmark, and by the Huns who by their magic arts defeated Sigisbert, King of Soissons, in the time of Chilperic, not to mention Haakon, Prince of Norway, who fought his enemies with storms of hail. But I mean that they could raise an army equal to that of Xerxes, although that was of eighteen hundred thousand men. For if it is true that Trois-eschelles, one of the best informed of their sect, declared in the time of Charles IX that there were in France alone three hundred thousand, or as some read, thirty thousand witches, at what figure can we estimate the number of those which could be found in all the different countries of the world? And must we not believe that since that time they have increased by more than half? For my part I have no doubt of it. For if we but look around among our own neighbors, we shall find them all infested with this miserable and damnable vermin. Germany is almost entirely occupied with building fires for them. Switzerland has been compelled to wipe out many of her villages on their account. Travelers in Lorraine may see thousands and thousands of the stakes to which witches are bound. We in Burgundy are no more exempt than other lands; for in many parts of our country we see that the execution of witches is a common occurrence. Returning again to our neighbors, Savoy has not escaped this pest; for every day she sends us a countless number of persons possessed of demons which, on being exorcised, say that they have been sent by witches into the bodies of these poor wretches; moreover, most of the witches whom we have burned here came originally from Savoy. And what shall we say of France? It is difficult to believe that she is purged of witches, considering the great number which she had in the time of Trois-eschelles. I say nothing of other more remote lands. No, no; there are witches by the thousand everywhere, multiplying upon earth even as worms in a garden. And this is a shame to the magistrates whose duty it is to punish felons and criminals; for if we had no more than the direct command of God to put them to death as being His bitterest enemies, why should we endure them any longer and thus disobey the Majesty of the Most High? In this we do even worse than the witches themselves; for disobedience is likened to idolatry and witchcraft by Samuel, speaking to Saul. And Saul found this to be true, to his own great damage; for because he did not slay all the Amalekites and their cattle as he had been commanded, God was angry with him and caused him to be defeated and killed, with his sons, by the Philistines.

Therefore we ought well to search our conscience, and fear lest it should happen to us as it did to Saul for that one disobedience. I pass over the fact that God at various times threatened cities and villages with destruction for this crime, and that He has sometimes brought them to utter ruin for the same crime of witchcraft. I say nothing, too, of the fact that the only delight of witches is to do ill, and that they gloat over the sickness and death of persons and cattle. This is but another reason why we should naturally be incited to punish them, provided that there is any humanity in us and if, to speak more strongly, we are at all worthy of the name of man. For even the most irrational beasts do not suffer amongst them those which league and conspire together against the rest, as we know from experience. Nature, or to speak more correctly, the Author of nature, naturally impresses this common duty on our minds; for otherwise the world could not continue. For these reasons, therefore, it is necessary that everybody should bear a hand in so good a work, and especially those in authority so that we may show ourselves to be what we were created to be, namely men and reasonable beings, and that we bring not upon us the destroying anger and indignation of the Living God. I know that there have before this been those who have not been able to believe that what is said of witches is true; but in these present days they are beginning to believe it, owing to a special grace of God, who has opened their eyes, which had been blinded by Satan that by this means he might, as he has done, increase his kingdom. These men, I say, are now busy in hunting down witches, so that not long ago they caused some to be put to death. And I take this as a sign that in a short time Satan and all his subjects will be overcome, and witches will no longer boast that they are able to make war upon a king, as they have done before now. I would have them to know that, if effect could be given to my wish, the earth would be immediately cleared of them; for I would that they should all be united in one single body, so that they might all be burned at once in a single fire. In the same way a certain emperor wished, but wished wrongly, that all the Romans might have but a single head, so that he might slay them with one blow. Meanwhile, I shall use every endeavor to make war upon them, both by bringing them to justice, and by my humble writings, as I now do with this treatise which I offer again to the public under your name, Monsieur, always presupposing that Monseigneur your uncle, to whom I dedicated it in the first place, will agree that during his absence you should take his place in this new edition, and that on your own part you will be pleased to accept my offer coming from one who has already devoted himself entirely to you and desires ever to be known, Monsieur, as your very humble servant, Henry Boguet. . . .

Chapter XI. Of the Copulation of the Devil with Male and Female Witches.

The third point in Françoise Secretain's confession was that she had had carnal relations with Satan. Clauda Jamprost, Jacquema Paget, Antoine

Tornier, Antoine Gandillon, Clauda Janguillaume, Thievenne Paget, Rolande du Vernois, Janne Platet and Clauda Paget confessed the same thing; and it has been revealed in the examination of witches that they all have connection with Satan. The Devil uses them because he knows that women love carnal pleasures, and he means to bind them to his allegiance by such agreeable provocations. Moreover, there is nothing which makes a woman more subject and loyal to a man than that he should abuse her body.

And since male witches are addicted no less to this pleasure, the Devil also appears as a woman to satisfy them. This he does chiefly at the Sabbat, according to the reports of the father and son, George and Pierre Gandillon, and of those women whom I have several times named, all who agree in saying that in their assemblies there are many demons, of whom some take the form of women for the men, and others that of men for the women. These demons are called incubi and succubi. And it is no new thing for Satan to draw us to him by these means; for we read that, in order to tempt St Anthony, St Jerome and other devout persons, who passed their life in the solitude of the desert, he commonly appeared to them in the form of a courtesan.

There is also another reason for the coupling of the Devil with a witch, which is that the son may thereby become the more grievous. For if God abominates the coupling an infidel with a Christian, how much more shall He detest that of a man with the Devil? Moreover, by this means man's natural semen is wasted, with the result that the love between man and wife is often turned to hatred, than which no worse a misfortune could happen to the state of matrimony.

Chapter XII. Whether such copulation exists in the imagination only.

But since here are some who maintain that the coupling of which we have just spoken exists in the imagination only, it will be well to say something here on this subject. For some treat the matter with derision, some are doubtful about it, and others firmly believe it to be a fact. St Augustine appears to be among these last, as also St Thomas Aquinas and several other later learned authorities. But the witches' confessions which I have had make me think that here is truth in this matter; for they have all admitted that they have coupled with the Devil, and that his semen was very cold; and this is confirmed by the reports of Paul Grilland and the Inquisitors of the Faith. Jacquema Paget added that she had several times taken in her hand the member of the Demon which lay with her, and that it was as cold as ice and a good finger's length, but not so thick as that of a man. Thievenne Paget and Antoine Tornier also added that the members of their demons were as long and big as one of their fingers; and Thievenne Paget said, moreover, that when Satan coupled with her she had as much pain as a woman in travail. Françoise Secretain said that, whilst she was in the act, she felt something burning in her stomach; and nearly all witches affirm that this coupling is by no means pleasurable to them, both because of Satan's ugliness and deformity, and because of the physical pain which it causes them, as we have just said.

The ugliness and deformity lies in the fact that Satan couples with witches sometimes in the form of a black man, sometimes in that of some animal, as a dog or a cat or a ram. With Thievenne Paget and Antoine Tornier he lay in the form of a black man; and when he coupled with Jacquema Paget and Antoine Gandillon he took the shape of a black ram with horns; Françoise Secretain confessed that her demon appeared sometimes as a dog, sometimes as a cat and sometimes as a fowl when he wished to have carnal intercourse with her. For all these reasons I am convinced that there is real and actual copulation between a witch and a demon; for what is there to prevent the Devil, when he has taken the form of an animal, from coition with a witch? In Toulouse and Paris women have been known to make sexual abuse of a natural dog; and it seems to me quite to the point to refer here to the legends of Pasiphae and other such women. . . .

When Satan means to lie with a witch in the form of a man, he takes to himself the body of some man who has been hanged. But even if he has only a body formed from the air, there is still nothing to prevent him from intercourse with a witch; for in that case he makes the body of air so dense that it is palpable (for air is, of itself, palpable) and consequently capable of coition with, and even defloration of a woman. And why should not this be easy for him, seeing that he is powerful enough to overthrow a town or a city or a kingdom? And as for his semen, he has but too plentiful a supply, even were there no other sources of it, in that which he receives when he acts as a succubus.

And therefore I thoroughly believe all that has been written of fauns, Satyrs and woodland gods, which were no more than demons, and were inordinately lustful and lascivious. Also I think that we may consider under this head the stories we are told of the wantonness of Numa, and of the nymph Egeria, and of several others whom the poets have particularly mentioned.

Similarly we find in the West Indies that their gods, which they call Cocoto, lay with women and had sexual intercourse with them; unless it was really certain lickerish men who abused them, as Decius Mundus, a Roman knight, whose story Josephus tells in his Antiquities, did to Paulina under pretence of being the god Anubis.

But to return to Françoise Secretain, it is a strange thing that Satan lay with her in the shape of a fowl. I am of opinion that she meant to say a gander instead of a fowl, for that is the form that Satan often takes, and therefore we have the proverb that Satan has feet like a goose. Yet it would be as easy for him to take the shape of a fowl as that of a gander. For we know that he has at different times assumed the shape of a dog for the same purpose, and we have two remarkable examples of this: one of a dog, said to be a demon, which used to lift up the robes of the nuns in a convent of the diocese of Cologne in order to abuse them; the other, of certain dogs found on the beds of the nuns of a convent on Mount Hesse in Germany.

17

NICOLAS REMY:
THE DEVIL'S MARK
AND FLIGHT TO THE
SABBATH, 1595

Nicolas Remy (c.1530–1612), the author of the witchcraft treatise *Demonolatry* (1595), had a distinguished judicial career in the French-speaking duchy of Lorraine, which lay on the eastern frontier of the kingdom of France. In 1576 Duke Charles III of Lorraine appointed Remy to serve on his ducal court, and in that capacity Remy conducted an intense campaign against witchcraft. Gaining a reputation as "the scourge of witches," Remy sent at least 800 witches to their deaths between 1576 and 1592. He continued these prosecutions in his capacity as *procureur général* for Lorraine, a post he held from 1595 until 1606. Like many other witchcraft treatises, *Demonolatry* was based on some of the cases that the author had adjudicated. Remy places great credence in virtually all aspects of witchcraft, including the Devil's mark and the flight of witches to the sabbath. The only witch-belief that Remy attributes to demonic illusion is metamorphosis, or the changing of a human being into the shape of a beast.

Source: Nicolas Remy, *Demonolatry*, trans. E. Ashwin (London, 1930), pp. 1–2, 9, 47–53, 56, 108–113.

Book I

Chapter I. The inducements by which men may first be led astray by demons, and so falling become dealers in magic.

Experience itself, to our own great loss and bane, affords us sad proof that Satan seizes as many opportunities of deceiving and destroying mankind as there are different moods and affections natural to the human character. For such as are given over to their lusts and to love he wins by offering them the hope of gaining their desires: or if they are bowed under the load of daily poverty, he allures them by some large and ample promise of riches: or he tempts them by showing them the means of avenging themselves when they have been angered by some injury or hurt received: in short, by whatever other corruption or luxury they have been depraved, he draws them as it were bound to him . . . Satan assails mankind not only through their secret and domestic affections and (if I may so express it) by burrowing into their very hearts, but also openly and in declared warfare, as it is called. For he openly addresses them by word of mouth, and appears in visible person to converse with them. . . . But this he does the more easily when he finds a man weakened by the hardships and cares of life; for then he suggests to the man that he is grieved at his misfortunes and is willing to come to help him. But not even so can he aid and assist any man unless that man has broken his baptismal pledge and agreed to transfer his allegiance to him and acknowledge him as his Master. But if he cannot gain his object in this way by mere persuasions, then Satan employs those allurements and temptations which I have already mentioned: he fabricates some fair and delectable body and offers it for a man's enjoyment: or he can do much by means of a false display of riches: or by providing drugs to poison those upon whom a man wishes to be avenged, or to heal those to whom a man owes a debt of gratitude: often, indeed, the demons forcibly drive and compel men into compliance by fierce threats and revilings, or by the fear of the lash or prison. For men may just as easily be led by violence to practise sorcery as by coaxing and blandishment. . . .

Chapter V. That it is not enough for demons to hold men bound and fettered by a verbal oath; but they furthermore mark them with their talons as an enduring witness of the servitude to which they have subjected them. In what part of the body this mark is most often made, and how that part is entirely insensitive and devoid of feeling.

And so today the Devil brands and seals those whom he has newly claimed as his own with such tokens of harsh and inhuman slavery, marking them especially (as some say) on that part of the body which was anointed by the priest on the day of their baptism; just as thieves change the brand on stolen cattle to change their own mark. . . .

And what may seem more wonderful is that the place is entirely blood-less and insensitive, so that even if a needle be deeply thrust in, no pain is felt and not a drop of blood is shed. This fact is held to be so certain a proof of capital guilt that it is often made the base of examination and torture. . . . At Porrentruy (30th Oct., 1590), again, Claude Bogart was about to be put to the torture and, as the custom is, had had her head shaved. A scar on the top of her forehead was thus plainly brought to light. Thereupon the Judge, suspecting the truth, namely, that this was the mark of the Demon's talon, which had before been hidden by her hair, ordered a pin to be thrust deeply into it; and when this was done it was seen that she felt no pain, and that the wound did not bleed in the very least. Yet she persisted in denying the truth, saying that her numbness to pain was due to an old blow from a stone; but after she was brought to the torture she not only acknowledged that the mark had been made by a demon, but recounted several other cruel injuries which she had received from him. . . .

Chapter XIV. That witches do often really and in fact travel to their nocturnal syna-gogues; and often again such journeyings are but an empty imagination begotten of dreams; and that they are equally right who support either of these opinions. Further, that these journeys are performed in various manners; and on what night they most commonly take place in Lorraine.

There is much controversy and dissension among those who treat of this aspect of witchcraft; as to whether witches do in fact fly to and bodily present themselves at the notorious evil assemblies of demons, or whether they are only possessed by some fantastic delusion, and, as happens when the empty mind is filled with dreams at night, merely imagine that they are so present. There are good arguments and examples on both sides in this dispute. Credible authors, such as Fr. à Turella and Jean Bodin in his *Daemonomania*, have vouched for cases where women have manifestly spent the whole night at home, and even in bed with their husbands, and yet on the next morning they have confidently recounted many details of the Sabbat at which they have affirmed they were present on the previous night. Other women, again, have been kept under express observation throughout the night by their friends and relations, as well as their neighbors, who had become suspicious of them because of certain rumours; and they have been seen to move spas-modically in their sleep as if they were smitten with some acute pain; or even to mount upon a chair or some other object and act as if they were spurring a horse to great speed; yet they did not go out of the house, but on awaking appeared as weary as if they had returned from a long journey, and told wonderful stories of what they imagined they had done, and were much offended and angry with those who would not believe them. . . .

On the other side there is no lack of well-reputed authors, for example Ulrich Molitor and Jean Bodin, who, both by argument and examples, main-tain the literal truth of this matter. For (they say) they have heard the evidence of those who have smeared and rubbed themselves with the same ointment that witches use, and have in a moment been carried with them to the Sabbat; though it cost them many days' journey to return from it when, as Apuleius says, the song was done and the blind force of conjured Powers was expended. They have heard also of those who have gone on foot to the Sabbat with their children, whom they meant to initiate at the solemn assembly, and were afterwards carried home through the air by the Demon. . . .

As Nicolette Lang-Bernhard was returning from the old mill of Guermingen to Assenoncour on the 25th July, 1590, and was going along a forest path at high noon, she saw in a field nearby a band of men and women dancing round in a ring. But because they were doing so in a manner contrary to the usual practice, with their backs turned towards each other, she looked more closely and saw also dancing around with the others some whose feet were deformed and like those of goats or oxen. Nearly dead with fright, she began (as we do when some sinister disaster threatens us) to call upon the saving Name of Jesus, and to beseech Him that she might at least return safe and unhurt to her house. Thereupon all the dancers seemed to vanish at once, except one named Petter Gross-Petter, who rose quickly into the air, and was seen to let fall a mop such as bakers use to clean out their ovens before putting in their dough. . . .

On the other hand, I am quite willing to agree with those who think that such Sabbat meetings at times exist only in dreams. It was very clearly stated not long since in her evidence by Catharine Prevotte (at Freiseen, September 1589) that sometimes witches are fully awake and actually present at these assemblies; but that often they are merely visited in their sleep by an empty and vain imagination. For the demons are equally ready either to transport them whither they wish when they are awake, or to impress the image of such a happening upon their minds while they are sleeping and (as Galen says . . .) influenced by a brief mania. . . .

The commonest practice of all witches is to fly up through the chimney. If anyone objects that chimneys are too small and narrow, or raises any other difficulties, he must know that, by virtue of that Demonolatry which makes all things monstrous and portentous, they are first bidden to exceed their natural limits; and, moreover, the matter becomes more intelligible when it is remembered that the chimneys are square and wide in all peasants' cottages, and that it is from this class that the vile rabble of sorcery is mostly derived.

Alexia Violet (in the district of Thann, 1583), Jeanne le Ban (Masmunster, July 1585), Claude Fellet (Mazieres, Nov. 1585), Dominique Petrone (Giron-court, Oct. 1585), and nearly all (Masmunster, July 1585) of those convicted of this crime, have by their free and several confessions borne witness to the truth of this fact. Nicole Ganette (Mazières, Dec. 1583) added that it was her custom, when she was preparing to start on that journey, to put one foot up into a basket after she had smeared it with the same ointment which she had used upon herself. François Fellet (at Vergaville, December, 1585) said that he used to place his left foot, not in a basket but on the ends of the backward bent twigs of a besom which he first anointed. Others, again, use other methods to fly to their assemblies. Margareta Doliar said that she had often been carried there riding upon a wicker net or a reed, after having pronounced certain requisite words. Alexia Bernard (in Guermingen, Jan. 1590) said that she rode upon a pig; and Hennezel Erik (at Vergaville, July 1586) that his father went upon a huge mighty bull, and his mother on a forked stick such as is used in stables . . . Jeanne Gransaint (at Conde-sur-l'Escaut, July 1582) of Montigny said that whenever she wished to make this journey there immediately appeared before her door a terrible black dog, upon which she boldly mounted as upon a well-tamed horse; and in payment for her passage, when she dismounted she was in her turn mounted and defiled by the dog; but first (as it seemed to her) it changed itself into a not uncomely young man. . . .

Chapter XV. That all kinds of persons attend the nocturnal assemblies of demons in large numbers; but the majority of these are women, since that sex is the more suscep-tible to evil counsels.

. . . But all those taken up for witchcraft are unanimous in their assertion that the Sabbats are attended by great numbers. Leanne le Ban (Masmunster, June 1585) and Nicole Ganète (July 1685) said that the numbers were so great whenever they were present that they felt little pity for the human race than when they saw how many enemies and traitors were opposed to it, and that it was most surprising that mortals did not suffer greater damage from them. Catharina Ruffa (Ville-dur-Moselle, June 1587) stated that she saw no less than five hundred on the night when she was first enticed into their company. Barbeline Rayel (Blainville, Jan. 1587) said that the women far exceeded the men in number, since it was much easier for the Demon to impose his deceits upon that sex. . . . Certainly I remember to have heard of far more cases of women than men; and it is not unreasonable that this scum of humanity should be drawn chiefly from the feminine sex, and that we should hear mostly of women simplists, wise women, sorceresses, en-chantresses, and masked Lombard women. For in estimating numbers and frequency it is enough to reckon those who form the majority. . . .

Book II

Chapter V. That the much-talked-of examples of metamorphosis, both in ancient and recent times, were true in appearance only, but not in fact; for the eyes are deceived by the glamorous art of the demons which cause such appearances . . .

The witches of Dieuze, Vergaville, and Forbach, and nearly all who have hitherto been tried for this crime in the kingdom of Austria, and whose confessions have come into my hands, have maintained that they changed themselves from men into cats as often as they wished to enter another man's house secretly in order to plant their poison there at night. These statements are borne out and substantiated by the evidence of many who have reported that they have been attacked by witches in such shape. . . .

Whenever (as so easily happens among neighbors and fellows) Petrone of Armentières (Dalheim, 1581) . . . was moved with hatred or envy against the herdsmen of neighbouring flocks, he used to utter certain words by which he was changed into a wolf; and being, in such disguise, safe from all suspi-cion of ill doing, he would then fall upon and rend in pieces every beast of the herd that he could find. . . . And not long ago the Dolonais witnessed the public execution of two werwolves who had been condemned to death by their Supreme Court. . . .

It is, therefore, absurd and incredible that anyone can truly be changed from a man into a wolf or any other animal. Yet there must be some foundation for the opinion so obstinately held by so many: the countless stories that are circulated about such happenings cannot be entirely without warrant. Nearly all who have deeply examined this whole question are convinced that such transformations are magical portents and glamours, which have the form but not the reality of their appearances; and that they can be caused in two ways.

The Demon can so confuse the imagination of a man that he believes himself to be changed; and then the man behaves and conducts himself not as a man, but as that beast which he fancies himself to be. . . .

Secondly, these illusions can be caused extrinsically, when the Demon causes an actual object to assume the apparent shape which suits his purpose at the time, and so deludes a man's senses into the belief that an object has been changed into a different form. . . .

But there is another far stronger argument which might appear to prove the actuality of these transformations. It is not only the external physical shape that appears to be changed; the witch is also endowed with all the natural qualities and powers of the animal into which she is seemingly changed. . . .

It must, then, be admitted that these things are actually what they appear to be; but that they are done through the agency of the Demon, who, by virtue of his immense preternatural powers, makes their accomplishment possible. (For it is written in Job that upon earth there is not his like.) Thus we must believe that it was by the strength of Satan that the demoniac was able easily to burst the chains and fetters with which he was bound (St Luke viii); for it is needless to say that he could not have done this of his own human strength. . . .

We will admit, therefore, that witches so well imitate the faculties, powers and actions of the beasts whose appearance they assume that they differ but little from actuality; but that they are in very truth actual will not easily be believed by anyone who will ponder upon the dignity and excellence of man; how he was created in God's own image, as a marvellous and transcendent type of the whole worldly creation, and has therefore been called a *microcosm*. For God made him a little lower than the angels, and put all things in subjection under his feet; and through baptism he wins atonement and absolution, and at last his body will be raised from the dead unto unchanging eternity. Who can think that a soul so largely and variously blessed can be put to such ludicrous humiliation as to be transferred into the carcass and entrails of the baser animals, and be there hid as in a sepulchre?

18

MARTÍN DEL RIO:
THE MALEFICIA OF
WITCHES, 1600

Martín Del Rio (1551–1608), a Jesuit theologian born of Spanish parents, wrote a number of devotional and scholarly works, as well as a history of the Spanish Netherlands (present-day Belgium), his native land. His most famous work, *Disquisitiones Magicae* [Investigations into Magic] (1599–1600) was a massive, six-volume work on the magical arts, especially witchcraft. The work achieved immense popularity among its scholarly audience of lawyers and theologians and went into several editions. It soon replaced the *Malleus maleficarum* as the most authoritative Catholic treatise on witchcraft, and it was cited widely by demonologists of all religious persuasions throughout the seventeenth century, even by those who displayed skepticism regarding certain witch-beliefs. In a certain sense it became an encyclopedia of witchcraft, containing information and commentary on almost all aspects of witchcraft. The following excerpts from Del Rio's work regarding the practice of magic reflect the scholarly and encyclopedic character of the work as well as the author's knowledge of classical antiquity and his use of scholastic categories, such as that of efficient cause, to explain witches' activities. The excerpt also underlines Del Rio's unqualified assertion that the power of witches to perform *maleficia* can only come through a pact made with the Devil.

Source: Martín Del Rio, *Investigations into Magic*, ed. and trans. by
P. G. Maxwell-Stuart (Manchester, 2000), pp. 68–73, 117–120.

Book 2. Magic involving Evil Spirits

Question I. Is there such a thing as magic involving evil spirits?
    Those who follow the Sadducees, Democritus, Aristotle, Averroes and Simplicius in asserting that evil spirits do not exist also say that this form

of magic does not exist. But this opinion of theirs is impious and heretical. Evil spirits do exist and so does the magic which involves them. Such a magic is not based upon the industry or inventiveness of human beings, nor does it rely upon natural causes. It rests, rather, on some kind of non-material, separate power. . . .

Question 2. Whence does this magic come? Who invented it?

There are those who say that evil spirits exist but deny that this type of magic is done by means of evil spirits or devils (*diaboli*), attributing its effects either to God operating directly through magicians of this kind, or to God using good angels in order to produce these effects. These people say that certain graces have been given freely (just as for example the gifts of language and of health are freely given) and that these gifts are not infrequently granted to people like Balaam and to other reprobates. I maintain first that this opinion is entirely blasphemous since it attributes to the magical arts something which belongs properly to graces feely given, and confuses genuine miracles with acts of trickery. Secondly, it makes the free gifts of God subject to human artifice and certain ridiculous practices. Thirdly it says that God would unreasonably and malevolently prohibit something which he himself graciously bestows upon human beings as a favour.

Question 3. The types of magic which involve evil spirits, and the books connected with this subject.

Since there is no such thing as theurgy or "white" magic it follows that all this magic of wonders is nothing other than *goetica* and "black" magic. This we usually call specialised magic. The Arch-magician [Agrippa] divided it into two types: (a) the one whose practitioners surrender themselves to an evil spirit, sacrifice to him, and worship him: and (b) the one which he would persuade us is free from a pact with evil spirits but which commands them by nods of the head and, through the power of divine names, summons, adjures, and compels them to obey. The former, he says, is forbidden by human and divine law, is particularly wicked, and should be punished with every type of fire. The latter, he says, accomplishes what it claims to do, especially with regard to compelling evil spirits (which he goes on to argue is a proper thing to do) although it is exposed to the manifest dangers of illusion. . . .

Question 4. The basis of this magic, that is to say a pact, explicit or implicit.

First conclusion: All material operations rest, as on a foundation, upon a pact made between the magician and an evil spirit. This, as often as the magician wishes to effect anything, he is constrained explicitly or implicitly by this prop to his art to demand that the evil spirit meet the terms of the agreement.

This is proved by the authority of the Church Fathers. Saint Cyprian says that magicians have a treaty with an evil spirit. Gratian recalls the words of Saint Augustine in the codex of his *Decretals*. These are as follows: "All arts of this kind, either of frivolous or harmful superstition, come from a certain established plague-bearing association, like a pact of faithless and deceitful friendship, between individuals and evil spirits." Secondly, it is proved by Imperial decree: "Many people use magical arts to disturb the elements. They do not hesitate to undermine the life of children and they dare to summon the spirits of the dead and expose them to the air, so that someone may destroy his enemies by means of their wicked arts. May a deadly plague carry these people off, since they are alien to nature."

Thirdly, one should believe the decree of the Articles of the School of Paris, which runs thus: ". . . We maintain that there is an implicit pact in all super-stitions observations whose effect one may not reasonably expect to come from God or from nature." . . .

Book 3: Harmful Magic and Superstition

Part I: Harmful Magic

Question 1: What is harmful magic and how many different kinds are there?

I am not arguing about whether it exists or not. I take for granted that it does. Those who deny this are contradicted by the precepts of Holy Scripture, canon and civil law, and by historians, poets, common belief and the testimony of all past ages. No branch of magic delights the evil spirit more because, as Synesius says, "the disasters of humankind are food and drink to evil spirits." By the word *malefice*, however, I do not mean just any kind of injury or sin, but rather a magical, superstitious sign or effect. The person who employs malefice is called *maleficus,* and the person who is injured by it is called *maleficatus*. So it can be described as follows: "Malefice is a type of magic by which an evil spirit intends to harm another individual."

I have said "a type of magic" in order to restrict what is rather a broad term to this kind of harmful activity, and I have added "by which some evil spirit" because if a pact or a treaty with the evil spirit were lacking, there would be no point in the subject's appearing in this treatise, any more than murder, rape of a virgin, theft, or larceny. Malefice can be subsumed under two headings: "Intention" and "Efficient Cause." By "efficient cause" I do not mean "the permission granted by God" or "the evil spirit who carries it out" or "the depraved free will of the evil magician who agrees to receive help from an evil spirit and cooperates with him" because these three things always go together in every act of malefice. For not a hair of one's head can fall without God's permission; nor can an evil spirit do more harm than God allows; nor can he bring to a conclusion what he is allowed to do unless the worker of harmful magic (*maleficus*) consents to the malefice. This last point is manifestly in sacrilegious imitation of Almighty God, who requires the consent of the minister so that he can grant salvation through the ministration of the sacraments. That such an intention on the part of the worker of harmful magic is a prerequisite is shown by the fact that we see that the touch or powders of witches (*striges*) harm only those the witches wish to harm, as many examples from Remy demonstrate; and indeed this is certainly true of the instruments of magic (*maleficia*) which are not composed of natural poisons. So by "efficient causes" I mean the instruments and material whereby people may be injured, which act together to harm without the need for an intermediary.

1) Witches do harm by means of certain very fine powders which they mix in food or drink, or rub on a naked body, or scatter over clothes. The powders which kill are black; those which simply cause illness are ash-coloured (or sometimes reddish-brown) whereas the powder which removes a spell and acts as a medicine is exceptionally white. The virtue of these powders, however, does not come from their colour or from any other quality but is entirely dependent upon a pact made with an evil spirit. The colours merely serve to clarify the intentions of those who attend sabbats, so that the witches (*striges*) may not make any mistake about which one should be used for which purpose ("what for what," as the saying goes). Hence one may conclude that the white powder used by one witch as medicine often proves lethal in the hands of a second, and the ash-coloured powder used by one to bring disease brings death when employed by another. What is more, one and the same witch (*saga*) may use the powder to bring death on one occasion and to cure illness on another. It all depends on the way the evil spirit is pleased to change its signification.

2) They work malefice with herbs, pieces of straw, and other rubbish such as that. This they do by throwing them on the ground, and when the person against whom they wish to work malefice walks over them, he will most certainly fall sick or die.

3) They use white or dull red ointments which have the consistency of tar. Droplets of white and bright yellow metal are mixed in with these ointments, which causes them to shine, and if you throw the ointment on the fire, it sparks and crackles, and emits a strong smell which is unlike anything else. Many witches always have some of it smeared on their hands so that no opportunity of doing harm may slip past them. The ointment is lethal if it rubs off on you or if it touches your outer garments.

4) They poison people merely by breathing or blowing on them. This is how they are accustomed to cause miscarriages, as well as very great danger to life.

5) They cause immense harm with words alone, as Lucan says, "Even when the mind has not been polluted by any poisonous oozing, it dies after it has been enchanted." Vergil says: "They have mingled herbs and words which are not without harmful intention." There can be no doubt this is

what the evil spirit has taught them. Therefore Ovid refers to the incantations of Hecate: "At once she pounded together herbs well-known to cause harm and juices which inspire terror, and when she had blended these together she added the incantations of Hecate." Seneca lists a good many poisons in his Medea: "To the poisons she adds words which are to be feared no less than they." The extraordinary thing is that sometimes they harm people by means of threats alone, or with loud, violent complaining – although I believe that this was not the way of the pagans. They used to wear a wreath round their heads while they caroused in order to counteract this particular evil. No, the practice belongs to our age, as experience has proved. Nevertheless, I maintain (and I emphasize) that all these things are accomplished, not by any power in the words, but by the operation of the Devil as a sign of his agreement and approval.

6) They do not hesitate to use sacred things. For example, a witch touched the holy water sprinkler with her powders, asperged another woman with holy water, and thereby made her ill. (See Remy.)

Finally, some witches proceed more openly, and with the help of an evil spirit cause someone to be strangled or to drop down dead. They suffocate very small children during the night by smothering them with the mattress; or they kill them by thrusting a needle behind their ear, as the midwife Helvetia did, according to Sprenger's account. They snatch children from the cradle and rend them in pieces; or they use them to make their ointments, as I have said elsewhere; or they eat them, a food they find very pleasing. . . . Sometimes they drop poison upon the children, and this either makes them die at once or causes them to waste away after a little while. Sometimes, too, they suck out their blood. This is the origin of the ancient belief about a bird, also known as the strix, which gnashes its teeth. For example, Quintus Serenus: "Moreover, if the dark strix presses down upon little children, squirting rank milk from its teats on the lips which are turned towards it"; while Ovid, in the following verse, accepts another theory: "They fly at night, seeking children without a nurse, and despoil their bodies after snatching them from their cradles. They are said to pluck the entrails out of the sucklings with their beaks, and their throats are filled with the blood they drink . . ."

These days they do not so much pretend to be nurses as take the appearance of wild animals, and attack those children who are left unguarded and suck out their lives along with their blood while they are asleep; or they kill them with a poison which makes them waste away. . . .

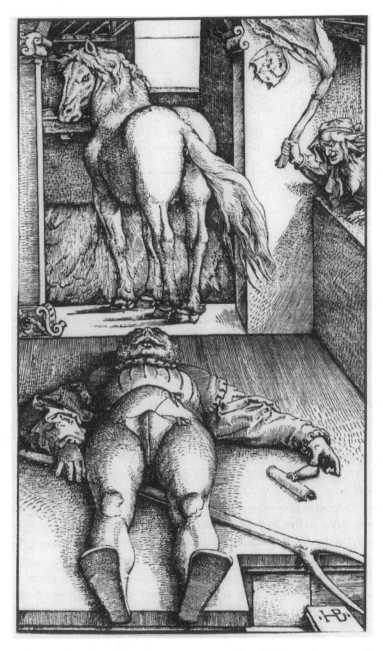

Figure 3 *The Bewitched Stable Groom.* This engraving by the sixteenth-century German artist Hans Baldung Grien depicts the death of a stableman by witchcraft. The witch, in the upper right hand corner, who conforms to the traditional stereotype of the witch as an old woman with exposed breasts, has used magic to cause the man's death.

19

WILLIAM PERKINS:
GOOD AND BAD WITCHES,
1608

—————————

William Perkins (1558–1602), an English Protestant minister and theologian, was one of a small group of English clergymen responsible for introducing continental European ideas of witchcraft into England in the late sixteenth and early seventeenth centuries. In his treatise, *The Damned Art of Witchcraft*, which was written around 1602 and published six years later, Perkins insisted that the pact with the Devil, rather than the practice of harmful magic, was the essence of the crime of witchcraft. This claim did not agree with the wording of the English witchcraft statute of 1563, which defined the crime exclusively in terms of *maleficium*. Nor did it reflect the content of most English witchcraft accusations, which villagers directed against their neighbors for harming them by magical means. Although all continental European demonologists held that the pact with the Devil was central to the crime of witchcraft, Protestant theologians placed a special emphasis on it. Perkins, who developed the covenant theology that found favor among Puritans in England and New England, used the idea of a covenant or pact with Satan as the antithesis of man's covenant with God. By identifying the pact with the Devil rather than *maleficium* as the essence of witchcraft, Perkins was led to argue that men as well as women could become witches, even though female witches were still more numerous than men. The logic of Perkins' position also led him to advance the argument, echoed by other Protestant ministers and theologians, that there was no difference between so-called good or white witches, who practised healing and other forms of beneficent magic, and bad witches. This was the same position that St Augustine had taken in Christian antiquity.

Source: William Perkins, *A Discourse of the Damned Art of Witchcraft* (1608), pp. 167–185.

Chapter V. What witches be and how many sorts.

A witch is a magician who either by open or secret league wittingly and willingly consenteth to use the aid and assistance of the Devil in the working of wonders.

First, I call the witch a magician to show what kind of person this is: to wit, such a one as doth profess and practise witchcraft. For a magician is a professor and a practiser of this art, as may appear [in] Acts 8:9, where Simon, a witch of Samaria, is called magus, or Simon the magician.

Again, in this general term I comprehend both sexes or kinds of persons, men and women, excluding neither from being witches. A point rather to be remembered, because Moses in this place setting down a judicial law against witches useth a word of the feminine gender (*mecashephah*), which in English properly signifieth a woman witch; whereupon some might gather that women only were witches. Howbeit Moses in this word exempteth not the male but only useth a notion referring to the female, for good causes, principally for these two:

First, to give us to understand, that the women, being the weaker sex, is sooner entangled by the Devil's illusions with this damnable art than the man. And in all ages it is found true by experience that the Devil hath more easily and oftener prevailed with women than with men. Hence it was that the Hebrews of ancient times used it for a proverb, "The more women, the more witches." His first temptation was with Eve, a woman, and since [then] he pursueth his practice accordingly, as making most for his advantage. For where he findeth easiest entrance and best entertainment, thither will he oftenest resort.

Secondly, to take away all exception of punishment from any party that shall practise this trade, and to show that weakness cannot exempt the witch from death. For in all reason, if any might allege infirmity and plead for favour, it were the woman, who is weaker than the man. But the Lord saith, if any person of either sex among his people be found to have entered covenant with Satan and become a practiser of sorcery, though it be a woman and the weaker vessel, she shall not escape; she shall not be suffered to live; she must die the death. And though weakness in other cases may lessen both the crime and the punishment, yet in this it shall take no place.

The second point in this description is consenting to use the help of the Devil, either by open or secret league, wittingly and willingly. Wherein standeth the very thing that maketh a witch to be a witch.; the yielding of consent upon covenant. By which clause two sorts of people are expressly excluded from being witches. First, such as be tainted with frenzy or madness or are through weakness of the brain deluded by the Devil. For these, though they may be said after a sort to have society with Satan, or rather he with them, yet they cannot give their consent to use his aid truly, but only in imagination; with the true witch it is far otherwise. Secondly, all such superstitious persons, men or women, as use charms and enchantment for the

95

effecting of anything upon a superstitious and erroneous persuasion, that the charms have virtue in them to do such things, not knowing that it is the action of the Devil by those means; but thinking that God put virtue in them, as he hath done into herbs for physic. Of such persons we have (no doubt) abundance in this our land, who, though they dealt wickedly and sin grievously in using charms, yet because they intend not to join league with the Devil, either secretly or formally, they are not to be counted witches. Nevertheless, they are to be advertised in the meantime, that their estate is fearful. For their present ungodly practises have prepared them already to this cursed trade, and may bring them in time to be the rankest witches that can be. Wherefore I advise all ignorant persons, that know not God, nor the Scriptures, to take heed and beware of this dangerous evil, the use of charms. For if they be once convinced in their consciences, and know that God hath given no power to such means, and yet shall use them, assuredly they do in effect consent to the Devil to be helped by him, and thereupon are joined in confederacy with him in the confidence of their own hearts, and so are become witches.

The third and last thing in the description is the end of witchcraft: the working of wonders. Wonders are wrought three ways (as hath been showed), either by divination or by enchantment or by juggling, and to one of these three heads all feats and practices of witchcraft are to be referred. . . .

Of witches there be two sorts: the bad witch and the good witch, for so they are commonly called.

The bad witch is he or she that hath consented in league with the Devil to use his help for the doing of hurt only, as to strike and annoy the bodies of men, women, children, and cattle with diseases and with death itself, so likewise to raise tempests by sea and by land, etc. This is commonly called the binding witch.

The good witch is he or she that by consent in a league with the Devil doth use his help for the doing of good only. This cannot hurt, torment, curse, or kill but only heal and cure the hurts inflicted upon men or cattle by bad witches. For as they can do no good but only hurt, so this can do no hurt but good only. And this is that order which the Devil hath set in his kingdom, appointing to several persons their several offices and charges. And the good witch is commonly termed the unbinding witch.

Now howsoever both these be evil, yet of the two the more horrible and detestable monster is the good witch; for look in what place soever there be bad witches that hurt only, there also the Devil hath his good ones, which are better known than the bad, being commonly called wisemen or wise-women. This will appear by experience in most places in this country. For let a man's child, friend or cattle be taken with some sore sickness or strangely tormented with some rare and unknown disease, the first thing he doth is to bethink himself and inquire after some wiseman or wisewoman, and thither he sends and goes for help. When he comes, he first tells him the state of the sick man. The witch, then being certified of the disease, prescribeth either charms of words to be used over him or other such counterfeit means wherein there is no virtue, being nothing else but the Devil's sacraments to cause him to do the cure if it come by witchcraft. Well, the means are received, applied, and used; the sick party accordingly recovereth; and the conclusion of all is the usual acclamation: Oh happy is the day that ever I met with such a man or woman to help me!

Here observe that both have a stroke in this action: the bad witch hurt him and the good healed him, but the truth is, the latter hath done him a thousand times more harm than the former. For the one did only hurt the body, but the Devil by means of the other, though he have left the body in good plight, yet he hath laid fast hold on the soul and by curing the body hath killed that. . . .

This point well considered yieldeth matter both of instruction and practice. Of instruction, in that it shows the cunning and crafty dealing of Satan, who afflicteth and tormenteth the body for the gain of the soul. And for that purpose hath so ordered his instruments that the bad witch gives the occasion by annoying the body or goods, and the good immediately accomplisheth his desire by entangling the soul in the bands of error, ignorance and false faith. Again, this showeth the blindness of natural corruption, especially in ignorant and superstitious people. It is their nature to abhor hurtful persons such as bad witches be, and to count them execrable, but those that do them good they honour and reverence as wise men and women., yea seek and sue unto them in times of extremity, though of all persons in the world they be the most odious, and Satan in them seems the greatest friend, when he is most like himself and intendeth greatest mischief. Let all ignorant persons be advised hereof in time, to take heed to themselves, and learn to know God and his word, that by light from thence they may better discern of the subtle practices of Satan and his instruments.

For matter of practice, hence we learn our duty to abhor the wizard as the most pernicious enemy of our salvation, the most effectual instrument of destroying our souls, and of building up the Devil's kingdom, yea, as the greatest enemy to God's name, worship and glory that is in the world, next to Satan himself.

Chapter VI. Of the punishment of witches.

In the judicial law of Moses (whereof this is one) the Lord appointed sundry penalties, which in quality and degree differed one from another, so as according to the nature of the offence was the proportion and measure of the punishment ordained. And of all sins, as those were the most heinous in account, which tended directly to the dishonour of God, so to them was assigned death, the greatest and highest degree of punishment. He that despised the law of Moses died without mercy under two or three witnesses, Hebrews 10:18; the punishment of the thief was restitution fourfold,

Exodus 22:1, but the murderer must be put to death, Numbers 35:31; the idolater and seducer were commanded to be slain, Exodus 22:20, Deut. 13:5; the blasphemer must be stoned, Leviticus 29:19. And the witch is numbered among these grievous offenders; therefore his punishment is as great as any other. For the text saith, he might not be suffered to live, Exodus 22:18.

But why should a witch be so sharply censured? And what should move the Lord to allot so high a degree of punishment to that sort of offenders? Answer: this cause was not the hurt which they brought upon men in body, goods, or outward estate. For they be such that never did harm, but good only. We read not of any great hurt that was done by the enchanters of Egypt or by the Pythoness of Endor or by Simon Magus in Samaria. And those divining witches, which have taken upon them to foretell things to come, hurt not any but themselves, yet they must die the death. This therefore is not the cause. But what if these do hurt or kill, must they not then die? Yes, verily, but by another law, the law of murder, and not by the law of witchcraft. For in this case he dieth as a murderer, and not as a witch, and so he should die, though he were no witch.

The cause then of this sharp punishment is the very making of a league with the Devil, either secret or open, whereby they covenant to use his help for the working of wonders. For by virtue of this alone it cometh to pass that witches can do strange things, in divining, enchanting, and juggling. Now let it be observed, of what horrible impiety they stand guilty before God, who join in confederacy with Satan. Hereby they renounce the Lord that made them; they make no more account of his favour and protection; they do quite cut themselves off from the covenant made with him in baptism, from the communion of the saints, from the true worship and service of God. And on the contrary they give themselves to Satan as their god, whom they continually fear and serve. Thus are they become the most detestable enemies of God and his people that can be. For this cause Samuel told Saul that rebellion was as the sin of witchcraft; that is, a most heinous and detestable sin in the sight of God. The traitor that doth no hurt to his neighbour but is willing and ready to do him the best services that can be desired is notwithstanding, by the law of nations, no better than a dead man, because he betrays his sovereign and consequently cannot be a friend unto the commonwealth. In like manner, though the witch were in many ways profitable and did no hurt but procured much good, yet because he hath renounced God his king and governor and hath bound himself by other laws to the service of the enemy of God and his Church, death is his portion justly assigned him by God; he may not live.

20

FRANCESCO MARIA GUAZZO: THE PACT WITH THE DEVIL, 1608

In 1608 Francesco Maria Guazzo, a brother in the Milanese Order of St Ambrose, published a demonological treatise, *Compendium maleficarum,* which went into a second edition in 1626. As the title indicates, the book presents a summary of information and arguments about witches. It draws on many earlier demonological works, including a number of Italian and French treatises of the sixteenth century, and provides numerous examples from court records. One striking contribution the book makes to demonological literature is its enumeration of the different steps taken in the negotiation of the pact with the Devil. The treatise also includes a number of woodcuts illustrating some of those ceremonies. Guazzo also includes in the *Compendium* an excerpt from a demonological work by Sebastian Michaelis, *Pneumanologie* (Paris, 1587), which summarizes all the alleged crimes of witches. This summary, which was presented in a sentence passed against a witch in a trial at Avignon in 1582, makes reference to many of the ceremonies that Guazzo discusses in his chapter on the pact. It also provides a fairly concise statement of the witch beliefs of continental European demonologists at the beginning of the most intense period of witch-hunting.

Source: *Compendium Maleficarum, Collected in Three Books from Many Sources by Brother Francesco Maria Guazzo*, ed. Montague Summers, trans. E. Ashwin (London, 1929), pp. 13–19, 135–136.

Book I

Chapter 6. Of the Witches' Pact with the Devil.
    . . . [T]here are certain matters common to all their pacts with the Devil, and these may be arranged under eleven heads.

First, they deny the Christian faith and withdraw their allegiance from God. They repudiate the protection of the Blessed Virgin Mary, heaping the vilest insults upon her and calling her Harlot, etc. And the devil arrogates honor to himself, as St Augustine notes . . . The Devil then places his claw on their brow, as a sign that he rubs off the holy chrism and destroys the mark of their baptism.

Second, he bathes them in a new mock baptism.

Third, they foreswear their old name and are given a new one; as, for example, della Rovere of Cuneo was renamed Barbicapra.

Fourth, he makes them deny their godfathers and godmothers, both of baptism and confirmation, and assigns them fresh ones.

Fifth, they give the Devil some piece of their clothing. For the devilish eager to make them his own in every particular; of their spiritual goods he takes their faith and baptism; of their bodily goods, he claims their blood, as in the sacrifices of Baal; of their natural goods he claims their children, as will be shown later; and of their acquired goods he claims a piece of their clothing.

Sixth, they swear allegiance to the Devil within a circle, traced upon the ground. Perhaps this is because a circle is the symbol of divinity, and the earth is God's footstool; and so he wishes to persuade them that he is the God of Heaven and Earth.

Seventh, they pray the devil to strike them out of the book of life, and to inscribe them in the book of death. So we can read written in a black book the names of the witches of Avignon.

Eighth, they promise to sacrifice to him; and certain fiendish hags, as Bartolomeo Spina tells, vow to strangle or suffocate for him one child every month or two weeks.

Ninth, they must every year make some gift to the demons their masters to avoid being beaten by them, or to purchase exemption from such of their pledged undertakings as are obnoxious to them; but, as Nicolas Remy says, these gifts are only legitimate when they are completely black in colour.

Tenth, he places his mark upon some part or other of their bodies, as fugitive slaves are branded; and this branding is sometimes painless and sometimes painful, as we learn from examples of it. He does not, however, mark them all, but only those whom he thinks will prove inconstant. And the mark is not always of the same description; for at times it is like the footprint of a hare, sometimes like that of a toad or a spider or a dog or a dormouse. Neither does he always mark them upon the same place: for on men it is generally found on the eye-lids, or the arm pit or lips or posterior; whereas on women it is found on the breasts or private parts, as has been observed by Lambert Daneau and Bodin and Gödelmann. And just as God in the Old Testament marked his own with the sign of circumcision and in the New Testament with the sign of the holy cross which took the place of circumcision, according to St Gregory Nazianen and St Jerome; so also the Devil, who loves to imitate God, has from the very infancy of the Church marked those heretics who were implicated in witchcraft with a certain sign. . . .

Eleventh, when they have been so marked they make many vows: as never to adore the Eucharist; that they will both in word and deed heap continual insults and revilings upon the Blessed Virgin Mary and the other saints; that they will trample upon and defile and break all the relics and images of the saints; that they will abstain from using the sign of the cross, holy water, blessed salt and bread and other things consecrated by the Church; that they will never make full confession of their sins to a priest; that they will maintain an obstinate silence concerning their bargain with the Devil, and that on stated days they will, if they can, fly to the witches' sabbat and zealously take part in its activities; and finally they will recruit all they can into the service of the Devil. And the Devil in his turn promises that he will always stand by them, that he will fulfill their prayers in this world and bring them to happiness after death.

Book II

Chapter 15. A Summary in a Few Words of All the Crimes of Witchcraft.

Sebastien Michaëlis in his *Pneumalogie* gives an example of a sentence passed at Avignon in 1582, as comprising in a little space the most execrable and abominable of the crimes of witches and sorcerers. The extract is as follows:

We N.N., having considered the charge wherewith you stand charged and accused before us, and having examined both the statements of your selves and your associates, and your own confessions made to us according to lawful requirements and often repeated upon oath, as well as the depositions and charges of the witnesses and the other legitimate proofs, basing our judgement upon that which has been said and done during this process, we are fully and lawfully agreed that you and your associates have denied God the Creator of us all and the Most Holy Trinity our maker, and that you have worshipped the Devil, that ancient and implacable enemy of the human race. You have vowed yourself to him forever, and have renounced your most Holy Baptism and your sponsors therein, together with your part in Paradise and the eternal heritage which our Lord Jesus Christ bought for you and the whole race of men by His death. All these you did deny before the said cacodemon in the form of a man, and that blatant Devil did baptise you with water, and you did change the names given to you at the holy font, and so took and received another false name in the guise of baptism. And as a pledge of your fealty sworn to the Devil you gave to him a fragment and particle of your clothing; and that the Father of Lies should have a care to delete and obliterate you from the book of life you did at his direction and command with your own hands write your names in the black book there prepared, the roll of the wicked condemned to eternal death; and that he might bind you with stouter bonds to so great a perfidy and impiety, he branded each of you with his mark as belonging to him, and you did swear homage and obedience to his behests upon a circle (the symbol of divinity) traced upon the earth (which is God's footstool); and each of you bound herself to tread under foot the image of the Lord and the cross; and in obedience to Satan, with the help of a staff smeared with some abominable unguent given to you by the Devil himself and placed between your legs, you were enabled to fly through the air at dead of night to the place ordained, at an hour fit for vilest criminals, and on stated days you were so carried and transported by the Tempter himself; and there in the common synagogue of witches, sorcerers, heretics, conjurers and devil-worshipers, you did kindle a foul fire and after many rejoicings, dancings, eating and drinking, and lewd games in honour of your president Beelzebub the prince of Devils in the shape and appearance of a deformed and hideous black goat, you did worship him in deed and word as very God and did approach him on bended knees as suppliants and offered him lighted candles of pitch; and (fie, for very shame) with the greatest reverence you did kiss with sacrilegious mouth his most foul and beastly posterior; and did call upon him in the name of the true God and invoke his help; and did beg him to avenge you upon all who had offended you or denied your requests; and, taught by him, you did wreak your spite in spells and charms against both men and beasts, and did murder any new-born children, and with the help of that old serpent Satan you did afflict mankind with curses, loss of milk, the wasting sickness, and other most grave diseases. And your own children, many of them with your own knowledge and consent, you did with those magic spells suffocate, pierce, and kill, and finally you dug them up secretly by night from the cemetery, where they were buried, and so carried them to the aforesaid synagogue and college of witches. There you did offer them to the Prince of Devils sitting upon his throne, and did draw off their fat to be kept for your use, and cut off their heads, hands, and feet, and did cook and stew their trunks, and sometimes roast them, and at the bidding of your aforesaid evil father did eat and damnably devour them. Then, adding sin to sin, you the men did copulate with succubi, and you the women did fornicate with incubi; moreover, in most bitter and icy connexion and foul coitus with demons, you did commit the unspeakable crime of buggery. And, most hateful of all, at the bidding of the aforesaid Serpent thrust from Paradise, you did keep in your mouths the most holy sacrament of the Eucharist received by you in the sacred church of God, and did execrably spit it out upon the ground that you might with the greatest of all contumely, contempt and blasphemy dishonour God, our true and sacred Hope, and promote the glory, honour, triumph, and kingdom of the Devil himself, and worship, honour and glorify him with all honour, praise, majesty, authority and adoration. All which most grave, abhorred and unspeakable crimes are directly contumacious and contemptuous of Almighty God the creator of all.

Figures 4 and 5 The Pact with the Devil. These woodcuts depict the conclusion of a formal, explicit pact with the Devil. Figure 4 shows the Devil baptizing his converts into the religion of their new master. Figure 5 shows a witch kissing the buttocks of the Devil, a ceremony that allegedly took place at the sabbath. From Francesco Maria Guazzo, *Compendium maleficarum* (Milan, 1610).

21

PIERRE DE LANCRE:
DANCING AND SEX
AT THE SABBATH,
1612

Pierre de Lancre, a French magistrate, was commissioned by Henry IV in 1606 to investigate witchcraft in the Basque-speaking southwestern French province of Labourd, bordering on the Spanish kingdom of Navarre. His witch-hunting ultimately resulted in the execution of approximately eighty persons for witchcraft, and his activities also led to the massive witch-hunt in the Basque region between 1609 and 1611 that is the subject of Document 53. In 1612 de Lancre published a treatise, *Description of the Inconstancy of Bad Angels and Demons*, in order to convince the reading public of the danger presented by witchcraft as well as to show how the law could counteract this menace. The work became the most comprehensive description of the witches' sabbath written during the seventeenth century. Like many demonological works, it uses the testimony of confessing witches to lend authority to his views. The treatise also included the most famous and sensational engraving of the witches' sabbath, by the Polish artist Jan Ziarnkov. De Lancre's description of the witches' sabbath is not only the most detailed available, but it is also the most sensational, emphasizing the Devil's copulation with witches and giving more attention to their obscene dances than any other demonological treatise. Its main value to historians of witchcraft is the insight it provides into the mind of de Lancre, a lay demonologist who was obsessed with the sexual elements of the witches' sabbath. De Lancre's treatise, presented in the first person and drawing extensively on the cases he prosecuted, serves more as a description of the sabbath than as a philosophical or theological analysis. De Lancre plays the role of eye-witness and observer, and in describing the ceremonies of the sabbath, especially the dances discussed in one of the sections excerpted here, he also assumes the role of ethnographer, showing how dancing reflected Spanish traditions of the people of Labourd.

Like many other demonologists, de Lancre emphasizes the fact that the great majority of the witches whom he tried were women, and he uses the theme of inconstancy to characterize women as well as demons.

Translated from Pierre de Lancre, *Tableau de l'inconstance des mauvais anges et démons, ou il est amplement traité des sorcierrs et de la sorcellerie* (1612), ed. Nicole Jacques-Chaquin (Paris, 1982), pp. 141–142, 189–190, 197–199.

Book II

Discourse I. A description of the Sabbath, of the poison that is made there, and some noteworthy depositions of sufficiently strong certain witches who clearly confirm the transport.

The description of the Sabbath, which occurs in various lands, seems to be somewhat diverse. The variety of the places where it is held, the master who presides over it, all diverse and variable, and the unpredictable moods of those who are called to it, create the diversity. But, taking everything into consideration, the main and the most important, most serious ceremonies are all consistent. This is why I will recount what we have learned from our proceedings, and will state simply what some notable sorcerers have put before us, without changing anything or altering their depositions, so that each person may take from it what he pleases.

In the proceedings of Ustaritz which is the seat of the Courts of Labourd, in the trial of Petri Daguerre, 73 years of age, who since has been executed as a notorious witch, two witnesses maintained that he was the Master of ceremonies and the governor of the Sabbath. That the Devil put into his hand a golden baton, with which as a Master of the camp, he put into order the people, and all things at the Sabbath: And when this was finished he gave this baton to the Grand master of the assembly.

Gentle Rivaffeau confessed in front of the Court that he had been at the Sabbath two times, without worshiping the Devil or acting like the others, because he had made such a pact with him, and he had torn open half of his left foot to have the ability to heal, and the liberty to simply see the Sabbath without being obligated to do other things. And he said that the Sabbath was held almost always around midnight, at an intersection, most often on Wednesday or Friday night: That the Devil looked for the stormiest night he could find, so that the winds and the storms would carry their powders further and more impetuously: That two notable Devils would preside at these Sabbaths, the great Negro who was called master Leonard, and another small devil that Master Leonard sometimes substituted in place of himself, whom they call master Jean Mullin: That they loved the Great master, and that after everyone had kissed his backside, there were around sixty who would dance without their cloaks, back to back, each with a large cat attached to the tail of their shirt, then they would dance completely naked.: That this master Leonard taking the form of a black fox would murmur a badly articulated word at the beginning, and that after this everyone was silent.

One witch among other very notorious ones told us that she had always believed that witchcraft was the best religion, itself founded on what she had often heard as some form of Mass with more pomp than in the real church. . . .

Discourse IV. Of the dance of the witches at the sabbath.

. . . And even more seriously and hideously at the Sabbaths, and obscene movements of the dances that are done at these unfortunate assemblies, and these indecent desires, that the Devil engenders in the hearts of an infinity of young virgins that are there: all in front of whom the Devil and an infinity of witches openly perform their demonic coupling.

These are not at all games and dances, they are acts of incest and other hideous crimes, which we can truthfully say came to us from this bad and pernicious neighboring of Spain: Where the Basques, and those of the country of Lambourd, are neighbors. Also, do they not have a noble dance like those that are popular in France: In this way all the most excitable dances, and those that agitate and torment the body the most, those which disfigure it the most, and all the most indecent dances came from there. All the Pyrrhonic, the Moorish, the perilous jumps, dances on ropes, the cascading from high ladders, the flying with fake wings, Pirouettes, the dancing on half lances, swinging, making circles, the forces of Hercules on the woman turned upside down without touching her back to the floor, the canaries of the feet and of the hands, almost all these atrocities came from Spain. And quite recently it gave us the new invention of the Chaconne or Saraband.

It's the most lewd and the most shameless dance that one can see, that which the Spanish courtesans who have since become comediennes, have made so fashionable in our theaters, so that now our littlest of girls make a profession of dancing it perfectly. Moreover it is the most violent dance and the most animated, the most passionate, in which the gestures, however mute, seem to demand more with silence, that the lewd man desires from a woman, over all others. Because the man and the woman cross each other several times at certain measured distances, one would think that each limb and little part of the body seeks out and takes its measure so as to join itself and associate itself with each other in time and space. The only Bergamask, which is not at all accompanied by dishonest gestures, but with very little respect of the other, came from Italy.

And yet, all of these dances are practiced still with much more liberty and more shamelessly at the Sabbath: for the wisest and the most moderate believe never to fail, in committing incest every night with their fathers, brothers and others closer, even in the presence of their husbands. And they take Royal titles as well, such as Queen of the Sabbath, of this miserable demon, to be publicly known as such before everyone: while his coupling is accompanied by a marvelous and horrible torment, as we would say in his place.

The dances of the witches almost make the men furious and force abortions on the women most often.

Discourse V. Of Satan's copulation with male and female witches, and whether that is capable of producing any offspring.

Several people have denied the coupling and contact of Satan with the male and female witches: which would be to completely deny what the incubus and the succubus say, and to destroy what antiquity and our proceedings allowed us to see. The truth is that the demons make themselves a body of air with which, while this seems to be something marvelous and quasi impossible, they can practice the acts of Venus.

And yet, this odious and accursed coupling comes after the dancing and the feasts. Coupling so abominable that it is a horror to tell of the particularities, to good girls and other Christian people as it makes them suffer. But I can say that some girls and women of Labourd, who have worshiped at the Sabbaths, instead of keeping quiet about this damnable coupling, instead of blushing and crying about it, they recount the dirtiest and the most obscene occurrences and deeds, with such liberty and gaiety, that they make saying it glorious, and take a certain pleasure in telling about it, taking the mating of this obscene demon to be more dignified than that of the most honest husband they could ever meet. They do not blush for anything, whatever impudent and sordid question or dirty interrogation is presented to them, in the way that our interpreter, who was an ecclesiastic, was more ashamed of asking them the questions than they were of answering them. The young girls of thirteen and fourteen years of age express themselves more openly than we do in asking them. And I know very well about the one who begged the Devil, since he wanted to carnally know her, to change her form. Here is what Marie Dindarte of Sare, seventeen years of age, excellent sorceress, and who brought children to the Sabbath, told us: That the Devil wanting to couple with a young witch, she instantly begged him to give her another form to make her not recognize him, which he did. Nevertheless, she recognized him, because the Devil does not hide from great witches like her. I am afraid that by writing about this, I will be esteemed more shameless than these women. But I would not know how to convince them of the effrontery if I did not say one thing about it, but that I will not say anything that will be embedded in our procedures, and I will be quiet about most of it.

Johannes d'Aguerre, says that the Devil, in the form of a billy goat, had his limb in the back and had sexual relations with the women by agitating and pushing with this against their fronts.

Marie de Marigrane aged fifteen years and resident of Biarritz said that she often saw the Devil coupling with an infinity of women that she names by name and surname: and that his custom is to have sexual relations with the beautiful women from the front, and the ugly ones from behind.

And yet, while this is obscene to pronounce, one can clearly see that she speaks the truth. While she is still very young, her youth is incapable of such a filthy invention. Since, if it is like this, as those that have even tried it have told us, (since the Devil only hides from children, who say they see the women with whom the Devil wants to have sexual relations separate themselves from the troupe, withdraw a little with him, and that they cannot see this execrable act because he puts in front of them some sort of dense, thick cloud: but they hear them screaming like people who are suffering from great pain, and they see them soon after come back to the Sabbath all bloody) I think that it is just as well from the front as from the back, depending on the place where he struck. And one should not doubt that he takes more pleasure in receiving sexual relations from the back than from the front; and moreover when he has relations with children or little girls, that he also takes more pleasure in sodomy, than in the most regulated and the most natural voluptuousness. Since he only seeks to offend God, affect nature, and corrupt and dishonor the human race. I will leave this distressing and dirty discourse, and will not engage myself either in that of the incubus and succubus to recount unaltered what our trials tell us about it.

Several people told us that at the Sabbath during or after the dancing, the Devil takes the most beautiful women to have carnal knowledge of them. But most often he gives this honor to the Queen of the Sabbath, and to the one whom he holds in high favor sitting next to him. Sometimes he also openly has sexual relations with several others: the dense cloud that he interposes being only for the children. About which an old lady told us a particularity, that the Devil has never become accustomed to having contact with virgins, because he cannot commit adultery with them, so he waits until they are married. And she told us about this, what the common rumor was among them, that the Master of the Sabbath retained a certain very beautiful girl until she married, not wanting to dishonor her, as if the sin was not so great to corrupt her virginity, without committing adultery with her. And those that are so privileged that he holds them by his side pompously clothed are generally held as and called the Queens of the Sabbath: while we have foreseen certain incidents, that often he loses all his respect, and takes the girls, as well as the women, and at the Sabbath and elsewhere he marries them and couples with them.

Figure 6 The witches' sabbath. This engraving, by the Polish artist Jan Ziarnkov, is the most detailed of all early modern depictions of the witches assemblies. It appeared in Pierre de Lancre's *Tableau de l'inconstance des mauvais anges et démons*, second edition (Paris, 1613) (see Chapter 21). In the top right witches sacrifice an infant to the Devil, seated on his throne, flanked by the queen and princess of the sabbath. At the bottom right witches and demons eat the dismembered parts of the sacrificed children. To the left and right witches dance naked. In the center witches fly to this assembly by various means. Below them witches stand over a cauldron, preparing potions that will be used to cause harm, showing that *maleficia* remained an essential dimension of the witches' crime at the sabbath.

22

COTTON MATHER:
THE APOCALYPSE AND
WITCHCRAFT, 1692

Cotton Mather, a Protestant minister in Boston, Massachusetts, was closely involved in the witch-hunt that took place at Salem in 1692. At the beginning of the investigations he had been a firm advocate of trying the witches, and even after the trials he continued to claim that the entire episode was a satanic conspiracy to prevent the spread of Christianity in the New World. His treatise, *Wonders of the Invisible World*, was prepared by October 1692 as an "account of the sufferings brought upon the country by witchcraft." The book was a collection of excerpts from demonological works (including that of William Perkins, the Puritan divine), accounts of five of the trials that had taken place at Salem, and narratives of other recent witchcraft prosecutions, such as those that had been held in Sweden between 1668 and 1676. The part of the book that was most relevant to the development of witch-beliefs was a sermon that Mather had given on 4 August 1692 at the height of the witch panic at Salem. Bearing the title of "A Discourse on the Wonders of the Invisible World," the sermon takes its text from Revelation 12:12. Revelation, the last book of the New Testament, prophesied the Second Coming of Christ, who would destroy the powers of evil. Revelation foretold that this event would be preceded by the appearance of the anti-Christ and the workings of the Devil on earth. Mather interpreted the signs of demonic possession visible in Massachusetts as evidence that the anti-Christ had appeared and that the Devil was loose. The proper Calvinist response to this apocalyptic challenge was to wage war against Satan by taking action against witchcraft. The interpretation of witchcraft in apocalyptic terms had been the work primarily of Protestant, and especially English, demonologists of the seventeenth century. The writers whom Mather read, including Perkins, Henry Holland, Alexander Roberts, and Thomas Cooper, had all associated witchcraft with the apocalypse. So too had John Stearne the colleague of the witch-finder Matthew Hopkins in 1645–1646, during the English Civil War. At that time apocalyptic thought had become a major theme of Protestant sermons and polemics. Now, in another period of crisis in British North America, when the colony of Massachusetts had lost its charter and Puritanism itself was being challenged from within, the theme was once again emphasized. It represents one of the few Protestant contributions to demonology made towards the end of the period of witch-hunting.

Source: Cotton Mather, *A Discourse on the Wonders of the Invisible World* (1692) in *Wonders of the Invisible World* (Boston, 1693).

Revel. XII.12

Woe to the inhabitants of the Earth and of the Sea, for the Devil is come down unto you, having great wrath, because he knoweth he hath but a short time.

The text is like the cloudy and fiery pillar vouchsafed unto Israel, in the wilderness of old; there is a very dark side of it in the intimation that *The Devil is come down having great wrath*; but it has also a bright side, when it assures us that *He has but a short time.* . . .

We are in the first place to apprehend that there is a time fixed and started by God for the Devil to enjoy a dominion over our sinful and therefore woeful world. . . . But we must likewise apprehend that in such a time the woes of the world will be heightened beyond what they were at any time from the foundation of the world.

If lastly we are inquisitive after instances of those aggravated woes with which the Devil will towards the end of his time assault us, let it be remembered that all the extremities which were foretold by the trumpets and vials in the apocalyptic schemes of these things to come upon the world were the woes to come from the wrath of the Devil upon the shortening of his time.

And besides all these things, and besides the increase of plagues and wars, and storms, and internal maladies in our days, there are especially two most extraordinary woes, one would fear, will in these days become very ordinary. One woe that may be looked for is a frequent repetition of earthquakes, and this perhaps by the energy of the Devil in the earth. The Devil will be clapped up as a prisoner in or near the bowels of the earth when once that conflagration shall be dispatched, which will make *The new earth wherein shall dwell righteousness*; and that conflagration will doubtless be much promoted by the subterraneous fires, which are a cause of the earthquakes in our days. . . .

And then another woe that may be looked for is the Devil's being now let loose in preternatural operations more than formerly, and perhaps in possessions and obsessions that shall be very marvelous. You are not ignorant that just before our Lord's first coming there were most observable outrages committed by the Devil upon the children of men. And I am suspicious that

there will again be an unusual range of the Devil among us, a little before
the second coming of our Lord, which will be to give the last stroke in
destroying the works of the Devil. The evening wolves will be much abroad
when we are near the evening of the world. The Devil is going to be dislodged
of the air, where his present quarters are; God will with flashes of hot lightning upon him cause him to fall as lightning from his ancient habitations;
and the raised saints will there have a new heaven, which we expect according
to the promise of God. Now a little before this thing you be like to see the
Devil more sensible and visibly busy upon Earth perhaps than ever he was
before. You shall oftener hear about apparitions of the Devil and about poor
people strangely bewitched, possessed and obsessed by infernal fiends. When
our Lord is going to set up his kingdom, in the most sensible and visible
manner that ever was, and in a manner answering the transfiguration in the
mount, it is a thousand to one but the Devil will in sundry parts of the
world assay the like for himself with a most apish imitation; and men, at
least in some corners of the world, and perhaps in such as God may have
some special designs upon, will to their cost, be more familiarized with the
world of the spirits than they had been formerly.

23

JAMES HUTCHINSON:
CHILDREN, THE
COVENANT, AND
WITCHCRAFT, 1697

<hr/>

During the last large witch-hunt in Scotland, which took place at Paisley in 1697, the minister of Kilallan, James Hutchinson, preached a sermon before the judges who had been appointed by the Privy Council to try those accused of the crime. This witch-hunt, which had begun with the possession of a young girl, Christian Shaw, led to the trial and execution of seven persons for witchcraft (Chapter 50). Sermons were instrumental in many witch-hunts, especially when the clergy were not involved in the actual trial of those prosecuted in the secular courts. This sermon reveals the strength of the belief in witchcraft among the clergy at a time when trials were declining in number and had long since come to an end in other parts of Europe. It is also significant in its discussion of the culpability of children for witchcraft, a phenomenon that became increasingly common in the seventeenth century and had been central to the large witch-hunt that took place in Sweden in 1668–1676. In that hunt many children had been accused of being taken to the sabbath. In the English-speaking world the large witch hunt at Salem, Massachusetts in 1692 had also led to the imprisonment, but not the execution, of a five-year-old girl in 1692. This sermon attributes the culpability of children to their parents. Finally, the sermon is significant in its exhortation to the judges to use the same means that were used to secure confessions to treason against the king. Hutchinson was reluctant to recommend specifically the use of torture, which in Scotland required a warrant from the Privy Council, but that was clearly his intent.

Source: The sermon is printed in George Neilson, "A Sermon on Witchcraft in 1697," *Scottish Historical Review* 7 (1910): 390–399. Spelling and punctuation have been modernized.

Sermon Preached by Mr James Hutchison before the Commissioners of Justiciary appointed for trial of several persons suspected guilty of witchcraft. At Paisley the 13 April 1697

Exodus 22, chapter 18 verse: Thou shalt not suffer a witch to live.

We have in this verse a precept of the law of God. In reference to a certain sort of malefactors to be found within the visible Church, even amongst the Israelites. These malefactors are there called witches. The person to whom this direction and command is given is not expressed or specified, but may be easily understood by the nature of the precept itself. It is a precept of the judicial law given to the people of Israel that was a national church as having the power of the sword given to them . . .

By a witch is understood a person that hath immediate converse with the devil, that one way or another is under a pact with him acted and influenced by him in reference to the producing such effects as cannot be produced by others without this compact. . . . The word here is in the feminine gender, a she-witch, yet [in] Leviticus 20:27 the spirit of God doth expressly mention either man or woman: the man or woman that hath a familiar spirit or a vizard shall surely be put to death; they shall stone them with stones. . . .

Now in the next place to come to the question proposed what constitutes formally a person to be a witch? . . . It requires that there be a real compact between Satan and that person either personally drawn up and made or mediately by parents immediate or mediate having power of the person, adding thereunto his mark. . . . No less doth Satan require of them that will follow in his way than either personal covenanting with him, and receiving his mark upon their flesh, or that the parents give their children to him and they receive his mark, and where this is, I doubt not such a person is really a witch or warlock, and even suppose it be a child it will be found afterwards (if the Lord's powerfully converting of the soul to himself prevent it not). That such persons will be as really in covenant with Satan as the children of professing parents receiving baptism will be found to be in covenant with God.

In the next place as to the nature of the compact that is between Satan and those that follow him, it must be no less than this, that they shall worship him as their God, that they shall follow him as their guide, that they shall be acted and influenced by him in his sinful ways and actings even in such wherein they could not produce any effect if Satan did not concur with them. . . .

As for the mark I think there is more weight to be laid upon it than many do. Satan must be in a manner God's ape. To follow and imitate him, he must give marks and impressions. And however doctors may say such and such things of it, we know not upon what ground. It may be they have been budded and bribed to say such things; yet they themselves may know, and if put to it, they will say that there is still a difference between that insensible mark that the devil gives and any other insensible mark that proceeds from any natural or physical cause whatsoever. . . .

[T]hese that have been by their parents mediately or immediately to Satan and follow his way and have received his mark and have been trained up by these parents in the way of witchcraft and have practised them may justly be looked upon as witches, formally constituted as being under a real covenant with Satan. Suppose that they have never renewed that covenant that was between their parents and Satan, yet they, having received his mark and being given by their parents and him, he keeps the grip he gets as long as he can, and so they, joining with witches and meeting at their meetings and consenting to their wicked actings, are to be judged witches. And the ground I give for this is, as really as children of professing parents receiving the external sign of God's covenant and coming to the assemblies of the people and joining with them in the ordinance and acts of worship, though they never come under a personal covenant with God themselves, yet they are constructed to be in covenant with God as well as the parents, I mean externally in covenant with God, just so may those be looked upon as professors of Satan and followers of his way. Secondly, these that upon a call from Satan keep the meetings with Satan with his followers and join with them in acts of murder or tormenting their neighbors old or young whether by ordinary means as a cord or napkin to strangle them or by a picture by putting pins in it or roasting it at the fire and flaming it with vinegar and brandy, and all to put the person to torment, these are not only murderers by the law of God but partakers of devilry and witchcraft because they make use of the means that Satan prescribes for the killing of such and such persons. Thirdly, another inference is that they that confess themselves that they have been frequently at the meetings of Satan with witches and have concurred with him in his wicked way by essaying to torment or murder old or young are to be looked upon as confessing witches as well as they that confess they had made a personal covenant with him themselves and had confessed they had renounced their baptism, because it supposes a real covenant, that is, that their parents or they that have the power of them have given them to Satan, they have his mark if they be well searched and have practised with Satan and have gone along with him in this horrid act of wickedness. A fourth inference is that they that confess they have been carried here and where to such assemblies with witches they know not how, but sometimes they have been at his call to go, are likewise to be looked upon as confessing witches. This I would a little amplify thus. The compact real or personal made between Satan and witches has this in it that they shall be guided and influenced by Satan and be at his call. Now this is the remark you will find from all confessing witches when Satan would have them at meetings, there needs no more but a call. There is no refusing this call; they must go whether they will or not, which is a strange kind of power that Satan has over these persons. They get not leave to be so deliberate as to choose or refuse to go, but go they must.

A fifth inference is that carnal dealing with Satan is so gross a crime and so opposite to that natural and moral honesty and chastity among all that those that confess that are to be looked upon as confessing witches. . . .

Now I would offer a word to the honourable judges here appointed for cognoscing this affair that we have been speaking of. And first I would lay before them that witchcraft is one of these evil deeds that the spirit of God enjoins death upon, and little wonder, for witches are the pests of congregations. . . .

Another thing I would propose is, the safety of professors is concerned in it. Therefore they to whom a matter of such importance is committed ought to beware that they be not trivial therein and that they do not burden and weary in searching it out, lest the Lord give them a reproof for being so weary of that which is his concern. . . .

Again further I would propose this: that confession of the witches being that which will clear the judges, most pains would be taken to bring them to a confession. Whatever lawful means may be used to bring a person guilty of treason against the king to a confession, the same is necessary to bring a witch to confession. But those methods I will not prescribe. Let the honourable judges think upon them as God shall give them direction.

Part IV

THE TRIAL AND PUNISHMENT OF WITCHES

Many of the demonological works of the fifteenth, sixteenth, and seventeenth centuries not only described in great detail the activities of witches but also provided instruction on how to identify, try, and punish them. The authors appealed to authorities to bring these confederates of Satan to justice, and they discussed the methods for securing convictions.

The discovery and punishment of witches was a process that was fraught with difficulty. Courts had to be given the authority to prosecute criminals who were being accused of both a secular and a spiritual crime. The crime by definition used occult or mysterious means, and it was performed secretly, sometimes at night, when the only witnesses were the witches' alleged accomplices. The refusal of witches to confess to their crime presented further juridical problems for prosecutors.

The primary concern of the literature on legal procedures in witchcraft cases was the use of judicial torture. This procedure began to be introduced into the ecclesiastical and secular courts of most European countries in the thirteenth century, and in some but not all jurisdictions it was routinely used to interrogate witches. The purpose of torture was to obtain confessions when the testimony of eye-witnesses could not be produced. Its use was regulated by a number of rules regarding the intensity and duration of the torture, but in their eagerness to obtain convictions many judicial officials often violated those rules on the grounds that witchcraft was an exceptional crime that had to be prosecuted at all costs. The result was that many accused witches were forced to confess to crimes they did not commit, and when they were tortured to find the names of their alleged accomplices, many other innocent persons were convicted and executed. Without torture, courts would never have been able to convict the large numbers of witches who were prosecuted during the early modern period.

The judicial literature on witchcraft also dealt with many other procedures used in the trial of witchcraft, including the techniques used to determine whether witches could be tried, the admissibility of evidence from certain types of witnesses in witchcraft trials, and the criteria for proving whether a witch was guilty. All these issues are discussed in the eleven documents included in this Part. The first five documents recommended the use of special procedures to try witches, while the final six urged caution or the abandonment of the trials on the grounds that innocent people were being executed. Chapter 24, a papal bull issued by Pope Innocent VIII in the late fifteenth century, was intended to facilitate the prosecution of witches by papal inquisitors. In Chapter 25, the main beneficiary of Innocent's edict, Heinrich Kramer, provides instruction for inquisitors regarding the use of torture. Jean Bodin, a secular judge writing almost a century after Kramer, justifies the use of special procedures against witches on the grounds that it is an excepted crime (Chapter 26), while Henri Boguet sets forth a number of rules to govern the conduct of a secular witchcraft judge (Chapter 27). King James VI of Scotland, who wrote a demonological treatise in 1597, discusses the techniques of swimming and pricking witches for the Devil's mark as part of a more general discussion of the punishment of witches (Chapter 28).

The remaining documents were written in response to the realization that innocent people were being executed as witches. Friedrich Spee, a German Jesuit priest who had served as a confessor to a number of witches, wrote a devastating critique of torture as used in witchcraft trials. His work contributed to a significant decline in the number of convictions and executions for witchcraft (Chapter 29). In England, where torture was not used, a witch-hunt in the county of Kent a few years later led Sir Robert Filmer to criticize the legal criteria proposed by William Perkins for establishing the guilt of witches (Chapter 30). In neighboring Scotland, Sir George Mackenzie, while still professing a belief in witchcraft, delivered a comprehensive indictment of the judicial procedures used to try witches at a time when the number of trials had begun to decline in his country (Chapter 31). In France, an edict of Louis XIV in 1682 put an end to most witchcraft trials in that country (Chapter 32), while in Prussia the Saxon jurist Christian Thomasius called not only for an end to witchcraft trials but also to the use of torture in all criminal investigations (Chapter 33). In 1736 a British statute repealed the English and Scottish witchcraft statutes upon which prosecutions in both countries had been based (Chapter 34). The statute reflects the recognition, shared by many Europeans in the early eighteenth century, that witchcraft was no longer a crime.

24

INNOCENT VIII:
PAPAL INQUISITORS AND
WITCHCRAFT, 1484

——————>◦◦◦<——————

In the first year of his pontificate Pope Innocent VIII issued a bull or edict known by its first Latin words, *summis desiderantes*. Its main purpose was to give juris-dictional authority to two inquisitors, Heinrich Kramer (identified in this document by his Latin name, Institoris) and Jacob Sprenger, to prosecute witches in various parts of Germany. These two German Dominicans, both professors of theology, had been encountering resistance to their inquisition from local secular author-ities, who also claimed jurisdiction over witchcraft. They also encountered resistance from some clerics who exercised episcopal authority in their dioceses. There was nothing special about this papal bull. Other popes had granted similar jurisdictional authority to its inquisitors in the name of protecting the faith. Nor did the bull mark a significant change in the definition of the crime of witchcraft, which it defined exclusively in terms of *maleficia*, especially the impeding of fertility. The bull refers to these witches giving themselves to devils male and female, but says nothing about the worship of the Devil at the sabbath. Nor does it comment on the preponderance of women among the accused, noting simply that people of both sexes were guilty of the crime. The only reason for the noto-riety of the document is that Kramer published it two years later as a preface to his witchcraft treatise, the *Malleus maleficarum* (1486). The bull makes it clear that even at this early date, ecclesiastical courts had no monopoly of jurisdic-tion over the crime of witchcraft. The bull also recommends, as does the *Malleus*, that the secular courts would need to cooperate with the inquisition in order to counteract the threat of witchcraft.

Source: The translation is based on that given in George L. Burr,
The Witch Persecutions (Philadelphia, 1902), pp. 7–10.

Desiring with supreme ardor, as pastoral solicitude requires, that the Catholic faith in our days everywhere grow and flourish as much as possible, and that all heretical pravity be put far from the territories of the faithful, we freely declare and anew decree this by which our pious desire may be fulfilled, and, all errors being rooted out by our toil as with the hoe of a wise laborer, zeal and devotion to this faith may take deeper hold on the hearts of the faithful themselves.

It has recently come to our ears, not without great pain to us, that in some parts of upper Germany, as well as in the provinces, cities, territories, regions, and dioceses of Mainz, Köln, Trier, Salzburg, and Bremen, many persons of both sexes, heedless of their own salvation and forsaking the Catholic faith, give themselves over to devils male and female, and by their incantations, charms, and conjurings, and by other abominable superstitions and sortileges, offences, crimes, and misdeeds, ruin and cause to perish the offspring of women, the foal of animals, the products of the earth, the grapes of vines, and the fruits of trees, as well as men and women, cattle and flocks and herds of animals of every kind, vineyards also and orchards, meadows, pastures, harvests, grains and other fruits of the earth; that they afflict and torture with dire pains and anguish, both internal and external, these men, women, cattle, flocks, and herds, and animals, and hinder men from begetting and women from conceiving, and prevent all consummation of marriage; that, moreover, they deny with sacrilegious lips the faith they received in holy baptism; and that at the instigation of the enemy of mankind, they do not fear to commit and perpetrate many other abominable offences and crimes, at the risk of their own souls, to the insult of the divine majesty and to the pernicious example and scandal of the multitudes. And although our beloved sons Henricus Institoris and Jacobus Sprenger, of the order Friars Preachers, professors of theology, have been and still are deputed by our apostolic letters as inquisitors of heretical pravity, the former in the aforesaid parts of upper Germany, including the provinces, cities, territories, dioceses, and other places as above, and the latter throughout certain parts of the course of the Rhine; nevertheless certain of the clergy and of the laity of those parts, seeking to be wise above what is fitting, because in the said letter of deputation the aforesaid provinces, cities, dioceses, territories and other places, and the persons and offences in question were not individually and specifically named, do not blush obstinately to assert that these are not at all included in the said parts and that therefore it is illicit for the aforesaid inquisitors to exercise their office of inquisition in the provinces, cities, dioceses, territories, and other places aforesaid, and that they ought not to be permitted to proceed to the punishment, imprisonment, and correction of the aforesaid persons for the offences and crimes above named. Wherefore in the provinces, cities, dioceses, territories, and places aforesaid such offences and crimes, not without evident damage to their souls and risk of eternal salvation, go unpunished.

120

We therefore, desiring, as is our duty, to remove all impediments by which in any way the said inquisitors are hindered in the exercise of their office, and to prevent the taint of heretical pravity and of other like evils from spreading their infection to the ruin of others who are innocent, the zeal of religion especially impelling us, in order that the provinces, cities, dioceses, territories, and places aforesaid in the said parts of upper Germany may not be deprived of the office of inquisition which is their due, do hereby decree, by virtue of our apostolic authority, that it shall be permitted to the said inquisitors in these regions to exercise their office of inquisition and to proceed to the correction, imprisonment, and punishment of the aforesaid persons for their said offences and crimes, in all respects and altogether precisely as if the provinces, cities, territories, places, persons and offences aforesaid were expressly named in the said letter. And, for the greater sureness, extending the said letter and deputation to the provinces, cities, dioceses, territories, and places aforesaid, we grant to the said inquisitors that they or either of them, joining with them our beloved son Johannes Gremper, cleric of the diocese of Constance, master of arts, their present notary, or any other notary public who by them or by either of them shall have been temporarily delegated to the provinces, cities, dioceses, territories and places aforesaid, may exercise against all persons, of whatever condition or rank, the said office of inquisition, correcting, imprisoning, punishing, and chastising, according to their deserts, those persons whom they shall find guilty as aforesaid.

And they shall also have full and entire liberty to propound and preach to the faithful the word of God, as often as it shall seem to them fitting and proper, in each and all the parish churches in the said provinces, and to do all things necessary and suitable under the aforesaid circumstances, and likewise freely and fully to carry them out.

And moreover we enjoin by apostolic writ on our venerable brother, the Bishop of Strasburg, that, either in his own person or through some others solemnly publishing the foregoing wherever, whenever, and how often soever he may deem expedient or by these inquisitors or either of them may be legitimately required, he permit them not to be molested or hindered in any manner whatsoever by any authority whatsoever in the matter of the aforesaid and of this present letter, threatening all opposers, hinderers, contradictors, and rebels, of whatever rank, state, decree, eminence, nobility, excellence, or condition they may be, and whatever privilege or exemption they may enjoy, with excommunication, suspension, interdict, and other still more terrible sentences, censures, and penalties, as may be expedient, and this without appeal and with power after due process of law of aggravating and reaggravating these penalties, by our authority, as often as may be necessary, to this end calling in the aid, if need be, of the secular arm.

And this, all other apostolic decrees and earlier decisions to the contrary notwithstanding; or if to any, jointly and severally, there has been granted by this apostolic see exemption from interdict, suspension, or excommunication, by apostolic letters not making entire, express, and literal mention of the said grant of exemption; or if there exist any other indulgence whatsoever, general or special, of whatsoever tenor, by failure to name which or to insert it bodily in the present letter the carrying out of this privilege could be hindered or in any way put off, – or any of whose whole tenor special mention must be made in our letters. Let no man, therefore, dare to infringe this page of our declaration, extension, grant, and mandate, or with rash hardihood to contradict it. If any presume to attempt this, let him know that he incurs the wrath of almighty God and of the blessed apostles Peter and Paul.

Given in Rome, at St Peter's, in the year of Our Lord's incarnation 1484, on the nones of December, in the first year of our pontificate.

25

HEINRICH KRAMER:
THE TORTURE OF
ACCUSED WITCHES,
1486

⸻◦◦◦⸻

Part III of Heinrich Kramer's *Malleus maleficarum* (1486), the first two parts of which are excerpted in Chapter 14, offers recommendations for the successful prosecution of witches. Kramer is willing to countenance just about any practice that would succeed in convicting the witch and thus do God's work. His recommendations are based on the assumption that witchcraft is a *crimen exceptum*, a special crime, in which the normal rules do not apply. According to Kramer, the testimony of all sorts of witnesses, including children, should be admitted; the judge should have complete discretion in setting procedures; defense advocates, though permitted, should not be allowed to use their skills to defend parties whom they know are guilty. Most important, Kramer gives great latitude to judges to elicit confessions by means of torture. The following excerpts from Kramer's treatise all deal with the application of torture, recommending when and how to employ this procedure.

Source: *The Malleus Maleficarum of Heinrich Kramer and James Sprenger*,
ed. Montague Summers (London, 1928), pp. 222–226.

Part I

Question XIII. Of the points to be observed by the judge before the formal examination in the place of detention and torture. This is the eighth action.

The next action of the Judge is quite clear. For common justice demands that a witch should not be condemned to death unless she is convicted by her own confession. But here we are considering the case of one who is judged to be taken in manifest heresy for one of the other two reasons set down in the First Question, namely direct or indirect evidence of the fact, or the legitimate production of witnesses; and in this case she is to be exposed to questions and torture to extort a confession of her crimes.

And to make the matter clear we will quote a case which occurred at Spires and came to the knowledge of many. A certain honest man was bargaining with a woman and would not come to terms with her about the price of some article; so she angrily called after him, "You will soon wish you had agreed." For witches generally use this manner of speaking, or something like it, when they wish to bewitch a person by looking at him. Then he, not unreasonably being angry with her, looked over his shoulder to see with what intention she had uttered those words; and behold! he was suddenly bewitched so that his mouth was stretched sideways as far as his ears in a horrible deformity, and he could not draw it back, but remained so deformed for a long time.

We put the case that this was submitted to the judge as direct evidence of the fact; and it is asked whether the woman is to be considered as manifestly taken in the heresy of witchcraft. This should be answered from the words of St Bernard which we have quoted above. For there are three ways in which a person may be judged to be so taken, and they not so closely conjoined as though it were necessary for all three to agree in one conclusion, but each one by itself, namely the evidence of the fact, or the legitimate production of witnesses, or her own confession, is sufficient to prove a witch to be manifestly taken in that heresy.

But indirect evidence of the fact is different from direct evidence; yet though it is not so conclusive, it is still taken from the words and deeds of witches, as was shown in the Seventh Question, and it is judged from witchcraft which is not so immediate in its effect, but follows after some lapse of time from the utterance of the threatening words. Wherefore we may conclude that this is the case with such witches who have been accused and have not made good their defense (or have failed to defend themselves because this privilege was not granted them; and it was not granted because they did not ask for it). But what we are to consider now is what action the judge should take, and how he should proceed to question the accused with a view to extorting the truth from her so that sentence of death may finally be passed upon her.

And here, because of the great trouble caused by the stubborn silence of witches, there are several points which the judge must notice, and these are dealt with under their several heads.

And the first is that he must not be too quick to subject a witch to certain signs which will follow. And he must not be too quick for this reason; unless God, through a holy angel, compels the devil to withhold his help from the witch, she will be so insensitive to the pains of torture that she will sooner be torn limb from limb than confess any of the truth.

But the torture is not to be neglected for this reason, for they are not all equally endowed with this power, and also the devil sometimes of his own will permits them to confess their crimes without being compelled by a holy angel. . . .

For there are some who obtain from the devil a respite of six or eight or ten years before they have to offer him their homage, that is, devote themselves to him body and soul; whereas others, when they first profess their abjuration of the faith, at the same time offer their homage. And the reason why the devil allows that stipulated interval of time is that, during that time, he may find out whether the witch had denied the faith with her lips only but not in her heart, and would therefore offer him her homage in the same way.

For the devil cannot know the inner thoughts of the heart except conjecturally from outward indications, as we showed in the First Part of this work where we dealt with the question whether the devil can turn the minds of men to hatred or love. And many have been found who, driven by some necessity or poverty, have been induced by other witches in the hope of ultimate forgiveness in confession, to become either total or partial apostates from the faith. And it is such whom the devil deserts without any compulsion by a holy angel; and therefore they readily confess their crimes, whereas others, who have from their hearts bound themselves to the devil, are protected by his power and preserve a stubborn silence.

And this provides a clear answer to the question how it comes about that some witches readily confess, and others will by no means do so. For in the case of the former, when the devil is not compelled by God, he still deserts them of his own will, in order that by temporal unhappiness and a horrible death he may head to despair those over whose hearts he could never obtain the mastery. For it is evident from their sacramental confessions that they have never voluntarily obeyed the devil, but have been compelled by him to work witchcraft.

And some also are distinguished by the fact that, after they have admitted their crimes, they try to commit suicide by strangling or hanging themselves. They are induced to do this by the Enemy, lest they should obtain pardon from God through sacramental confession. This chiefly happens in the case of those who have not been willing agents of the devil; although it may also happen in the case of willing agents, after they have confessed their crimes; but then it is because the devil has been compelled to desert the witch.

In conclusion we may say that it is as difficult, or more difficult, to compel a witch to tell the truth as it is to exorcise a person possessed of the devil. Therefore the judge ought not to be too willing or ready to proceed to such examination unless, as has been said, the death penalty is involved. And in this case he must exercise great care, as we shall show; and first we shall speak of the method of sentencing a witch to such torture.

Question XIV. Of the method of sentencing the accused to be questioned; and how she must be questioned on the first day; and whether she may be promised her life. The ninth action.

Secondly, the judge must take care to frame his sentence in the following manner.

We the judge and assessors, having attended to and considered the details of the process enacted by us against you N. of such a place in such a diocese, and having diligently examined the whole matter, find that you are equivocal in your admissions; as for example, when you say that you used such threats with no intention of doing an injury, but nevertheless there are various proofs which are sufficient warrant for exposing you to the question and torture. Wherefore, that the truth may be known from your own mouth, and that henceforth you may not offend the ears of the judges, we declare, judge and sentence that on this present day at such an hour you be placed under the question and torture. This sentence was given, etc.

Alternatively, as had been said, the judge may not be willing to deliver the accused up to be questioned, but may punish her with imprisonment with the following object in view. Let him summon her friends and put it to them that she may escape the death penalty, although she will be punished in another way, if she confesses the truth, and urge them to try to persuade her to do so. For very often mediation, and the misery of imprisonment, and the repeated advice of honest men, dispose the accused to discover the truth.

And we have found that witches have been so strengthened by this sort of advice that, as a sign of their rebellion, they have spat on the ground as if it were in the devil's face, saying "Depart, cursed devil: I shall do what is just"; and afterwards they have confessed their crimes.

But if after keeping the accused in a state of suspense, and continually postponing the day of examination, and frequently using verbal persuasions, the judge should truly believe that the accused is denying the truth, let them question her lightly without shedding blood; knowing that such questioning is fallacious and often, as has been said, ineffective.

And it should be begun in this way. While the officers are preparing for the questioning, let the accused be stripped; or, if she is a woman, let her first be led to the penal cells and there stripped by honest women of good reputation. And the reason for this is that they should search for any instrument of witchcraft sewn into her clothes; for they often make such instruments, at the instruction of devils, out of the limbs of unbaptized children, the purpose being that those children should be deprived of the beatific vision. And when those instruments have been disposed of, the judge shall use his own persuasions and those of other honest men zealous for the faith to induce her to confess the truth voluntarily; and if she will not, let him order the officers to bind her with cords, and apply her to some engine of torture; and then let them obey at once but not joyfully, rather appearing to be disturbed by their duty. Then let her be released again at someone's earnest request, and taken on one side, and let her again be persuaded; and in persuading her, let her be told that she can escape the death penalty. . . .

But if neither threats nor such promises will induce her to confess the truth, then the officers must proceed with the sentence, and she must be examined, not in any new or exquisite manner, but in the usual way, lightly or heavily, according as the nature of her crimes demands. And as she is being questioned about each several point, let her be often and frequently exposed to torture, beginning with the more gentle of them; for the judge should not be too hasty to proceed to the graver kind. And while this is being done, let the notary write all down, how she is tortured and what questions are asked and how she answers.

And note that, if she confesses under torture, she should then be taken to another place and questioned anew, so that she does not confess only under the stress of torture.

The next step of the judge should be that, if after being fittingly tortured, she refuses to confess the truth, he should have other engines of torture brought before her, and tell her that she will have to endure these if she does not confess. If then she is not induced by terror to confess, the torture must be continued on the second or third day, but not repeated at that present time unless there should be some fresh indication of its probable success.

26

JEAN BODIN:
WITCHCRAFT AS AN
EXCEPTED CRIME,
1580

Jean Bodin (1530–1596), a lawyer and scholar best known for his writing on political theory, most notably *The Six Books of the Republic* (1576), also wrote a highly influential work on witchcraft. *Démonomanie des sorciers* [The Demon-Mania of Witches] was first published at Paris in 1580. The book became enormously popular, going into 23 editions in four languages. Bodin's interest in witchcraft originated in a witchcraft trial that he adjudicated in 1578 at Lyons, where he held a minor official post. The treatise, which begins with a reprinting of the condemnation of magic by the theologians at the University of Paris in 1398 (Chapter 12), exhibits a deep hostility to all forms of magic, especially sorcery. Bodin includes in the *Demon-mania* a sustained attack on the skeptical views of the demonologist Johann Weyer, who denied the culpability of witches (Chapter 50). The most extreme views reflected in the book however, are the unorthodox judicial tactics Bodin sanctions in the investigation and trial of witches. These appear in Book Four, which was intended to be a manual for lay judges. Arguing that witchcraft was an exceptional crime against God and also a crime that was difficult to prove, Bodin recommends the admissibility of the testimony of the witch's accomplices, the secret initiation of cases by judges rather than by prosecutors, anonymous denunciations of witches by the community, conviction of the witch on the basis of testimony by witnesses to separate crimes, the interpretation of an obscure testimony by a witch as a confession, and the consideration of a person's refusal to confess under torture as half a confession justifying punishment. Bodin's determination to prosecute witches at all costs contrast markedly with his commitment to religious toleration.

Source: Jean Bodin, *Demon-Mania of Witches*, trans. Randy A. Scott
(Toronto, 2001), pp. 173–195.

Book 4

Chapter 1 On the Investigation of Witches.

... But of all the sins which entail their own penalty, such as avarice, envy, drunkenness, wantonness, and other such things, there is none which punishes its victim more cruelly, nor longer than witchcraft, which takes revenge both on the soul and the body. ...

We have shown that their craft cannot enrich them nor give them pleasure, honour, or knowledge but only the means to commit base filth and wickednesses, in which Satan employs them. And for reward in this world he forces them to renounce God and to worship him and to kiss his rear in the form of a he-goat or some other foul animal. And instead of resting, he transports his slaves at night to commit the filthy acts which we have described. Thus the death penalty prescribed for witches is not to make them suffer more than they are suffering by punishing them, but to bring an end to the wrath of God on the whole people; also in part to bring them to repentance and to cure them, or at least until they will not change their ways, to reduce their number, surprising the wicked and preserving the elect. It is therefore, a very salutary thing for the whole body of a state diligently to search out and severely punish witches. Otherwise there is a danger that the people will stone both magistrates and witches. This happened a year ago at Haguenone when two witches who rightly deserved death were sentenced one to the lash, and the other to be in attendance. But the people seized them, stoned them and drove off the officers. Another very notorious witch living at Verigni, who died last April, took children, and after being accused of many sorceries, was acquitted. But she avenged herself so effectively that she killed both people and countless livestock, as I learned from the inhabitants. And I have marvelled at why many princes have set up inquiries and named special commissioners to conduct the trials of thieves, financiers, usurers, and highway robbers – and have left unpunished the most detestable and horrible wickedness of witches. ...

Since Satan and witches enact their mysteries at night, and witches' works are hidden and concealed and they cannot be easily sighted, the investigation and proof are difficult. This is what prevents judges from passing sentence or convicting people of such a despicable crime: a crime which involves every wickedness imaginable, as we have shown above. It is necessary therefore in a case of this nature, where such abominable crimes are done so secretly that one cannot discover them through respectable people, to verify them through accomplices, and people guilty of the same crime, just as is done with thieves; and only one is needed to denounce an infinite number of them. ...

Now there are several ways to proceed with the punishment of witches: either through regular judges or special magistrates. For in addition to the regular judges, it is necessary to establish special magistrates for that purpose, at least one or two in each province. But I do not mean, however, that either from bias or rivalry, but rather that they will lend mutual assistance in such a holy task. In earlier times ecclesiastical judges had this authority to the exclusion of lay judges. There is extant a decree of Parlement issued in the proceedings against the bishop of Paris in 1282. But later, authority was granted to civil magistrates while excluding churchmen by decree of the same Parlement in 1390, which was solemnly set forth. Subsequently Poulallier, the Provost Marshal of Laon, after arresting a number of witches, tried to bring that under his jurisdiction, but his suit was dismissed by decree of the court. It was then that Satan succeeded so well that people were of opinion that what was said about him was nonsense. In order then that judges not wait until a complaint is lodged, or until the king's prosecutors wake up, they must without request give information about suspects, which is the most secret method, and perhaps the best. But since some are frightened, and others do not wish to get involved with documenting evidence themselves, it is very necessary that crown prosecutors, and their deputies, become complainants. This is the second way. For it is really their responsibility to attend to everything and to prepare the prosecution for heinous crimes. Now since crown prosecutors very often are more negligent in their responsibilities than judges, it is advisable that each be admitted as a plaintiff in this crime, including the crown prosecutor. If, however, he does not wish to be involved, let private individuals nevertheless be permitted to lay charges for the prosecution and conviction of this crime; and without delay, whether it is a matter of personal interest or not, as is required in this realm for all other crimes, provided that in this case one respect the requisite solemnities of common law stated in the law, "*qui accusare, de publicis iudiciis*" [who has the right to accuse concerning public judgments]. This is the third form of proceedings that one can adopt.

The fourth will be effected by denunciations without the crown prosecutors having to name the informers, unless slander is very apparent (and the accused then is fully absolved in accordance with the Edict of Moulins) and unless the prisoner is released "*quousquei*" [provisionally], or it is announced that he will be more fully investigated, as must be done if there is any evidence or presumption. Now since this plague of witches is more common in villages and in areas outside towns, and poor simple people fear witches more than they do God or all the magistrates, and do not dare to come forward as accusers or as informers, it is necessary to implement for the detection of this crime which is so odious the praiseworthy custom of Scotland, practiced at Milan, which is called "Indict"; namely, that there be a box in church, where it will be easy for anyone to deposit a piece of paper with the name of the witch, the act committed by him, the place, the time and the witnesses. Then, in the presence of the judge and the crown prosecutor, who would each have a key to the box fastened with two locks, the box will be opened every fifteen days to inform secretly against those who are named. This is the fifth and most reliable way of proceeding. . . .

Chapter 2. On the Evidence Required to Prove the Crime of Witchcraft.

Among the proofs upon which a sentence can be based, there are three that may be called necessary and indisputable. The first is the truth of the acknowledged and concrete fact. The second is the voluntary confession of the one who is charged and convicted of the crime. The third is the testimony of several sound witnesses. As for evidence such as public reputation, forced confession, presumptions of law or other such things, one can say that they are "presumptions," some of which are greater than others, but not indisputable proofs.

Now the truth of the acknowledged and concrete fact is the clearest proof. . . . Thus when poisons and spells are found on the witch who is arrested with them, or in her room, or in her chest, or she is discovered digging beneath the doorway of a stable, and the poisons are found there that she was caught hiding, and livestock dies, one can assert that it is a clear and concrete fact. If one finds the person who is accused of being a witch in possession of toads, hosts, human members, or waxen images pierced with needles, in the prosecution of this crime these are concrete facts in such cases.

If one sees a witch or suspected witch kill a child . . . one can assert that is a clear fact in order to convict her of being a witch, even if she had confessed (as she did) that the Devil made her do it, inasmuch as she was not insane . . . For there is nothing more normal for witches than to murder children. If one sees a witch threaten her enemy who is hale and hearty, or she touches him, and instantly he falls dead, or he becomes a leper, or suddenly he becomes deformed or crippled or struck by a sudden illness, as we have shown by many examples – it is clear and concrete fact, if as well it is rumoured that she is a witch. . . . If one finds the agreement and the mutual compact between the witch and the Devil, signed by him, in his chest, as I remarked above, it is a concrete fact if the witch's signature is acknowledged by him. The clearest and the strongest proof then is one which brings to light the truth that one is seeking through tangible items. . . .

It is also a clear fact if the witch at one moment is discovered missing from her bed and her house, with the doors locked, after retiring at night to the same bed, then later she is found in her bed as we have previously shown in a number of examples. In all these cases and other comparable ones of clear facts which come before judges, they may base a conviction according to the respective facts, as we shall describe later – even if the witch refuses to confess; the more so if the witch's confession is concurrent with the clear fact; and even more if there are sound witnesses. . . .

The second means of clear and certain proof is when there are several sound witnesses who testify about tangible things by perceptions, and about intangible matters by arguments and sound reasonings. For the clarity of an acknowledged fact must be evident to the judges and to others present, and it does not suffice if it is apparent to the judge alone, or only to others . . .

When I said "several sound witnesses" the law stipulates at least two. But one must not look for a great number of witnesses for such despicable things which are done at night, or in grottoes or secret places. But what shall we say if three witnesses give evidence about three entirely different acts? That is, the first testifies to having seen a witch hollow out and dig beneath the threshold of a door, or at a crossroads, for that is normally where witches place their spell; and then that people or livestock have died there. Another testifies that after the same witch had touched someone, he suddenly fell dead. The third that after she had threatened her neighbour, he fell into a languor. I maintain that these three sound witnesses, with some other presumption, are adequate grounds for a death sentence, even though the witnesses each tell of different acts. For they are universally associated with the crime of witchcraft. In this case all authorities are in agreement that the proof is sufficient for hidden crimes such as fraud, murder, usury, adultery and other crimes which are committed as secretly as possible, and especially the casting of spells. . . .

In Germany they have a very bad custom of not putting the guilty person to death unless he confesses, although he is convicted with a thousand witnesses. It is true that they apply the question so violently and cruelly that the person remains crippled for the rest of his life. Now since this does not happen except in "exceptional crimes" and not in others, as the doctors state, who do not even consider accomplice witnesses with presumption sufficient to apply the question. Thus it is necessary that in exceptional crimes such as poisoning and witchcraft, the crime of treason, or murder, accomplices of the same act be admissible to give full evidence, unless there is a pertinent objection, such as the accomplice is a great enemy of the one whom he accuses of being involved in the evil spell. . . .

Thus a witness who has come forward without being called to testify against a witch must be heard, even though in another matter he might not be admissible. I shall make exception only for the objection of a major enmity arising from a cause other than witchcraft. . . . And even though a witness in other cases be convicted of perjury, and must be rejected, nonetheless in this crime he will be admitted along with others, unless he bears some outstanding hatred for the defendant. Furthermore, although a lawyer and a prosecutor cannot and must not be obliged to testify concerning their clients, nevertheless they must be compelled to do so in this crime, since many have argued that they can be forced to give evidence about their clients if the opposing party calls for it, either in a civil or a criminal action. Also, although accomplices do not constitute necessary proof in other crimes, nonetheless fellow witches denouncing or giving testimony against their accomplices constitute sufficient proof to pass sentence, especially if there are a number of them. For it is quite well known that only witches can testify about being present at the assemblies which they attend at night. . . . But it is absolutely necessary to bear in mind that the crime of witchcraft must not be treated in the same way as others. One must, rather, adopt an entirely different and exceptional approach for the reasons which I have set out. . . .

Chapter 3. Of the Voluntary and Forced Confessions of Witches.

Now there are two kinds of confession: one voluntary and the other forced. Both may be given in court or outside of court. The one given outside of court may be in the presence of many people or just one, either friend, relative, enemy or confessor. All these circumstances are to be taken into account, not because the truth is more true in court than outside of court, nor before an audience than before a confessor. Indeed on the contrary, most people conceal in public what they confess in private, either from shame or fear, as is often seen with thieves who reveal to their confessor what they would never say in court. The proof, however, is not as strong from an extrajudicial confession as a judicial one; nor from a forced as from a voluntary one. And among voluntary confessions, one made before interrogation has more effect. For sometimes the judge tricks the one whom he is questioning, and on occasion puts words into his mouth. . . .

The judge, nevertheless, must first proceed with tortures, according to the rank of the persons, against the one accused of witchcraft who will not answer anything, providing there is a good witness or several presumptions. And if he will not say anything under torture, the crime will be half confessed, and punished in accordance with the amount of proof. . . . Also in such a case one who purposely give an obscure answer is deemed to have confessed. Although legally speaking, such an answer is not enough proof for other crimes when it concerns corporal punishment, unless there are witnesses – which is not necessary with a clear and voluntary confession – with this crime, however, so secret and loathsome, it is sufficient along with other presumptions. And although doctors have established confession as one of the necessary and indubitable proofs, as holds in civil actions, nevertheless there are noteworthy differences in the circumstances of the place, the time, the people and the crime, such as the confession of a child or an elderly man, of a wise man or a fool, of a man or a woman, of a friend or an enemy, in court or outside of court, of an injury or of a parricide, under torture or without torture. This diversity must be carefully weighed by a wise and expert judge. . . .

With respect to witches who have a formal compact with the Devil, and who confess to having been at the assemblies, and other wickedness which cannot be learned except by their confession or from their accomplices, such a confession free of torture constitutes a proof, if made by the one who is charged, especially if he is suspected and reputed as such, even though it is not apparent that he caused death to people or livestock. For that wickedness is more detestable than any parricide imaginable. And if it is proposed that one must not concentrate upon the confession of something unnatural, as some state, it would not be necessary then to punish filthy Sodomites, who confess the unnatural sin. But if one means "unnatural" as something "impossible," that is wrong. For what is unnatural by nature, is not impossible; such as all the actions of the intelligences, and the works of God contrary to the course of nature, which one often witnesses; and even Hippocrates remarked that all the common illnesses come from God, or in his words, have something "divine and counter the course and order of natural causes," about which physicians know nothing. . . .

Now to confirm the proof of the witches' confessions, one must link them with the confessions of other witches. For the actions of the Devil are always consistent in every country, just as an ape is always an ape, dressed in sackcloth or in royal purple. This is why one finds that the confessions of witches in Germany, Italy, France, Spain, and the ancient Greeks and Romans are similar. And most often witches are denounced by each other . . .

27

HENRI BOGUET:
THE CONDUCT OF
A WITCHCRAFT JUDGE,
1602

As an Appendix to his *Discourse of Witchcraft* (1602), the Burgundian judge and demonologist Henri Boguet presented a series of articles regarding the proper procedure for trying witches. Recognizing witchcraft as an excepted crime, Boguet gives the judge sufficient latitude to prosecute witches successfully, including permission to arrest an alleged accomplice named by only one other witch. But Boguet also recommends restraint in the application of torture, rejects the swimming test approved by James VI of Scotland (Chapter 28), and condemns the false promise of immunity to witches.

Source: Henri Boguet, *An Examen of Witches*, trans. E. A. Ashwin (London, 1929), pp. 212–226.

The Manner of Procedure of a Judge in a
Case of Witchcraft

Article I

The judge in this country can by himself conduct the trial of witches when there is definite evidence of the fact: this was decreed by the Court on the 28th September, 1598. This is also the practice today in France.

Article II

Witchcraft is a crime apart, both on account of its enormity, and because it is usually committed at night and always secretly. Therefore the trial of this crime must be conducted in an extraordinary manner, and the usual legalities and ordinary procedure cannot be strictly observed.

Article III

The judge must decide whether the presumptions and conjectures are enough to warrant his committing the accused to prison; for we can give no certain rule as to this. Yet I shall always maintain that a person should always be imprisoned on the accusation of even only a single accomplice. For it has been noted that witches who have confessed have as a rule never laid information against any who were not of their brotherhood, or at least were not deeply suspected. In fact Binsfeld, Suffragan of Trèves, wrote that of a hundred witches he hardly found one who made false accusation against another.

The same applies when the person is accused by common rumour; for this is almost infallible in the matter of witchcraft. . . .

Article VIII

Sprenger and Bodin have given instructions as to what questions the judge should put, and reference may be made to their works. But I would add that the judge must question the accused without interruption and strongly press him, always with gentle words: that if the accused refuses to answer one question, he must pass on to another, and afterwards go back to the former one, and must repeat the same question again and again. The accused will then, if he be guilty, be very easily trapped into contradicting himself.

Article IX

The judge must also ask the accused whether he has any children, whether they are dead, and if so of what sickness they died. For it has been noted that witches ordinarily dedicate their children to the Devil, or else kill them in their mother's womb or as soon as they are born. . . .

Article XV

There are others who make use of the ducking stool. But I doubt whether this practice does not serve rather to tempt God than to prove anything against the witch who is ducked. For Satan may let a guilty one sink to the bottom, or an innocent one float on the water, so that he may cause an innocent man to be put to death wrongfully and so protect the guilty. Also, the ducking stool is condemned by the Canons; as is also the ordeal by red-hot iron, so that the Suffragan of Trèves even says that it is a sin to practise it. . . .

Article XX

Judges have been known to extract the truth from witches by means of a promise of impunity, yet have not failed to put them to death afterwards. This practice is used by many today, and it seems to be approved by the common opinion of the Doctors of Civil Law. Yet I feel great doubt as to the morality of this; for it is unlawful for us to deceive our neighbour in any way by a lie; neither ought we ever to do evil that good may come of it, as St Paul says. The practice is also condemned by the theologians, and fully refuted by Binsfeld where he replies to Bodin.

Article XXI

But above all the advocate of the accused must particularly beware against doing so as one did whom I know. This man cunningly got the truth from a witch and then revealed it to the judge. The judge then confronted the witch with the advocate, and the witch confessed. It is beyond doubt that it is unlawful for the advocate to reveal matters which are prejudicial to his client. This is so incontestably true that the theologians hold that he who acts in such a way is guilty of mortal sin if his revelation is notably prejudicial to his client. The advocate may certainly decline to continue the defence; but, according to the opinion of St Thomas, approved by Navarro, he must not discover anything which might injure his client.

Article XXII

The judge must avoid torture as much as possible; for, besides the spells for maintaining silence which witches hear about them, they have other charms which prevent them from feeling any pain. This secret is known also to nearly all other criminals, so that today torture has become almost without effect. And with particular reference to witches, Sprenger writes that it is as difficult to apply torture to a witch as it is to exorcise a demoniac. . . .

Article XXVII

In the first place, a confession made out of court is a sufficient reason for resorting to torture against one accused of witchcraft. This rule is observed with regard to other crimes also.

We must go even further, according to the opinion of Julius Clarus, in the case of a prisoner who has recanted his confession made out of court, for otherwise no confession made out of court would be of any effect.

But this has particular reference to the crime of witchcraft, seeing that it is a crime in a class by itself, which is very difficult to bring home against the accused.

The same must be said of a case where the accused has confessed before an incompetent judge.

Yet, if the confession has been made in error, and the accused offers to rectify the error, the torture should be postponed, and the accused granted a hearing. . . .

Article XXVIII

Secondly, a witch's confession is warrant enough for the employment of torture against his accomplice, if such confession is substantiated by some other presumption or indication.

And although the common opinion of the doctors is that in this case the accomplice is not to be accredited, if he should not abide by his confession under torture, yet this rule is not observed in this country any more than it is in many other places. And this seems to me to be very reasonable; for what need is there again to extort by torture a confession which has been voluntarily made without it, seeing that a voluntary confession is always of greater weight than one which is forced by torture? . . .

Article XXIX

Thirdly, the familiarity and association of the accused with a witch is enough to warrant the same procedure, if it is substantiated by other evidence or indication. This rule is founded upon Holy Scripture, which declares that good brings good, and evil evil. . . .

Article XXXII

Sixthly, common rumour, combined with other indications, is also sufficient. It does not seem to me necessary in this case to particularise the circumstances requisite for the verification of a common rumour with regard to other crimes; for the crime of witchcraft is one which is called exceptional, and one which is very difficult of proof. Else common rumour would never be of any account; for it is so difficult to prove that even lawyers themselves, when produced as witnesses, have found themselves at a loss to give reasonable evidence, as Clarus says.

And therefore we require some indications in support of the common rumour, to supply the want of such circumstances; for otherwise only a common rumour duly verified would be enough to warrant torture, as some have thought. . . .

Article XLIII

If the accused confesses under torture, he must be made to repeat his confessions some time later, say twenty-four hours, and in another place than that of torture. But it is very necessary to take care that one of his accomplices does not speak to him in the meanwhile, lest he should corrupt him. Also it is well not to leave him alone, for fear lest the devil may likewise come to advise him.

Article XLIV

If he recants, he must be again exposed to the torture. This the judge may do three times, but no more.

Article XLV

And then, if the accused continues to persist in his denials, he must be released. But there is great doubt whether he may be fully and absolutely released, or only subject to being again called for trial.

The common opinion of the doctors on this question as it affects other crimes is that if all the indications against the accused are entirely purged, then he must be fully and absolutely discharged; but if they are not, his discharge may be conditional upon his being liable for recall.

But I shall always hold that one accused of witchcraft must never be unconditionally discharged, whatever torture he may have suffered, if there remains the slightest indication against him. For, as we have seen, he who has once given himself to the Devil cannot easily withdraw from his clutches: so that, after having been detained by justice, he will be even busier in evil-doing.

Article XLVI

In any case, if the indications were very strong and almost beyond doubt, the judge could proceed to sentence the accused notwithstanding the fact that he had suffered torture; but he should not then sentence him to the usual punishment of witches, but to something extraordinary, such as banishment, etc. This practice is observed in some countries in the case of other crimes. . . .

28

KING JAMES VI:
THE SWIMMING
AND PRICKING OF
WITCHES, 1597

King James VI of Scotland, (1567–1625), a highly educated ruler, wrote a treatise on witchcraft in 1597 that was widely circulated not only in Scotland but also in England, where he became king in 1603. James had had a personal experience with witchcraft in 1590, when a conspiracy of witches had allegedly tried to prevent the arrival of his bride, Princess Anne of Denmark, in Scotland. The witches had also allegedly tried to use witchcraft to murder him. At that time the government had given legal sanction to a large witch-hunt, which claimed a large number of victims. James's treatise on witchcraft, written in 1597, in the wake of another large Scottish witch-hunt, was intended mainly as a response to skeptical witchcraft treatises written by Johann Weyer and Reginald Scot in 1563 and 1584 respectively (Chapters 51 and 52). The most relevant and widely cited part of the treatise, which takes the form of a dialogue between Philomathes and Epistemon, is its final chapter, which deals with the discovery and punishment of witches. The king takes a hard line regarding the punishment of offenders, including those who counsel witches. The only exception he allows is that of children [bairns] who have not reached the age of reason. James urges the appropriate caution of judicial authorities in adjudicating witchcraft cases, lest the innocent suffer, but the seriousness of the crime leads him to permit the testimony of children, wives, and confessing witches. He also allows the use of spectral evidence (the visions afflicted persons saw of the witches as they were allegedly causing them harm), the pricking of witches to detect the Devil's mark, and the swimming of witches (the old water ordeal). In approving this last provision, which was used mainly by local communities in an extra-judicial manner, James was taking a position with which few of his contemporaries, even the avid witch-hunter Jean Bodin, agreed.

Source: James VI, *Daemonologie* (Edinburgh, 1597), pp. 77–81.

Book III

Chapter VI.
Argument: Of the trial and punishment of witches. What sort of accusation ought to be admitted against them. What is the cause of the increasing so far of their number in this age.

PHILOMATHES: Then, to make an end to our conference since I see it draws late, what form of punishment think ye merit these magicians and witches? For I see that ye account them to be all alike guilty?

EPISTEMON: They ought to be put to death according to the law of god. The civil and imperial law, and the municipal law of all Christian nations.

P: But what kind of death, I pray you?

E: It is commonly used by fire, but that is an indifferent thing to be used in every country according to the law or customs thereof.

P: But ought no sex, age nor rank to be exempted?

E: None at all, being so used by the lawful magistrate, for it is the highest point of idolatry, wherein no exception is admitted by the law of God.

P: Then bairns may not be spared?

E: Yea, not a hair the less of my conclusion, for they are not that capable of reason to practise such things. And for any being in company and not revealing thereof, their less and ignorant age will no doubt excuse them.

P: I see ye condemn them all that are of the counsel of such crafts.

E: No doubt, for as I said, speaking of magic, the consulters, trusters in, overseers, entertainers, or stirrers up of these craftsfolks are equally guilty with themselves that are the practisers.

P: Whether may the prince then, or supreme magistrate, spare or oversee any that are guilty of that craft upon some good respects known to him?

E: The prince or magistrate, for further trial's cause may continue the punishing of them such a certain space as he thinks convenient. But in the end to spare a life and not to strike when God bids strike, and so severely punish in so odious a fault and treason against God, it is not only unlawful but doubtless no less sin in that magistrate nor it was in Saul's sparing of Agag. And so comparable to the sin of witchcraft itself as Samuel alleged at that time. (1 Samuel 15).

P: Surely then, I think, since this crime ought to be so severely punished, judges ought to beware to condemn any but such as they are sure are guilty, neither should the clattering report of a carling [an old woman] serve in so weighty a case.

E: Judges ought indeed to beware whom they condemn, for it is as great a crime (as Solomon saith) (Proverbs 17), "To condemn the innocent, as to let the guilty escape free." Neither ought the report of any one infamous person be admitted for a sufficient proof, which can stand of no law.

P: And what may a number, then, of guilty persons' confessions work against one that is accused?

E: The assize [a Scottish jury] must serve for interpreter of our law in that respect. But in my opinion, since in a matter of treason against the prince, bairns, or wives or never so defamed persons may of our law serve for sufficient witnesses and proofs. I think surely that by a far greater reason such witnesses may be sufficient in matters of high treason against God; for who but witches can be witnesses and proves [those who provide proof] and so witnesses, of the doings of witches?

E: Indeed, I trow they will be loath to put any honest man upon their counsel. But what if they accuse folk to have been present at their imaginary conventions in the spirit, when their bodies lie senseless, as ye have said.

E: I think they are not a hair the less guilty, for the devil durst never have been at it. And the consent in these turns is death of the law.

P: Then Samuel was a witch, for the devil resembled his shape and played his person in giving response to Saul.

E: Samuel was dead as well before that, and so none could slander him with meddling in that unlawful art. For the cause why, as I take it, that God will not permit Satan to use the shapes and similitudes of any innocent person at such unlawful times, is that God will not permit that any innocent person shall be slandered with that vile defection, for then the devil would find ways anew to calumniate the best. And this we have in proof by them that are carried with the fairy, who never see the shadow of any in that court but of them that thereafter are tried to have been brethren and sisters of that craft. And this was likewise proved by the confession of a young lass troubled with spirits laid on her by witchcraft, that although she saw the shapes of diverse men and women troubling her, and naming the persons whom these shadows represent, yet never one of them is found to be innocent, but all clearly tried to be most guilty, and the most part of them confessing the same. And besides that I think it hath been seldom heard tell of that anywhom persons guilty of that crime accused, as having known them to their marrows by eye-sight and not by hearsay, but such as were accused of witchcraft, could not be clearly tried upon them, were at least publicly known to be of a very evil life and reputation; so jealous is God, I say, of the fame of them that are innocent in such causes. And besides that, there are two other good helps that may be used for their trial: the one is their finding of their mark and the trying the insensibleness thereof. The other is their floating on the water for, as in a secret murder, if the dead carcass be at any time thereafter handled by the murderer, it will gush out of blood, as if the blood were crying to the heaven for revenge of the murderer, God having appointed that secret supernatural sign for trial of that secret unnatural crime. So it appears that God hath appointed, for a supernatural sign of the monstrous impiety of the witches, that the water shall refuse to receive them in her bosom that have shaken off them the sacred water of baptism, and willfully refused the benefit thereof. Not so much as their eyes are able to shed tears (threaten and torture them as ye please) while first they repent (God not permitting them to dissemble their obstinacy in so horrible a crime) albeit the womenkind especially be able otherways to shed tears at every light occasion when they will, yea, although it were dissemblingly like the crocodiles.

P: Well, we have made this conference to last as long as leisure would permit. And to conclude then, since I am to take my leave of you, I pray God to purge this country of these devilish practices, for they were never so rife in these parts as they are now.

E: Pray God that so be too. But the causes are over-manifest that make them to be so rife. For the great wickedness of the people, on the one part, procures this horrible defection whereby God justly punisheth sin by a greater iniquity. And on the other part, the consummation of the world, and our deliverance drawing near, makes Satan to rage the more in his instruments (Revelation 12), knowing his kingdom to be so near an end. And so farewell for this time.

Figure 7 Swimming the witch. This procedure originated in the medieval ordeal. If the bound person floated, she was considered guilty, since the water, which was blessed beforehand, rejected her. If she sank, she was innocent, although her life was nonetheless in danger. The ordeals were banned by the Fourth Lateran Council of 1215, but the swimming test was often employed by local communities during the period of witch-hunting. Most demonologists, including Remy (Chapter 27) denied its validity, but James VI of Scotland accepted it as a proof of witchcraft (see Chapter 28). From E. D. Hauber, *Bibliotheca sive Acta et Scripta Magica*, vol. I (Lemgo, 1738).

29

FRIEDRICH SPEE:
A CONDEMNATION OF
TORTURE, 1631

The most well known and eloquent attack on the conduct of witch-trials came from the pen of a Jesuit priest, Friedrich Spee von Langenfeld (1591–1635). Spee was a professor of moral theology at the University of Paderborn during a period of intense witch-hunting in the city and the surrounding region. During those years he also served as a confessor to many accused witches. Spee became convinced that the great majority of accused and convicted witches, having been forced to confess under severe torture, were innocent. His opposition to the use of torture in these trials on the grounds that witchcraft was an excepted crime led to the formulation of a critique of the entire process by which witches were identified, interrogated, and tried. He criticized the way in which prosecutions arose on the basis of rumours. He insisted on the right of witches to a lawyer. He directed his most severe criticisms, however, against the princes of the various German territories and the judges who conducted the trials. Spee raised the question whether these men had sinned in their treatment of witches. His exposé, entitled *Cautio Criminalis*, was addressed to the Holy Roman Emperor. The book was published anonymously in Latin at Rinteln, in 1631. It incurred fierce attacks from the political and ecclesiastical establishment.

Spee was not the first critic of witch trials. Sixteenth-century skeptics like Johann Weyer, Reginald Scot, and Cornelius Loos had exposed their evidentiary and procedural weaknesses. The Jesuit Adam Tanner, a contemporary of Spee who taught at the University of Ingolstadt, included a devastating critique of the trials in *Theologia Scholastica* (1626/7). Spee's book, however, reached a far larger audience than Tanner's. It was soon translated into every major European language, and it contributed to a reduction in the intensity of witchcraft prosecutions in Germany and many surrounding countries. It also inspired a number of late seventeenth- and early eighteenth-century criticisms of witch-hunting, especially that of Christian Thomasius (Chapter 33).

Spee never denied the reality of the crime of witchcraft; he simply claimed that there were very few witches. Nor did he deny the reality of demonic power. He admitted for example that the Devil could represent innocent people at the sabbath in order to lead to their execution. Spee directed his wrath solely against the way in which trials were conducted. He thus joined the ranks of those judicial skeptics who tried to bring the trials to an end while still admitting the possibility of the crime. Only in the eighteenth century did scholars take the more radical step of claiming that witches did not exist. The following chapter of Spee's book summarizes the various arguments he had developed more fully in the preceding chapters. His main argument is that anyone accused of witchcraft in Germany was condemned to die, one way or another.

Source: Friedrich Spee von Langenfeld, *Cautio Criminalis, or a Book on Witch Trials*, ed. Marcus Hellyer (Charlottesville, Va., 2003), pp. 214–222.

Question 51: What is a brief summary of the method use by many judges in witch trials today fitting for the noble Emperor to comprehend and Germany to study?

I answer, any reader could fashion a summary of this treatise himself, but because I can do it more easily I shall do it myself here, omitting, however, many things which cannot be conveniently inserted. For such matters consult what I have said already and, likewise, if you should want to know more details concerning those things which are set down here. So here is the summary:

1. It is incredible what superstitions, jealousies, lies, slurs, mutterings, and the like there are among the common people in Germany, particularly (it is embarrassing to say) among Catholics, which the authorities do not punish nor preachers reproach, and which first arouse the suspicion of magic. All divine punishments which God threatens in the Holy Scriptures are committed by witches. God no longer does anything, nor nature, but everything is done by witches.

2. Thus everyone shouts with great passion that the authorities should therefore investigate the witches – of which they themselves created so many with their own tongues.

3. The princes therefore command their judges and counselors to begin to try witches.

4. At first these men do not know where to begin for they have neither evidence nor proof, and they do not dare in good conscience to undertake anything without good cause.

5. Meanwhile they are admonished two to three times to begin the trials. The common people shout that this delay is itself not without suspicion. So, advised by I know not whom, the princes convince themselves of virtually the same thing.

146

6. In Germany it is a serious matter to offend the princes and not obey them immediately. Most people, even clergymen, excessively approve of almost everything as long as it pleases the princes, nor do they notice who is often inciting the princes, however much the princes themselves may have the best nature possible.

7. Therefore the judges finally accede to the princes' will and at least find some way to begin the trials.

8. If the judges still delay and abhor dealing with such a perilous matter, then a specially appointed inquisitor is sent. If he brings with him a certain inexperience or passion, as is normal in human affairs, it changes its complexion and name in this matter and becomes nothing other than pure justice and zeal, which no doubt his hope for monetary gain does not diminish, particularly in a rather poor and greedy man who has a family full of children, when a bounty of several thalers has been arranged for him for every criminal he burns, in addition to the incidental monies and contributions which inquisitors may liberally extract from the peasants, as I mentioned above.

9. So if the possessed should say anything, or if the malign and spurious (for it is never proven) rumor of the day falls heavily upon some poor, common Gaia, then she is the first.

10. Lest they should appear to try her on the basis of the rumor alone without any other evidence, as they call it, look! suddenly some evidence is at hand by means of this dilemma: either the Gaia led an evil and immoral life or a good and virtuous one. If evil, then they say that is strong evidence, for from evil to evil is an easy assumption. If, however, it was a good life, then this is equally strong evidence, for they say that is the way witches cover themselves, for they usually try to appear to be especially virtuous.

11. Gaia is ordered to be taken to the prison, and look! more evidence comes from this dilemma: either she now shows that she is afraid, or she does not. If she shows fear (and naturally so since she has heard what severe tortures are normally used in these matters), then this is evidence because they say that her conscience is accusing her. If she does not show fear (and naturally so, for she is confident of her innocence) then this is also evidence because they say that it is quite peculiar to witches to boast that they are innocent and hold their heads high.

12. But if he does not yet have much evidence against her, then the inquisitor has his men, often immoral and disreputable ones, inquire into everything in her past, and of course it cannot happen otherwise than something which she has either said or done presents itself which those men with their mean-spirited interpretation can easily twist and turn into proof of magic.

13. If there are any people who ever wanted to do her harm, they now have a wonderful opportunity to hurt her. They can allege whatever they want, they will easily find things. So they shout from all sides that she is incriminated by strong evidence.

14. Therefore she is dragged off to be questioned as soon as possible, unless she was already led off on the very day that she was arrested, as often occurs.

15. Nobody at all is granted a lawyer or a completely unbiased defense, since everyone shouts that this is an excepted crime, so anyone who wants to defend her and speak for her also comes under suspicion of this crime. It is the same with those people who wish to say something on the matter and admonish the judges to use caution, for they are immediately called patrons of witches. In this way everyone's mouths are shut and quills dulled so that they neither speak nor write.

16. Generally, however, lest it seem that the judges have not given Gaia at least a chance to defend herself, they lead her into an appearance in court and the evidence is read out and examined, if that really is an examination.

17. Even if she refutes the evidence and accounts for all the separate charges, they neither notice nor record it. The charges retain their strength and validity, no matter how well her answers strip them away. They just order her to be led away in chains, so that she may carefully consider whether she wishes to persist in her obstinacy. For she is already obstinate, since she has defended herself. In fact, if she thoroughly vindicates herself, then this is new evidence, since naturally they say that she would not be so eloquent if she were not a witch.

18. After she has considered matters, they lead her back in again the next day and read the decree of torture to her, just as if she had not said anything in reply to the accusations and refuted them.

19. However, before he tortures her, the torturer leads her aside. So that she may not strengthen herself against the pain with some kind of magic charm, he shaves and searches her entire body – even that part by which her sex shows is most impudently searched. Of course to this day nothing has ever been found.

20. But why not do that to a woman when it is also done to consecrated priests, even by the inquisitors and ecclesiastical officials of Church princes? For German judges do not consider the brute thunderbolts which the papal bull *Coena* casts at those people who try clerics without the special and specific permission of the Apostolic Chair. But the inquisitors make sure that the most pious princes, those most obedient to the Roman See, learn nothing and thus do not rein in the trials.

21. Once Gaia has been searched and shaved, she is tortured so that she recounts the truth, that is, she simply pronounces herself to be guilty. Whatever else she might say is not the truth, nor can it be.

22. However, they subject her to torture of the first kind, that is, the more mild kind, which one should understand this way: it actually is very severe, but it is mild in comparison with the following kinds. Therefore, if she confesses they say and circulate that she confessed without torture.

23. Who among the princes and others who hear this would not think that she is most certainly guilty, since she admitted of her own accord without torture that she is guilty?

24. After this confession she is executed without a thought. She is executed even if she did not confess, for once the torture has begun, the die has been cast; she can no longer escape; she must die.

25. So either she confesses or she does not. Whatever happens, she is done for in either case. If she confesses, the matter is clear, as I said, and she is executed. Any retraction is made completely in vain, as we showed above. If she does not confess, then the torture is repeated two, three or four times. Whatever the judges want is permitted. For there is no rule governing the duration, severity, or repetition of torture in excepted crimes. The judges do not think that they have committed any sin here which they will have to confront in the court of their own conscience.

26. Should Gaia in her torment roll her eyes in agony or stare, then this is new evidence. If she rolls her eyes, look! they say, she is searching for her concubine! If she stares, look! they say, she has already found him; she is looking at him. But if she does not break her silence after several rounds of torture, if her face is twisted in pain, if she sinks into unconsciousness, etc., they shout that she is laughing or sleeping during the torture, that she is using the sorcery of silence, and she must be so much the guiltier. How fitting then that she be burned alive. This was recently done to several women who did not want to confess despite being tortured repeatedly.

27. Then even confessors, even regular clergy [i.e., clergy in monastic orders] call that dying obstinate and impenitent. She did not want to repent or abandon her concubine, but wanted to remain faithful to him.

28. But if it should happen that someone yields up her spirit after such torture, they say that the devil broke her neck, and they prove it with this irrefutable argument, which you may take if you wish to use it: there is not a single person who was not killed by the devil in this way, as I showed above.

29. Therefore, of course, her body may be taken out and deservedly buried beneath the gallows by the executioner.

30. But if Gaia does not die and some scrupulous people do not dare either to torture her further without her confession, then they keep her in prison bound in tight chains and there is to be tormented for up to a whole year until she is overcome.

31. But she can never clear herself through torture and wash away the crime once tainted with it, as the law intends. To let her go once she has been arrested would disgrace the inquisitors. Once the chains have embraced her, she must be guilty by hook or by crook.

32. Meanwhile, as well as before and after, ignorant, impetuous priests are sent to her who are more troublesome than the torturers, Their purpose is to harass the unfortunate in every way possible to the point that she finally

confesses that she is guilty, whether she is or not. If she does not confess, they shout she cannot be saved nor fortified with the sacraments. . . .

34. While Gaia is still kept in the dungeon in the way I said and is harassed by those who ought to do it the least, there is no shortage of beautiful discoveries with which diligent judges may not only find new evidence against the witch but can also prove (God save us!) her guilt to her face, so that they may proclaim that she may be burned alive in accordance with the ruling of the Academies of Doctors, as has been discussed earlier. . . .

35. Some men, however, order that Gaia be exorcised to excess, transferred to another place, and then tortured again, as if perhaps by this purging and change of location her spell of silence can be broken. But if they can make no progress this way, then finally they commit her living to the flames. Since she dies whether she confesses or not, I would like to know, may God love me, how she can ever escape, no matter how innocent she may be? You miserable woman! What are you hoping for? Why did you not declare yourself guilty when you first entered the prison? Why, you foolish and insane woman, do you wish to die many times when you can do it just once? Follow my advice, and before any torture just say that you are guilty and die. You will not escape, for this, after all is the catastrophe of Germany's zeal.

36. One can hardly say what misery this is if any woman falsely states that she is guilty because of the violence of her pain, since in most courts there are no means available by which she might escape. She is forced to accuse others whom she does not know, whom her questioners not infrequently place in her mouth or the torturer suggests, or who they have heard are already infamous, or denounced, or already arrested once and released. And those women must in turn denounce others, and they in turn still others, and so on. Who does not see that this must go on infinitely.

37. Therefore the judges must either break off their trials and damn their own art, or they must in the end burn their own families, themselves and everyone else, for these completely false denunciations will eventually reach everyone, and if only torture can follow them, then it will reveal that they are guilty.

38. Thus those people who at the beginning actually shouted the loudest that the bonfires be constantly fed are themselves finally entangled. For these short-sighted fools do not see that their turn must also come. And indeed it will be God's just judgment on them, for it was they who created so many witches for us with their pestilent tongues and added so many innocent people to the flames.

39. But how many more prudent and learned people have begun to see little by little and, as if aroused from a deep sleep, are opening their eyes and are using cruelty more slowly and cautiously.

40. Although the judges deny that they move on to torture on denunciations alone, I have shown above that they really do this. Consequently they deceive their own good princes when they deny it. For the rumor they usually

link to the denunciations is always invalid and null, since not one has ever been legitimately proven. As for the rubbish which they talk about stigmata, I am amazed that wise men have never noticed that they are deceptions performed by torturers.

41. But while the trials boil along and women diligently denounce others when compelled by the harshest torment possible, it soon trickles out just who has been denounced. This is the meaning of secrecy for those present at the interrogation, and it is not without profit for them because in this way they can at once seize evidence against those denounced through this dilemma: if people hear that they have been informed on, as they certainly do hear, either they then take flight so that they are not arrested, or they stay in place. If they take flight then the judges say that this is great evidence of their guilt and fearful consciences. However, if they stay, then this is also evidence, because the devil, it is said, holds them so they cannot leave, as I recently have had to listen to more than once with a groan.

42. Furthermore, if someone goes to the investigators to ask them whether what he has heard is true, so that he may have time to defend himself and counteract his impending troubles by legal means, this is also taken to be evidence, as if someone against whom the inquisitors had not yet undertaken anything must have been motivated by his bad conscience and guilt.

43. But whatever he does, he binds the rumour to himself, which, having matured sufficiently after a year or two and combined with denunciations, suffices for torture, even though the rumor itself first arose through denunciations, for I have seen examples of this.

44. Things happen in a similar way with those people who endure some calumny which arose out of malice. For they will either defend themselves in court, or they will not. If they do not defend themselves, this is evidence of their guilt because they are silent. However, if they do defend themselves, the calumny spreads further and arouses suspicion and the curiosity to find out more in those who knew nothing about it before, and soon a rumor is circulating which can never be suppressed.

45. So nothing is more likely to happen than those who are tortured in the meantime and forced to denounce others readily denounce those about whom the rumor spread.

46. From this a particular COROLLARY follows which one should note in red. If we constantly insist on conducting trials, no one of any sex, fortune, condition, or rank whatsoever who has earned himself even one enemy or slanderer who can drag him into the suspicion and reputation for witchcraft can be sufficiently safe in these times. So wherever I turn, the condition of our times is certainly the most miserable possible, unless care is taken otherwise. I said above, and I will repeat my words, that this plague, whatever it may be, cannot be destroyed by fire, but it can be very effectively in another way through which hardly any blood will flow. But who wants to know this? Pain overwhelms me as I try to say more, so that I cannot carefully bring

this summary to a perfect end, nor can I contemplate writing a German version, which would not be without its uses; perhaps there will be those who will carefully complete it out of love for their fatherland and innocent people. Finally, I entreat all learned and pious, prudent and moderate appraisers of affairs (for I care nothing for the rest) for the sake of the court of the omnipotent Judge to diligently read through and consider what I have written in this treatise [NB in margin]. All rulers and princes put their eternal salvation in great danger, unless they are willing to be as careful as possible. They should not be astonished if I harshly admonish them from time to time, for it is not fitting for me to be among those whom the Prophet calls mute dogs who are not strong enough to bark. Let our rulers take care of themselves and their whole flock, for one day GOD will require as accurate an accounting as possible for it from their hands.

Figure 8 Torture by means of the strappado. This brutal procedure was usually not used unless other instruments of torture, such as the thumbscrews, had not resulted in a confession. The pain could be increased by jerking the ropes, hitting the ropes with a stick, or adding weights (depicted here in the center foreground) to the ankles. This illustration of the strappado comes from Empress Maria Theresa's reform of the criminal law in 1769. In 1776 torture was abolished throughout the empire. Niclas Fiedler in Chapter 35, Johannes Junius in Chapter 39, and the unidentified witch in Chapter 40 were all tortured by the strappado. From *Constitutio Criminalis Theresiana* (Vienna, 1769), Appendix.

30

SIR ROBERT FILMER: THE DISCOVERY OF WITCHES, 1652

Sir Robert Filmer (*c*.1588–1653) was an educated country gentleman from the English county of Kent. He owes his fame mainly to his work in political theory, especially his defense of the absolute power of the king in *Patriarcha*, a treatise written during the late 1630s before the English Civil War and published in 1680. *The Advertisement*, published anonymously in the year of Filmer's death, was occasioned by a set of witchcraft trials that resulted in the execution of six women, at Maidstone, Kent, in the summer of 1652. Filmer objected to the grounds upon which these women had been convicted. The *Advertisement* is directed mainly against the arguments advanced by William Perkins, the author of *The Damned Art of Witchcraft* (Chapter 19) and a zealous promoter of witch-hunting. Perkins belongs to a small group of English clerical writers who were in large part responsible for introducing continental European ideas of witchcraft (those which emphasized the demonic nature of the crime) into England. Perkins also proposed that English judicial authorities use Continental standards of proof in the investigation and trial of witches. These included interrogation on the basis of sufficient presumptions of guilt, the administration of torture, and the conviction of witches on the basis of the Roman-canonical law of proof, which demanded either a confession or the testimony of two eye-witnesses in all capital cases. In responding to Perkins, Filmer attacks the validity of these presumptions and proofs, and he points out that torture could be used in England only in cases of treason. What is left unsaid in this critique of Perkins is the fact that there was no official law or standard of proof in English criminal prosecutions; juries could and sometimes did convict witches on the basis of circumstantial evidence. Nevertheless, Filmer's treatise stands as a firm statement of the growing difficulty seventeenth-century judicial authorities had in establishing evidence of the witches' crime. In this way the *Advertisement* contributed to the greater caution that many judicial authorities exercised in prosecuting witches in the late seventeenth century, and it led ultimately to the realization that the crime could not be proved.

Source: Sir Robert Filmer, *An Advertisement to the Jury-Men of England Touching Witches* (London, 1653) sig. A2–A3, pp. 9–15.

The late execution of witches at the summer assizes in Kent occasioned this brief exercitation, which addresses itself to such as have not deliberately thought upon the great difficulty in discovering what or who a witch is. To have nothing but the public faith of the present age is none of the best evidence unless the universality of elder times do concur with these doctrines, which ignorance in the times of darkness brought forth, and credulity in these days of light hath continued.

Such as shall not be pleased with this tractate are left to their liberty to consider whether all those proofs and presumptions numbered up by Mr. Perkins for the conviction of a witch be not all condemned or confessed by himself to be insufficient or uncertain . . .

And as Mr. Perkins weakens and discredits all his own proofs, so he doth the like for all those of King James, who as I remember hath but three arguments for the discovery of a witch. First, the secret mark of a witch, of which Mr. Perkins saith it hath no power by God's ordinance. Secondly, the discovery by a fellow witch; this Mr. Perkins by no means will allow to be a good proof. Thirdly, the swimming of a witch, who is to be slung crosswise into the water . . . ; against this trial by water, together with a disability to shed tears (which King James mentions) Delrio and Mr. Perkins both argue, for it seems they both write after King James, who put forth his *Book of Daemonologie* in his youth, being in Scotland, about his age of thirty years.

It concerns the people of this nation to be more diligently instructed in the doctrine of witchcraft than those of foreign countries, because here they are tied to a stricter or exacter rule in giving their sentence than others are, for all of them must agree in their verdict, which in a case of extreme difficulty is very dangerous, and it is a sad thing for men to be reduced to that extremity, that they must hazard their consciences or their lives.

Of the discerning and discovery of a Witch.

A magistrate, saith Mr. Perkins, may not take upon him to examine whom, and how he willeth of any crime, nor to proceed upon slight causes, or to show his authority, or upon sinister respects, or to revenge his malice, or to bring parties into danger, and suspicion, but he must proceed upon special *presumptions*.

He calls those presumptions which do at least probably and conjecturally note one to be a witch, and are certain signs whereby the witch may be discovered. I cannot but wonder that Mr. Perkins should say that presumptions do at least probably and conjecturally note, and are certain signs to discover a witch; when he confesseth that though presumptions give occasion to examine, yet they are no sufficient causes of conviction; and though presumptions be never so strong, yet they are not proofs sufficient for conviction, but only for examination. Therefore no credit is to be given to those presumptions he reckons up. 1. For common fame, it falls out many times, saith he, that the innocent may be suspected, and some of the better sort notoriously defamed. 2. The testimony of a fellow witch, he confesseth doth not probably note one to be a witch. The like may be said of his third and fourth presumption, if after curing or quarreling or threatening there follow present mischief. And the fifth presumption is more frivolous, which is if the party be the son or daughter, or servant, or friend near neighbour, or old companion of a witch. . . .

Touching examination, Mr. Perkins names two kinds of proceedings, either by simple question or by torture. Torture, when besides the enquiry by words the magistrate uses the rack or some other violent means to urge confession, this he saith may be lawfully used, howbeit not in every case, but only upon strong and great presumptions and when the party is obstinate. Here it may be noted that it is not lawful for any person, but the judge only to allow torture; suspicious neighbours may not of their own heads use either threats, terrors, or tortures. I know not any one of those presumptions before cited to be sufficient to warrant a magistrate to use torture, or whether when the party constantly denies the fact, it must be counted obstinacy. In case of treason sometimes, when the main fact hath been either confessed or by some infallible proofs manifested, the magistrate for a farther discovery of some circumstance of the time, the place, and the persons, or the like, have made use of the rack, and yet that kind of torture hath not been of ancient usage in this kingdom. . . .

From presumptions Mr. Perkins proceeds to proofs of a witch, and here he hath a neat distinction of proofs, less sufficient or more sufficient; by less sufficient he means insufficient . . . Those unsufficient sufficient proofs are weaker and worse than his presumptions which he confesseth are no proofs at all, yet we must reckon them up. His first less sufficient proof is the ancient trial of taking red hot irons or putting the hand in hot scalding water. This he saith hath been condemned for diabolical and wicked, as in truth it is, for an innocent man may thereby be condemned, and a rank witch escape unpunished. A second insufficient proof is scratching of the suspected party and the present recovery thereupon. A third is the burning the thing bewitched, as a hog, an ox, or another creature; it is imagined a forcible means to cause the witch to discover herself. A fourth is the burning the thatch of the suspected party's house. . . .

At the last Mr. Perkins comes to his more sufficient proofs, which in all are but two: the confession of the witch or the proof of two witnesses. Against the confession of a witch Mr. Perkins confesseth, it is objected that one may confess against himself an untruth being urged by force, or threatening, or the desire upon some grief to be out of the world, or at least being in trouble, and persuaded it is the best course to save their lives and obtain their liberty they may upon simplicity be induced to confess that they never did, even against themselves . . .

Now Mr. Perkins will confess that the examination and confession of a suspected witch is always after such time as her covenant is made, when she is by his confession deluded and not fit to give testimony against herself.

His second more sufficient proof (he saith, if the party will not confess as commonly it falleth out) is two witnesses avouching upon their own knowledge, either that the party accused hath made league with the Devil or hath done some known practices of witchcraft, or hath invocated the Devil, or desired his help. But if every man that hath invocated the Devil or desired his help must have formerly made a league with him, then whole nations are every man of them witches, which I think none will say. . . .

It remains that if the two true proofs of Mr. Perkins, which are the witches' confession or sufficient witnesses, fail, we have not warrant, as he saith, in the word to put such an one to death.

31

SIR GEORGE MACKENZIE: JUDICIAL CAUTION IN THE TRIAL OF WITCHES, 1678

Sir George Mackenzie (c.1636–1691), a Scottish lawyer and judge, played a central role in the decline of witchcraft prosecutions in Scotland. Known by his Presbyterian adversaries as "Bloody Mackenzie" for his harsh treatment of religious dissenters during the reign of Charles II, Mackenzie was much more lenient in dealing with witches. As an advocate he defended a witch named Maevia, and he published his argument on her behalf in his *Pleadings in Remarkable Cases* (1672). As Lord Advocate of Scotland he was directly responsible for the acquittal or the setting at liberty of a number of witches. Mackenzie, like most educated Scots in the late seventeenth century, believed firmly in the reality of witchcraft and in the suitability of the death penalty for the crime. He agreed with other demonologists, especially Martín Del Rio, that the Devil could inflict and cure diseases and even transport witches to the sabbath. At the same time, however, he thought it unlikely that witches would make pacts with the Devil, and he denied the Devil's ability to change the shape of men or beasts. Mackenzie's importance, however, lies not in the content of his witch-beliefs but in his recommendations regarding the discovery and trial of witches. As a lawyer and judge who had participated in the Scottish witch-hunt of 1661–1662, he was aware of the many miscarriages of justice that had taken place in witchcraft trials and demanded that of all crimes witchcraft required the clearest proof. In *The Laws and Customs of Scotland in Matters Criminal* (1678), a summary of Scots criminal law, Mackenzie explains why many innocent people were accused of, and sometimes confessed to, a crime they did not commit. He also criticizes many of the judicial practices that facilitated their conviction, including the torture of witches by those who took custody of them, the pricking of them for the Devil's mark, and the trial of witches by local authorities who have no knowledge of the crime and who allow the testimony of unqualified witnesses. Mackenzie's skepticism, therefore, relates more to the legitimacy of the procedures used to try witches than to the reality of witchcraft itself. His criticism of the trials led to their abandonment long before Scots and many other Europeans denied the reality or possibility of the crime.

Source: Sir George Mackenzie, *Laws and Customs of Scotland in Matters Criminal* (Edinburgh, 1678), pp. 80–108.

That there are witches, divines cannot doubt, since the word of God hath ordained that no witch shall live; nor lawyers in Scotland, seeing our law ordains it to be punished with death. And though many lawyers in Holland and elsewhere do think that albeit there were witches under the law, yet there are none under the gospel, the Devil's power having ceased as to these, as well as in his giving responses by oracles. . . .

Albeit witchcraft be the greatest of crimes, since it includes in it the grossest of heresies and blasphemies and treasons against God, in preferring to the Almighty his rebel and enemy, and in thinking the Devil worthier of being served and reverenced, and is accompanied with murder, poisoning, bestiality and other horrid crimes. Yet I conclude only from this that when witches are found guilty, they should be most severely punished, not with scourging and banishment, as the custom of Savoy was related to be by Gothofred . . . but by the most ignominious of deaths. Yet from the horridness of this crime I do conclude that of all crimes it requires the clearest relevancy and most convincing probation. And I condemn next to the witches themselves those cruel and too forward judges who burn persons by thousands as guilty of this crime, to whom I shall recommend these considerations:

I. That it is not presumable that any who hear of the kindness of God to men and of the Devil's malice against them; of the rewards of Heaven and torments of Hell, would deliberately enter into the services of that wicked spirit; whom they know to have no riches to bestow, nor power to help, except it be allowed by permission, that he may tempt men: and that he being a liar from the beginning, his promises deserve no belief, especially since in no man's experience he hath ever advantaged any person, whereas on the contrary his service hath brought all who entered in it to the stake.

II. Those persons who are ordinarily accused of this crime are poor ignorant creatures and oft-times women who understand not the nature of what they are accused of; and many mistake their own fears and apprehensions for witchcraft; of which I shall give you two instances, one of a poor weaver, who after he had confessed witchcraft, being asked how he saw the devil, he answered "like flies dancing about the candle." Another of a woman who asked seriously when she was accused "if a woman might be a witch and not know it." And it is dangerous that these who are of all others the most simple should be tried for a crime which of all others is most mysterious.

III. These poor creatures when they are defamed become confounded with fear and the close prison in which they are kept and so starved for want of meat and sleep (either of which wants is enough to disorder the strongest reason) that hardly wiser and more serious people than they would escape distraction. And when men are confounded with fear and apprehension, they will imagine things very ridiculous and absurd, and as no man would escape a profound melancholy upon such an occasion, and amidst such usages. Therefore I remit to physicians and others to consider what may be the effects of melancholy, which hath oft made men, who appeared otherways solid enough, imagine they were horses, or had lost their noses, etc. And since it may make men err in things which are oblivious to their senses, what may be expected as to things which transcend the wisest men's reason?

IV. Most of these poor creatures are tortured by their keepers, who being persuaded they do God good service, think it their duty to vex and torment poor prisoners. And I know *ex certissima scientia* [from most certain knowledge], that most of all that ever were taken were tormented after this manner, and this usage was the ground of all their confession; and albeit the poor miscreants cannot prove this usage, the actors being the only witnesses, yet the judge would be afraid of it, as that which at first did elicit the confession, and for fear of which they dare not retract it.

V. I went when I was a justice-depute to examine some women who had confessed judicially, and one of them, who was a silly creature, told me under secrecy, that she had not confessed because she was guilty, but being a poor creature, who wrought for her meat, and being defamed for a witch, she knew she would starve, for no person thereafter would either give her meat or lodging, and that all men would beat her, and hound dogs at her, and that therefore she desired to be out of the world, whereupon she wept most bitterly, and upon her knees called God to witness what she said. Another told me that she was afraid the Devil would challenge a right to her, after she was said to be his servant and would haunt her, as the minister said when he was desiring her to confess; and therefore she desired to die. And really ministers are oft-times indiscreet in their zeal to have poor creatures to confess and in this. And I recommend to judges that the wisest ministers should be sent to them, and those who are sent should be cautious in this.

VI. Many of them confess things which all divines conclude impossible, as transmutation of their bodies into beasts and money into stones, and their going through walls and closed doors, and a thousand other ridiculous things, which have no truth nor existence but in their fancy.

VII. The accusers here are masters or neighbors who had their children dead and are engaged by grief to suspect these poor creatures. I knew likewise one burnt because the lady was jealous with her husband. And the crime is so odious that they are never assisted or defended by their relations.

VIII. The witnesses and assizers [i.e. jurors] are afraid that if they escape that they will die for it, and therefore they take an unwarrantable latitude.

160

And I have observed that scarce ever any who were accused before a country assize of neighbors did escape that trial.

IX. Commissions are granted ordinarily to gentlemen and others in the country who are suspect upon this account and who are not exactly acquainted with the nature of this crime, which is so debatable among the learned. Nor have the panels [the defendants] any to plead for them, and to take notice who are led as witnesses, so that many are admitted who are *testes inhabiles* and suspect. And albeit their confessions are sent to and advised by the council before such commissions be granted, yet the council cannot know how these commissions were emitted, nor all the circumstances which are necessary and cannot be known at a distance. Very many of these poor silly women do reseal at the stake from the confessions they emitted at the bar and yet have died very penitent. And as it is presumable that few will accuse themselves or confess against their own life, yet very many confess this crime . . .

The relevancy of this crime being thus discussed, the ordinary probation of it is by confession or witnesses, but the probation here should be very clear, and it should be certain that the person who emitted it is not weary of life, or oppressed with melancholy. Albeit *non requiritur hic ut constet de corpore delicti* [this does not require that there be factual evidence], this being a crime which consists oft times in spirit, yet it ought to be such as contains nothing in it that is impossible or improbable. And thus albeit Isobel Ramsay did upon the 20 of August 1661 confess that the Devil gave her six pence and said that God desired him to give it her, and at another time a dollar, which turned thereafter in a slate stone, the justices did not find this confession, though judicial, relevant. And to know what things are of themselves impossible for the Devil to do, or at least what is believed to be impossible, may be seen very fully treated in Del Rio's second book, where it is condescended that *succubi et incubi sunt possibiles*, that is that the Devil may lie in the shape of a man with a woman, or in the shape of a woman with a man, having first formed to himself a body of condensed air, and upon such a confession as this Margaret Lauder and others were convict. It is likewise possible for the Devil to transport witches to their public conventions, from one place to another, which he may really do by carrying them, and sundry witches were in *anno* 1665 burnt in Culross upon such a confession as this. . . .

The Devil cannot make one solid body to penetrate another . . . and therefore I think that article libeled against Margaret Hutchison of coming to John Clark's house when doors and windows were shut should not have been admitted to probation, since it is very probable they would have searched the house after the second or third night's fear, and she could not penetrate doors nor walls.

The Devil cannot transform one species into another, as a woman into a cat, for else he behooved to annihilate some of the substance of the women, or create some more substance to the cat, the one being much more than the

161

other; and the Devil can neither annihilate nor create, nor could he make the shapes return. . . . But if we consider the strange tricks of jugglers and the strange apparitions that Kercher and others relate from natural causes, we may believe that the Devil may make a woman appear to be a beast and the contrary. . . .

The Devil may inflict diseases, which is an effect he may occasion *applicando activa passivis*, and by the same means he may cure, a clear instance whereof appears in the marriage knot. And not only may he cure diseases laid on by himself, as Wierus observes, but even natural diseases, since he knows the natural causes and the origin of even these natural diseases better than physicians can, who are not present when diseases are contracted, and who, being younger than he, must have less experience. And it is as untrue that . . . cures performed by the Devil cannot continue, since his cures are not natural. And since he may make sick and may make whole, it follows that he may transfer a disease from one person to another. . . .

It is ordinarily doubted whether confessions emitted before the kirk sessions in this case be sufficient . . . Only here I should observe that Christian Stewart was found Art and Part of the bewitching of Patrick Ruthven by laying on him a heavy sickness with a black clout, which she herself had confessed before several ministers, notaries and others at diverse times, all which confessions were proved. . . . And if the confession be not fully adminiculate, lawyers advise that confessors should be subjected to the torture, which is not usual in Scotland. And it is very observable that the justices would not put James Welch to the knowledge of an inquest, though he had confessed himself a witch before the presbytery of Kirkcudbright, because he was a minor when he confessed the crime and the confession was only extra-judicial and that he now retracted the same; but because he had so grossly prevaricated and had delated so many honest persons, they ordained him to be scourged and put in the correction house. . . .

The probation by witness in this crime is very difficult, and therefore *socii criminis* [accomplices in the crime] or other confessing witches are adduced, but though many of them concur, their depositions solely are not esteemed as sufficient.

32

KING LOUIS XIV OF FRANCE: THE DECRIMINALIZATION OF FRENCH WITCHCRAFT, 1682

―――――――⋙◊◊◊◊⋘―――――――

In July 1682 the government of Louis XIV (r. 1643–1715) issued an edict that laid the foundation for the decriminalization of witchcraft in France. The edict was one of a number of efforts made by the French government in the late seventeenth century to place limits on the prosecution of witches, especially in the outlying regions of the country. The edict did not deny the reality of witchcraft, and in fact it never used the word witchcraft (*sorcellerie*) as such. Identified by its title as an ordinance against various "diviners, magicians, and enchanters," it ordered such persons to leave the kingdom on pain of corporal punishment, while prescribing summary punishment for practitioners of "pretended" magic and superstition according to the gravity of their offenses. The death penalty was reserved for those who compounded superstition with impiety and sacrilege, as well as for poisoners, even if their victims did not die. These latter provisions, as well as a number of articles governing the production and sale of poisons, were included mainly in response to a scandal, known as the Affair of the Poisons, which had rocked the highest levels of Parisian society, including the royal court, between 1676 and 1681. The affair, which centered on the activities of a widow known as La Voisin, not only involved the discovery of poison, infanticide, and alleged child-sacrifice but also the saying of amatory masses.

The implications of the edict of 1682 for witchcraft were two-fold. On the one hand witchcraft was implicitly reclassified as practical superstition and pretended magic, thereby dissociating it from the diabolism with which the crime had become closely identified while at the same time denying that the magic had any efficacy. It thus combined skepticism with a redefinition of the crime itself. On the other hand, the edict provided for greater leniency in the prosecution of what once passed as witchcraft by reserving the death penalty to cases involving sacrilege, blasphemy, or poisoning. The provision for punishing witches according to the gravity of the offense, however, left open the possibility of harsh treatment for reputed witches, while the prohibition of sacrilege could be extended to include the diabolism that had been excluded from the definition of the crime. Sorcerers could still be charged with profaning the sacred host, renouncing God, and adoring the demon, as they were at Marseilles in 1693. The edict did not therefore, ban all witchcraft trials or even result in the reversal of all capital sentences on appeal. But the few trials that did take place under the terms of the edict employed the more precise language of the new jurisprudence.

Source: *Édit du Roi, pour la punition de différens crimes . . . 1682*
(Paris, 1776)

Edict of the King

For the punishment of different crimes, notably of Poisoners, those who claim to be Diviners, Magicians and Enchanters and for regulation for the Grocers and Apothecaries. Given at Versailles, in the month of July 1682.

Registered in the Parlement August 31 of the same year.

Louis, by the grace of God, King of France and Navarre; to all present and to come, greetings. The execution of our preceding ordinances of the king, against those who call themselves diviners, magicians, and enchanters, having been long since neglected, and this slackening having attracted from foreign countries into our kingdom, several of these imposters, it has happened that under the pretext of horoscope and divination, and by means of the illusions of the workings of pretended magic and other similar illusions that these sorts of people have become accustomed to using, they have deceived numerous ignorant or gullible individuals, who identifiably engaged in dealings with them, by passing from vain curiosities to superstitions, and from superstitions to impieties and to sacrileges. And by a fatal sequence of events those who abandon themselves the most to the behavior of these seducers will be carried to an extreme criminality as to add sorcery and poison to the impieties and to the sacrileges, to obtain the effect of the promises of the said seducers, and to fulfil their wicked predictions. These practices having come to our attention, we have used all possible pains to end them and to stop by appropriate means the progress of these detestable abominations: And well after the punishment which was carried out against the principal authors and accomplices of these crimes, we had hoped that these people would be forever banished from our dominions, and our subjects would be safe from their deceit. However, as the experience of the past allowed us to understand just how dangerous it is to suffer the smallest abuse that crimes of this quality entail, and just how difficult it is to uproot them, since by dissimulation or by the number of guilty individuals they became public crimes, not wanting moreover to omit anything from what could be the greatest glory of God and the security of our subjects, We have deemed it necessary to renew the old ordinances, and adding to this, to take new precautions with regard to all those who use evil spells and poisons, as well as to those who under the vain profession of diviners, magicians, witches or other similar names, condemned by divine and human laws, infect and corrupt the spirit of the people by their speeches and practices, and by the profaning of the most holy religion. Know that we, for these causes and others which move us, and by our own movement, certain knowledge, full royal power and authority, have said, declared, and ordered . . . that which follows:

I. That all persons associated with the act of divination, and calling themselves fortune-tellers will, after the publication of our present declaration, leave the kingdom immediately on the pain of corporal punishment.

II. We prohibit all superstitious practices, by action, in writing, or in word, either abusing the text of the Holy Scripture or the prayers of the Church, or saying or doing things that have no connection with natural causes. We want that all those who find that they have taught them, along with those who put them to use, and those who have made use of them for whatever purpose, be singled out for exemplary punishment, and in proportion to the exigency of the case.

III. And if in the future it is found that some rather evil people add to superstition and compound it with impiety and sacrilege, under the pretext of operations of pretended magic, or another pretext of a similar kind, we want those who are convicted of it to be punished by death.

IV. All those who are convicted of poisoning by magical or natural means, whether death follows or not, like those who are convicted of concocting or distributing poison for the purpose of poisoning, will be punished by similar means. And because the crimes that are committed by poison are not only the most detestable and the most dangerous of all, but also the most difficult to discover, we require that all those, without exception, who will have knowledge of those who have worked to make poison, who have requested or given some, be obliged immediately to indicate what they know to our public prosecutors or to their surrogates, and in their absence to the first public officer of the locality, on the pain of an extraordinary proceeding against them, and be punished according to the circumstances and the requirements of each case, as the abettors and accomplices of the said crimes. Neither are the informants subjected to any punishment, not even to civil claims, when they have declared and articulated facts or important pieces of evidence which are found to be truthful and in keeping with their denunciation, though afterwards the individuals cited in the said denunciations be acquitted of the charges, to that end departing from Article 73 of the Ordinance of Orléans for the effect of magical and natural poison only, except to punish the slanderers according to the strictness of the stated ordinance.

33

CHRISTIAN THOMASIUS: THE PROHIBITION OF TORTURE, 1705

Christian Thomasius, a jurist who became the chancellor of the University of Halle in Brandenburg, wrote commentaries on criminal procedure and witchcraft during the period when witchcraft prosecutions were still occasionally taking place in some German territories. His most famous work, *Dissertatio de crimine magiae* (1701), was largely concerned with questions of judicial proof. Taking issue with the influential Saxon jurist Benedict Carpzov, Thomasius recommended that when cases of witchcraft came before the courts, judges needed to proceed with great caution, investigate the possibility of deception, and demand more proof than was required under existing criminal law. Even if it could be proved that the Devil had been responsible for the injury or illness that had been inflicted (a point on which Thomasius was himself highly dubious), one could not prove that the accused was responsible for the deed by means of the pact. Thomasius concluded that the entire procedure for trying witches was worthless and demanded that all witchcraft prosecutions cease. Fourteen years later King Frederick William I of Prussia issued an edict ending all witchcraft prosecutions in his jurisdiction.

In addition to his condemnation of witch trials, Thomasius formulated a more general critique of torture in all criminal prosecutions. In 1705 he published *Dissertation concerning Torture*. The treatise revealed the influence of Friedrich Spee (Chapter 29) and other earlier critics of torture, including Adam Tanner and Johann Meyfarth. In these concluding sections, Thomasius rebuts the arguments that had been made in defense of judicial torture. He concludes that the practice was irreligious and unjust and must be prohibited. The government of Prussia did not act on his recommendation until 1754, when it became the first country in continental Europe to abolish torture.

Source: Christian Thomasius, *Über Die Folter,* ed. R. Lieberwirth
(Weimar, 1986), pp. 178–187.

Part II

*Chapter 8. The same arguments that are customarily produced by the adversaries to
defend torture are answered. The argument from the requirement of Roman law.*

Therewith we have concluded the arguments against torture. Now we
shall also elucidate those which tend to be produced in its defense. The first
argument in defense of torture is its longstanding use and its deep-rooted
usage by so many people. For even before the foundations of the city of Rome,
this practice, in truth, had already come into use among the Athenians and
the Rhodians (from whom the Romans have acquired not a small part of
their laws.) But because long usage should have no less force than the law
itself, they stubbornly insist that torture, on account of its great antiquity,
gains strength from the agreement of all people and must necessarily be
treated as a law in the state. But who does not see the weakness of this argument based on antiquity? I do not deny that custom must be protected by
the authority of the law. But neither age alone nor the frequency of practices nor even the agreement of many peoples is sufficient to designate
anything at all as a genuine custom and attain the force of law, because a
large number of errors does not remove or correct the disgrace of error, nor
do the defenders of many bad causes make them just.

But it is moreover necessary that the custom is reasonable and not be
introduced in the first place through error. . . . Bad customs are confirmed
neither through length of time nor through long usage. If therefore it is
proper on the basis of Imperial evidence that a custom must be reasonable
and cannot be introduced through error, in order that it enjoy the authority
of the law, it follows in general that this extremely unreasonable practice of
torture, which was introduced by a very serious mistake, does not deserve
the name of a custom. Another argument in defense of torture goes back to
the authority of Justinian or another Roman emperor. For the defenders of
this hangman's bloodthirsty duty insist that whatever was included in the
sacred institutes of Roman law enjoys the authority of law among our countrymen, and thus in as much as the laws enacted concerning this question
[of torture] were confirmed by Justinian and other emperors, the authority
of those legislators cannot abrogate those enacted laws. But, by God, this
argument in favour of horrible torture is feeble, for it is known that no prince
who has supreme authority in his dominions must obey the laws of another
sovereign prince. And because today each and every prince can do in his
territory what the emperor can in the empire, so it follows that each and
every ruler in his territory can abolish bad laws and substitute equitable ones
in their place.

Chapter 9. The argument from necessity is refuted. It is shown that torture is a false means for discovering the truth.

In defense of putting defendants to the question, the adversaries customarily reply also very passionately that such a practice cannot be permitted without the most serious inconveniences for the courts, for, as an accused person whose innocence is established must be acquitted, and that person whose guilt for a crime is evident must be condemned to deserved punishment, so must a means be discovered by which the judge can determine either the innocence of the suspects or their guilt (to speak barbarously) so that the accused can either be acquitted or absolved.

For that reason torture must be maintained in our courts since it is useful to a high degree, so argue its supporters. But this objection is without foundation, for who does not see that torture is a fallacious, dangerous and erroneous thing, and the judge would have no more certainty after the applied torture about the crime that has been perpetrated than before the accused was placed on "the little horse." Moreover the adversaries themselves know that no one can be acquitted or convicted if the innocence or the committed crime can not be clearly established. But what is being considered here is torture as the means to discover the guilt or innocence of an accused man. A just judge can convict or acquit someone with calm certainty whether torture is administered or not. Who of course is not aware of the so many intrigues connected with torture not only to demonstrate the entire thing but also to make it more suspicious than it was before. Therefore it should be sufficiently clear that those err most grievously who contend that torture is a means by which suspects can either be set at liberty or convicted.

Chapter 10. Refutation of the opposing opinion regarding the customs of other people, among whom the practice of torture does not take place. Just as a defendant who has endured torture must be acquitted, even if he might have committed the crime, so in occult crimes he is to be prosecuted without torture. The punishment of occult crimes is to be entrusted to God, who can read the soul. It is proven that torture is a punishment to the entire body, and that if suspects are punished in this manner, it is an injustice.

The defenders of torture consider it unjust to acquit or condemn suspects on the basis of many pieces of circumstantial evidence. To refute this opinion I cite the customs of the English, the Dutch, and other peoples who do not use torture today yet where the suspect is neither unconditionally acquitted nor condemned; rather they keep those suspected of a crime in chains and conduct an extremely thorough investigation. But if by means of this investigation neither their innocence nor their guilt for the crime can be sufficiently established, after trusted individuals report to the court, they are acquitted for the time being, until more weighty evidence for a renewed investigation be brought against them. . . .

Chapter 11. It will be objected by those who disagree that by means of torture secret crimes can be discovered. Experience is opposed to the counter-argument of these objectors. The words of Holy Scripture will be cited where God has forgiven the wicked what he had threatened the godless because until then few of them were just.

Finally the patrons of that hangman's duty call upon experience, saying that if wicked people who tell the truth under torture have often experienced deserved punishment and that they could not, if the torture were not permitted, be punished in any other way. And so the patrons are of the opinion that the welfare of the state demands that wicked men be punished. And therefore they believe with a word that torture should be permitted everywhere in well ordered states as the most certain means to discover the truth. And I recognize that, but I assert on the other hand that the state is still more concerned not to torture the innocent harshly nor to punish them with an undeserved death. They appeal to experience, which more often taught us that malicious men receive just punishment through a confession extracted under torture, and I appeal to experience in defense of my opinion; for it is apparent that many, if not most, who endure this torture have not done anything and in this way either experience unjust punishments or die undeserved deaths. . . . I believe with Trajan that it is preferable to let the crime of a guilty person go unpunished than to convict an innocent person.

This moreover is confirmed in Genesis 18:23, where Abraham tried to use questions to avert the destruction which God had threatened the Sodomites on the grounds that there were still righteous and holy men among those people who would perish together with the others. Further proof of this comes in a parable of Christ: in Matthew 13:20: Do not destroy the wheat together with the weeds; let them grow together until the harvest. And so can a judge by analogy of these words set free ten guilty men whose crimes are not surely known to him rather than to assign an innocent man to the torture and through coerced testimony condemn him to an undeserved death. I contend that it appears from what has already been clarified what I have asserted in the title of this dissertation that torture, which is an irreligious, unjust thing and stands in contradiction of divine and natural law must be prohibited.

34

THE REPEAL OF
THE ENGLISH AND
SCOTTISH WITCHCRAFT
STATUTES, 1736

Most witchcraft prosecutions in the secular courts in Europe were authorized by specific statutes, edicts, or other legislation identifying the crime of witchcraft and authorizing its prosecution. When prosecutions for witchcraft declined and came to an end, authorities sometimes repealed the statutes upon which the trials had been based. In most cases the repeal of witchcraft laws came many years after the last witch had been tried. That was the case in Great Britain, where the English witchcraft statute of 1604 and the Scottish statute of 1563 were both repealed by the British parliament in 1736. (The parliaments of the two countries had been united in 1707.) The last witchcraft trial in England had taken place in 1717, almost twenty years before the act of repeal, while the last Scottish prosecution had occurred in 1727. For all practical purposes, therefore, the act of 1736 simply ratified the fact that British authorities no longer considered witchcraft to be a crime. This did not mean that those authorities, much less the uneducated people, denied the reality of witchcraft. Those beliefs, especially in Scotland, continued well into the eighteenth century. Nor did this act completely eliminate all judicial penalties regarding witchcraft. By the terms of this statute, it became a crime to *pretend* to be a witch. This provision of the act reflected the same concern of French royal authorities in Louis XIV's edict of 1682 (Chapter 32). That crime remained on the statute book until 1951.

Source: *Statutes at Large from the Third Year of the Reign of King George the Second to the Twentieth Year of the Reign of King George the Second* (London, 1769), vol. 6. pp. 206–207.

AN ACT TO REPEAL THE STATUTE MADE IN THE FIRST YEAR OF THE REIGN OF KING JAMES THE FIRST, ENTITLED AN ACT AGAINST CONJURATION,

171

WITCHCRAFT AND DEALING WITH EVIL AND WICKED SPIRITS, EXCEPT SO MUCH THEREOF AS REPEALS AN ACT OF THE FIFTH YEAR OF THE REIGN OF QUEEN ELIZABETH, AGAINST CONJURATIONS, ENCHANTMENTS AND WITCHCRAFTS, AND TO REPEAL AN ACT PASSED IN THE PARLIAMENT OF SCOTLAND IN THE NINTH PARLIAMENT OF QUEEN MARY, ENTITLED ANENTIS WITCHCRAFTS, AND FOR PUNISHING SUCH PERSONS AS PRETEND TO EXERCISE OR USE ANY KIND OF WITCHCRAFT, SORCERY, ENCHANTMENT OR CONJURATION

Be it enacted by the King's most Excellent Majesty, by and with the consent of the Lords Spiritual and Temporal, and Commons, in this present parliament assembled, and by the authority of the same, that the statute made in the first year of the reign of King James the First, entitled *An Act against Conjuration, Witchcraft, and dealing with evil and wicked Spirits*, shall from the twenty-fourth day of June next, be repealed and utterly void and of none effect (except so much thereof that repeals the statute made in the first year of the reign of Queen Elizabeth, intitled, *An Act against conjurations, enchantments and Witchcrafts.*)

II. And be it further enacted by the authority aforesaid, that from and after the said twenty-fourth day of June, the act passed in the parliament of Scotland in the ninth parliament of Queen Mary, entitled *Anentis Witchcrafts*, shall be and is hereby repealed.

III. And be it further enacted that from and after the said twenty-fourth day of June no prosecution suit or proceeding shall be commenced or carried on against any person or persons for witchcraft, sorcery, enchantment, or conjuration, or for charging another with any such offence, in any court whatsoever in Great Britain.

IV. And for the more effectual preventing and punishing any pretences to such arts or powers as are before mentioned, whereby ignorant persons are frequently deluded and defrauded, be it further enacted by the authority aforesaid, that if any person shall, from and after the said twenty-fourth day of June, pretend to exercise or use any kind of witchcraft, sorcery, enchantment or conjuration, or undertake to tell fortunes, or pretend from his or her skill or knowledge in any occult or crafty science to discover where or in what manner any goods or chattels, supposed to have been stolen or lost, may be found; every person so offending, being thereof lawfully convicted on indictment or information in that part of Great Britain called England, or on indictment or libel in that part of Great Britain called Scotland, shall for every such offence suffer imprisonment by the space of one whole year without bail or mainprize, and once in every quarter of the said year in some market town of the proper county upon the market day, there stand openly on the pillory by the space of one hour, and also shall (if the court by which judgment shall be given think fit), be obliged to give sureties for his or her good behaviour, in such sum, and for such time, as the said court shall judge proper according to the circumstances of the offence, and in such case shall be further imprisoned until such sureties be given.

Part V

WITCHCRAFT TRIALS
IN THE SIXTEENTH
AND SEVENTEENTH
CENTURIES

Between 1400 and 1750 perhaps as many as 100,000 persons were tried for the crime of witchcraft in Europe and colonial North America. Approximately half of those alleged witches were executed, many by burning at the stake. Most of the trials, especially those after 1580, when the most intense period of witch-hunting began, took place in the secular courts, which administered justice in kingdoms, principalities, counties, and towns. Ecclesiastical courts had taken a major role in witch-hunting during the fifteenth century, and they continued to conduct some prosecutions after that time, but many of those trials were for practising lesser forms of magic and superstition. Cases involving serious *maleficia*, such as causing the illness or death of a person, were usually held in the secular courts, which had a more clearly defined juris-diction and greater procedural latitude.

The records of witchcraft trials during the sixteenth and seventeenth centuries are both incomplete and difficult to use. Many records have been lost, and of those that have been preserved, few give a full account of the proceedings. The records nonetheless provide a wealth of information regarding the ways in which educated and illiterate Europeans understood the crime of witchcraft and how they perceived the threat it represented. When the records include the depositions of the witch's neighbors, they delineate the circumstances in which the original accusations arose. The formal charges brought against the accused and the confessions adduced under torture show how these societies understood the nature of the crime. The records of the interrogations reveal how prosecutors were able to shape the testimony of the accused to conform to what they believed the parties had done. Those same records often reveal how witches were able to profess their innocence until the application of torture forced them to incriminate themselves. Torture also influenced the content of the witch's confessions. References to the worship of the Devil, especially collective worship, and flight to the sabbath almost always appear in the trial records after torture had been administered.

Trials that occurred in the same jurisdiction often resembled each other closely, mainly because court officials suspected that all witches performed the same deeds and therefore asked the same leading questions. Throughout Europe, however, there were great procedural variations, and these produced trials with marked variations in content and style. The greatest differences existed between those countries that followed an inquisitorial system of criminal procedure, in which the officials of the court controlled every stage of the judicial process, including the determination of guilt or innocence, and an accusatorial system in which lay members of the community played a role in bringing formal charges against witches and in determining their guilt. The trials in England, New England, and to a lesser extent Scotland (Chapters 38, 41, and 43) followed accusatorial procedure, whereas those in Trier, Lorraine, Bamberg, Eichstätt, and Russia (Chapters 35, 36, 39, 40, and 42) followed inquisitorial procedure. The trial in Guernsey, a French-speaking island in the English Channel whose courts followed a mixture of English and French criminal procedure, remains a special case (Chapter 37).

35

THE CONFESSION
OF NICLAS FIEDLER AT
TRIER, 1591

Between 1589 and 1591 a severe witch-hunt occurred in the German electorate of Trier, a territorial state ruled by a prince-archbishop who was one of the electors of the Holy Roman Emperor. Witchcraft trials in the electorate had begun in the late fifteenth century, but harsh economic conditions encouraged a spate of accusations during this late sixteenth-century period. The number of accusations and trials increased dramatically as accused witches were forced to name accomplices. As the hunt careened out of control, many individuals of high social rank were included among the victims. Among them was Dr Dietrich Flade, the former Vice Governor of Trier and rector of its university, who was executed in 1589, and Niclas Fiedler, the former mayor of the city. During Fiedler's examination, which took place two years after Flade's execution, the accused confessed that he had seen Flade at the witches' sabbath. The prosecution of Fiedler, like many other German witchcraft trials, reveals the crucial role that torture played in securing witches' confessions.

Source: This account of Fiedler's confession is translated from Rita Voltmer, *Hexenprozesse in der Stadt Trier und im Herzogtum Luxemburg Geständnisse (Auszüge aus Prozessakten)*, in Rosemaries Beier-de Haan, Rita Voltmer und Franz Irsigler (eds), *Hexenwahn: Ängste der Neuzeit* (Wolfratshausen, 2002), pp. 72–81.

Confession of the former mayor of Trier,
Niclas Fiedler, who was executed on
1 October 1591 (Abstract)

On the same day in the afternoon between three and six o'clock appeared once again in the council chamber on behalf of the governor: his secretary

Jakob, the jurymen Hans Philipp Botzheim and Johann Tholes, the city clerk as well as the tithe collector Wilhelm, who was ordered to bring in the prisoner. Scarcely had Fiedler sat down when his confession that was taken today was once again read aloud by Botzheim; Fiedler immediately began to say he was an unfortunate man and that only under pain had he confessed things that were not true. If he admitted this, then he would damn his soul, because he would thereby do wrong to himself and other men. He had nothing to do with these things. Since he persisted in his denial despite all warnings, he was handed over to the hangman so that he could perform his duty. The hangman led him to the place of torture, bound him, pulled him up high, secured the cord to the wall and beat on the rope with a stick, thereby inflicting great pain on the bound prisoner, as indicated by his screams. After Fiedler had been suspended and beaten in this manner for half an hour, he began to confess as follows:

That approximately twelve years ago, when his wife had been sick for a long time, he had experienced great sadness and depression; during which time a black man appeared to him in the courtyard of his house between day and night, who had comforted him with the words that all would turn out well and who had demanded of him that he should swear adherence to him and help with murders as well as to renounce Christ crucified, Mary, who is the Devil's whore, and all the saints whom he, the tempter, had named. Those things he, Fiedler, had done. The Devil had placed in his cap money which in reality was horse manure and had promised to bring him to and from [the sabbath] unnoticed and not to remain there long. After eight days the Devil had come to him again and had said, you must be off. In his courtyard Fiedler mounted a billy-goat from the left side and with the Devil flew off to Franzenknüppchen [a place on a mountain overlooking Trier where witches allegedly gathered], where they would dance and make merry. Except for [Hans] Kesten and Maria the hatter, who lives above St John's Hospital in the Brotgasse, he recognized no one; the others were strangers to him. Fiedler believed that he had also seen Johannet Trommen as well as the zum Drachens and their daughter. Each of those who were there at that time has agreed to destroy wine and corn.

During this confession Dr. Hulzbach, the village mayor, came up, remained standing outside the room, heard how the proceedings were going and how moreover the accused under torture admitted that he had also been to St Mattheisser's Kopf [a place where witches allegedly gathered] between Niedermennig and St Matthias; that he had been brought there by a billy-goat which he himself had obtained. At this place he had seen the wife of Georg von Niedermennig, whose father was a tanner. Moreover the wife of Arnold from Konz, known as Konzer Beel, had been there.

When the village mayor noted that the degree of the torture had been excessive, he demanded several times that the poor man be let down, for the confessions and the statements of the poor criminal would be of little value when made under torture and should not be recorded, yet his demand was not met. Thereupon he entered the room and ordered the torturers to stop the torture and to loosen the ropes, which was done.

When Fiedler was released from the torture and brought down, the village mayor demanded of him now to acknowledge the real truth how he had fallen into demonic temptation and what of relevance he had helped promote in this situation. Fiedler said that for twelve years he had encountered something uncanny in the courtyard of his house, yet he had seen no one and not observed anything there.

Warned that he should not proceed, and that he should admit the truth, he said that a black man appeared to him who commanded him to renounce God, Christ crucified, his mother Mary, whom he called a whore, and the saints, and to swear allegiance to him. He had placed money in his cap, but it was not money but dung. The Devil called not himself but him, Fiedler, Greiss; he also gave him no mark [i.e. he did not scratch off the baptismal chrism]. After that the Devil came to him again and ordered that he should ride out with him to Franzenknüppchen. He, Fiedler, agreed and at that moment he was taken to Franzenknüppchen on a billy-goat. There he saw [Dietrich] Flade and Hans Kesten. Eight years before he had observed there Johannet Trommen and Maria the hatter, who lives beneath his house "Zum Rat."

Asked what they were doing there [at the place of dancing], he answered they had been plotting to destroy the wine and grain harvest but their plan had miscarried, for the prayer of godly people had prevented it.

They also had gathered on the Niederrmenniger heights for festivals and to make merry, but there it was not as usual for them to be there to celebrate, but to engage in a miserable, abominable business. It happens at night; it appears as if there is light somewhere but in reality there is none. People do not sit but stand at these gatherings. Fiedler believes Flade had intended to destroy everything.

On the Hetzerather Heide [an alleged central place for witches' assemblies in Trier and Luxembourg] they must gather on each ember week, and one time he had arrived there on a billy-goat and had been at that place.

This May there were no more than ten persons there; it happened over the cross on the Hetzerather Heide, on the right side. Fiedler believed he was there physically but he did not know whether Kesten and the others were really there. He insisted on saying this to Kesten face to face.

They would dance around clumsily in a circle like round wooden blocks, and it was only a small amusement. He, Fiedler, danced with the shoemaker, who lives opposite the Rathaus, and with Ursel, who was her maid. One whistled with a horrible tone. He paid no money for it. Then around Easter time, he agreed to destroy corn.

Flade has made the proposal to destroy the corn and has ordered the women who were there, namely Anna von Ruwer and the female tanner in the

Neugassen to accomplish this task. The women know, for example, how a storm is made: the Devil stirs it up for that purpose. They beat on a stream or on a surface of water in the Devil's name, and from that would come cold mist, rain, and other harms.

36

THE TRIAL OF FRANÇATTE CAMONT IN LORRAINE, 1598

━━━━◦◦◦━━━━

The duchy of Lorraine, on the eastern border of France, was the center of some of the most intense witch-hunting of the sixteenth century. The duchy was independent of both the French royal government and the Holy Roman Empire, although it technically lay within the boundaries of the Empire. The official who prosecuted many of the witches in Lorraine was Nicolas Remy, who used the evidence drawn from many of the cases he tried in writing his witchcraft treatise, *Demonolatry* (see Chapter 17). One of the cases that Remy prosecuted after he became the *procureur général* of Lorraine in 1595 was that of Françatte, wife of Jean Camont, of Laygoutte, in the late spring and early summer of 1598. The prosecution, which lasted more than two months, begins with depositions taken from many witnesses, all of whom reveal the basis for their suspicion of Françatte. The uncertainty that some of the witnesses expressed regarding Françatte's responsibility for their misfortunes adds weight to the integrity of these depositions as reliable statements of peasant belief. None of the deponents, moreover, mentions the Devil, whose activities were of little concern to Françatte's neighbors, except when Françatte herself referred to him. Only when Remy asked for torture did she confess to having been seduced by a demon, named Persin, and to having attended the sabbath. She also named one accomplice.

Source: the Archives of the Meurthe-et-Moselle Department at Nancy, B 8682, no. 8. The transcript of this case was prepared by Robin Briggs.

April 1598. Depositions.

1. Magdelaine, wife of Colas Cointzelin, of Raves, 23, deposed that the accused had a long reputation for witchcraft. Four or five years earlier she had been guarding animals with the daughter of the accused when she came and

rebuked her, saying "might she have ill health," and even drawing her knife to strike her. This was because animals had strayed and had been fined by Colas de Bonipaire; she said that as the eldest witness she should have prevented this. Three or four years earlier she had married and then became ill after the pregnancy; she sent for Françatte to visit her, suspecting she was the cause of her illness, but she pretended she was absent even though she was at home. She still has not properly recovered or is able to walk. If Françatte was a witch as reputed, in view of her threats, she thought she was the cause.

2. Jean Claude Maimbourg, 50, testified that during the 20 years she had been in the village, he had various quarrels with her, and she usually threatened him, saying he would repent. These threats were normally followed by the death of animals, and in one period of two years he lost eight horses and during a winter four oxen, so that since she and her husband were his neighbors he had lost animals to the value of over 1000 francs. In view of her reputations and the threats she made, he was sure she had caused most of these deaths. Seven or eight years earlier his wife had died after an illness lasting a fortnight, during which she often asked her daughters and others to persuade Françatte to visit her, since she suspected her of being the cause, but she only came to the funeral procession.

3. Demenge Colas Jacquemin, of Raves, 40, had served seven years in the house of the widow of Jacquat Rolbel, hostess at Layegoutte. During this time his mistress was ill and sent him to consult a woman at Fertrupt on her behalf. He left early one morning, and as he left the village he fell, dislocating his shoulder, which he had to have set by a doctor at St Marie. On his return he told his mistress about this, and she said Françatte had joined another woman by spring after he left, saying "that the hostess had sent her valet to the Devil, and that she wished to make him sick as well as her." Nevertheless he did not think she had caused his fall, and if she had he forgave her.

4. Thoussainct Grand Didier, of Raves, 40, deposed that more than 20 year ago Françatte and her husband, who had no property, came to live at Raves. After three or four years they wanted to go to Lubine, but the villagers would not receive her, saying she was rumoured to be a witch. This is why they went to Layegoutte; she had always been reputed a witch since then. He had a quarrel with her husband over tithes, which led to a lawsuit, after which a horse broke his leg and died. He then lost a series of animals over two years and was unable to keep any calves successfully. If she was a witch, as reputed, he believed she had caused these losses, in view of their quarrel and the fact that the husband had said in public before the church at Betrimoustier, "that all those who attacked her would gain nothing." He also thought she might have caused the illness of his wife, which began on the day of the quarrel over tithes. Since then she had been unable to keep food down without vomiting, and she was not cured despite all efforts; she had eaten nothing since last Friday.

180

5. Andreu Gerardin, of Combrimont, servant to the widow Jacquot Rolbel of Layegoutte, had heard her reputed as a witch as long as he had known her. Three years earlier, when there was a large company in the tavern, he had a quarrel with her husband and told him that "he lived and slept with a witch." There was no reaction, and no reparation was sought. . . .

7. Jean Colin, 54, had various quarrels with her and her husband, notably some twelve years earlier over a meadow they rented jointly. They had cut the hay first and had taken more than their share; then he took some of what they had cut and she was very angry, leading to a violent quarrel. He had had various losses, although he could not now remember the details; one of his children died and many of his animals. To find out the truth he went to Val de Villers, where there was a woman "who engaged in divination" and asked her who had caused the losses. After some speech between them she said, "that it was the work of the woman he suspected, and to confirm what she said took a glass in which she put something like a round apple, and after performing some trick she made him see the effigy of a woman resembling the said Françatte, asking him if it was the one he suspected, and after looking hard several times, he replied that he recognized it was her." In view of this and her reputation he suspected that she had caused his losses. . . .

10. Jean Claude Epurat, 40, testified that six or seven years earlier the prisoner had brought back two pigs she had found in her garden, saying "that little profit might he have from them, and it would turn out so." The pigs then became ill and were unable to walk, so after two weeks his wife obtained some bread from the children of the accused by means of a servant, and the pigs recovered after eating this. Frightened that they might still be bewitched, he sold the pigs at Ste Marie; he was convinced that she was responsible. He had later heard that she had learned about the use of the bread, had been very angry, and forbad the children to give any in the future. He also had a sow which became ill. This time he was unable to obtain anything to give it, and it died. . . .

13. Demenge Jean Gerardin, of Combrimont, 45, testified that some fifteen years earlier, while living at Bonipaire, he had met often with her husband, and one day she spoke to his late wife, asking how they could separate their husbands, who got together to drink. Five or six weeks later he was at the husband's forge with some miners, and they sent for a pot of wine. She drank some from a glass, then handed the rest to the witness, who drank it, but was soon afflicted by "a cold sickness" through his whole body, lost the use of his limbs, and after three months had to take to his bed. He sent his friend Olry Jeandel, who is now dead, to consult a doctor on his behalf, who said that he had taken ill by eating a salad and drinking from a glass given him by a woman at the same time. To obtain a cure he was told to bathe himself for nine days, and three or six days later the woman who had made him ill would come to visit him, asking where he had sent to the diviner, at which point he should strike her with his fist. He followed

this advice, and on the third day Françatte appeared, asked him about the diviner, and also demanded repayment of four or five gros he owed her. He was too weak to punch her, but within a few days he started to feel rather better, so he took courage and went on horse to visit the "physician" at Naterodes. He told him what had happened, to which he replied "that she had not completely cured him, but that with God's grace he would cure him of all and would operate in such a manner that one would know from her [i.e. the prisoner's] face that she was the cause of the whole sickness." On his return his sister, who lived at Layegoutte, told him Françatte's face was all black, as if she had been beaten. He took the trouble to go and see for himself, and he soon made a complete recovery. He could only think that she had bewitched him. . . .

19. Margueritte, wife of Didier Tixerand, de Grand Rux, 34, told how her first husband, Demenge Aubert, before their marriage, had been asked by Françatte to help her with enclosing a field. He had said he was too busy, but she kept pressing him, and he finally agreed. In the evening, when it was late and too dark to see properly, she gave him some tripes, and there was a piece he could not chew. Since she was sitting next to him and he was afraid of her, he swallowed it rather than spit it out, after which he had a pain in his stomach and became very swollen, feeling he had an animal inside him. After a year he was rather better and able to work and he then married the witness. He was well for six weeks but then the illness returned. He said that he had an animal inside him that was eating his heart and asked her to listen to it crying, especially when the weather was changing; she did sometimes think she heard it cry. He finally died in Easter Week, having often said "that he had been careful not to visit the house of the said Françatte but had not been careful enough, and it was there he had taken the morsel of death." He had sent to someone to ask about the illness, and they said Françatte was responsible. That person also gave her some dried herb, saying that when these were boiled in a new earthenware pot the woman who had made him ill would appear; when this was done Françatte appeared, sat by him where he was in bed by the fire, and asked how he was. . . .

Interrogation: She said that she was a native of a village named Baignon, near Verzou in Burgundy. Her father's name was Jean, and she had never known her mother. Her father was a "cousturier," who also begged his living, and he had one other child. She had been to see a relative at Kayserberg when they all caught the plague. The others died, while she was ill and taken to hospital, which she left three weeks later. She went around begging until she was employed by a lieutenant at Bruyeres to keep animals, which she did for five years. She had another seven years and a half in service with five masters, starting in Ban de Corcieux and ending up in Wisembach. When she was about 20 she married her husband, who was a blacksmith from France, and had been married some thirty years; she thought she was about 54.

She had eight children, of whom six were alive. Two were in Allemaigne; the others were at home learning the trade of smith. She agreed that the previous years she had a quarrel with the wife of Jean Epural, because their daughter did not help the daughter of the accused as she should have done with the herd of pigs. Epural's wife called her "rascal" on this occasion, but that was all. Had not been to visit Jean Claude Maimbourg's wife because she was "a bad neighbour and a bad woman."

Asked about Andreu Gerardin's claim in the tavern, that her husband slept with a witch, she said that her husband had retorted by saying that he lied like a witch and had obtained informal reparation before "gens de bien." As for the late wife of Demenge Gerardin, she had been a very good woman and neighbour. She did go and see her sometimes during her illness, but not as often as she would have wished because she had to help her husband with the forge. She claimed that Demenge Gerardin had made her reputation for words he had spoken against her.

She denied most suggestions of quarrels and said "that the false witnesses could not make her bad; that the more there were, the worse; and that it would be much better if they were all burned."

19 May 1598. The Change de Nancy requested that she be confronted with witnesses. Françatte denied all charges. When confronted with them she made numerous general remarks that they were liars, bore false witness, were children of witches, etc.

1 June 1598. Nicolas Remy asks for torture.

Interrogation under torture. Racked severely, but would confess nothing, insisting she was a good Christian. Either later the same day or subsequently she was tortured again, being racked "very severely," and finally asked to be released, saying she had been seduced by Persin the previous year. When sat down by the fire she said the seduction had been ten years earlier. She had been very angry with her son Jacquot, who had returned from Allemaigne. He had refused to guard the animals, so she beat him. Persin gave her a purse, offering her a bigger one which he showed her. She went to the sabbat once, but only identified one of those who were dancing, Dedielle, the wife of Michiel Claudel of Ginfosse.

She had tried out the powder on her cat, which died. Then she killed a series of animals, in revenge for minor offences in most cases. She had made the servant of Jacquot Rolbel's widow lame by sprinkling powder on his foot after he stole some of her oats at the mill, then finally felt sorry for him and healed him. He had also made Demenge Jean Gerardin ill by putting powder in the glass when he shared wine with her but then finally felt sorry for him and did the same with yellow powder to heal him. She was angry because he had encouraged her husband to go drinking, and there was not enough money for their food. She also seems to have killed a beggar woman who asked importunately for bread when she was kneading dough and had none cooked.

She said she had paid the rent of a chicken to be let off regular attendance at the sabbat, but then said she had been more times than she could remember. She confessed to the usual activities of damaging crops. She added to the names of those she had seen there Gregoire Matthis and his daughter, of Bertrimoutier, both executed, the late Dion Bouray of Raves, Dedielle (already named), Jennon, la mother superior of Wisembach, and Laurence, wife of Colas Mandray of Wisembach.

11 June 1598. Interrogation. Confirmed earlier confessions. Asked if she had taken any of her children to the sabbat, she insisted she had not. Remy then asked for execution.

15 June 1598. The Change de Nancy approved this request, subject to reiteration of confessions without any threat of torture. Reiteration of torture had been "directly contrary to law and good practice."

27 June 1598. Interrogation. She now said she was not a witch and had only confessed this because of torture, but was content for them to put her to death nevertheless. On the suggestion that Persin must have visited her in prison to persuade her to say this, she then agreed that the confessions had been true.

7 July 1598. Sentence carried out.

37

THE CONFESSIONS OF WITCHES IN GUERNSEY, 1617

The trial, conviction, and execution of three women – a widow, her married daughter, and a married woman – for witchcraft on the isle of Guernsey in 1617 provides an illuminating commentary on the way in which torture influenced the content of witches' confessions. The trial took place in a French-speaking possession of the English crown in the English Channel. The legal procedures used in criminal cases were a hybrid between English and French practice. The presentation of criminals by a jury followed English custom, and the trial was also apparently conducted by a petty jury of twelve men, but following sentence the prisoners were tortured in order to reveal the names of their accomplices, a procedure that was prohibited by English common law. This sequence makes it possible to see how the demonic aspects of witchcraft, including the worship of the Devil at the sabbath, were adduced only after torture was applied. Before the confessions of the three witches, the trial concerned only *maleficia*, which included the infliction of many strange diseases on men, women, and children as well as beasts. Only when the first witch named in the record, Collette du Mont, was tortured did she reveal the content of her crimes, which now included temptation by the Devil and flight to the sabbath. At the sabbath she confessed to having joined 15 or 16 other witches, copulated with the Devil in the form of a dog, danced, and drunk wine. At the end of the sabbath the Devil gave her the powders with which she could continue her practice of harming her neighbors by magical means. The confessions of the other two witches added details regarding the sabbath, flight, and copulation with the Devil. The three witches were executed by hanging, as was the practice in England, but their bodies were afterwards burned, which was the practice in France.

Source: *Witchcraft and Devil Lore in the Channel Islands: Transcripts from the Official Records of the Guernsey Royal Court*, ed. J. L. Pitts (Guernsey, 1886), pp. 9–18.

Before Amice de Carteret, Esq., Bailiff and the Jurats, July 4, 1617

Sentence of death

Collette du Mont, widow of Jean Becket; Marie, her daughter, wife of Pierre Massy; and Isabel Becquet, wife of Jean Le Moygne, being by common rumour and report for a long time past addicted to the damnable art of witchcraft, and the same being thereupon seized and apprehended by the officers of His Majesty [James I], after voluntarily submitting themselves, both upon the general inquest of the country, and after having been several times brought up before the court, heard, examined, and confronted, upon a great number of depositions made and produced before the court by the said officers; from which it is clear and evident that for many years past the aforesaid women have practiced the diabolic art of witchcraft, by having retained in languor through strange diseases, many persons and beasts; and also cruelly hurt a great number of men, women, and children, and caused the death of many animals, as recorded in the informations thereupon laid, it follows that they are clearly convicted and proved to be witches. In expiation of which crime it has been ordered by the court that the said women shall be presently conducted, with halters about their necks, to the usual place of punishment, and shall there be fastened by the executioner to a gallows, and be hanged, strangled, killed, and burnt, until their flesh and bones are reduced to ashes, and the ashes shall be scattered; and all their goods, chattels and estates, if any such exist, shall be forfeited to His Majesty. In order to make them disclose their accomplices, they shall be put to the question before the court, previous to being executed. . . .

Confession of Collette Du Mont

First, the said Collette immediately after the said sentence was pronounced, and before leaving the court, freely admitted that she was a witch; and at the same time, not wishing to specify the crimes which she had committed, she was taken, along with the others, to the torture chamber, and the said question being applied to her, she confessed that she was quite young when the Devil, in the form of a cat, appeared to her, in the parish of Torteval, as she was returning from her cattle, it being still daylight, and that he took occasion to lead her astray by inciting her to avenge herself on one of her neighbours, with whom she was then at enmity, on account of some damage which she had suffered through the cattle on the latter; that since then when

186

she had a quarrel with anyone, he appeared to her in the aforesaid form; and sometimes in the form of a dog, inducing her to take vengeance upon those who had angered her, persuading her to cause the death of persons and cattle.

That the Devil, having come to fetch her that she might go to the Sabbath, called for her without anyone perceiving it, and gave her a certain black ointment with which (after having stripped herself), she rubbed her back, belly and stomach; and then again having put on her clothes, she went out of her door, when she was immediately carried through the air at a great speed; and she found herself in an instant at the place of the Sabbath, which was sometimes near the parochial burial ground, and at other times near the sea-shore in the neighbourhood of Rocquaine Castle, where, upon arrival, she met fifteen or sixteen wizards and witches with the devils who were there in the form of dogs, cats, and hares; which wizards and witches she was unable to recognize, because they were all blackened and disfigured. It was true, however, that she had heard the Devil summon them by their names, and she remembered among others those of Fallaise and Hardie; confessed that on entering the sabbath, the Devil wishing to summon them, commenced with her sometimes. Admitted that her daughter Marie, wife of Massy, now condemned for a similar crime, was a witch, and that she took her twice to the Sabbath with her. At the Sabbath, after having worshipped the Devil, who used to stand up on his hind legs, they had connection with him under the form of a dog; then they danced back to back. And after having danced, they drank wine (she did not know what colour it was), which the Devil poured out of a jug into a silver or pewter goblet; which wine did not seem to her so good as that which was usually drunk; they also ate white bread which he presented to them – she had never seen any salt at the Sabbath.

Confessed that the Devil had charged her to call, as she passed, for Isabel le Moygne, when she came to the sabbath, which she had done several times. On leaving the sabbath the Devil incited her to commit various evil deeds; and to that effect he gave her certain black powders, which he ordered her to throw upon such persons and cattle as she wished. With this powder she perpetrated several wicked acts which she did not remember. Among others she threw some upon Mr. Dolbell, parish minister, and was the occasion of his death by these means. With this same powder she bewitched the wife of Jean Maugues, but denied that the woman's death was caused by it. She also touched on the side, and threw some of this powder over the deceased wife of Mr. Perchard, the minister who succeeded the said Dolbell in the parish, she being *enceinte* at the time, and so caused the death of her and her infant – she did not know that the deceased woman had given her any cause for doing so.

Upon the refusal of the wife of Collas Tottevin to give her some milk, she caused her cow to dry up, by throwing upon it some of this powder, which cow she afterwards cured again by making it eat some bran and some terrestrial herb that the Devil gave her.

Confession of Marie Becquet

Marie, wife of Pierre Massy, after sentence of death had been pronounced against her, having been put to the question, confessed that she was a witch; and that at the persuasion of the Devil, who appeared to her in the form of a dog, she gave herself to him; that when he gave herself to him he took her by the hand with his paw; that she used to anoint herself with the same ointment as her mother used; and had been to the sabbath upon the bank near Rocquaine Castle with her, where there was no one but the Devil and her as it seemed, in the aforesaid form in which she had seen him several times. She was also at the Sabbath on one occasion among others in the road near Collas Tottevin's. Every time that she went to the Sabbath the Devil came to her, and it seemed as though he transformed her into a female dog. She said that upon the shore, near the said Rocquaine, the Devil, in the form of a dog, having had connection with her, gave her bread and wine, which she ate and drank.

The Devil gave her certain powders, which powders he put into her hand, for her to throw upon those whom he ordered her. She threw some of them by his orders upon persons and cattle, notably on the child of Pierre Brehaut. Item, on the wife of Jean Bourgaize, while she was *enceinte*. Item, upon the child of Leonard le Messurier.

Confession of Isabel Becquet

Isabel, wife of Jean le Mogne, having been put to the question, at once confessed that she was a witch, and that upon her getting into a quarrel with the woman Girarde, who was her sister-in-law, the Devil, in the form of a hare, took occasion to tempt her, appearing to her in broad daylight in a road near her house, and pursuing her and inciting her to give himself to him, and that he would avenge herself on the said Girarde, and everybody else; to which persuasion she would not at the moment condescend to yield. So he at once disappeared. But very soon he came again to her in the same road, and pursuing his previous argument, exhorted her in the same terms as above. That done, he left her and went away, after having previously put her a sackful of parsnips. She then took a certain black powder wrapped in a cloth which he placed [there], which powder she kept by her. He appeared to her another time under the same form in the town district, inciting her anew to give herself to him, but she not wishing to comply, he next made a request to her to give him some living animal, whereupon she returned to her dwelling and fetched a chicken, which she carried to him to the same place where she had left him, and he took it. And after having thanked her he made an appointment for her to be present the next morning before daylight at the Sabbath, promising that he would send for her, according to which promise, during the ensuing night, the old woman Collette du Mont came to fetch her and gave her some black ointment, which she had had from the Devil. With this (after having stripped herself) she anointed her back and belly. Then, having dressed herself again, she went out of her house door, when she was instantly caught up and carried across hedges and bushes to the bank of the seashore in the neighbourhood of Rocquaine Castle, the usual place where the Devil kept his Sabbath. No sooner had she arrived there than the Devil came to her in the form of a dog, with two great horns sticking up, and with one of his paws (which seemed to her like hands) took her by the hand, and calling her by name, told her that she was welcome. Then immediately the Devil made her kneel down, while he himself stood up on his hind legs. He then made her express detestation for the Eternal in these words: "I renounce God the Father, God the Son, and God the Holy Ghost," and then caused her to worship and invoke himself in these terms: "Our Great Master, help us!" with a special compact to be faithful to him. And when this was done, he had connection with her in the aforesaid form of a dog, but a little larger. Then she and the others danced with him back to back. After having danced, the Devil poured out of a jug some black wine, which he presented to them in a wooden bowl, from which she drank, but it did not seem to her so good as the wine which is usually drunk. There was also bread – but she did not eat any. Confessed that she did give herself to him for a month. They returned from the Sabbath in the same manner that they went there.

38

THE TRIAL AND
CONFESSION OF
ELIZABETH SAWYER,
1621

———❦———

The actual trial records of English witchcraft are very sparse. Most English witches were tried at the semi-annual assizes of the counties, and the records of those prosecutions are limited to the indictment and the indication of the outcome of the trial. The richest source in witchcraft trials, the written depositions of witnesses, have for the most part been lost or destroyed. The best accounts of most English trials, therefore, come from the pamphlets that provide a narrative of the trial and summarize the evidence presented against the witch. The following narrative recounts the trial of Elizabeth Sawyer, a witch from the village of Edmonton, near London, in 1621. Like many English witches Sawyer, a poor woman who was deformed in body, imposed upon her neighbors by asking them for charitable assistance. She was suspected of performing various *maleficia*, including the death of Agnes Ratcliffe and other unnamed children and cattle.

The trial also serves as a commentary on the legal procedures used in English trials. First, as in all English witchcraft trials, the outcome was decided by a jury. In this case the jurors brought in a verdict of guilty on the charge that she had bewitched Agnes Ratcliffe to death but not on the other charges of *maleficia*. Secondly, the jury convicted Sawyer without having secured a confession, which was unnecessary at English law. After the trial, however, Henry Goodcole, the minister who wrote the account of the trial, extracted a confession from Sawyer with great difficulty, and that confession was read at the time of her execution. Third, the trial reveals the limited role of diabolism in English witchcraft prosecutions. The only reference to the Devil in the trial appears in the charge that she harmed people with the Devil's help, which was provided by the imps or familiars who sucked blood from the small teat found on her body. All other

190

references to the demonic nature of her crime appear in the confession secured, with leading questions, by Goodcole.

The trial owes its fame not only to the widespread circulation of this pamphlet but to a contemporary play written by William Rowley and Thomas Dekker, first performed in December 1621 and published in 1658. The play draws directly on this published account of the trial. The author of the pamphlet also reports that ballads sung after the trial, to which he objected, attributed additional activities to Elizabeth Sawyer.

Source: Henry Goodcole, *The Wonderful Discoverie of Elizabeth Sawyer, a Witch, late of Edmonton, her conviction and condemnation and death* (London, 1621).

A true declaration of the manner of proceeding against Elizabeth Sawyer, late of Edmonton, spinster, and the evidence of her conviction.

A great and long suspicion was held of this person to be a witch, and the eye of Mr. Arthur Robinson, a worthy Justice of the Peace, who dwelleth at Tottenham near to her, was watchful over her and her ways, and that not without just cause; still, having his former long suspicion of her, by the information of her neighbours that dwelt about her; from suspicion to proceed to great presumptions, seeing the death of nurse children and cattle strangely and suddenly to happen. And to find out who would be the author of this mischief, an old ridiculous custom was used, which was to pluck the thatch of her house and burn it, and it being burned, the author of such mischief should presently then come. And it was observed and affirmed to the court that Elizabeth Sawyer would presently frequent the house of them that burnt the thatch, which they plucked of her house, and come without any sending for.

This trial, though it was slight and ridiculous, yet it settled a resolution in those whom it concerned, to find out by all means they could endeavour her long and close carried witchery, to explain it to the world; and being descried to pay in the end such a worker of iniquity her wages, and that which she had deserved (namely, shame and death) from which the Devil, that had so long deluded her, did not come as she said to show the least help of his unto her to deliver her, but being descried in his ways and works, immediately he fled, leaving her to shift and answer for herself, with public and private marks on her body as followeth:

1. Her face was most pale and ghost-like without any blood at all, and her countenance was still dejected to the ground.

2. Her body was crooked and deformed, even bending together, which so happened but a little before her apprehension.

3. That tongue which by cursing, swearing, blaspheming, and imprecating, as afterward she confessed, was the occasioning cause of the Devil's

access unto her, even at that time, and to claim her thereby as her own, by it discovered her lying, swearing and blaspheming, as also evident proofs produced against her, to stop her mouth with truth's authority. At which hearing she was not able to speak a sensible or ready word for her defence but sends out in the hearing of the judge, jury, and all good people that stood by many most fearful imprecations for destruction against herself then to happen, as heretofore she had wished and endeavoured to happen on divers of her neighbours, the which the righteous Judge of Heaven, whom she thus invocated, to judge then and discern her cause did reveal.

Thus God did wonderfully overtake her in her own wickedness to make her tongue the means of her own destruction, which had destroyed many before.

And in this manner, namely, that out of her false swearing the truth whereof she little thought should be found, but by her swearing and cursing blended, it thus far made against her that both judge and jury, all of them grew more suspicious of her, and not without great cause, for none that had the fear of God or any the least motion of God's grace left in them would, or durst, to presume so impudently with execrations and false oaths to affront justice.

On Saturday, being the fourteenth day of April, Anno Dom. 1621, this Elizabeth Sawyer, late of Edmonton, in the county of Middlesex, spinster, was arraigned and indicted three several times at Justice Hall in the Old Bailey in London in the parish of St Sepulchers, in the ward of Farrington Without, which indictments were, *viz.*:

That she the said Elizabeth Sawyer, not having the fear of God before her eyes, but moved and seduced by the Devil, by diabolical help did out of her malicious heart (because her neighbours where she dwelt would not buy brooms of her) would therefore thus revenge herself on them in this manner, namely, witch to death their nurse children and cattle. But for brevity's sake I here omit forms of law and informations.

She was also indicted for that she, the said Elizabeth Sawyer, by diabolical help and out of her malice afore-thought, did witch unto death Agnes Ratcliffe, a neighbour of hers, dwelling in the town of Edmonton where she did likewise dwell, and the cause that urged her thereunto was because that [Agnes] Ratcliffe did strike a sow of hers in her sight for licking up a little soap where she had laid it, and for that Elizabeth Sawyer would be revenged of her and thus threatened Agnes Ratcliffe that it would be a dear blow unto her, which accordingly fell out and suddenly. For that evening Agnes Ratcliffe fell very sick and was extraordinarily vexed and in a most strange manner in her sickness was tormented. Oath whereof was by this Agnes Ratcliffe's husband given to the court, the time when she fell sick, and the time when she died, which was within four days after she fell sick; and further then related that in the time of her sickness his wife Agnes Ratcliffe lay foaming at the mouth and was extraordinarily distempered, which many of his neighbors seeing as well as himself, bred suspicion in them that some mischief was done against her, and by none else, but alone by this Elizabeth Sawyer it was done, concerning whom the said Agnes Ratcliffe, lying on her death-bed, these words confidently spoke: namely, that if she did die at that time, she would verily take it on her death that Elizabeth Sawyer her neighbour, whose sow with a washing-beetle she had stricken, and so for that cause her malice being great, was the occasion of her death. . . .

The jury hearing this evidence given unto oath by the husband of the above named Agnes Ratcliffe and his wife's speeches relating to them likewise on oath, as she lay on her death-bed, to be truth, that she had said unto her husband; namely, that if she died at that time, she the said Elizabeth Sawyer was the cause of her death and maliciously did by her witchery procure the same.

This made some impression in their minds and caused due and mature deliberation, not trusting their own judgments what to do in a matter of such great import, as life, they deemed might be conserved.

The foreman of the jury asked of Master Heneage Finch, recorder, his direction and advice, whom he Christianlike thus replied, "Do it as God shall put in your hearts."

Master Arthur Robinson, a worshipful justice of the peace dwelling at Tottenham, had often and divers times, upon the complaints of the neighbors against this Elizabeth Sawyer, laboriously and carefully examined her, and still his suspicion was strengthened that doubtless she was a witch. An information was given unto him by some of her neighbors, that this Elizabeth Sawyer had a private and strange mark on her body, by which their suspicion was confirmed against her, and he sitting in the court at the time of her trial informed the Bench thereof, desiring the Bench to send for women to search her presently, before the jury did go forth to bring in the verdict concerning Elizabeth Sawyer whether that she was guilty or no, to which motion of his they most willingly condescended.

The Bench commanded officers appointed for those purposes, to fetch in three women to search the body of Elizabeth Sawyer, to see if they could find such unwonted marks as they were informed of. One of the women's names was Margaret Weaver, that keeps the Sessions House for the City of London, a widow of an honest reputation, and two other grave matrons brought in by the officer out of the street, passing by there by chance, were joined with her in this search of the person named, who fearing and perceiving that she should by that search of theirs be discovered, behaved herself most sluttishly and loathsomely towards them, intending whereby to prevent their search of her. . . . And they all three said, that they a little above the fundament of Elizabeth Sawyer the prisoner, there indicted before the Bench for a witch, found a thing like a teat the bigness of the little finger and the length of half a finger, which was branched at the top like a teat, and seemed as though one had sucked it, and that the bottom thereof was blue and the top of it was red. This view of theirs and answer that she had such a thing about her, which boldly she denied, gave some insight to the jury of her, who upon their consciences returned the said Elizabeth Sawyer to be guilty by diabolical help of the death of Agnes Ratcliffe only, and acquitted her of the other two indictments. And thus much of the means that brought her to her deserved death and destruction.

I will address to inform you of her preparation unto death, which is alone pertinent to my function, and declare unto you her confession verbatim, out of her own mouth, delivered to me the Tuesday after her conviction, though with great labour it was extorted from her, and the same confession I read unto her at the place of execution, and there she confessed to all people that were there, the same to be most true, which I shall here relate.

And because it should not be thought that from me alone this proceeded, I would have other testimony thereof to stop all contradictions of so palpable a verity, that heard her deliver it from her own mouth in the chapel of Newgate the same time.

A true relation of the confession of Elizabeth Sawyer, spinster, after her conviction of witchery, taken on Tuesday, the 17th day of April, anno 1621, in the gaol of Newgate, where she was prisoner, then in the presence and hearing of divers persons whose names to verify the same are here subscribed to this ensuing confession made unto me, Henry Goodcole, minister of the word of God, ordinary and visitor for the goal of Newgate. In dialogue manner are here expressed the persons that she murdered and the cattle that she destroyed with the help of the Devil.

In this manner was I forced to speak unto her because she might understand me and give unto me answer according to my demands, for she was a very ignorant woman.

Question. By what means came you to have acquaintance with the Devil, and when was the first time that you saw him, and how did you know that it was the Devil?

Answer. The first time that the Devil came unto me was, when I was cursing, swearing, and blaspheming. . . .

Question. What said you to the Devil, when he came unto you and spake unto you, were you not afraid of him if you did fear him, what said the Devil then unto you?

Answer. I was in very great fear, when I saw the Devil, but he did bid me not to fear him at all, for he would do me no hurt at all but would do for me whatsoever I should require of him. And as he promised unto me, he always did such mischief as I did bid him to do, both on the bodies of Christians and beasts. If I did vex them to death, as oftentimes I did so to bid him, it was then presently by him so done. . . .

Question. Of what Christians and beasts, and how many were the number that you were the cause of their death, and what moved you to prosecute them to the death?

Answer. I have been by the help of the Devil the means of many Christians' and beasts' death. The cause that moved me to do it was malice and envy, for if anybody had angered me in many manner, I would be so revenged of them, and of their cattle. And [I] do now further confess that I was the cause of those two nurse-children's death for the which I was now indicted and acquitted by the jury.

Question. Whether did you procure the death of Agnes Ratcliffe for which you were found guilty by the jury?

Answer. No, I did not by my means procure against her the least hurt.

Question. How long is it since the Devil and you had acquaintance together, and how oftentimes in the week would he come and see you and you company with him?

Answer. It is eight years since our first acquaintance and three times in the week the Devil would come and see me, after such his acquaintance gotten of me. He would come sometimes in the morning and sometimes in the evening.

Question. In what shape would the Devil come unto you?

Answer. Always in the shape of a dog and of two collars, sometimes of black and sometimes of white.

Question. What talk had the Devil and you together when that he appeared to you, and what did he ask of you, and what did you desire of him?

Answer. He asked me when he came unto me how I did and what he should do for me, and demanded of me my soul and body, threatening then to tear me in pieces if that I did not grant unto him my soul and my body which he asked of me.

Question. What did you after such the Devil's asking of you to have your soul and body, and after this his threatening of you, did you for fear grant unto the Devil his desire?

Answer. Yes, I granted for fear unto the Devil his request of my soul and body, and to seal this my promise made unto him. I then gave him leave to suck of my blood, the which he asked of me.

Question. In what place of your body did the Devil suck of your blood, and whether did he himself choose the place or did yourself appoint him the place? . . .

Answer. The place where the Devil sucked my blood was a little above my fundament, and that place chosen by himself; and in that place by continual drawing, there is a thing in the form of a teat, at which the Devil would suck me. And I asked the Devil why he would suck my blood, and he said it was to nourish him.

Question. Whether did you pull up your coats or no when the Devil came to suck you?

Answer. No, I did not, but the Devil would put his head under my coats, and I did willingly suffer him to do what he would.

Question. How long would the time be that the Devil would continue sucking of you, and whether did you endure any pain the time that he was sucking of you?

Answer. He would be sucking of me the continuance of a quarter of an hour, and when he sucked me, I then felt no pain at all. . . .

Question. By what name did you call the Devil, and what promises did he make to you?

Answer. I did call the Devil by the name of Tom, and he promised to do for me whatsoever I should require of him. . . .

Question. Did the Devil at any time find you praying when he came unto you, and did not the Devil forbid you to pray to Jesus Christ but to him alone? And did not he bid you pray to him the Devil, as he taught you?

Answer. Yes, he found me once praying, and he asked of me to whom I prayed, and I answered him to Jesus Christ, and he charged me then to pray no more to Jesus Christ, but to him the Devil, and he the Devil taught me this prayer: *Santibicetur nomen tuum.* Amen.

Question. Were you ever taught these Latin words before by any person else, or did you ever hear it before of any body, or can you say any more of it? . . .

Answer. No, I was not taught it by anybody else, but by the Devil alone; neither do I understand the meaning of these words, nor can speak any more Latin words.

Question. What moves you now to make this confession? Did any urge you to it, or bid you do it? Is it for any hope of life you do it?

Answer. No, I do it to clear my conscience, and now having done it, I am the more quiet and the better prepared and willing thereby to suffer death, for I have no hope at all of my life, although I must confess, I would live longer if I might.

Figure 9 Elizabeth Sawyer, the witch of Edmonton. Sawyer conformed to the stereotype of the witch as an old woman who was dependent upon the community. Her trial and confession is recounted above in Chapter 38. From Henry Goodcole, *The Wonderful Discoverie of Elizabeth Sawyer, a Witch, late of Edmonton, her conviction and condemnation and death* (London, 1621).

39

THE CONFESSIONS
OF JOHANNES JUNIUS
AT BAMBERG,
1628

The witch-hunt conducted in the German city of Bamberg between 1626 and 1630 was one of the most intense in all of Europe. More than 630 people were accused of witchcraft, and many of them were executed. Prominent among the victims was Johannes Junius, the mayor of the city. The trials at Bamberg were noteworthy not only for the number of victims, but also for the pattern of accusations. The practice of torturing confessing witches to name their accomplices was widespread in Europe, and at Bamberg it had a snowball effect, driving up the number of accused at an alarming rate. As this occurred, the witches conformed less and less to the traditional stereotype of an old, poor woman. By the time the trials ended this stereotype broke down completely, and prominent citizens, including Junius, were sucked into the web of accusations, tortured, and forced to confess. The account of this trial reveals the way in which torture, if applied without restraint, was able to force innocent people to confess to witchcraft. The case of Junius is unique, however, in the survival of a letter written to his daughter, explaining how torture and the threat of further torture forced him to confess and to name a number of innocent accomplices.

Source: *The Witch Persecutions*, ed. George L. Burr (Philadelphia, 1902), pp. 23–28.

On Wednesday, June 28, 1628, was examined without torture Johannes Junius, Burgomaster at Bamberg, on the charge of witchcraft: how and in what fashion he had fallen into that vice. Is fifty-five years old, and was born at Niederwaysich in the Wetterau. Says he is wholly innocent, knows nothing of the crime, has never in his life renounced God; says that he is wronged before God and the world, would like to hear of a single human being who has seen him at such gatherings [as the witches' sabbaths].

Confrontation of Dr. Georg Adam Haan. Tells him to his face that he will stake his life on it, that he saw him, Junius, a year and a half ago at a witch-gathering in the electoral council-room, where they ate and drank. Accused denies the same wholly.

Confronted with Hopffens Elsse. Tells him likewise that he was on Haupts-moor at a witch-dance; but first the holy water was desecrated. Junius denies. Hereupon he was told that his accomplices had confessed against him, and was given time for thought.

On Friday, June 30, 1628, the aforesaid Junius was again without torture exhorted to confess, but again confessed nothing, whereupon, . . . since he would confess nothing, he was put to the torture, and first the

Thumb screws were applied. Says he has never denied God his Saviour nor suffered himself to be otherwise baptized; will again stake his life on it; feels no pain in the thumbscrews.

Leg-screws. Will confess absolutely nothing; knows nothing about it. He has never renounced God; will never do such a thing; has never been guilty of this vice; feels likewise no pain.

Is stripped and examined; on his right side is found a bluish mark, like a clover leaf, is thrice pricked therein, but feels no pain and no blood flows out.

Strappado. He has never renounced God; God will not forsake him; if he were not such a wretch he would not let himself be so tortured. God must show some token of his innocence. He knows nothing about witchcraft. . . .

On July 5, the above named Junius is without torture, but with urgent persuasions, exhorted to confess, and at last begins and confesses:

When in the year 1624 his law-suit at Rothweil cost him some six hundred florins, he had gone out, in the month of August, into his orchard at Friedrichsbronnen; and as he sat there in thought, there had come to him a woman like a grass-maid, who had asked him why he sat there so sorrowful; he had answered that he was not despondent, but she had led him by seductive speeches to yield him to her will. . . . And thereafter this wench had changed into the form of a goat, which bleated and said: "Now you see with whom you have had to do. You must be mine or I will forthwith break your neck." Thereupon he had been frightened, and trembled all over for fear. Then the transformed spirit had seized him by the throat and demanded that he should renounce God Almighty, whereupon Junius said: "God forbid," and thereupon the spirit vanished through the power of these words. Yet it came straightway back, brought more people with it, and persistently demanded of him that he renounce God in Heaven and all the heavenly host, by which terrible threatening he was obliged to speak this formula: "I renounce God in Heaven and his host, and will henceforward recognize the Devil as my God."

After the renunciation he was so far persuaded by those present and by the evil spirit that he suffered himself to be otherwise baptized in the evil spirit's name. The Morhauptin had given him a ducat as dower-gold, which afterward became only a potsherd.

He was then named Krix. His paramour he had to call Vixen. Those present had congratulated him in Beelzebub's name and said that they were now all alike. At this baptism of his there were among others the aforesaid Christiana Morhauptin, the young Geiserlin, Paul Glaser. After this they had dispersed.

At this time his paramour had promised to provide him with money and from time to time to take him to other witch gatherings. . . . Whenever he wished to ride forth [to the witch-sabbath] a black dog had come before his bed, which said to him that he must go with him, whereupon he had seated himself upon the dog, and the dog had raised himself in the Devil's name and so had fared forth.

About two years ago he was taken to the electoral council-room, at the left hand as one goes in. Above at a table were seated the Chancellor, the Burgomaster Neydekher, Dr. Georg Haan [and many others]. Since his eyes were not good, he could not recognize more persons.

More time for consideration was now given him. On July 7 the aforesaid Junius was again examined, to know what further had occurred to him to confess. He confesses that about two months ago, on the day after an execution was held, he was at a witch-dance at the Black Cross, where Beelzebub had shown himself to them all, and said expressly to their faces that they must all be burned together on this spot, and had ridiculed and taunted those present. . . .

Of crimes. His paramour had immediately after his seduction demanded that he should make away with his younger son Hans Georg, and had given him for this purpose a gray powder; this, however, being too hard for him, he had made away with his horse, a brown, instead.

His paramour had also often spurred him on to kill his daughter . . . and because he would not do this he had been maltreated with blows by the evil spirit.

Once at the suggestion of his paramour he had taken the holy wafer out of his mouth and given it to her. . . .

A week before his arrest, as he was going to St Martin's Church, the Devil met him on the way, in the form of a goat, and told him that he would soon be imprisoned, but that he should not trouble himself – he would soon set him free. Besides this, by his soul's salvation, he knew nothing further; but what he had spoken was the pure truth; on that he would stake his life. On August 6, 1628, there was read to the aforesaid Junius that his confession, which he then wholly ratified and confirmed, and was willing to stake his life on it. And afterward he voluntarily confirmed the same before the court.

[So ended the trial of Junius, and he was accordingly burned at the stake. But it so happens that there is also preserved in Bamberg a letter, in quivering hand, secretly written by him to his daughter while in the midst of his trial (July 24, 1628):]

Many hundred thousand good-nights, dearly beloved daughter Veronica. Innocent have I come into prison, innocent have I been tortured, innocent must I die. For whoever comes into the witch prison must become a witch or be tortured until he invents something out of his head and – God pity me – bethinks him of something. I will tell you how it has gone with me. When I was the first time put to the torture, Dr. Braun, Dr. Kötzendörffer, and two strange doctors were there. Then Dr. Braun asks me, "Kinsman, how come you here?" I answer, "Through falsehood, through misfortune." "Hear you," he says, "you are a witch; will you confess it voluntarily? If not, we'll bring in witnesses and the executioner for you." I said, "I am no witch, I have a pure conscience in the matter; if there are a thousand witnesses, I am not anxious, but I'll gladly hear the witnesses." Now the chancellor's son was set before me . . . and afterward Hoppfen Elss. She had seen me dance on Haupts-moor . . . I answered. "I have never renounced God, and will never do it – God graciously keep me from it. I'll rather bear whatever I must." And then came also – God in highest heaven have mercy – the executioner, and put the thumb-screws on me, both hands bound together, so that the blood ran out at the nails and everywhere, so that for four weeks I could not use my hands, as you can see from the writing. . . . Thereafter they first stripped me, bound my hands behind me, and drew me up in the torture. Then I thought heaven and earth were at an end; eight times did they draw me up and let me fall again, so that I suffered terrible agony . . . And this happened on Friday, June 30, and with God's help I had to bear the torture. . . . When at last the executioner led me back into the prison, he said to me: "Sir, I beg you, for God's sake confess something, whether it be true or not. Invent something, for you cannot endure the torture which you will be put to; and even if you bear it all, yet you will not escape, not even if you were an earl, but one torture will follow after another until you say you are a witch. Not before that," he said, "will they let you go, as you may see by all their trials, for one is just like another." . . .

And so I begged, since I was in wretched plight, to be given one day for thought and a priest. The priest was refused me, but the time for thought was given. Now, my dear child, see in what hazard I stood and still stand. I must say that I am a witch, though I am not – must now renounce God, though I have never done it before. Day and night I was deeply troubled, but at last there came to me a new idea. I would not be anxious, but, since I had been given no priest with whom I could take counsel, I would myself think of something and say it. It were surely better that I just say it with mouth and words, even though I had not really done it; and afterwards I would confess it to the priest, and let those answer for it who compel me to do it. . . . And so I made my confession as follows; but it was all a lie.

201

Now follows, dear child, what I confessed in order to escape the great anguish and bitter torture, which it was impossible for me longer to bear.

[*Here follows his confession, substantially as it is given in the minutes of his trial. But he adds*:]

Then I had to tell what people I had seen [at the witch-sabbath]. I said that I had not recognized them. "You old rascal, I must set the executioner at you. Say – was not the chancellor there?" So I said yes. "Who besides?" I had not recognized anybody. So he said: "Take one street after another; begin at the market, go out on one street and back on the next." I had to name several persons there. Then came the long street. I knew nobody. Had to name eight persons there. Then the Zinkenwert – one person more. Then over the upper bridge to the Georgthor, on both sides. Knew nobody again. Did I know nobody in the castle – whoever it might be, I should speak without fear. And thus continuously they asked me on all the streets, though I could not and would not say more. So they gave me to the executioner, told him to strip me, shave me all over, and put me to the torture. "The rascal knows one on the market-place, is with him daily, and yet won't name him." By that they meant Dietmeyer, so I had to name him too.

Then I had to tell what crimes I had committed. I said nothing . . . "Draw the rascal up!" So I said that I was to kill my children, but I had killed a horse instead. It did not help. I had also taken a sacred wafer, and had desecrated it. When I had said this, they left me in peace.

Now, dear child, here you have all my confession, for which I must die. And they are sheer lies and made-up things, so help me God. For all this I was forced to say through fear of the torture which was threatened beyond what I had already endured. For they never leave off with the torture till one confesses something; be he never so good, he must be a witch. Nobody escapes, though he were an earl. . . .

Dear child, keep this letter secret so that people do not find it, else I shall be tortured most piteously and the jailers will be beheaded. So strictly is it forbidden . . . Dear child, pay this man a dollar. . . . I have taken several days to write this: my hands are both lame. I am in a sad plight . . .

Good night, for your father Johannes Junius will never see you more. July 24, 1628.

[*And on the margin of the letter he adds*:]

Dear child, six have confessed against me at once: the Chancellor, his son, Neudecker, Zaner, Hoffmaisters Ursel, and Hoppfen Elsse – all false, through compulsion, as they have all told me, and begged me for forgiveness in God's name before they were executed . . . They know nothing but good of me. They were forced to say it, just as I myself was.

40

THE WITCH-HUNT
AT EICHSTÄTT, 1637

The territory of Eichstätt in southern Germany was the center of intense witch-hunting beginning in 1617, and in 1637 a series of trials took place that resulted in scores of executions. Like many witchcraft trials throughout Europe, the first step in this particular prosecution was the taking of depositions from neighbors, but after fifteen of these depositions were recorded, the court took the initiative and, using torture, obtained the rest. Although it is unclear how all the original accusations were initiated, the ruling elite took control of the proceedings and used the tactics of secret interrogations and torture to secure confessions and convictions. The following transcript of the interrogation of an unnamed woman in 1637 provides a vivid illustration of how the court was capable of extracting the confessions that it expected.

Source: The account comes from a book written in 1811, from which the names of all the parties were removed and indicated simply by "N.N." It was reprinted in the Appendix to Hugo J. J. Zwetsloot, *Friedrich Spee und die Hexenprozesse* (Trier, 1954), pp. 310–318.

Present: the Herr Chancellor, the Herr Municipal Judge, the Herr Doctor, the Herr Secretary, and the Herr Recorder.

Monday, 15 November 1637.
    After serious consideration by the civil councillors of the court, the prisoner, N.N. commonly known as N.N., having been taken into custody on suspicion of witchcraft, and on fifteen sworn depositions, meriting death, is thoroughly examined as follows:
    Q. What is her name?

A. N.N., aged forty years, does not know the names of either her father or mother, or when they were born, or where they were brought up, or when they died. She has lived with her husband twenty-three years, and during that time has borne eight children, five of whom are still living. Of the three deceased, one died of smallpox twenty-one years ago; another died eight or nine years ago at the age of six, on acount of which she was told to appear at the town hall because of these suspicious circumstances of death; and the third had died six years ago, also of smallpox.

Q. Whether she knows the reason why she was ordered to appear at the town hall?

A. She knows of no reason other than the accusation of being a witch.

Q. That is true: otherwise she would not have been brought here. Therefore she should make a start at admitting her guilt, and not look round for any excuses.

A. She will suffer anything, but cannot admit that she is a witch.

Then the judges exhort her as strongly as possible to confess, but all is in vain; so the prepared list of depositions and completed indictment are read to her and specifically discussed.

While the first deposition is being read to her, she laughs heartily at the charge and declares she prefers death. She replies how could she have done anything when she had not been anywhere. She admits she might possibly have been guilty of the second denunciation. Regarding denunciations 3, 4, 5 and 6 she says that never during her entire life has she been at a sabbat. Says she has no knowledge of denunciations 7, 8, 9, 10 and 11. Again, to denunciations 12, 13, 14 and 15, she denies again any participation.

Thus, although she is in no way answerable or responsible for these charges, yet again she states she will gladly accept death.

Q. Whether she wishes to die like a witch?

A. Whatever God wishes, that is her wish too.

Q. Indeed. Therefore she should start making her confession and tell how long she has been engaged in this vice, and how she was first enticed into it.

A. Yes, your Lordships, I shall willingly go wherever you wish, but I am not a witch, as true as Christ was tortured and made to suffer.

Then she is examined for the Devil's mark, which is found on the right side of her back, near the shoulder blade, about the size of a half-kreutzer. Then, the mark is pricked and found to be insensitive; however, when she is pricked in other places, she immediately behaves as if she is mad. Many more suspicious marks are observed. She is questioned:

Q. Where did these Devil's marks come from?

A. She does not know. Moreover, the Devil had nothing to do with her.

Inasmuch as the accused does not respond to merciful treatment, she is brought into the torture chamber.

Evidence taken down in the torture chamber.

After being tied to the pulley [the strappado], and hoisted up a little, she says, that, yes, she could be a witch, yet when released, she announces she is not a witch. Therefore she is pulled up somewhat higher, and then a second and third time, and then released on the admission that she is a witch. But immediately she becomes stubborn and denies she is a witch. Then again she is pulled even more tightly on the ropes. She confesses that fourteen years ago, when she was unmarried, she had become a witch.

Q. But since she had testified that she had been married for twenty-three years, how could it be only fourteen years ago that she became a witch?

A. At this, she asked to be let down, when she would tell the truth.

Q. No, she must first begin confessing; she deserves to remain as she is.

When she finds out that she is not going to be released, she says that about eighteen years ago, once her husband had come home drunk and wished the Devil would take her (at that time she had just given birth to another child) and her children, young and old alike. And she thought, Oh, when would he come! Oh, soon! And at one time she had an illicit love affair with a hangman, and the Devil presented himself the next day during the night in the guise of the same hangman. In fact, he arrived during the first night, but since a light was burning continuously, therefore he could not get anywhere with her. And since she was under the impression that he was the hangman, the next night about ten o'clock she had intercourse with him, and his member was very cold. After having had intercourse a second time, the Devil revealed who he was, talking lewdly, and demanded that she give herself to him, and renounce God and our dear Lady and all the saints. He threatened her so she had to submit to him, but now she was penitent and wanted to turn to God again.

Q. Whether the Devil did not demand anything more of her?

A. To do evil everywhere.

Q. What methods was she supposed to employ to work evil?

A. Eight days after her seduction the Devil gave her a green powder and a black ointment in an earthen dish, which she used on man and beast.

Q. Whether she still had any of this material?

A. No, she threw it into the water four weeks ago.

Q. Whether she had been forewarned of her impending arrest?

A. No, nothing beyond what her sister had warned her.

Q. Whether she had flown also with her sister?

A. No. But they have seen each other at the Devil's sabbath.

Q. What did the Devil call her, and what name did she call the Devil?

A. She called the Devil *Gokhelhaan* [rooster] and he called her *Shinterin* [bone-breaker]. Three weeks after her seduction, the Devil baptized her and poured something over her head.

Q. Is all that she is saying true?

A. Yes.

She is led out of the torture chamber.

Tuesday, 16 November 1637.

Present: the Deputies, the Herr Municipal Judge, the Herr Doctor, and the Herr Recorder. The accused is brought in and the usual prayers are read.

Q. Whether she could truly confirm with heart and mouth what she had confessed yesterday?

A. Yes, and her whole confession as previously given is true. She said, moreover, she is afraid that because of her great sins she cannot pray to God any more. The Devil made her obey him by beating her often and severely. Only last night she twice heard a rustling sound in her cell. Even now during this examination she hears rustling sounds.

Q. The court then gave her good advice how to protect herself from the wicked enemy and insure her salvation.

A. Yes this is true. If she had remained outside the Church, she would never have found salvation. If it is the will of God that the whole world should be a witness to her evil doings, she is willing to make a public confession; and she desires to pray for their worships the Herr Chancellor and the Herr Doctor because they ordered her to appear in this court. The Devil often caused her pain while they were in bed together so that she screamed out and awakened her husband, who soon after began to sleep in a separate bed. "O Jesus Christ, be with me, and because I have grievously sinned against thee, please dear God, open your ears again to me."

Q. How often did she receive powder and ointment from the Devil? Whether she had any more powder in her possession?

A. Yes, in her store, to the left as one enters from the alley, there is a box which has four drawers on top; in one of these is the ointment.

After searching the store a court officer found three small boxes of ointment and one box with powder, which he delivered to the town hall.

Q. Whom did she injure with this material?

A. First, about eight or nine years ago, she was ordered by the Devil to smear the ointment on a cherry and give it to her six-year old daughter to eat, intending to poison her. Then the child became ill, and within one hour passed from life to death. As a result of this she was told to appear at the town hall. Incidentally, if her husband had not been so religious, the Devil would have killed him too.

Second, about thirteen or fourteen years ago, one night while her husband was asleep, the Devil sprinkled a powder on him so that he should not wake up, and smeared ointment on his feet and hands, back and neck so that he should die. Within three days her husband got bladder incontinence, which still troubles him to this day. She says she did not confess this crime because, if she confessed, the Devil would appear and give her no peace. . . .

Third, three years ago she mixed the Devil's ointment into a stew and gave it to the four-year-old son of her former mistress. The boy instantly caught the gangrenous plague and died within two days. . . .

Seven, eight years ago she killed her own black cow using a diabolical powder that she mixed in its mash. It was healthy but died within two or three days.

Eighth, six years ago she sprinkled the powder on her brown horse in the name of the Devil, and it collapsed.

Friday, 19 November 1637.

The prisoner is led out again and questioned.

She says and announces publicly that all her life she never saw the Devil nor had intercourse with him. All her previous testimony was false. Neither her conscience nor her devotion and love to Jesus Christ permit her to continue these lies. She reached this decision just last night. If she could have found a knife to thrust into her breast she would have killed herself. Indeed, she had asked the guard to let her have a knife, giving as an excuse that the collar of her smock was too tight and she wanted to loosen it.

The judges listened to this revocation and recognized her stubborn devilish heart. Her eyes were red as if the Devil had tried to pull them out of their sockets. The hangman was ordered to stretch her on the ladder. Soon after, she asked to be released and promised to tell everything she had done during her life.

Q. Is her preceding testimony true?

A. Yes, unfortunately, not only this but everything else she will reveal.

Q. What was the cause of her revocation?

A. The Devil visited her last night at twelve o'clock and fornicated with her and commanded her to deny everything she had testified previously, saying he would help her, whereupon she was released from the thought of renewed torture.

Saturday, 20 November 1637.

. . . Q. How often then during each month and each year did she go out? Where did she go, and for what purpose?

A. Twice a month, twenty-four times a year, on a pitchfork that the Devil brought to her, which was always smeared with an ointment. She could mount the fork only in the kitchen, the bedroom, hall, or loft, where the Devil met her, so that she could not awaken her husband, and so the Devil sprinkled a powder over him. Whenever she wanted to depart for the sabbath, she recited this charm: "Whoosh! Up the chimney, up the window hole! In the name of the Devil, out and onward!" The Devil always sat in front, and she sat behind. While riding the pitchfork, the Devil emitted fiery streams so that she could see very little. The assembly places, so far as she knew, were the pasture, the gallows, and the mountain. At first it seemed they had lots to eat and drink, roasts and stews, served in green dishes. But the food was insipid as well as moldy, completely black, very sweet, indistinguishable, and badly prepared. She never saw bread or salt, and she drank white wine from wooden or clay cups. The wine was brought in pitchers or leather skins. They sat on seats and benches as well as on the gallows. During the meal they blasphemed God and plotted how to commit *maleficia*. . . .

These departures occurred on Thursday and Saturday nights at ten and twelve o'clock, according to the season of the year. The place was illuminated by lights held by poor old women; she herself had once held a light by her arm in the midst of them. After that the dancing began. The chief devil was seated in an easy chair, and special honor was paid him by curtsying with their backsides. After dancing round together in no set pattern, couples paired off to commit lewdness on the side. She thought the musicians were pipers and fiddlers, but she did not know any of them. About fifty people, some wearing masks, attended these assemblies. . . . They all sat at a round table. But when a general assembly took place, the witches were so numerous that they could not be counted. When the time for departure came, the chief devil said, "Whoosh! Away with you, in the name of the Devil." They left in the same way they came. Specifically she saw the following at the diabolical meals: . . .

{*During the following days, to November 26, the accused identified 45 accomplices. For every person named, she described characteristic clothing and actions, and the attendant incubus and succubus*}

Friday, 26 November 1637.

The accused says that during the time she was under the influence of the Devil she had been to confession and had received holy communion fifteen times. But fourteen years ago, while receiving communion, she put the sacred host into a handkerchief and took it home and threw it away into a horrible place. Twelve years ago she had dishonored the sacred host in the same way.

Six years ago, when she had received communion, she retained the sacred host in her mouth and took it into her garden and placed it on the cover of the well. She stabbed it with a knife many times until the holy and pure blood ran out; then she threw it with a little cloth into the well. Instead of saying her prayers she prayed that thunder and hail might bring on destruction. . . .

She is suspected of storm-raising and passing through locked doors in to cellars.

Saturday, 27 November 1637.

The accused said she had thought about storm-raising for a long time, and had helped cause eight tempests. The first storm she had made fifteen years ago, between midday and one o'clock, in her own garden, spurred on by the Devil to make the fruit drop so that it would not ripen, and this had in fact occurred.

Q. With what materials did she raise storms, or how else did she do it? . . .

A. She says that the Devil supplied her with a powder made from children's corpses and told her to use it for raising storms.

Friday, 3 December 1637.

She says that once, seven, eight or nine years ago, she helped [a named person] exhume her own child from the cemetery. This child had already lain in the grave for six years, and its body had completely decayed. They took the remains home, stirred them for two days and nights, then put them in a pot, pounded them into a powder, and gave it to the Devil. . . .

Saturday, 11 December 1637.

She passed through closed doors into the wine cellars of [five names given] about forty times. Also present were two witches, identified by name, who drank wine from the measure or right from the casks.

Q. What other crimes can she think of, and are there other things she can remember? This question is discussed.

A. No, but what she has testified is the truth, for which she is responsible before God and the world. She wishes to live and die according to this testimony and be justified by the verdict of the court. Whereupon she is led back to the torture chamber and the list of accomplices is read to her, and she confirms it.

Friday, 17 December 1637.

She dies penitent.

41

THE TRIAL OF
JANET BARKER AND
MARGARET LAUDER
AT EDINBURGH, 1643

Witchcraft prosecutions in Scotland were much more numerous than in neigh-boring England, and they claimed many more lives. It is estimated that whereas as few as 500 witches were executed in England, as many as 1500 Scottish witches perished. When the trials of Scottish witches were conducted by local authorities on the basis of commissions granted by the Privy Council, more than 90 percent of those tried were executed. Even when the trials were conducted in the Court of Justiciary in Edinburgh, as this trial was, more than half of those accused were convicted and executed. One reason for the high intensity of witch-hunting in Scotland was the use of torture – almost always applied illegally – at the time of the witches' arrest. The ability of the Lord Advocate to bring charges against witches by his own authority, without the approval of a grand jury, also facilitated successful prosecution. The main difference between Scotland and England in this regard, however, was that Scottish witches were often charged with worshipping the Devil collectively and having sex with him. This contributed to the growth of large witch-hunts, which occurred at various intervals in Scottish history. One of those large hunts took place in 1643, when Scotland had already experienced a revolution and its armies had just entered the English Civil War on the side of the English Parliament. The trial of Janet Barker and Margaret Lauder before the Justiciary Court is typical in its emphasis on the demonic aspect of the crime of witchcraft rather than on the witches' exercise of malefi-cent magic. The only reference to *maleficium* in this case is the report that Janet Barker cured George Scott of a grievous sickness inflicted on him by another witch, Janet Cranstoun. Scottish words have been anglicized or their equivalents inserted in brackets. Punctuation and capitalization have also been modernized.

Source: The transcript of the trial is preserved in the National Archives of
Scotland, JC 2/8, pp. 347–349.

The same day, viz. The 28 of December 1643, Janet Barker and Margaret
Lauder, indwellers in Edinburgh, being entered upon panel, delated, accused
and pursued by dittay at the instance of Thomas Hope of Craighall, knight
baronet, Advocate of our sovereign Lord for his Highness's interest, of the
crimes of sorcery and witchcraft and keeping company with Satan, the enemy
of man and woman their salvation, specified in their dittay, viz. – For as
much as by the divine law of the almighty God, mentioned in his sacred
word, all users and practisers of witchcraft, sorcery, charming and sooth-
saying, or keeping of company, trysts, or meeting with the Devil or his
wicked instruments are ordained to be punished to the death, and such by
divers Acts of Parliament of this kingdom, namely the 73 Act of the
Parliament of our sovereign lord's dearest grandmother, Queen Mary of good
memory [1563], it is stated and ordained that no manner of person or persons,
of whatsoever estate, condition or degree they be of, presume nor take upon
hand to use any manner of witchcraft, sorcery, nor necromancy, nor give
themselves out to have any such craft or knowledge thereby to abuse His
Majesty's good subjects and people, and that no person or persons seek any
help, response or consultation from the Devil or any of his wicked instruments, uses and abuses foresaid, under the pain of death, as in the said laws
and acts of parliament at length is contained. Notwithstanding whereof, it
is of verity that the said Janet Barker, understanding that the son of George
Scott was visited with a grievous sickness, which was laid about him by the
late Janet Cranstoun, a witch and her door neighbour, come to the young
youth the said John Scott his son, and by her sorcery, witchcraft and charming
practised by her upon him, cured him of the said sickness or evil that was
laid upon him, which the said Janet Barker has confessed by her depositions.

Likewise she has confessed and declared that her first acquaintance with
the Devil was by the said the late Janet Cranstoun her [means] and induce-
ment; and that the said Janet Barker and the said Janet Cranstoun had divers
meetings with the Devil, who at his first meeting with the said Janet Barker
desired her to be his servant, and that she should be as trimly clad as the
best servant in Edinburgh and that he would give her a red wyliecoit [waist-
coat] or red kirtle [gown] and that thereupon she condescended to be his
servant for half a year if he would keep promise, and that she refused the
red kirtle and was content to take a white plaid coat or white wyliecoit.

As also has confessed in her examination that she has had divers times
carnal copulation with the Devil both in her own little shop and in the said
late Janet Cranstoun her house and had ado with him [in her] naked bed,
who was heavy above her like an ox and not like another man; and that after
she had cured the said George Scott's son, the said Janet Barker received
from the Devil a black card, which be the Devil's direction she put under

the said George Scott his door, but noways would confess the cause wherefore that card was put under the said door; and further has granted and confessed that she was the Devil's servant the space of four years and used not oftentimes to keep the kirk [attend church], and when she kept the kirk worst, the Devil come oftenest to her.

As also she confessed that after her coming to the jail or the wardhouse in the New Wark, the Devil appeared to her in the likeness of a dog and forbad her to tell or confess anything, and in so doing nothing should ail her. And further has confessed that the Devil gave her no new name when she agreed to be his servant, but that he gave her his mark upon the back near to her left shoulder; and that she with the said Janet Cranstoun and Margaret Lauder had divers times been in company with the Devil, specially she and the said Margaret Lauder, being within the said Janet Cranstoun's house, two pints of beer were drunk by them there together in the said house, at which the Devil appeared to them in the likeness of a trim gentleman and drank with them all three, and that he embraced the said Margaret Lauder in his arms at the drinking of the beer, and put his arm around her waist.

Likewise seen the said Janet Barker her taking and examination upon her former witchcraft, James Scobie, indweller in Musselburgh, being sent for and brought in before the said Janet Barker, as he that had knowledge in finding and trying out the Devil's mark, he found out the same mark betwixt her shoulders, in the which he did thrust a long pin, the which pin waited sticking in the said mark the space of three quarters of an hour, and yet the said pin was noways felt sensible by the said Janet, and at the outdrawing thereof she confessed that not only she herself but also the said late Janet Cranstoun had received the Devil's mark about the same part where her mark was marked. . . .

And likewise the said Margaret Lauder, being indicted and accused . . . that at her first meeting with the Devil he desired of her to be her servant, which she yielded unto, but in her examination [before the kirk-session] she cursed the time that she ever knew the said late Janet Cranstoun or saw her, declaring that she was the only woman that made that unhappy acquaintance. And further the said Margaret Lauder has confessed in her depositions that the Devil did lie with her and had carnal dealing with her, but at her first meeting with him, and that before they departed asunder she knew and took him up to be the Devil . . .

Upon the which seventh day of December instant the said Margaret Lauder in her deposition confessed that at the time when the Devil got a promise of her to become his servant, he desired her to renounce her baptism, which she then did and promised to quit Christ and become the Devil's servant. Likewise in her examination the said day the said Margaret, being demanded how long it was since the Devil had last lain with her, she confessed that six or seven weeks ago the Devil come and lay with her after a beastly manner, like a dog. . . .

After the reading of the which two dittays and their accusation of the heinous crimes foresaid mentioned thereunto, which was confessed judicially by the said Janet Barker to be of verity but denied and past from by the said Margaret Lauder, albeit clearly verified by her confession specified in her deposition produced by His Majesty's advocate for proving thereof, the Justice, finding the same relevant, referred the dittays above written and crimes therein contained to the knowledge of an assize . . . They removed to the assize house [where] all in one voice they . . . found them guilty. For he which cause the Justice, by the mouth of Patrick Barrie, dempster of court, determined and adjudged the said Janet Barker and Margaret Lauder and either of them, to be taken to the Castle Hill of Edinburgh and there to be wired to a stake until they be dead, and thereafter their bodies to be burnt in ashes, as culpable and convicted of the said crimes; which was pronounced for judgment.

42

A RUSSIAN WITCH-TRIAL
AT LUKH, 1657

Witchcraft prosecutions took place in all European countries including Russia, known during the early modern period as Muscovy. In the autumn of 1657 the townspeople of the provincial town of Lukh, northeast of Moscow, submitted a petition to their local town governor, Nazarii Alekseev, complaining that a number of their wives had been bewitched (literally, "spoiled") with malevolent curses. They now were suffering from a particular form of magical affliction, called *klikushestvo*, translated as "shrieking" or "spirit possession." All official business in Muscovy was conducted by petition, usually addressed directly to the Tsar, but actually submitted to local authorities or central administrative agencies. Thus most of these court documents are framed as petitions. In keeping with Russian custom, petitioners usually referred to themselves as slaves or orphans of the emperor. This case appears to have been the largest and most lethal of all the witchcraft incidents of the seventeenth century in Russia. Different forms of the same proper name, such as the nickname Tereshka for Terentei, have been standardized to some extent.

Source: *Rossiiskii gosudarsvennyi arkhiv drevnikh aktov*, trans. and ed. Valerie A. Kivelson fond 210, opis' no. 13, ed. khr. 300, fols 39–40, 54–56, 58, 61–68 (folios presented here out of order).

To the Tsar Sovereign and Grand Prince Aleksei Mikhailovich, Sovereign of all Great, Small and White Russia!

I, Petrushka Vasil'ev, of the town of Lukh, petition you. Sovereign, I want to lodge a complaint against Lukh townsman Terentei, son of Kalinii Malakurov. In this year 7166 (1657) on St Nicholas Day Terentei bewitched my wife, Irinitsa. He cast a shrieking curse on her, motivated by some unknown grudge or scheme. Merciful Sovereign, Tsar and Grand Prince Aleksei Mikhailovich of all Great and Small and White Russia Sovereign,

214

favor me, your orphan! Order Terentei interrogated to see what he was scheming when he bewitched my wife or what grudge he had against us. Tsar, Sovereign, have mercy!

In response to this petition, Tereshka Malakurov and his wife were interrogated to see what he was scheming when he bewitched Petr Maslenikov's wife and during the interrogation in the torture chamber, in sight of the instruments of torture, he did not incriminate himself and said nothing.

Clerks of the central chancellery in Moscow routinely summarized the cases that came to them from the provinces and collected all of the relevant documents, gluing them together and rolling them up into a long scroll. The clerks' notes introduce petitions and documents sent from Lukh.

In the chancellery was written out:

In past year, 1657, [Lukh Governor] Nazarii Alekseev wrote to the tsar. A bewitchment had broken out in Lukh, afflicting the wives of towns people with magical bewitchment and hiccupping and racking pain, and all kinds of bestial cries. In that bewitchment they accused Lukh townspeople Tereshka Malakurov, Igoshka and Ianka Salautin, Fedka Kuzmin, and Tereshka Malakurov's wife, Olenka. They also accuse Prince Ivan Khvorostinin's peasant Ianka Erokin and the monastic peasant Arkhipko Fadeev.

The case proved to be too difficult for the local governor to handle, so a special investigator, Ivan Romanchiukov, was dispatched to conduct the investigation. He sent a report on the situation to Moscow, explaining all the steps he had taken, and then appended transcripts of the interrogation of the suspects.

To Sovereign Tsar and Grand Prince Aleksei Mikhailovich, Sovereign of all Great, Small and White Russia!

Your slave Ivashka Romanchiukov petitions you. I, your slave, was ordered to go to Lukh because [the town governor] Nazarii Alekseev had written to you from Lukh saying that in the town of Lukh, the female sex was suffering from a terrible magical affliction, and the townspeople of Lukh had petitioned you [about the bewitchment of their wives]. And they accuse some townsmen of Lukh, Igoshka and Ianka Salautin and Tereshka Malakurov, and Fedka Kuzmin of causing that criminal witchcraft and bewitchment. And they also accuse the monastic peasant Arkhipko Fadeev and Prince Ivan Khvorostinin's peasant from . . . Lukh Province, Ianka Erokhin.

And I, your slave, having arrived in Lukh according to your sovereign order, took the townspeople's bewitched wives . . . and asked them who had bewitched them. And they, Sovereign, in their testimony didn't accuse anyone of having bewitched them, saying that they didn't know. I also interrogated the Lukh townspeople, and they didn't accuse anyone either. In their report they only said that they had petitioned to you, Great Sovereign. . . . , about Lukh townspeople Ignashka and Ianka Salautin and Tereshka Malakurov and Fedka Vasilev, and Prince Ivan Fedorovich Khvorostinin's

215

peasant Ianka Erokhin and the monastery peasant Arkhipko Fadeev because the bewitched people cry out their names when they are stricken with their affliction. And the bewitched people have no memory of what they cry [during their affliction].

So I, your slave, tortured Ignashka Salautin and his comrades without mercy, and after three rounds of torture, he, Ignashka, still said nothing to incriminate himself or the others. But with torture, his comrades Tereshka Malakurov and Ianka Salautin and the monastic peasant Arkhipko Fadeev admitted to that criminal witchcraft. They confessed that they had bewitched all those townspeople of Lukh of the male sex and of the female sex. During torture, Tereshka Malakurov also accused his wife, Olenka. He admitted that he had taught his wife to practice witchcraft. His wife, Olenka, also confessed under torture that she had bewitched people with her husband, Tereshka. Tereshka also confessed, under torture, that the townsman Fedka Vasilev and Prince Ivan Khvorostinin's peasant Ianka Erokhin were in league with them. I questioned him, Tereshka about whom else he had taught to practice witchcraft, but even with torture he did not confess anything more, and said he had not taught anyone other than his wife.

Having been tortured, the monastic peasant Arkhipko Fadeev said that he had not taught criminal witchcraft to anyone except Ianka Salautin, and he confessed that they bewitched people together. He denied knowing about any other witchcraft. And they did not say which people they had bewitched, but Arkhipko said that his uncle, called Eremka Kiianov, taught him. His uncle was a peasant who belonged to Temka Fedorov Belianikhin. And Arkhipko said that Tereksha Malakurov was taught by Prince Fedor Nikitin Boriatinskoi's peasant, a horse-healer called Oska. Arkhipko said that he could not remember Oska's father's name, and anyway, both of those men, their teachers, died long ago. I investigated widely to find out about Oska and Eremka, and in investigation, [local residents] said that Oska drank himself to death with wine, and Eremka died.

And in September of this year 1658, Ivan Romanchiukov wrote [to the tsar] from Lukh and sent the interrogation speeches of the suspects.

Transcript of the interrogation of Tereshka Malakurov, townsman of Lukh.

In his interrogation Tereshka Malakurov said he had never bewitched any townspeople and he didn't heal the sick, or he would heal without taking any money: he eased hernias and quieted blood-flow with words. He learned those words in the village of Malechkino 20 years ago from a horse-healer, but what the horse-healer was called, he cannot remember. And he says that horse-healer died.

And Tereshka Malakurov was tortured about his magical criminality three times, burned with pincers.

With the first application of torture, he said he had tried to cure the wife of Priest Matvei of the Church of the Resurrection, and townsman Fedor

Stepanov's daughter-in-law and he took money from them for the healing, but he wasn't able to heal them and the priest's wife died of that illness.

And with the second round of torture he began to incriminate himself more. He learned witchcraft from that same horse-healer Oska, on the estate of Prince Fedor Boriatinskoi in the village of Malechkino, and he said that the horse-healer died. And he said this was his third year bewitching people with criminal witchcraft. He said his spells over salt and then swept that bewitched salt along the streets and at intersections of roads, and he set his spells loose on the wind, so whoever [they touched] would be overcome with melancholy and would begin to cry out with all kinds of voices, and others will hiccup and bite themselves. . . . But he bewitched people because he hoped to cure the bewitched and thereby earn a living and feed himself.

With the third torture he accused himself further. He bewitched the townsman Fedka Marteanov and his wife Matrenka, and also the widow Tatianka, and Ofronska, Fedka Martynov's daughter-in-law, and Arinka, Petrushka Maslenikov's wife, and Matrenka, Senka Belianinov's wife, and Dashka, Isachka Sidorov's wife, and Ogrofonka, Kiriusha Tretiakov's wife, and Fedorka, Sershka Tretiakov's wife. He bewitched all the bewitched people in Lukh with salt, and he sent forth that bewitched salt with his wife, and his wife bewitched people as he had taught her. And Ianka Erokhin and Fedka Vasilev also bewitched people with him, all of them together.

Five local officials and five prison guards testified against Tereshka. They said Tereshka told them that when he fell asleep, there came to him in his sleep many people and there was noise, and they suffocated him, Tereshka, but who the people were who came to him he doesn't remember.

Transcript of the interrogation of Olenka, wife of Tereshka Malakurov.

And in questioning and with [the first application of] torture Tereshka Malakurov's wife Olenka didn't confess anything about bewitchment against herself or her husband.

And with the second torture she accused herself. She had bewitched some townspeople's wives: Fedka's widow and Shelma's daughter-in-law, Tanka, Kiriushka Tretiakov's wife, Fedorka, Fedka Martynov's wife, Matrenka and his daughter-in-law, Ofroska, Petrushka Maslenikov's wife, Irinka, with salt, and she learned that witchcraft from her husband Tereshka, but she hadn't taught anyone herself.

Transcript of the interrogation of the monastic peasant Arkhipko Fadeev.

The peasant Arkhipko Fadeev was tortured twice without mercy and burned with pincers and crushed in his secret places with pincers. And with torture he confessed that he had healed little children of hernias and blood-flow and he fended off evil magic at weddings and cured two townsmen of impotence, and he tied off hernias.

And Arkhipko Fadeev after torture and on another day confessed that he had tied off a hernia on Ianka Salautin. And he had bewitched some townspeople: Mikishka Molchanov's wife and Fedor Lydin's daughter-in-law, and he doesn't remember any others. He released his spells to the wind, and in houses, and he learned to bewitch people from his uncle, Eremka, and [from him he learned] how to release spells and which wind will carry the bewitchment and bring trembling and chills and racking pain and crying out.

Arkhipko Fadeev was tortured a third time and with torture confessed that he bewitched [people], and he bewitched them with three words. Whomever he would look in the face, would be bewitched. He confessed that he taught witchcraft to Ianka Salautin and that Igoshka Salautin had asked him for spells so that his cows wouldn't stray or scatter, but he didn't give him the spell, and he didn't teach him that witchcraft and he doesn't know anything against him.

Transcript of the interrogation of Krestinka, Arkhipko Fadeev's wife.

And Arkhipko's wife Krestinka in interrogation and with torture said her husband whispers spells over little children, cured Ianka Salautin of a hernia by tying it off, but she didn't confess anything against herself.

Transcript of the interrogation of Ianka Salautin, townsman of Lukh.

Ianka Salautin was tortured twice without mercy and burned with pincers and crushed in his secret places with pincers.

With the first torture he said that Arkhipko Fadeev had tied off a hernia on him but he said that the bewitched people have not accused him of bewitchment and have not cried out against him.

But with the second torture Ianka Salautin confessed that he had bewitched [some people]. He set spells loose in the wind and in smoke. Whomever he looks in the face, even if from afar, will be struck by that bewitchment. And Ianka Erokhin and Fedka Vasilev went to Tereshka to learn, but he didn't teach anyone any witchcraft. Ianka said nothing to incriminate his brother Igoshka. He said he had learned magical bewitchment from Arkhipko Fadeev.

Conclusion of the case: Conviction, Sentencing, and Execution.

By your sovereign order, I, your slave Ivashka Romanchiukov, took those brigands, Tereshka Malakurov, Ianka Salautin, and monastic peasant Arkhipka Fadeev and Tereshka Malakurov's wife Olenka, and I publicly proclaimed their guilt in the presence of many people on a market day. I then ordered Tereshka and Ianka and Arkhipko executed by beheading, and Tereshka's wife Olenka I ordered buried in the earth. And I have investigated in full truth and have carried out everything fully, according to your sovereign order. I am writing to you, Great Sovereign, as you ordered me, about everything that has been done, and which people will be executed. And I will remain in Lukh until you order otherwise.

And for criminal witchcraft, Tereshka Malakurov, Ianka Salautin, and Arkhipka Fadeev had their sentences carried out: their heads were cut off. But Tereshka's wife Olenka was buried in the earth.

43

THE SALEM
WITCHCRAFT TRIALS,
1692

The witch-hunt that took place at Salem, Massachusetts in 1692 is one of the most famous episodes in the history of witchcraft. As the only major witch-hunt in the British North American colonies, it has been the subject of voluminous scholarship and has also provided the setting for Arthur Miller's play, *The Crucible*. The case began when a group of young girls, some of whom were in the household of Samuel Parris, the Puritan minister of Salem Village, began to experience the symptoms of demonic possession. These girls ultimately named a number of women as the source of their affliction, claiming to see their specters as they experienced fits and convulsions. The girls' accusations spread outside of Salem village, and other residents of the area also brought charges against their neighbors. The total number of persons who were formally accused reached 164. A special criminal court was set up to try the accused, and those trials led ultimately to the conviction of 30 witches, of whom 19 were executed. Doubts about the guilt of those executed led to a reconsideration of the procedures used to discover and prosecute the accused, and the governor of the colony stopped the trials suddenly in the autumn of 1692. The following year the Salem jurors who had convicted the witches admitted that they had been mistaken, although the attainders passed on seven of those convicted were not lifted until 2001. The following excerpts come from the trial records of three of the accused witches: Tituba, Bridget Bishop, and Susannah Martin.

Tituba, an Indian woman who was a member of the Parris household, may have instilled the fear of witchcraft among the afflicted girls. Her confession, laced with ideas drawn from widely circulated European witch-beliefs, gave credence to the suspicion of the residents of Salem village that the afflictions of the girls were the result of witchcraft. Tituba remained in prison during the entire episode and might very well have been executed at the end of the trials, but she was released in the general pardon given by the governor. The second set of documents concern Bridget Bishop, who professed her innocence but who was executed after her conviction by the jury. She was convicted on the basis of depositions from witnesses, including not only the afflicted girls, but others who made her the scapegoat of their misfortunes. The depositions of John and William Bly formed the basis of the charge that Bishop practised image magic using puppets that were found in her house. The third accused witch was Susannah Martin, who had been prosecuted as a witch in 1669 but had been discharged without trial. Her reputation as a witch, however, made her vulnerable to accusation when the Salem witch-hunt began. The proceedings against her began with an effort to identify her as a cause of the afflicted girls' fits, but other witnesses accused her of performing other *maleficia*, including the affliction of Elizabeth Brown with a distemper and attacking Robert Browner in the shape of a cat. Susannah Martin was one of the nineteen witches executed at Salem.

Source: *Salem Witchcraft Papers: Verbatim Transcripts of the Legal Documents*, ed. Paul Boyer and Stephen Nissenbaum (New York, 1977), 3: 746–749, 753; 1: 85–87, 94–95, 101, 103; 2: 553, 558–559, 564, 572, 573–574, 575.

1. Tituba

Tituba, an Indian woman brought before us by Constable Joseph Herrick of Salem upon suspicion of witchcraft by her committed according to the complaint of Joseph Hutcheson and Thomas Putnam, etc., of Salem Village, as appears per warrant granted [at] Salem 29 February 1691/2. Tituba, upon examination and after some denial, acknowledged the matter of fact according to her examination given in more fully will appear and who also charged Sarah Good and Sarah Osborne with the same. Salem Village, March the 1st, 1691/2 . . .

Examination of Tituba

HATHORNE: Tituba, what evil spirit have you familiarity with?
TITUBA: None
H: Why do you hurt these children?
T: I do not hurt them.
H: Who is it then?
T: The devil for ought I know.
H: Did you never see the devil?
T: The devil came to me and bid me serve him.
H: Who have you seen?
T: Four women sometimes hurt the children.

H: Who were they?

T: Goody Osborne and Sarah Good and I do not know who the others were. Sarah Good and Osborne would have me hurt the children, but I would not. (She further saith there was a tall man of Boston that she did see.)

H: When did you see them?

T: Last night at Boston.

H: What did they say to you?

T: They said hurt the children.

H: And did you hurt them?

T: No, there is four women and one man. They hurt the children and lay all upon me, and they tell me if I will not hurt the children, they will hurt me.

H: But did you not hurt them?

T: Yes, but I will hurt them no more.

H: Are you not sorry you did hurt them?

T: Yes.

H: And why then do you hurt them?

T: They say hurt children or we will do worse to you.

H: What have you seen?

T: A man come to me and say serve me.

H: What service?

T: Hurt the children, and last night there was an appearance that said, "Kill the children," and if I would not go on hurting the children they would do worse to me.

H: What is this appearance you see?

H: Sometimes like a hog, sometimes like a great dog.

H: What did it say to you?

T: The black dog said serve me, but I said I am afraid. He said if I did not, he would do worse to me.

H: What did you say to it?

T: I will serve you no longer. Then he said he would hurt me, and then he looks like a man and threatens to hurt me. (She said that this man had a yellow bird that kept with him) and he told me he had more pretty things that he would give me if I would serve him.

H: What were these pretty things?

T: He did not show me them.

H: What else have you seen?

T: Two rats, a red rat and a black rat . . .

H: What did they say to you?

T: They said serve me.

H: When did you see them?

T: Last night, and they said serve me, but she said I would not.

H: What service?

T: She said hurt the children.

H: Did you not pinch Elizabeth Hubbard this morning?
T: The man brought her to me and made me pinch her.
H: Why did you go to Thomas Putnam's last night and hurt his child?
T: They pull and haul me and make [me] go.
H: And what would [they] have you do?
T: Kill her with a knife.

(Lieutenant Fuller and others said at this time when the child saw these persons and was tormented by them, that if she did complain of a knife, that they would have her cut her head off with a knife.)

H: How did you go?
T: We ride upon sticks and are there presently.
H: Do you go through the trees or over them?
T: We see nothing but are there presently.
H: Why did you not tell your master?
T: I was afraid. They said they would cut off my head if I told.
H: Would you have not hurt others if you could?
T: They said they would hurt others but they could not.
H: What attendants hath Sarah Good?
T: A yellow bird and she would have given me one.
H: What meat did she give it?
T: It did suck her betweeen her fingers. . . .
H: Did you not hurt hurt Mr. Currin's child?
T: Goody Good and Goody Osborne told that they did hurt Mr. Curren's child and would have had me hurt him too, but I did not.
H: What hath Sarah Osborne?
T: Yesterday she had a thing with a head like a woman with two legs and wings. (Abigail Williams, that lives with her uncle Mr. Parris, said that she did see the same creature and it turned into the shape of Goody Osborne.)
H: What else have you seen with Goody Osborne?
T: Another thing hairy. It goes upright like a man. It hath only two legs.
H: Did you not see Sarah Good upon Elizabeth Hubbard last Saturday?
T: I did see her set a wolf upon her to afflict her.

(The persons with this maid did say she did complain of a wolf. She further said that she saw a cat with Good at another time.)

H: What clothes doth the man go in?
T: He goes in black clothes, a tall man with white hair, I think.
H: How doth the woman go?
T: In a white hood and a black hood with a top knot.
H: Do you see who it is that torments these children now?
T: Yes, it is Goody Good. She hurts them in her own shape.
H: And who is it that hurts them now?
T: I am blind now; I cannot see. . . .

223

(The children having fits at this very time, she was asked who hurt them. She answered Goody Good, and the children affirmed the same, but Hubbard being taken in an extreme fit after she was asked who hurt her, and she said she could not tell, but said they blinded her and would not let her see, and after that was once or twice taken dumb herself.)

2. Bridget Bishop

Examination of Bridget Bishop. April 19, 1692.

(Bridget Bishop, being now coming in to be examined relating to her accusation of suspicion of sundry acts of witchcrafts, the afflicted persons are now dreadfully afflicted by her, as they do say.)

MR. HATHORNE: Bishop, what do you say, you stand here charged with sundry acts of witchcraft by you done upon the bodies of Mercy Lewes and Ann Putnam and others?

BISHOP: I am innocent. I know nothing of it. I have done no witchcraft.

H: Look upon this woman and see if this be the woman that you have seen hurting you. Mercy Lewes and Ann Putnam and others do now charge her to her face with hurting of them. What do you say now you see they charge you to your face?

B: I never did hurt them in my life. I did never see these persons before. I am innocent as the child unborn.

H: Is not your coat cut?

B: Answers no, but her garment being looked upon, they find it cut or torn two ways. Jonathan Walcott saith that the sword that he struck at Goody Bishop with was not naked but was within the scabbard, so that the rent may very probably be the very same that Mary Walcott did tell that she had in her coat by Jonathan's striking at her appearance.
The afflicted persons charge her with having hurt them many ways and by tempting them to sign the devil's book, at which charge she seemed to be very angry and shaking her head at them, saying it was false. They are all greatly tormented [as I conceive] by the shaking of her head.

H: Goody Bishop, what contract have you made with the devil?

B: I have made no contract with the devil. Anne Putnam saith that she calls the devil her God.

H: What say you to all this that you are charged with? Can you not find in your heart to tell the truth?

B: I do tell the truth.

MERCY LEWES: Oh, Goody Bishop, did you not come to our house the last night, and did you not tell me that your master made you tell more than you were willing to tell?

H: Tell us the truth in this matter. How come these persons to be thus tormented and to charge you with doing?

B: I am come here to say I am a witch to take away my life.

H: Who is it that doth it if you do not? They say it is your likeness that comes and torments them and tempts them to write in the book. What book is [it] that you tempt them with?

B: I know nothing of it. Am innocent.

H: Do you not see how they are tormented? You are acting witchcraft before us. What do you say to this? Why have you not an heart to confess the truth?

B: I am innocent. I know nothing of it? I am no witch. I know not what a witch is.

H: Have you not given consent that some evil spirit should do this in your likeness?

B: No, I am inocent of being a witch. I know no man, woman or child here.

MARSHALL HERRICK: How came you into my bed chamber one morning and asked me whether I had any curtains to sell? (She is by some of the afflicted persons charged with murder)

H: What do you say to these murders you are charged with?

B: I am innocent. I know nothing of it. (Now she lifts up her eyes, and they are greatly tormented again)

H: What do you say to these things here horrible acts of witchcraft?

B: I know nothing of it. I do not know whether [there] be any witches or no.

H: No, have you not heard that some have confessed?

B: No, I did not.

(Two men told her to her face that they had told her here she is taken in a plain lie. Now [that] she is going away, they are dreadfully afflicted. Five afflicted persons do charge this woman to be the very woman that hurts them.)

Samuel Gray of Salem, aged about 42 years, testifieth and saith that about fourteen years ago, he going to bed well one one Lord's Day at night, and after he had been asleep some time, he awakened and looking up, saw the house light as if a candle or candles were lighted in it and the door locked, and that little fire there was raked up. He did then see a woman standing between the cradle in the room and the bedside and seemed to look upon him. So he did rise up in his bed and it vanished or disappeared. The he went to the door and found it locked, and unlocking and opening the door, he went to the entry door and looked out and then again did see the same woman he had a little before seen in the room and in the same garb she was in before. Then he said to her, "What in the name of God do you come for?" Then she vanished away, so he locked the door again and went to bed, and between sleeping and waking he felt something come to his mouth or lips cold, and thereupon started and looked up again and did see the same woman with some thing between both her hands holding before his mouth upon which she moved. And the child in the cradle gave a great screech out as if it was greatly hurt and she disappeared, and taking the child up could not quiet it in some hours from which time the child that was before a very lively, thriving child did pine away and was never well, although it lived some months after, yet in a sad condition and so died. Some time after within a week or less he did see the same woman in the same garb and clothes that appeared to him as aforesaid, and although he knew not her nor her name before, yet both by the countenance and garb doth testify that it was the same woman that they now call Bridget Bishop, alias Oliver, of Salem. Sworn Salem, May 30th 1692.

June 12th 1692 John Bly, senior, aged about 57 years and William Bly, aged about 15 years, both of Salem, testifieth and saith that being employed by Bridget Bishop, alias Oliver, of Salem to help take down the cellar wall of the old house she formerly lived in, we the said deponents in holes of the said old wall belonging to the said cellar found several puppets made up of rags and hog's brissels with headless pins in them with the points outward, and this was about seven years past.

Marty Warren, aged 20 years or thereabouts testifieth and saith that severall times after the nineteenth day of April last when Bridget Bishop alias Oliver who was in the gaol at Salem, she did appear to this deponent tempting her to sign the book and oft times during her being in chains said thoiugh she could not do it, she would bring one that should do it, which now she knows to be Mr. [Cary] that then came and afflicted her. Sworn to us this the 1 day of June 1692.

3. Susannah Martin

Examination of Susannah Martin 2 May 1692.

As soon as she came into the meeting house, many fell into fits

Hath this woman hurt you?

Abigail Williams said it is Goody Martin; she hath hurt me often. Others by fits were hindered from speaking.

Elizabeth Hubbard said she had not hurt her. John Indian said he never saw her. Mercy Lewes pointed at her and fell into a fit. Ann Putnam threw her glove in a fit at her.

What do you laugh at it?

Well I may at such folly.

Is this folly, to see these so hurt?

I never hurt man, woman or child.

Mercy Lewes cried out, she hath hurt me a great many times and plucks me down.

Then Martin laughed again.

Mary Walcott said this woman hath hurt her a great many times and pucks me down.

Then Martin laughed again.

Mary Walcott said this woman hath hurt her a great many times.

Susannah Sheldon also accused her of hurting her.

What do you say to this?

I have no hand in witchcraft.

The deposition of William Brown of Salisbury, aged 70 years or thereabout, who testifying saith that about one of two and thirty years ago, Elizabeth his wife being a very rational woman and sober and one that feared God, as was well known to all that knew her, and as prudently careful in her family, which woman going upon a time from her own house towards the mill in Salisbury did there meet with Susannah Martin, the then wife of George Martin of Amesbury. Just as they came together [the] said Martin vanished away out of her sight, which put the said Elizabeth into a great fright, after which time the said Martin did many times afterward appear to her at her house and did much trouble her in any of her occasions, and this continued until about February following. And then when she did come, it was as birds pecking her legs or pricking her with the motion of her wings, and then it would rise up into their her stomach with pricking paion as nails and pins of which she did bitterly complain and cry out like a woman in travail, and after that it would rise up to her throat in a bunch, like a pullett's egg. And then she would turn back her head and say, "Witch, you shan't choke me." In the time of this extremity the church appointed a day of [humiliation] to seek God on her behalf, and thereupon her trouble ceased, and she saw goodwife Martin no more. For a considerable time for which the church instead of the day of humiliation gave thanks for her deliverance, and she came to meeting and went about her business as before. This continued until April following, at which time summonses were sent to the said Elizabeth Brown and Goodwife Osgood by the court to give their evidences concerning the said Martin, and they did before the grand jury give a full account.

After which time the said Elizabeth told this deponent that as she was milking of her cow the said Susannah Martin came behind her and told her she would make her the miserablest creature for defaming her name at the court and wept grieviously as she told it to this deponent.

About two months after this deponent came home from Hamptoon and his said wife would not own him but said that they were divorced and asked him whether he did not meet with one Mr. Bent of Abey in England by whom he was divorced. And from that time to this very day have been under a strange kind of distemper and frenzy incapable of any rational action though strong and healthy of body. He further testifieth that when she came into that condition, this deponent procured Doctors Fuller and Crosby to come to her for her release, but they did both say that her distemper was supernatural and no sickness of body but that some evil person had betwitchced her. Sworn the seventh day of May 1692.

The deposition of Joseph Ring at Salisbury, aged 27 years, being sworn, saith that about the latter end of September last, being in the wood with his brother Jarvis Ring hewing of timber, his brother went home with his team and left this deponent alone to finish the hewing of the piece for him for his brother to carry when he came again. But as soon as his brother was gone there came to this deponent the appearance of Thomas Hardy of the great island at Puscataway, and by some impulse he was forced to follow him to the house of Benovy Tucker, which was deserted and about a half a mile from the place he was at work in, and in that house did appear Susannah Martin of Amesbury and the aforesaid Hardy and another female person which the deponent did not know. There they had a good fire and drink – it seemed to be cider. There continued most part of the night, [the] said Martin being then in her natural shape and talking as if she used to. But towards the morning the said Martin went from the fire, made a noise, and turned into the shape of a black hog and went away, and so did the other. Two persons go away, and this deponent was strangely carried away also, and the first place he knew was by Samuel Woods' house in Amesbury.

The deposition of Robert Downer, of Salisbury, aged 52 years, who testify and say that several years ago Susannah Martin the then wife of George Martin, being brought to court for a witch, the said Downer having some words with her (she at that time attending Mrs. Light at Salisbury), this deponent among other things told her [he] believed she was a witch by what was said or witnessed against her, at which she, seeming not well affected, said that a or some she-devil would fetch him away shortly, at which this deponent was not much moved. But at night as he lay in his bed in his own house alone, there came at his window the likeness of a cat and by and by came up to his bed, took fast hold of his throat, and lay hard upon him a considerable while and was like to throttle him. At length he minded what Susannah Martin threatened him with the day before. He strove what he could and said avoid thou she-devil in the name of the Father and the Son and the Holy Ghost. And then it let him go and slumped down upon the floor and went out the window again.

The deposition of Thomas Putnam, aged 40 years and [Edward Putnam] aged 38 years, who testify and say that we have been conversant with the afflicted persons or the most of them, as namely Mary Walcott, Mercy Lewes, Elizabeth Hubbard, Abigail Williams, Sarah Bibber and Ann Putnam junior and have often heard the aforementioned persons complain of Susannah Martin of Amsbery torturing them, and we have seen the marks of several bites and pinches which they say Susannah Martin did hurt them with, and also on the second day of May 1692, being the day of the examination of Susannah Martin, the aforenamed persons were most grievously tortured during the time of her examination, for upon a glance of her eyes they were struck down or almost choked and upon the motion of her finger we took notes they were afflicted, and if she did but clench her hands or hold her head aside the afflicted persons aforementioned were most grievously tortured, complaining of Susannah Martin for hurting them.

The deposition of Elizabet Hubbard, about 17 years, who testifieth and saith that I have often seen the apparition of Susannah Martin amongst the witches, but she did not hurt me til the second day of May, being the day of her examination. But then she did afflict me most grievously during the time of her examination, for if she did but look personally upon me she would strike me down or almost choke me. And several times since the apparition of Susannah Martin has most grievously afflicted me. Also on the day of her examination I saw the apparition of Susannah Martin go and afflict and almost choke Mary Walcott, Mercy Lewes, Abigail Williams, and Ann Putnam junior.

Part VI

DEMONIC POSSESSION AND WITCHCRAFT

The phenomenon of demonic possession has its own history, but at various times it has intersected with that of witchcraft. There were reports of possession long before witchcraft prosecutions began in the fifteenth century, and they continued long after those prosecutions came to an end in the eighteenth century. But during the period of witch-hunting, especially in the late sixteenth and seventeenth centuries, cases of possession were often attributed to witchcraft. According to early modern demonological theory, a demon could enter a person's body either directly or at the command of a witch. When possession was attributed to witchcraft, its physical symptoms were identified as *maleficia*. Henri Boguet reported in 1598 that in Savoy a countless number of demoniacs claimed that witches were responsible for their affliction (Chapter 16). Two of the witchcraft trials documented in Part IV – those at Lukh in Muscovy (Chapter 42) and at Salem, Massachusetts (Chapter 43) – were prompted by cases of demonic possession.

The symptoms of possessions are not always the same, but they often involve bodily contortions and convulsions, the ability to perform great feats of strength, temporary loss of memory, sight, and speech, lesions on the skin, the vomiting of nails or other foreign objects, insensitivity to pain, a transformation of the victim's personality, knowledge of previously unknown foreign languages, speaking in strange voices, and hallucinations. In some recorded instances of possession in early modern Europe, entire groups of individuals, very often nuns or children, manifested such symptoms. Some of the most famous group possessions took place at Cambrai (1491), Wertet (1550), Rome (1555), Aix-en-Provence (1611), Loudun (1634), Louviers (1647), and Auxonne (1660). All these epidemics suggest that possession could be contagious. All these cases of group possession, moreover, involved charges of witchcraft.

In the Middle Ages the Church relied upon the process of exorcism to cast the demons out of the bodies that they allegedly inhabited. Exorcism was an elaborate ceremony based upon the example of Christ and the apostles. In the long history of the Church it has been intended not just to relieve afflicted persons but also to convert pagans, prove the holiness of the exorcist, or validate the Catholic Church's claim to be the one true church established by Christ. At the time of the Reformation Protestants rejected the Catholic ritual of exorcism but used their own methods of prayer and fasting to drive out demons.

The alleged possession of human beings has always met with a certain amount of skepticism. In the Middle Ages the Church itself required the administration of a series of tests to determine whether a possession was genuine. Skeptics regarding the possibility of possession generally subscribe to one of two general interpretations. The first is that the possessions were counterfeit or fraudulent. Demoniacs, according to this point of view, simulate the effects of possession in order to draw attention to themselves, engage in unconventional, disobedient, or immoral behavior, or retaliate against their enemies. In some cases, according to skeptics, possessed persons allegedly stage such fraudulent exhibitions at the behest of their parents or superiors, or at the very least they respond to promptings by members of their communities, thus acting out a script written by others.

The second interpretation of possession is that the victims, rather than actually being inhabited and controlled by demons, were plagued by some physical, neurological, or psychological disorder. Among the many maladies that have been identified with instances of alleged possession are hysteria, chorea or St Vitus' dance, ergot poisoning, catatonic schizophrenia, and Tourette's syndrome. A medical or psychological explanation of possession, such as that presented by Edward Jorden in Chapter 47, does not rule out the possibility that the victim could also be responding to the promptings of others or using his or her condition to relieve tension or express hostility. Nor does it rule out the possibility that the demoniac actually learned the specific symptoms that were recognized by others as the signs of possession. A person could suffer from a psychiatric illness and at the same time make the symptoms of the disorder conform to those of other demoniacs.

This chapter contains seven documents. In Chapter 44, Johann Weyer's commentary on the possession of the nuns at Wertet in 1550, presents a challenge to the contemporary view that the possession was caused by witchcraft. Weyer, a skeptic regarding the culpability of witches, accepted the reality of some cases of possession. This is followed by contemporary accounts of two individual possessions that took place in France in the late 1590s. The first, the possession of Loyse Maillat in Perche in 1598, led to the prosecution of Françoise Secretain for witchcraft (Chapter 45). The second, that of Marthe Brossier in Romorantin in 1599, who also claimed to have been possessed by the command of another witch, was written by one of the physicians who examined the demoniac and concluded that her possession was fraudulent (Chapter 46). About the same time as these two possessions, an English witch was executed for causing the possession of Mary Glover.

A treatise written by an English physician, Edward Jorden, argued that Glover's affliction was caused by a mental disease (Chapter 47). This is followed by a contemporary account, also written by a skeptical physician, of the collective possession of the nuns at Loudun (Chapter 48). The final two documents concern possession and witchcraft in Protestant communities. The first occurred in Boston, Massachusetts, four years before the famous case of witchcraft and possession at Salem (Chapter 49). The second narrates the possession of a young girl near Paisley, Scotland in 1697 (Chapter 50). Both of those later cases also resulted in the execution of witches for causing the possessions.

44

JOHANN WEYER:
THE POSSESSION OF
THE NUNS AT WERTET,
1550

Johann Weyer (1515–1588) was one of the most famous and most controversial demonologists of the sixteenth century. Born in Brabant, a Dutch province close to the border of Germany, Weyer had strong cultural ties with both German and Dutch culture, and he spelled his name in the Dutch manner (Wier) as well as the German (Weyer). Weyer was an evangelical Protestant who belonged to the same reform tradition as his fellow Dutchman, the Catholic scholar Erasmus of Rotterdam. The recipient of a humanist education, Weyer received his degree in medicine from the University of Paris, and he became the court physician to Duke William of Cleve, Jülich and Berg. While in the duke's service he wrote his most famous book, *De Praestigiis Daemonum*, which became widely known for its skepticism regarding witchcraft. Drawing on the arguments of the canon *Episcopi*, Weyer argued that the pact with the Devil was illusory and that the miserable women who confessed to being witches were afflicted with melancholy. Excerpts from Weyer's treatise illustrating this skepticism appear in Chapter 50. Weyer's skepticism was based not only on his medical knowledge but also on the authority of the Bible, which said nothing about witchcraft in the early modern sense of the word. Weyer never denied, however, the power of the Devil; quite to the contrary, he argued, in the tradition of the canon *Episcopi*, that the Devil was responsible for the illusions that deceived those who confessed to witchcraft. His belief in demonic power made him vulnerable to his more credulous critics, who insisted that if the Devil could deceive witches, he could also make covenants with human beings. Weyer also believed that the Devil could possess people's bodies. Although he dismisses some cases of possession as the result of fraud, he argued that others were genuine. In keeping with his skepticism regarding witchcraft, however, he contended that the Devil possessed the demoniacs directly, not as the result of witchcraft. In this section he argues that the nuns at the convent at Wertet, who were considered to have been bewitched by *Lamiae* (Weyer's word for witches), were actually possessed by the Devil.

Source: *Witches, Devils, and Doctors in the Renaissance: Johann Weyer,*
De praestigiis daemonum, ed. George Mora (Binghamton, NY, 1991),
pp. 304–307.

Some young female religious who were really possessed by demons were thought to be bewitched by Lamiae.

Some nuns cloistered at Wertet in the county of Horn were harassed by demons, and they suffered marvelous and dreadful vexation. They say that the problem started when a poor woman borrowed three pounds of salt (commonly called a quart in our country) during the Lenten season, and repaid almost double that amount at Eastertime. Thereafter little white spheres were found in the dormitory, like sugar-covered seeds but salty to the taste, but the nuns did not eat them, nor did they know whence they had come. Later, in the same place, they observed the entry of something that was groaning like a sick human being; from time to time they also heard a voice urging many of the nuns to get up and to draw near the fire with "her" because she was ill. And when they had arisen to go to the aid of their afflicted sister, they found nothing. Sometimes when they took a chamber pot and tried to urinate in it, it was violently snatched from them and they defiled the bed with urine. On other occasions, they were dragged from their beds by their feet for a distance of several paces, and the soles of their feet were sometimes tickled so much that they feared they would die from excessive laughter. Their torture took many forms; some had pieces of flesh torn from their bodies, while others had their legs, arms, and face wrenched totally backwards. Still others were carried up higher than a man's head and then cast down again. Some were tormented in such a way that, although they had nothing for fifty-two days save turnip soup without bread, they still vomited quantities of a black liquid like writing ink, which was said to be so sharp and bitter that it took a layer of skin off their mouths. And no sauce could be made up which would appeal to them. Once, when the sick women were calm and in good spirits, about thirteen of their male friends came into the convent to cheer them up, and the women fell down from their place at table, voiceless and without understanding, and some of them lay as though dead with their legs and arms contorted. One of the women was raised on high, and although the onlookers laid hold of her and struggled, she was still snatched up over their heads and then hurled down again in such a manner that she was thought to be dead. Later, regaining her senses as though she had been asleep, she returned from the hospital to the convent with no ill effects. Other nuns walked on the base of their shin-bones like [footless ones], not using their feet. (Their feet gave the appearance of being dragged along behind in a sack, as though the ligaments had been greatly loosened.) They would also climb trees like cats, and wriggle down again without any bodily harm. Once also, when the Superior of the convent, whom they address as "Mother," was on the grounds conversing with the noble and most pious Lady Margaret, countess of Buren (may the Father of mercies remember her in the resurrection of the just), flesh was torn from the nun's thigh, and she cried out in pain and was put to bed. Her wound was partly leaden in color and partly black; but it was cured. There was another instance when two of the nuns were sitting together laughing and enjoying themselves and talking about a black cat that had been shut inside a basket in the dormitory by a woman (they mentioned her name) who lived in the town. Their conversation was secretly observed by a third nun, who was a person of sound mind; she and the Superior and two or three other nuns found the basket and opened it up, whereupon the cat jumped out and ran away. As a result, the woman was branded as guilty and thrown into jail on a charge of witchcraft, along with seven other persons, including an elderly matron who, according to the testimony of the poor and of her neighbors, was so merciful and generous to the needy that she was in want herself. When she was subjected to the questioning by the torturer, no amount of torture could force her to admit to the crime. Finally, when the Burgrave offered her the usual sustenance, she said that she was too weak to take food and wanted only something to drink. This was at once provided by the Burgrave; and she then took hold of his robe, slid down against his leg, and breathed her last. Other marvelous things were also witnessed at this convent, and these manifest torments lasted for three years, after which time they were covered in silence.

It cannot be doubted that in fact Satan had possessed these maidens. Thinking that an opportunity for mocking had been conveniently afforded when the woman returned the salt, he strove to impose a belief in witchcraft upon the gullible nuns and to brand an innocent woman with an indelible mark of guilt. He therefore sprinkled about the semblance of seeds – sugar-covered, as it seemed – in order to entice the maidens to taste. But he added a salty flavor, the better to introduce suspicion concerning the woman who had returned the salt. And his attempts succeeded. God allowed him in this power of causing great distress in order that the nuns might be tempted or chastized, or else on account of their lack of belief. They were clearly shown to be of wavering faith, because they referred the causes of their torments not to the will of God but to women. Hence, too, the satanic counsel of the two young religious was originated by the Devil's shrewdness; he directed their lying remarks in order that the stigma of witchcraft might be impressed upon an innocent matron, and in order that the sequence of jail, torture, and death might be set in motion. If the cat was real, no doubt a demon conveyed it thither, yet I am more inclined to believe that it was a demon who had assumed the likeness of a cat. One can also see that precise limits are set upon the demon's power to do injury: even though one young woman appeared to be dead as a result of her being carried on high and cast down headlong, she experienced no injury, and she went off as though she had awakened from sleep.

A similar thing once happened in a convent located not far from Xanten, to some young women living under the strict rules of St Bridget. They were assailed in wondrous ways, many of them leaping up and sometimes bleating and making horrible sounds. Occasionally, too, they were shoved out of their appointed seats in church; and their veils would sometimes be pulled from their heads. Sometimes, too, their gullets were clamped shut so that they could take no food. This dreadful and manifold misfortune lasted up to ten years in many cases. The cause of the tragedy was imputed to a maiden once smitten with love for a young man not deemed worthy of her family by her parents. She was accordingly plunged into deep sorrow, and a demon presented himself to her in the guise of the young man, trying to force her into religious vows. Hearkening to his words, she allowed herself to be shut behind bars. Thus cloistered, she seemed driven by frenzy and she exhibited before all a frightening spectacle, which took many forms. The illness spread like a contagion to many of the nuns, and because of the woman's own confession, they were sure that she was the source of all this wretchedness. She was then arrested and taken away to another area, where she was twice impregnated by the prison guard and bore his offspring. Finally, she was released, and I believe she led out her life free from any suspicion of witchcraft. It was all a delusion engineered by the Devil, whereby she was duped into confessing that she had done deeds which are peculiar to Satan himself. . . .

Some nuns in the convent of Hessenberg at Nijmegen were beset by a demon for several years, as I have heard. He would enter their dormitory by night amidst a sort of whirlwind, and he would seem to play so sweetly upon the lyre and the cithara that the maidens might easily have been induced to dance in chorus. Then, in the form of a dog, he would leap into the bed of one of the nuns, and the suspicion would fall upon her of having committed the "silent sin," as they call it. . . .

I also know of another famous religious community on the borders of the province of Cologne, where eight years ago a demon in the form of a dog ran forth in broad daylight and went up under the inner garments of some religious maidens, and from the outer movements of the habits, gave indications of a sordid sexual skirmish. Demons did the same thing at Hensberg in the duchy of Jülich under the form of cats.

45

HENRI BOGUET: THE POSSESSION OF LOYSE MAILLAT, 1598

One indication of the growing importance of demonic possession in both the theory and practice of witchcraft was the attention given to the phenomenon in the literature of witchcraft. In 1602 Henri Boguet, a judge in the county of Burgundy, chose to begin the second edition of *Discours des Sorciers* [A Discourse on Witches], by discussing a classic case of demonic possession involving witchcraft. In 1598 Françoise Secretain, a poor woman who had asked for lodging in the house of Claude Maillat and Humberte of Coyrieres in Perche, had been accused of sending five devils into Loyse Maillat, the daughter of Claude and Humberte. Secretain confessed not only that she had bewitched this young girl but that she had attended the sabbath, danced with demons, and had copulated with the demon. Boguet used this case to raise the question whether witches could send demons into the body of another person, which he answered in the affirmative. In the concluding chapters of his treatise Boguet returned to the theme of possession, discussing another case of possession and defending the Roman Catholic use of exorcism to drive out demons.

Source: Henry Boguet, *An Examen of Witches*, trans. E. A. Ashwin, ed. Montague Summers (London, 1929), pp. 1–14.

Chapter I. Loyse Maillat, eight years old, is possessed of five devils and later delivered of them and Françoise Secretain made prisoner for casting the spell.

On Saturday the fifth of June in the year 1598 Loyse, the eight-years-old daughter of Claude Maillat and Humberte of Coyrieres in Perche, was stuck helpless in all her limbs so that she had to go on all fours; also she kept twisting her mouth about in a very strange manner. She continued thus afflicted for a number of days, until on the 19th of July her father and mother, judging from her appearance that she was possessed, took her to the Church of Our Saviour to be exorcised. There were then found five devils, whose names were Wolf, Cat, Dog, Jolly and Griffon; and when the priest asked the girl who had cast the spell on her, she answered that it was Françoise Secretain, whom she pointed out from among all those who were present at her exorcism. But as for that day, the devils did not go out of her.

But when the girl had been taken back to her parents' house, she begged them to pray God for her, assuring them that if they fell to their prayers she would quickly be delivered. Accordingly they did so at the approach of night, and as soon as her father and mother had done praying, the girl told them that two of the devils were dead, and that if they persevered with their devotions they would kill the remaining ones also. Her father and mother were anxious for their daughter's health and did not cease praying all night. The next morning at dawn the girl was worse than usual and kept foaming at the mouth; but at last she was thrown to the ground and the devils came out of her mouth in the shape of balls as big as the fist and red as fire, except the Cat, which was black. The two which the girl thought to be dead came out last and with less violence than the three others; for they had given up the struggle from the first, and for this reason the girl had thought they were dead. When all these devils had come out, they danced three or four times round the fire and then vanished; and from that time the girl began to recover her health.

For the rest: Late on the fourth of June Françoise Secretain had come to the house of Loyse Maillat's parents and had asked for lodging for that night. In the absence of her husband, Humberte had at first refused, but had in the end been forced by Françoise's insistence to give her lodging. When she had been received into the house, and Humberte had gone out to attend to her cattle, Françoise went up to Loyse and two of her younger sisters as they were warming themselves by the fire, gave Loyse a crust of bread resembling dung and made her eat it, strictly forbidding her to speak of it, or she would kill her and eat her (those were her words); and on the next day the girl was found to be possessed. Her mother bore witness to her refusal to give Françoise lodging, her father and mother together gave evidence of their daughter's malady, and this was confirmed by the girl, who gave evidence as to all the rest; and although she was so young she was so unshakable in her testimony that she compelled belief just as if she had been thirty or forty years old.

The judge, being fully convinced as to what had happened, had Françoise Secretain seized and put in prison.

Chapter II. The means by which the truth was drawn from Françoise Secretain.

For three days of her imprisonment Françoise Secretain refused to confess anything, saying that she was innocent of the crime of which she was accused and that they did her great wrong to detain her. To look at her, you would have thought she was the best woman in the world; for she was always talking of God, of the Virgin Mary, and of the Holy Saints of Paradise, and she had in her hand a long rosary which she pretended to say without interruption. But the truth is that the Cross of this rosary was defective, and it will be seen that this fact furnished evidence against her.

Further, it was observed that during her examination, although she strove her utmost to do so, she could not shed a single tear. For this reason she was more closely imprisoned, and certain threats were used to her. The following day she was pressed to tell the truth, but without success. Accordingly it was decided to shave off her hair and change her garments, and to search her to see if she were marked in any way. She was therefore stripped, but no mark was found; and when they came to cut the hair of her head, she submitted with the utmost confidence. But no sooner was her hair cut than she grew perturbed and trembled all over her body, and at once confessed, adding to her first confessions from day to day. I shall set down only the principal parts of her confession, following my undertaking to be brief.

Chapter III. The Principal Points in the Confession of Françoise Secretain.

First, that she had wished five devils on Loyse Maillat.

Second, that she had long since given herself to the Devil, who at that time had the likeness of a big black man.

Third, that the Devil had four or five times known her carnally, in the form sometimes of a dog, sometimes of a cat, and sometimes of a fowl; and that his semen was very cold.

Fourth, that she had countless times been to the Sabbat and assembly of witches near the village of Coyrieres in a place called Combes by the water; and that she went there on a white staff which she placed between her legs.

Fifth, that at the Sabbat she had danced, and had beaten water to cause hail.

Sixth, that she and Groz-Jacques Bocquet had caused Loys Monneret to die by making her eat a piece of bread which they had dusted with a powder given to them by the Devil.

Seventh, that she had caused several cows to die, and that she did so by touching them with her hand or with a wand while saying certain words. . . .

Chapter V. Whether it be Possible for One to Send Demons into the Body of Another.

Françoise Secretain confessed in the first place that she had wished five devils on Loyse Maillat; and in the first chapter we have told of the means she used to this end. But it is no easy matter to determine whether a person has the power to send demons into the body of another; there are those who have considered it not to be possible, and it is even said that formerly some maintained this opinion before Pope Paul IV.

The whole truth is that this thing is possible with the permission of God; for we have read that St Paul sent Satan into the body of the Corinthian fornicator, and into Hymenaeus and Alexander the heretics. And David says

241

in Psalm 78 that God "cast upon them the fierceness of His anger, wrath and indignation and trouble, by sending evil angels among them:" a passage which Jean Benedicti, the Franciscan theologian, quotes in his account of Perrenette Pinay in proof of my contention. Thyraeus is also of this opinion in his treatise on demoniacs.

There is no lack of examples. Simon Magus frequently caused those to be possessed who called him sorcerer. Theodoret tells of a young girl who was possessed by means of the spells and enchantments of a sorcerer, though he adds that the Devil betrayed the sorcerer and revealed the whole secret of the matter. Jacques Bocquet wished upon Rollande du Vernois two devils, of whom one was named Cat and the other Devil; and in this case Jacques confirmed the statement which had previously been made by Rollande. This woman was put in prison in the year 1598 under a charge of witchcraft, and after a long imprisonment was in the end burned. Later we shall speak of her fully, as her case deserves. Perrenette Pinay was found to be possessed by six devils, after having eaten at the instigation of a witch an apple and a piece of beef. Another witch sent three devils into the body of Catherine Pontet in the year 1554. The Jews of Rome caused eighty girls and women to be possessed by the Devil; and in the year 1552 the nuns of the Convent of Kendiorp were also tormented in this manner by means of their cook. Caron in his "Antichrist Unmasked" narrates that Catherine Boyraionne sent a number of demons into one Magdelaine, a woman of about twenty-two; and that another old woman cast a devil into one Marie. In each case the devils entered into the possessed by means of some nuts which they ate. Fernel also tells of a man who was thirsty and, for want of water, ate an apple, whereon he was at once possessed by a devil. But of what use is it to linger over such examples? Every day in our own town we continually meet with large numbers of persons who, for the most part, impute their possession to certain Vaudois or sorcerers. The truth is confessed by the devils themselves, being wrung from them by the might and virtue of exorcisms, and of the glorious body of St Claude, who, being descended from the counts of Palatine of Salins, after having governed the archbishopric of Besançon, came to this place to live the life of a hermit until his death in the year 650. By this he gained such favour with Heaven that from that time his body may be seen laid out whole upon the altar of the church in the eternal triumph of countless miracles which are performed upon those who resort to him; and demoniacs especially are every moment being healed by his prayers and intercessions.

46

THE POSSESSION
OF MARTHE BROSSIER,
1599

The alleged possession of the French woman Marthe Brossier in 1599 gained attention in England as well as France. Brossier was the youngest of four unmarried daughters of Jacques Brossier, a draper in Romorantin. In 1598 she claimed to have been possessed as the result of a bewitchment by one of her neighbors. Other recent cases of possession in her village had also led to charges of witchcraft. Marthe Brossier certainly knew of these cases, and the narrative of her possession suggested that she was also familiar with a famous case of possession that had occurred at Laon, France in 1566. This knowledge of other possessions clearly shaped her behaviour as a demoniac, whether or not she was acting fraudulently. Like many cases of French possession, the attempt to exorcise the demoniac supported attempts by Roman Catholics to prove that theirs was the true religion. The case took place just after the Edict of Nantes of 1598 had given Huguenots freedom of worship in France, and Marthe's statements made hostile references to the French Calvinists. Public exorcisms of Marthe at Orléans and Paris had been attended by large crowds and the king, Henry IV, ordered that Marthe and her father be returned to Romorantin, where the local judge was instructed to keep her from travelling to other areas. In December 1599 she was, however, abducted by the prior of a monastery and was taken to Tarascon and Avignon to give further anti-Huguenot performances. From there she went to Rome to see the pope, Clement VIII. She remained in Italy at least until 1604, when she was reported as having convulsions in Milan. This particular narrative, written by the physician Michel Marescot and his colleagues and published by royal command in 1599, argues that the possession was fraudulent, thereby challenging that of a less skeptical group of physicians who had reported on 3 April that Marthe was genuinely possessed.

Source: *A True Discourse upon the Matter of Martha Brossier of Romorantin, Pretended to be Possessed by a Devil*, from Abraham Hartwell (trans.), *Discours veritable sur la faict de Marthe Brossier de Romorantin pretendue demoniaque* (London, 1599), pp. 1–34.

As faith is the gift of God, and a virtue inspired by divinity, whereby we do steadfastly believe such things as do not appear unto us, neither by sense nor by natural reason; so is too great credulity a vice that proceedeth from an infirmity or weakness of a man's mind, and that often times by suggestion of the wicked Spirit. . . . The faith of Christians is greatly commended, but the credulity of magicians is much reprehended, as being so great that it taketh away belief from all things, and is the cause that by believing everything (though never so absurd) in the end men will believe anything at all. Credulous antiquity hath been deceived by the delusions of devils, and drawn to superstition and idolatry, but Christian religion hath been always contrary to such deceits, to the end that the honor of the true God and sincerity of faith might be preserved. . . . This difference of faith and credulity may be showed by many examples of ancient times, but there is none of them more worthy to be written than the history of Martha Brossier of Romorantin, pretended to be possessed with a spirit.

On Tuesday, the 30 of March 1599 at the commandment of the right reverend, the Bishop of Paris, there met together Marescot, Ellain, Hautin, Riolan, and Duret, within the Abbey of Geneussua in the hall of My Lord Abbot, where was brought before them one Martha Brossier, who (they said) was possessed of a wicked spirit, and this was in the presence also of the said Lords the Bishop and the Abbot, and many other persons of note. By the commandment of the said Lord Bishop, Marescot (as the ancientest of the rest) questioned with her in Latin (for the rumour went that she spake all manner of languages) but she answered not a word.

She being back upon her knees praying to God, and making the sign of the cross, presently tumbled herself backward, first upon her buttocks, then upon her back, fetching her breath very deep, and quaking in her flanks (like a horse after he hath run) she turned her eyes in her head, blared out her tongue, and told the bishop that he had not his miter, and bid him that he should go and fetch it. Then they caused certain relics of the very true cross to be brought unto her, which she endured to be put in her mouth. They presented also unto her a doctor's hood, which she stoutly rejected, as though the hood of a divine or the miter of a bishop had more virtue and more divinity in them then the relics of the very cross. . . .

The day following, which was Wednesday the last day of March, Ellain and Duret met together, and when the exorcisms or conjurations were again repeated, the said Martha fell down at the rehearsal of certain words, raised herself up again very lustily, made moves upon the exorcists even to their faces, and nothing else was then done, saving that Duret pricked her with a pin between the thumb and the forefinger. . . .

Upon Thursday the first day of April all mysteries were employed and used; none of the remedies were forgotten that are proper to the driving out of devils. They settled themselves to prayers. She blared out her tongue, turned her eyes, and at the pronouncement of certain words she fell as before and used such motions as they do that are troubled with a convulsion. Yet all these actions seemed to the physicians to be merely counterfeit. The exorcisms or conjurations were begun again, and the woman hearing the words *Et homo factus est*; And he was made man, she labored with all her strength and forces to make her gambols, and being upon her back, in four or five skips removed herself from the altar to the chapel door, which indeed did astonish all the company. . . .

And touching the thesis and general proposition, there was never any doubt of it. For we do believe, according to the Christian faith, that there are devils, that they enter into men's bodies, and that they torment them in sundry sorts, and all whatever the Catholic Church hath determined of their creation, nature, power, effects and exorcisms, we hold to be true, firm and stable, as the Pole of heaven. But touching the hypothesis, that is to say, that Martha Brossier is or hath been possessed of a devil, we say it is absurd, false and without any likelihood. And to prove it we will conclude by this general syllogism:

Major: Nothing ought to be attributed to the Devil that hath not something extraordinary above the laws of nature.

Minor: The actions of Martha Brossier are such as have nothing extraordinary above the laws of nature.

Conclusion. And therefore the actions of Martha Brossier ought not to be attributed to the devil.

Those that are exercised in the knowledge of the signification and equipollence of propositions, and in the art of syllogisms, will confess that it is concluded very well in *secundo modo prima figura*, that is, in the second mode of the first figure. The major or the propositions is very evident and Plato in his *Apology* is of opinion that there are devils because there be so many things whereof a man can give none other reasons but that it is the Devil, as being extraordinary effects and surpassing the forces of nature. The minor or the assumption may be known by an induction of all the actions of the said Martha Brossier For what hath she done? Marry, she hath blared forth her tongue, she hath rolled her eyes in her head, she hath showed divers motions like to convulsions, and being laid upon her back she hath shaken her flanks. There is never a one, I do not speak of these tumblers but even of the very lackeys of the court that cannot do so much. And by this reason that excellent dancer upon the rope was rather to be counted a demoniac and possessed with a devil than she is. Martha therefore hath done no action that we ought to attribute to the Devil, as hereafter shall be more at large declared. Moreover, it is likely that after fifteen months being so often vexed and tormented she should remain fat and in good liking? Considering that even in the gospel it is noted that such as were possessed with devils waxed dry and very slender? We are yet at this day all of us of one mind and opinion that these motions like to convulsions in Martha proceeded not of any sickness or disease, because while she was in them, keeping her eyes half shut and half open, she perceived and saw whatsoever was done, and did of her own free will and power move her eye, and by consequence all her body. Again, such as have a true convulsion indeed use to bite those which come unto them and put their fingers into their mouths. Yes, if a man put a cudgel between their teeth, they will crack it, and withal have their limbs so stark and stiff that they cannot be bended. Martha seeing herself stayed and holden by any, or hearing certain words of the priest, wherewith she was before instructed, lifted herself up lustily, as though she had no fit at all. These motions then proceeded not of any disease and therefore they were counterfeit, as we have always maintained, or else they proceeded from the Devil, as some held opinion grounded upon very slight reason, which we will thoroughly examine. . . .

But let us not rest upon this, seeing we are all agreed that the motions of this proceeded not from any disease, and let us examine the reasons you allege for the Devil.

The first reason is, for that she being pricked very deep with a pin, she never made any semblance that she felt it. Out of all question, when she was but slightly pricked on the side of her neck, she turned herself and felt it indeed. And then father Seraphin used his wonted excuse and said, "Here is nothing else but Martha." Well, a little after, being pricked somewhat deeper, she dissembled her pain. And therefore, has she the Devil in her body? The lackeys of the court, which diverse times will of themselves thrust a pin very deep into some fleshy part, as in the thigh, or in the arm, are they therefore possessed with a spirit? . . .

But you will say that Martha was pricked without any blood following. Assuredly we did see a show and a mark of red. And you must understand that when a pin is pricked directly and uprightly into a fleshy part, wherein there is no notable vein, it will make a very small and narrow hole, out of which blood doth not issue, especially if the blood be earthy and melancholic. Upon such a like argument as yours is, we have seen poor souls condemned to be burned for witches, and afterwards absolved and let go by the judges of the court. A dangerous argument for such witches, yet in this question now in hand much less pricking than a pin. . . . Cease therefore to conclude that Martha was possessed with a devil because she was not moved with the pricking of a pin; conclude rather that she was not possessed because she felt not the pricking. For there is no likelihood in it, and it is a thing incompatible (not agreeing with itself) that the Devil should quite take away the feeling of pain from those whom he meaneth to torment. Nay he would rather augment and increase the same to make them feel the greater pain. . . .

The second reason to prove that Martha was possessed with a devil is that there appeared in her mouth a certain kind of thin foam. Who did ever hear any speech of the Devil's foam? If it be so, there should have been added that it was also black. For all that cometh from him being of hell, must needs be black. Yea, our good old women used to say, "That the Devil hath no white at all in his eye." Who can forbear laughter to hear that a woman is known to be possessed with a spirit by her foam and spittle?

The third reason to prove that Martha was possessed with a spirit is because she had certain marvellous violent motions without any alteration either in her pulse, or in her breathing, or in her colour. . . . Yet this signifieth that her blood was very thick and earthy and so could not easily be kindled. And therefore we say with Gwln that the pulse of such people is very rare. We have sometimes seen sundry melancholic persons, not only many days and months but also many years, to have run up and down crying very strangely and howling like dogs without any change, either in pulse or in breathing or in colour. . . . How many things are there which we do daily see in nature to be far more strange, admirable and incredible which, notwithstanding are not attributed to devils but to the hidden secrets of nature.

The fourth reason, if it were true, would necessarily conclude that is to say, if she had spoken Greek and English, having never before learned either of those languages, it would be a certain and sure argument of her possession with a devil. But that is altogether false. For she never spoke any other language than the French tongue, and the proper speech of Romorantin, although false rumours have been spread abroad thereof to the contrary. But (say they) indeed she never spoke either Greek or English, but she answered to the purpose, when a question was demanded of her in Greek. One asked her [in Greek] "How camest thou into the body?" She answered in French, "For the glory of God." Now the very selfsame question in Greek had been made unto her before at Clery, as master Lieutenant Criminal hath seen in his informations. It is manifest therefore that there was a collusion in it. Besides, she answered not to the purpose, for she was asked the means how he had entered into the body and the answer was made of the end, that is to say, wherefore it entered into the body. . . .

Those that have thought themselves to be somewhat more wise than the rest, as being skillful in the law, and making profession thereof have oftentimes objected against us: "If Martha were not possessed of a wicked spirit, *cui bono?*" Whose benefit was it? . . . The father of Martha was always factious by common report. He saw that his daughter, who, as also the rest of his other children did, was ever reading of books touching devilry, and especially and principally that book of the devil of Laon was a very proper and fit book for these devilish feats and counterfeitings, adding thereunto that many priests, and namely the Theologal of Orleance, by that which she told unto us, confirmed her in this opinion, that she had the Devil in her body. And therefore he carried her to our Lady of Ardiliers to Saulmur, to Angers, to Clery, to Orleance and now at the last to Paris. Whether this were done upon a folly, thinking indeed that his daughter had the Devil in her body, or thereby to make some stir and altercation or covetousness God knoweth, for that belongeth to the parliament to look unto. But the very truth is that many bestowed money on her father, as namely Monsieur de S.M. twenty crowns, others thirty, some more, some less. Yea, her father, being at Paris, went up and down begging money of the churchmen, even of simple religious persons, to bring this holy enterprise to good perfection. And it is not to be doubted but if the matter had fallen out accordingly, there would have been good store of money gained by it, and she should have been carried from house to house to gather a benevolence, as was the mother of Friar Clement, that wicked and cursed apostate and runagate (the friar that murdered King Henry III of France), the remembrance of whom breedeth a horror in my soul. And thus much for those that ask, "*Cui bono?*" Who had benefit by it? . . .

Another pretty trick was that my masters of the clergy in Orleans would needs make experiment of the grand remedy to drive away the Devil, and that is called the perfume. They did set fire to this perfume, and offered those villainous and stinking vapours to her nose, she in the meanwhile being bound to a chair, but her feet at liberty to play withal, and then began she to cry out: "Pardon me. I am choked. He is gone away."

47

EDWARD JORDEN:
DEMONIC POSSESSION
AND DISEASE, 1603

⚊⚊⚊◆◆◆⚊⚊⚊

Edward Jorden, an English physician, became involved in a highly publicized and politicized case of possession in 1602. The case began when Mary Glover, the fourteen-year-old daughter of a London shopkeeper, displayed many of the signs of demonic possession. These included fits, writhing, contortions, loss of consciousness, and falling into trances. Glover accused an old woman, Elizabeth Jackson, with whom she had long been at odds, of having caused her afflictions by means of witchcraft. Jorden was one of four doctors called to testify at Jackson's trial. His argument was that Mary Glover's fits were not caused by supernatural means. He had difficulty proving this point, however, and he did not argue that she was faking the symptoms. With the judge, Edmund Anderson, strongly supporting the prosecution, Jackson was convicted and executed. Her death, however, did not end the controversy over Mary Glover's possession, especially after a group of Puritan preachers dispossessed Mary Glover. This action angered Richard Bancroft, the bishop of London, and his chaplain Samuel Harsnett, both of whom rejected the claims of Catholic and Puritan exorcists that they had a power, received directly from God, to cast out devils. Jorden wrote his treatise to provide scientific support for the arguments Harsnett made in his pamphlet, *A Declaration of Egregious Popish Impostures* (1603). Jorden's position was that the symptoms of possession were caused by disease, not by supernatural, demonic power. The book also made the original claim that Glover's symptoms were attributable to hysteria, then known as the suffocation of the mother, rather than to melancholy.

Source: These excerpts are taken from the dedication of Edward Jorden,
A Brief Discourse of a Disease Called the Suffocation of the Mother
(London, 1603).

The Epistle Dedicatory

To the Right Worshipfull the President and Fellows of the College of Physicians in London.

. . . I thought good to make known the doctrine of this disease so far forth as may be in a vulgar tongue conveniently disclosed, to the end that the unlearned and rash conceits of divers might be thereby brought to better understanding and moderation, who are apt to make everything a supernatural work which they do not understand, proportioning the bounds of nature unto their own capacities, which might prove an occasion of abusing the name of God, and make us to use holy prayer as ungroundedly as the Papists do their prophecy tricks, who are ready to draw forth their wooden dagger if they do but see a maid or woman suffering one of these fits of the Mother, conjuring and exorcising them as if they were possessed with evil spirits. And for want of work will oftentimes suborn others that are in health to counterfeit strange motions and behaviours, as I once saw in the Santo in Padua five or six at one sermon interrupting and reviling the preacher until he had put them to silence by the sign of the cross, and certain powerless spells.

Wherefore it behoveth us as to be zealous in the truth, so to be wise in discerning truth from counterfeiting and natural causes from supernatural power. I do not deny but that God doth in these days work extraordinarily for the deliverance of his children and for other ends best known unto himself, and that among other, there may be both possessions by the Devil and obsessions and witchcraft, etc. and dispossession also through the prayers and supplications of his servants, which is the only means left to us for our relief in that case. But such examples being very rare nowadays, I would in the fear of God be very circumspect in pronouncing of a possession both because the impostures be many and the effects of natural diseases be strange to such as have not looked thoroughly into them.

But let us consider a little the signs which some do show of a supernatural power in these examples. For if they say there need no such signs appear, because the Devil by witchcraft may inflict a natural disease, then I ask them what they have to do with the Devil or with dispossessing of him, when he is not there present, but hath been only an external source of a disease by kindling or corrupting the humours of our bodies, which disease as well as other will submit itself to physical indications, as is shewed, Chapter 1. Wherefore they must needs make him to be an internal cause, and to possess the members and faculties of the body, and hold them to his use; or else they understand not what they say when they do peremptorily disclaim natural means and avouch that they speak certain words and perform certain voluntary motions upon his incitation, and are hindered by him from speaking other words which they would fain utter. And therefore to this end diverse signs and symptoms are alleged by them as arguments of a super-natural and extraordinary power inherent in the body.

One of their signs is insensibility, when they do not feel being pricked with a pin or burned with fire, etc. Is this so strange a spectacle when in the palsy, the falling sickness, apoplexis, and divers other diseases it is daily observed? And in these fits of the Mother it is so ordinary as I never read any author writing of this disease who doth not make mention thereof. This point you shall find proved both by authorities and examples in the fourth Chapter.

There also you shall find convulsions, contractions, distortions and such like to be ordinary symptoms in this disease.

Another sign of a supernatural power they make to be the due and orderly returning of the fits when they keep their just day and hour, which we call periods or cicuits. This accident, as it is common to divers other chronical diseases, as headaches, gouts, epilepsies, Tertians, Quartans, etc., so it is often observed in this disease of the Mother, as is sufficiently proved in the second Chapter.

Another argument of theirs is the offence in eating or drinking, as if the Devil meant to choke them therewith. But this symptom is also ordinary in uterine affects, as I show in the sixth chapter. And I have at this time a patient troubled in like manner.

Another reason of theirs is the coming of the fits upon the presence of some certain person. The like I do show in the same Chapter, and the reasons of it from the stirring of the affections of the mind.

Another main argument of theirs is the deliverance upon fasting and prayer, which we will imagine to be so indeed without any counterfeiting in that point. You shall see in the seventh Chapter how this may be a natural remedy [in] two manner of ways: the one by pulling down the pride of the body and the height of the natural humours thereof, a very convenient means and often prescribed by our authors in young and lusty bodies; the other by the confident persuasion of the patient to find release by that means, which I show in that Chapter by rules and authorities in our profession and also by examples to be a very effectual remedy in curing divers diseases of this nature.

At any other such like instances they may produce according unto everyone's several conceit, which were in vain for me to repeat particularly unless I knew wherein they would principally insist. But in the discourse following I have as near as I could described all the symptoms of this disease, whereby every man may readily find answers to his several objections.

48

THE POSSESSIONS AT
LOUDUN, 1634

The demonic possession of several nuns in an Ursuline convent at Loudun in France between 1632 and 1637 and the prosecution and execution of Urban Grandier, a parish priest in that town, for having caused the possessions, is one of the most famous episodes in the history of witchcraft. Grandier became the target of witchcraft accusation because of his scandalous personal life in Loudun (he had impregnated the daughter of one of the town's leading officials) and his apparent sympathy for the Huguenots. He had also incurred the enmity of the bishop of Poitiers and Jean Martin de Laubardemont, a counsellor of King Louis XIII. Grandier's enemies used the apparent possession of Jeanne des Anges, the mother superior of the Ursuline convent in Loudun, and many other nuns in that convent, to destroy him. The case assumed national prominence when Cardinal Richelieu, the king's minister, at the behest of Laubardement supported Grandier's prosecution. The possession of the nuns and the attempts to exorcise them in public attracted enormous crowds to Loudun and became widely known throughout Europe. As in many other cases of possession, the exorcisms were intended to prove that the Catholic Church was the one true church. Under torture Grandier confessed to having made a pact with the Devil and having caused the nuns' affliction. He was executed in 1634. This account of the episode comes from a French contemporary, des Niau, who wrote *La veritable histoire des diables de Loudun* (Poitiers, 1634). Des Niau, a counsellor at la Flèche, accepted the possessions as genuine. Contemporary scholarship has tended to view the possessions as deriving from a mixture of imagination, mental illness, and deliberate deceit. Regardless of the explanation, the behaviour of the nuns conformed to the stereotype of demoniacal behavior that was current at the time.

Source: The translation of des Niau's account appears as *The History of the Devils of Loudun: The Alleged Possession of the Ursuline nuns, and the trial and execution of Urbain Grandier, told by an eye witness*, translated from the original French in Edmund Goldsmid (ed.), *Collectanea Adamantea*, vol. XXI (privately printed, Edinburgh 1887–1888), vol. I, pp. 36–43; vol. II, pp. 7–46; vol. III, pp. 6–8.

Vol. I.

The choice [of a confessor] fell upon Canon Mignon, a man of considerable merit and in whom spiritual gifts were only equalled by intellectual ones. Grandier, already irritated at his own want of success, was still more annoyed at Mignon's appointment. The contrast in all points between his character and that of the Canon was too great for any other result to have been looked for. Every honest man takes a pride in the blamelessness of his profession, and cannot look favourably on a colleague who dishonours it, nor speak favourably of him. The curate, then, had nothing to expect from the Canon, who was very intimate with the Bishop, and he had already been made aware of the opinions Mignon had expressed at the time of the first trial. These circumstances were not likely to induce Grandier to look with a kindly eye on his successful competitor, and he consequently determined to give plenty of work to the confessor and to his penitents.

Of the various functions the priest is called upon to perform, none requires such delicacy of treatment as the ministry of penitence. It becomes still more delicate where the consciences of nuns are concerned. But the burden is intolerable, and few could bear it, if extraordinary agencies are employed to increase the difficulty. The anxiety of a newly appointed confessor in such a situation would be easily understood by Grandier, and would tend to console him for his failure in obtaining the coveted position.

However this may be, extraordinary symptoms began to declare themselves within the convent, but they were hushed up as far as possible, and not allowed to be known outside the walls. To do otherwise would have been to give the new institution a severe blow and to risk ruining it at birth. This the nuns and their confessor understood. It was therefore decided to work in the greatest secrecy, and to cure, or at least mitigate, the evil.

It was hoped that God, touched by patience with which the chastisement was borne, would Himself, in His mercy, send a remedy. . . .

As usually happens, the extraordinary phenomena displayed in the persons of the nuns were taken for the effects of sexual disease. But soon suspicions arose that they proceeded from supernatural causes; and at last they perceived what God intended every one to see.

Thus the nuns, after having employed the physicians of the body, apothecaries and medical men, were obliged to have recourse to the physicians of the soul, and to call in both lay and clerical doctors, their confessor no longer being equal to the immensity of their labour. For they were seventeen in number; and everyone was found to be either fully possessed, or partially under the influence of the Evil One.

All this could not take place without some rumours spreading abroad; vague suspicions floated through the city; had the secret even been kept by the nuns, their small means would soon have been exhausted by the extraordinary expenses they were put to in trying to hide their affliction, and this, together with the number of people employed in relieving them, must have made the matter more or less public. But their trials were soon increased when the public was at last made acquainted with their state. The fact that they were possessed of devils drove everyone from their convent as from a diabolical residence, or as if their misfortune involved their abandonment by God and man. Even those who acted thus were their best friends. Others looked upon these women as mad, and upon those who tended them as visionaries. For in the beginning, people being still calm, had not come to accuse them of being imposters.

Their pupils were first taken from them; most of their relations discarded them; and they found themselves in the deepest poverty. Amidst the most horrible vexations of the invisible spirit, they were forced to labour with their hands, to earn their bread. What was most admirable was that the rule of the community was never broken. Never were they known to discontinue their religious observances, nor was divine service ever interrupted. Ever united, they retained unbroken the bonds of charity which bound them together. Their courage never failed, and when the seizure was past, they used to return to their work or attend the services of the church with the same modesty and calmness as in the happy days of yore. I know that malice will not be pleased at such a pleasing portraiture. But this base feeling, too natural in the human heart, should be banished thence by all men of honour, who know its injustice and only require that history should be truthful. Probability itself is in favour of our statements. For when God permits us to be attacked so violently by our common enemy, it is as a trial to ourselves, to sanctify us and raise us to a high degree of perfection, and simultaneously He prepares us for victory, and grants us extraordinary grace, which we have only to assimilate and profit by.

It became necessary to have recourse to exorcisms. This word alone is for some people a subject of ridicule, as if it had been clearly proved that religion is mere folly and the faith of the Church a fable. True Christians must despise these grinning imposters. Exorcisms were then employed. The demon, forced to manifest himself, yielded his name. He began by giving these girls the most horrible convulsions; he went so far as to raise from the earth the body of the Superior who was being exorcised, and to reply to secret thoughts, which were manifested neither in words nor by any exterior signs. Questioned according to the form prescribed by the ritual, as to why he had entered the body of the nun, he replied, it was from hatred. But when, being questioned as to the name of the magician, he answered that it was Urbain

Grandier, profound astonishment seized Canon Mignon and his assistants. They had indeed looked upon Grandier as a scandalous priest; but never had they imagined that he was guilty of magic. They were therefore not satisfied with one single questioning; they repeated the interrogatory several times, and always received the same reply. . . .

Vol. II.

The king had resolved to raze the castles and fortresses existing in the heart of the kingdom, and commissioned M. de Laubardemont to see to the demolition of that of Loudun. He arrived and saw what a ferment the town was in, the animosity that reigned there, and the kind of man who caused the commotion. The complaints of those who were victims of the debaucheries, of the pride, or of the vengeance of the curate, touched him, and it seemed to him important to put an end to the scandal. On his return he informed the king and the Cardinal-Minister of the facts. Louis XIII, naturally pious and just, perceived the greatness of the evil, and deemed it his duty to put a stop to it. He appointed M. de Laubardemont to investigate the matter without appeal; with others he chose in the neighbouring jurisdictions the most straightforward and learned judges. The commission is dated 30th November, 1633.

Nothing less was needed to bring to justice a man upheld by a seditious and enterprising party, and so well versed in the details of *chicannerie*: an art always shameful in any man, but especially to an ecclesiastic. The king issued at the same time two decrees, to arrest and imprison Grandier and his accomplices. . . .

The Commissioner now leaned of what Grandier and his art were capable. The witnesses were so intimidated that none would speak, and it required all the Royal Authority to reassure them. He therefore issued a proclamation forbidding the intimidation of witnesses, under penalty of prosecution. . . . The evidence of the nuns was also heard, and that of lay persons of both sexes, amongst others of two women, the one of whom confessed having had criminal relations with Grandier, and that he had offered to make her Princess of Magicians, whilst the second confirmed the evidence of the first.

As regards the nuns, they deposed that Grandier had introduced himself into the convent by day and night for four months, without anyone knowing how he got in; that he presented himself to them whilst standing at divine service and tempted them to indecent actions both by word and deed; that they were often struck by invisible persons; and that the marks of the blows were so visible that the doctors and surgeons had easily found them, and that the beginning of all these troubles was signalized by the apparition of Prior Moussaut, their first confessor. The Mother Superior and seven or eight other nuns, when confronted by Grandier, identified him, although it was ascertained that they had never seen him save by magic, and that he had never had anything to do with their affairs. The two women formerly mentioned and the two priests maintained the truth of their evidence. In a word, besides the nuns and six lay women, "sixty witnesses deposed to adulteries, incests, sacrileges, and other crimes committed by the accused, even in the most secret places of his church, as in the vestry, where the Holy Host was kept, on all days and at all hours." . . .

The examination lasted forty days, during which demons gave them the clearest proofs of their presence in the bodies of the persons exorcised, and every day added new evidence against Grandier, and yet never said anything against him, which did not turn out strictly true. These assertions merit distinct proof, which will be found interesting.

As regards the presence of devils in the possessed, the Church teaches us in its ritual that there are four principal signs by which it can be undoubtedly recognised. These signs are the speaking or understanding of a language unknown to the person possessed; the revelation of the future or of events happening far away; the exhibition of strength beyond the years and nature of the actor; and floating on the air for a few moments.

The Church does not require, in order to have recourse to exorcisms, that all these marks should be found in the same subject; one alone, if well authenticated, is sufficient to demand public exorcism.

Now they are all to be found in the nuns of Loudun, and in such numbers that we can only mention the principal cases.

Acquaintance with unknown tongues first showed itself in the Mother-Superior. At the beginning she answered in Latin the questions of the ritual proposed to her in that language. Later, she and the others answered in any language they thought proper to question in.

M. de Launay de Razilli, who had lived in America, attested that, during a visit to Loudun, he had spoken to them in the language of a certain savage tribe of that country, and that they had answered quite correctly, and had revealed to him events that had taken place there.

Some gentlemen of Normandy certified in writing that they had questioned Sister Clara de Sazilli in Turkish, Spanish, and Italian and that her answers were correct.

M. de Nismes, Doctor of the Sorbonne, and one of the chaplains of the Cardinal de Lyon, having questioned them in Greek an German, was satisfied with their replies in both languages. . . .

M. Chiron, prior of Maillezais, desiring to strengthen his belief in demoniacal possession . . . whispered to M. de Fernaison, canon and provost of the same church, that he wished the nun to fetch a missal then lying near the door, and to put her finger on the introit of the mass of the Holy Virgin, beginning "Salve, Sancta parens." M. de Morans, who had heard nothing, ordered Sister Clara, who was likewise ignorant of what had been said, to obey the intentions of M. Chiron. This young girl then fell into strange convulsions, blaspheming, rolling on the ground, exposing her person in the most indecent manner, without a blush, and with foul and lascivious expressions and actions, till she caused all who looked on to hide their eyes with shame. Though she had never seen the prior, she called him by his name, and said he should be her lover. It was only after many repeated commands, and an hour's struggling, that she took up the missal, saying "I will pray." . . .

The corporal effect of possession is a proof which strikes the coarsest minds. It has this advantage, that an example convinces a whole assembly. . . .

Now the nuns of Loudun gave these proofs daily. When the exorcist gave some order to the Devil, the nuns suddenly passed from a state of quiet into the most terrible convulsions, and without the slightest increase of pulsation. They struck their chests and backs with their heads, as if they had their neck broken, and with inconceivable rapidity; they twisted their arms at the joints of the shoulder, the elbow and the wrist two or three times round; lying on their stomachs they joined their palms of their hands to the soles of their feet; their faces became so frightful one could not bear to look at them; their eyes remained open without winking; their tongues issued suddenly from their mouths, horribly swollen, black, hard, and covered with pimples, and yet while in this state they spoke distinctly; they threw themselves back till their heads touched their feet, and walked in this position with wonderful rapidity, and for a long time. They uttered cries so horrible and so loud that nothing like it was ever heard before; they made use of expressions so indecent as to shame the most debauched of men, while their acts, both in exposing themselves and inviting lewd behaviour from those present would have astonished the inmates of the lowest brothel in the country; they uttered maledictions against the three Divine Persons of the Trinity, oaths and blasphemous expressions so execrable, so unheard of, that they could not have suggested themselves to the human mind. They used to watch without rest, and fast five or six days at a time, or be tortured twice a day as we have described during several hours, without their health suffering; on the contrary, those that were somewhat delicate appeared healthier than before their possession.

The Devil sometimes made them fall suddenly asleep. They fell to the ground and became so heavy that the strongest man had great trouble in even moving their heads. Françoise Filestreau having her mouth closed, one could hear within her body different voices speaking at the same time, quarrelling, and discussing who should make her speak.

Lastly, one often saw Elizabeth Blanchard, in her convulsions, with her feet in the air and her head on the ground, leaning against a chair or a window sill without other support.

The Mother Superior from the beginning was carried off her feet and remained suspended in the air at the height of 24 inches. A report of this was drawn up and sent to the Sorbonne, signed by a great number of witnesses, ecclesiastics and doctors, and the judgement thereon of the Bishop of Poitiers who was also a witness. The doctors of the Sorbonne were of the same opinion as the Bishop and declared that infernal possession was proved.

Both she and other nuns lying flat, without moving foot, hand, or body, were suddenly lifted to their feet like statues.

In another exorcism the Mother Superior was suspended in the air, only touching the ground with her elbow.

Others, when comatose, became supple like a thin piece of lead, so that their body could be bent in every direction, forward, backward, or sideways, until their head touched the ground; and they remained thus so long as their position was not altered by others.

At other times they passed the left foot over their shoulder to the cheek. They passed also their feet over their head till the big toe touched the tip of the nose.

Others again were able to stretch their legs so far to the right and left that they sat on the ground without any space being visible between their bodies and the floor, their bodies erect and their hands joined.

One, the Mother Superior, stretched her legs to such an extraordinary extent, that from toe to toe the distance was 7 feet, although she was herself but 4 feet high. . . .

Vol. III.

Any man whose own writing testifies against him is lost. Now this is what Grandier experienced. The devils in several instances confessed four pacts he had entered into.

The word, Pact, is somewhat equivocal. It may mean either the document by which a man gives himself to the Devil, or the physical symbols whose application will produce some particular effects in consequence of the pact. Here is an example of each case. Grandier's pact, or magical characters, whereby he gave himself to Beelzebub, was as follows: "My Lord and Master Lucifer, I recognise you as my God, and promise to serve you all my life. I renounce every other God, Jesus Christ, and all other saints; the Catholic, Apostolic and Roman Church, its sacraments. with all prayers that may be said for me; and I promise to do all the evil I can. I renounce the holy oil and the water of baptism, together with the merits of Jesus Christ and his Saints; and should I fail to serve and adore you, and do homage to you thrice daily, I abandon to you my life as your due."

These characters were recognised as being in Grandier's own hand.

Now there is a specimen of the other kind of pact or magical charm. It was composed of the flesh of a child's heart, extracted in an assembly of magicians held at Orléans in 1631, of the ashes of a holy wafer that had been burnt, and of something else which the least straight-laced decency forbids me to name.

A most convincing proof of Grandier's guilt is that one of the devils declared he had marked him in two parts of his body. His eyes were bandaged and he was examined by eight doctors, who reported they had found two marks in each place; that they had inserted a needle to the depth of an inch without the criminal having felt it, and that no blood had been drawn. Now this is a most decisive test. For however deeply a needle be buried in such marks no pain is caused, and no blood can be extracted when they are magical signs. . . .

What criminals could ever be condemned if such proofs were not deemed sufficient? The certainty of the possessions; the depositions of two priests who accused him of sacrilege; those of the nuns, declaring that they saw him day and night for four months, though the gates of the convent were kept locked; the two women who bore witness that he offered to make one of them Princess of the Magicians; the evidence of sixty other witnesses; his own embarrassment and confusion on so many occasions; the disappearance of his three brothers, who had fled and were never seen again; his pact and the magic characters that were afterwards burnt with him; all these placed his guilt beyond doubt.

Figure 10 The execution of Urbain Grandier, who was convicted of causing the possession of the nuns at Loudun. In the rear left an exorcism of one of the nuns is taking place, and a black demon is shown leaving her body. See above, Chapter 48. From *Effigie de la condemnation de mort et execution d'Urbain Grandier* (Paris, 1634).

49

COTTON MATHER:
THE POSSESSION OF THE
GOODWIN CHILDREN,
1688

⸺⸺❍⸻⸻

This account of the possession of the children of John Goodwin in Boston, Massachusetts, conforms to the pattern of many of the possession cases in late sixteenth- and seventeenth-century England. Like many of those cases, it resulted in the execution of a witch for causing the possession of children. In this case the accused witch was a poor Irish laundress. The response to the possession of the children conformed to the official Protestant demand that only prayer and fasting be used to dispossess the victims. This case possesses special significance in that it occurred four years before the famous witch-hunt at Salem, which also began with the possession of a group of young girls. This account comes from the hand of Cotton Mather, the cleric who played a central role in the Salem episode. At the end of the account Mather uses this case of possession to confirm his belief in the existence of witches and devils.

Source: Cotton Mather, *Memorable Providences Relating to Witchcrafts and Possessions* (Boston, 1689), pp. 1–41.

Sect. I. There dwells at this time in the south part of Boston a sober and pious man whose name is John Goodwin, whose trade is that of a mason and whose wife (to which a good report gives a share with him in all the characters of virtue) has made him the father of six now living children. Of these children, all but the elder, who works with his father at his calling, and the youngest, who lives yet upon the breast of its mother, have laboured under the direful effects of a (no less palpable than) stupendous witchcraft. Indeed, that exempted son had also, as was thought, some lighter touches of it, in unaccountable stabs and pains now and then upon him, as indeed every person in the family at some time or other had, except the godly father and the sucking infant, who never felt any impressions of it. . . .

Sect. II. The four children (whereof the oldest was about thirteen, and the youngest was perhaps about a third part so many years of age) had enjoyed a religious education. . . . Their parents also kept them to a continual employment, which did more than deliver them from the temptations of idleness, and as young as they were, they took a delight in it; it may be as much as they should have done. In a word, such was the whole temper and carriage of the children that there cannot easily be anything more unreasonable than to imagine that a design to dissemble could cause them to fall into any of their odd fits, though there should not have happened, as there did, a thousand things wherein it was perfectly impossible for any dissimulation of theirs to produce what scores of spectators were amazed at.

Sect. III. About midsummer in the year 1688 the eldest of these children, who is a daughter, saw cause to examine their washerwoman upon their missing of some linen, which twas feared she had stolen from them; and of what use this linen might be to serve the witchcraft intended the thief's tempter knows! The laundress was the daughter of an ignorant and scandalous old woman in the neighbourhood, whose miserable husband before he died had sometimes complained of her that she was undoubtedly a witch, and that whenever his head was laid, she would quickly arrive unto the punishments due to such an one. This woman, in her daughter's defense, bestowed very bad language upon the girl that put her to the question, immediately upon which the poor child became variously indisposed in her health, and visited with strange fits, beyond those that attend an epilepsy, or a catalepsy, or those that they call the diseases of astonishment.

Sect. IV. It was not long before one of her sisters and two of her brothers were seized, in order one after another, with affects like those that molested her. Within a few weeks they were all four tortured everywhere in a manner so very grievous that it would have broke an heart of stone to have seen their agonies. Skillful physicians were consulted for their help, and particularly our worthy and prudent friend Dr. Thomas Oakes, who found himself so affronted by the distempers of the children that he concluded nothing but an hellish witchcraft could be the original of these maladies. And that which yet more confirmed such apprehension was that for one good while the children were tormented in the same part of their bodies all at the same time together; and though they saw and heard not one mother's complaints, though likewise their pains were swift like lightning, yet when (suppose) the neck, or the hand, or the back of one was racked, so it was at that instant with the other too.

Sect. V. The variety of their tortures increased continually, and though about nine or ten at night they always had a release from their miseries, and ate and slept all night for the most part indifferently well, yet in the daytime they were handled with so many sorts of ails that it would require of us almost as much time to relate them all as it did of them to endure them. Sometimes they would be deaf, sometimes dumb, and sometimes blind, and often all this at once. One while their tongues would be drawn down their throats, another while they would be pulled out upon their chins to a prodigious length. They would have their mouths opened unto such a wideness that their jaws went out of joint, and anon they would clap together again with a force like that of a strong spring-lock. The same would happen to their shoulder blades and their elbows and their hand wrists and several of their joints. They would at times lie in a benumbed condition and be drawn together as those that are tied neck and heels, and presently be stretched out, yea, drawn backwards to such a degree that it was feared the very skin of their bellies would have cracked. They would make most piteous outcries that they were cut with knives and struck with blows that they could not bear. Their necks would be broken so that their neck bone would seem dissolved unto them that felt after it, and yet on the sudden it would become again so stiff that there was no stirring of their heads; yea, their heads would be twisted almost round; and if main force at any time obstructed a dangerous motion which they seemed to be upon, they would roar exceedingly. Thus they lay some weeks most pitiful spectacles, and this while as a further demonstration of witchcraft in these horrid effects, when I went to prayer by one of them that was very desirous to hear what I said, the child utterly lost her hearing till our prayer was over.

Sect. VI. It was a religious family that these afflictions happened unto, and none but a religious contrivance to obtain relief would have been welcome to them. Many superstitious proposals were made unto them by persons that I know not who, nor what, with arguments fetched from I know not how much necessity and experience, but the distressed parents rejected all such counsels with a gracious resolution to oppose devils with no other weapons but prayers and tears unto Him that has the chaining of them, and to try first whether graces were not the best things to encounter witchcrafts with. Accordingly they requested the four ministers of Boston, with the minister of Charlestown, to keep a day of prayer at their thus haunted house, which they did in the company of some devout people there. Immediately upon this day the youngest of the four children was delivered and never felt any trouble as afore. But there was yet a greater effect of these our applications unto our God!

Sect. VII. The report of the calamities of the family for which we were thus concerned arrived now unto the ears of the magistrates, who presently and prudently applied themselves with a just vigour to enquire into the story. The father of the children complained of his neighbour, the suspected ill woman, whose name was Glover, and she being sent for by the justices, gave such a wretched account of herself that they saw cause to commit her unto the gaoler's custody. Goodwin had no proof that could have done her any hurt, but the hag had no power to deny her interest in the enchantment of the children; and when she was asked whether she believed there was a God, her answer was too blasphemous and horrible for any pen of mine to mention. . . . Upon the commitment of this extraordinary woman, all the children had some present ease, until one (related unto her) accidentally meeting one or two of them, entertained them with her blessing, that is, railing; upon which three of them fell ill again, as they were before.

Sect. VIII. It was not long before the witch thus in the trap was brought upon her trial; at which, through the efficacy of a charm, I suppose, used upon her by one or some of the crew, the court could receive answers from her in none but Irish, which was her native language, although she understood the English very well and had accustomed her whole family to none but that language in her former conversation. . . . It was long before she could with any direct answers plead unto her indictment, and when she did plead, it was with confession rather than denial of her guilt. Order was given to search the old woman's house, from whence there were brought into the court several small images, or puppets, or babies made of rags and stuffed with goat's hair and other such ingredients. When these were produced, the vile woman acknowledged that her way to torment the objects of her malice was by wetting of her finger with her spittle and stroking of those little images. The abused children were then present, and the woman still kept stooping and shrinking as one that was almost pressed to death with a mighty weight upon her. But one of the images being brought unto her, immediately she started up after an odd manner and took it into her hand.; but she had no sooner taken it than one of the children fell into sad fits before the whole assembly. . . .

Sect. XI. When this witch was going to her execution, she said the children should not be relieved by her death, for others had a hand in it as well as she, and she named one among the rest whom it might have been thought natural affection would have advised the concealing of. It came to pass accordingly that the three children continued in their furnace as before, and it grew rather seven times hotter than it was. All their former ails pursued them till, with an addition of (tis not easy to tell how many) more, but such as gave more sensible demonstrations of an enchantment growing very far towards a possession of evil spirits.

Sect. XII. The children in their fits would still cry out upon *they* and *them* as the authors of all their harm, but who that *they* and *them* were, they were not able to declare. At last the boy obtained at some time a sight of some shapes in the room. . . .

Sect. XIII. The fits of the children yet more arrived unto such motions as were beyond the efficacy of any natural distemper in the world. They would bark at one another like dogs and again purr like so many cats. They would sometimes complain that they were in a red-hot oven, sweating and panting at the same time unreasonably; anon, they would say cold water was thrown upon them, at which they would shiver very much. They would cry out of dismal blows with great cudgels laid upon them, and though we saw no cudgels or blows, yet we could see the marks left by them in red streaks upon their bodies afterward. And one of them would be roasted upon an invisible spit, run into his mouth and out at his foot, he lying and rolling and groaning as if it had been so in the most sensible manner in the world. And then he would shriek that knives were cutting of him. Sometimes he would have his hand so forcibly, though not visibly, nailed unto the floor that it was as much as a strong man could do to pull it up. One while they would all be so limber that it was judged every bone of them could be bent, another while they would be so stiff that not a joint of them could be stirred. They would sometimes be as though they were mad, and then would climb over high fences, beyond the imagination of them that looked after them. Yea, they would fly like geese and be carried with an incredible swiftness through the air, having but just their toes now and then upon the ground, and their arms waved like the wings of a bird. . . .

Sect. XXXIII. I have writ as plainly as becomes a historian, as truly as becomes a Christian, though perhaps not so profitably as became a divine. But I am resolved after this never to use but one grain of patience with any man that shall go to impose upon me a denial of devils or witches. I shall count that man ignorant who shall suspect, but I shall count him downright impudent if he assert the non-existence of things which we have had such palpable convictions of.

50

THE POSSESSION OF
CHRISTIAN SHAW, 1697

The possession of the eleven-year-old Scottish girl Christian Shaw in 1697 is one of the last cases of possession in Europe that led to charges and convictions of witchcraft. Christian was the daughter of John Shaw, the laird of Bargarran, who lived near Paisley in Renfrewshire, Scotland. Like many victims of possession she came from a fairly prosperous family and had received proper religious instruction. The fits she experienced were similar to those of other demoniacs, and it is likely that reports of those possessions had a bearing on both her behavior and the community's interpretation of that behavior. The accusations laid by Christian Shaw against her alleged tormentors led to the indictment of twenty-one individuals for witchcraft. In the trials that followed three men and four women were convicted. There are resemblances, therefore, between this case and that of the Goodwin children of Boston in 1688 and the large witch-hunt that followed the possession of a group of young girls at Salem in 1692. This case is also noteworthy in that the young demoniac was described as resisting temptation to become a witch herself. Shaw's behaviour was interpreted by eighteenth-century commentators as fraudulent, as were many cases of alleged possession. The most important consideration in studying the case, however, is the way in which the experience of Christian Shaw and the response of the community to her affliction was culturally shaped by contemporary views of possession, especially in England and New England. The narrative of this possession is taken from an anonymous pamphlet, *True Narrative of the Sufferings and Relief of a Young Girl* (1698), which has been attributed to Francis Grant, the prosecutor of the witches accused of causing her possession, and John MacGilchrist, a Glasgow solicitor who was Christian's uncle. The same pamphlet was published in London the same year under the title *Saducismus Debellatus* [Saducism conquered]. Its purpose was to use the evidence of Christian's possession to prove the existence of spirits at a time when many intellectuals,

266

referred to by their opponents as Sadducees, denied the existence of both good and bad spirits.

Source: The pamphlet was reprinted in *The History of the Witches of Renfrewshire*, ed. John Millar (Paisley, 1877), pp. 71–125.

Christian Shaw, daughter to a gentleman of good account, called John Shaw, laird of Bargarran, in the parish of Erskine, within the shire of Renfrew, a smart lively girl, and of good inclinations, about eleven years of age, perceiving one of the maids of the house, named Katherine Campbell, to steal and drink some milk, she told her mother of it; whereupon the maid Campbell (being a young woman of a proud and revengeful temper, and much addicted to cursing and swearing upon any like occasion, and otherwise given to purloining) did in a most hideous rage, thrice imprecate the curse of God upon the child; and at the same time did thrice utter these horrid words, "The devil harle (that is, drag) your soul through hell." This passed upon Monday, August 17, in presence of several witnesses, who afterwards made evidence of it.

Upon the Friday following, being August 21st, about sunrise, one Agnes Naesmith, an old widow woman, ignorant and of a malicious disposition, addicted to threatenings (which sometimes were observed to be followed with fatal events), who lived in the neighbourhood, came to Bargarran's house where, finding the child Christian in the court with her younger sister, she asked how the lady and the young sister did, and how old the young suckling child was; to which Christian replied, what do I know? Then Agnes asked, how herself did, and how old she was; to which she answered, that she was well, and in the eleventh year of her age.

On the Saturday night thereafter, being August 22, the child went to bed in good health; but so soon as she fell asleep began to struggle and cry Help, help! And then suddenly got up and did fly over the top of a resting bed, where she was lying (her father, mother, and others being in the room, and to their great astonishment and admiration) with such violence, that probably her brains had been dashed out if a woman, providentially standing by, and supported by a door at her back, had not broke the force of the child's motion; who, being laid in another bed, remained stiff and insensible as if she had been dead for the space of half an hour; but for forty-eight hours thereafter she could not sleep, crying out of violent pains through her whole body, and no sooner began to sleep or turn drowsy but seemed greatly affrighted, crying still, Help, help.

After this the pain fixed in her left side, and her body was often so bent and rigid, as she stood like a bow on her feet and neck at once and continued without power of speech, except in some short intervals, for eight days, during which time she had scarce half an hour's intermission together, the fits taking her suddenly, and both coming on and going off by a swerff or short deliquium, but appeared perfectly well and sensible in the intervals.

But about the middle of September her fits returned in a manner differing from the former, wherein she seemed to fight and struggle with something that was invisible to spectators, and her action appeared as if she had been defending herself from some who were assaulting or attempting to hurt her, and this with such force that she did cry and screech with such vehemence as if they had been killing her but could not speak.

Before this time, as she was seized with the trouble, her parents had called for physicians from Paisley, viz. John White, apothecary, a near relation, and afterwards Dr. Johnstone, who took blood and applied several things, both at first and afterwards, without any discernible effect upon the patient, either to the better or worse; and she all the while of these latter fits being afflicted and extraordinary risings and fallings of her belly, like the motion of a pair of bellows, and such strange movings of her body as made the whole bed she lay on shake, to the great consternation of spectators.

Some days thereafter was an alteration in her fits, so far, that she got speaking during the time of them; and while she was in the fits, fell a crying that Katherine Campbell and Agnes Naesmith were cutting her side and other parts of her body; which parts were in that time violently tormented. And when the fit was over she still averred that she had seen the same persons doing the same things which she complained of while under the fit, (it being remarkable that in the intervals she was still as well and sensible as ever) and would not believe but that others present saw them as well as she! In this condition she continued with some but not very considerable variation, either as to the fits or intervals, for the space of a month.

After which time she was conveyed to Glasgow, where Dr. Brisbane, a physician deservedly famous for skill and experience, did by Mr. Henry Marshall, apothecary, apply medicine to her; after which, having stayed in Glasgow about ten days, and being brought home to the country, she had near a fortnight's intermission. But then her fits returned, with this difference that she knew when they were coming, by a pain in her left side, which she felt before they came; and in these fits her throat was prodigiously drawn down towards her breast, and her tongue back into her throat, her whole body becoming stiff and extended, as a dead corpse, without sense or motion; and sometimes her tongue was drawn out of her mouth over her chin to a wonderful length, her teeth setting together so fast upon it, that those present were forced to thrust something betwixt her teeth for saving her tongue; and it was oft observed that her tongue was thus tortured when essayed to pray. And in this condition she was for some time, with sensible intervals wherein she had perfect health and could give a full account of what she was heard to utter while in the fit.

For several days these fits continuing with some variation, her parents resolved to return her to Glasgow, that she might there have the more conveniency of being under the doctor's oversight and care for furthering discerning the nature of her trouble, and making use of the most probable natural remedies. But being on the way to her grandmother's house at Northbar, she did thrust or spit out of her mouth parcels of hair, some curled, some plaited, some knotted, of different colours, and in large quantities; and this she continued to do in several swooning fits every quarter of an hour. . . . and thereafter from Monday to Thursday following she put out of her mouth coal cinders about the bigness of chestnuts, some whereof were so hot that they could scarcely be handled, one of which, Dr. Brisbane being by her when she took it out of her mouth, felt to be hotter than the heat of anyone's body make it. Then for the space of two days in these swooning fits, as formerly, there was put, or taken out of her mouth, straw in great quantities, though but one straw at once folded up together, which when put out, returned to its length, was found to be both long and broad, and it was remarkable that in one of them there was a small pin found. Thereafter were put out of her mouth bones of various sorts and sizes, as bones of fowls, and small bones of the heads of kine, and then some small sticks of candle fir (a sort of fir in the country that burns like candle), one of which was about three or four inches long; which when any upon sight of either bones or sticks took hold of to pull out, they found them either held by her teeth set together upon them, or forcibly drawn back into her throat. . . . It is to be noticed that she never knew how these things were brought into her mouth, and when they were got out of it, she immediately recovered of her fit for that time. . . .

Sometime after the putting out of her mouth the trash above-mentioned, she fell into extremely violent fits, with lamentable crying, – four persons being hardly able to withhold her from climbing up the walls of the chamber, or from otherways doing herself hurt, meantime having no power of speech while in the fit, but the back and the rest of her body grievously pained, in which condition she continued four or five days, with the usual sensible intervals, in which she declared that four men, Alexander and James Andersons and other two, of whom she gave particular and exact marks, but knew not their names, were tormenting her. It was observed that many of these she named were known to be persons of ill fame, as these last two persons last named were. It is also remarkable that for some time she knew not the name of the said Alexander Anderson, till one day he came a-begging to the door of the house where the damsel was, whom she seeing, immediately cried out, "that was he whom she had seen among the crew." . . .

About the eighth of December, being brought home again from Glasgow, and having had six or seven days respite from her fits, she afterwards fell into frightful and terrifying fits; the occasion whereof she declared to be, her seeing the devil in prodigious and horrid shapes, threatening to devour her, and then she would fall dead and stiff with all the parts of her body distended and stretched out as a corpse, without sense or motion, which fits as they came suddenly on without her knowledge, so she did as suddenly recover and grow perfectly well. . . .

Before we proceed further in the relation, let it be noticed first that the foresaid Agnes Naesmith, being brought by the parents a second time to see the damsel, did (though not desired) pray for her, viz. "that the lord of heaven and earth might send the damsel her health and try out the verity." After which the damsel declared that though the said Agnes had formerly been very troublesome to her, yet, from that time forth, she did no more appear to her as her tormentor, but, on the contrary, as she apprehended, defending her from the fury of the rest. Second, it is further here to be noticed, that the forenamed Katherine Campbell could by no means be prevailed with to pray for the damsel, but upon the contrary, when desired by some, cursed them and all her family of Bargarran, and in particular the damsel and all that belonged to her, withal adding this grievous imprecation, "The devil never let her grow better, nor any concerned in her, be in a better condition than she was in, for what they had done to her." . . .

It is not to be omitted that as soon as the damsel's affliction was observed to be extraordinary and preternatural, there were (besides times formerly set apart in a more private way) at the desire of the parents and minister, and by the presbytery's special order, a minister or two appointed to meet every week, at the house of Bargarran, to join with the family, the minister of the parish, and other good Christians of the neighbourhood, in fasting and praying, which usually fell to be on the Tuesday. . . .

About this time nothing in the world would so discompose her as religious exercises. If there were any discourses of God or Christ, or of any of the things which are not seen and are eternal, she would be cast into grievous agonies; and when she essayed in her light fits to read any portion of the Scriptures, repeat any of the Psalms, or answer any questions of our catechisms (which she could do exactly at other times) she was suddenly struck dumb, and lay as one stiff dead, her mouth opened to such a wideness that her jaw appeared to be out of joint, and anon would clap together with incredible force. The same happened to her shoulder blade, her elbow, and hand wrists. She would at other times lie in a benumbed condition, and be drawn together as if she had been tied neck and heels with ropes; yet on a sudden would with such force and violence be pulled up and tear all about her, that it was as much as one or two could do, to hold her fast in their arms. But when ministers and other good Christians (seeing her in such intolerable anguishes) made serious application by prayer to God on her behalf, she got respite from grievous fits of this kind, and was ordinarily free of them during the time of prayer, though seized of them before; and albeit, usually, when ministers began to pray, she made great disturbances by idle loud talking, whistling, singing and roaring, to drown the voice of the person praying. . . .

Feb. 2. The girl being in the chamber with her mother and others, was on a sudden struck with great fear and consternation, and fell a-trembling upon the sight of John Lindsay in Barloch, talking with her father in the hall. She said to her mother that foresaid Lindsay had been always one of her most violent tormentors, and that she had been threatened with extreme tortures, if she should offer to name him. Whereupon she was desired to go towards the place where he was and touch some part of his body in a way unknown to him, which having done with some version, was instantly seized with extreme tortures in all the parts of her body. After which Lindsay was put to it and interrogated thereupon, but he, giving no satisfying answer, was desired to take the damsel by the hand, which he being unwillingly induced to do, she was immediately upon the touch cast into intolerable anguishes, her eyes being almost twisted round in her head, and all the parts of her body becoming rigid and stiff, fell down in the posture of one that had been laid for some days dead, and afterwards got up in a sudden, and tearing her clothes, threw herself with violence upon him, and when her fit was over, spectators did also take this damsel by the hand, yet no such effect followed. . . .

Before this time the lamentable case of the afflicted damsel had been represented to His Majesty's most honourable privy council, who upon serious application made to them, worthily and piously granted a commission to a noble lord and some worthy gentlemen to make inquiry into the same. By virtue of this commission some suspected persons were seized; particularly, Feb. 4, Alexander Anderson, an ignorant, irreligious fellow, who had been always of evil fame, and accused by the afflicted damsel, by a special order from the commissioners for inquiry was apprehended and committed to prison, as was also Elizabeth Anderson, his daughter, upon flagrant presumptions of witchcraft; for the other year, Jean Fulton, her grandmother, an old scandalous woman, being cited before the kirk-session, and accused for hideous cursing and imprecating mischief upon several persons, which had been followed with fatal events; the forementioned Elizabeth Anderson, her grandchild, who lived in the house with her, did declare before the session she had frequently seen the devil in company with the grandmother, in the likeness of a small black man, who usually did vanish on a sudden within the walls of the house when anybody came to the door. Upon this presumption was the said Elizabeth Anderson seized with her father, and committed to custody; but at first most obstinately denied accession any manner of way to the sin of witchcraft, until afterwards, when seriously importuned and dealt with in the prison by two gentlemen, did, before she came to Bargarran's house, confess her guilt without Bargarran's knowledge at the time. And that she had been at several meetings with the devil and witches and, amongst others, she did declare her own father and the forementioned Highland fellow to have been active instruments of the girl's trouble, and gave, before she was confronted with him, exact marks of the Highland body, and though she was declared she knew not his name, yet, when confronted with him she did accuse him, and affirm he was the person she spoke of . . .

February 5, a quorum of the commissioners being met at Bargarran, and the persons thus delated by Elizabeth Anderson to have been at meetings with the devil, and active instruments of the damsel's trouble, viz., Alexander Anderson, her father, Agnes Naesmith, Margaret Foulton, James Lindsay alias Curat, John Lindsay alias Bishop, Katherine Campbell were all of them (excepting John Lindsay alias bishop, who was not then apprehended) confronted with Katherine Shaw before the lord Blantyre, and the rest of the commissioner at Bargarran, and several other gentlemen of note, and ministers then present, and accused by her as her tormentors. And they having all touched her in presence of the commissioners, she was at each of their touches seized with grievous fits, and cast into intolerable anguishes, others then present touching her in the same way, but no such effect followed. And it is remarkable, when Katherine Campbell touched the girl, she was immediately upon her touch seized with more grievous fits, and cast into more intolerable torments than what followed upon the touch of the other accused persons, whereat Campbell herself being damped and confounded, though she had formerly declined to bless her, uttered these words, "The Lord God of heaven and earth bless thee, and save thee both soul and body." After which the damsel, when the fits were over, in which she had been a most pitiful spectacle, did declare she was now loosed, and that she might freely touch any of the accused persons, or they her after this, without trouble, which accordingly upon trial fell so out; and being inquired how she came to the knowledge of that, answered as formerly in the like case: that something speaking distinctly as it were above her head suggested this to her; and likewise usually gave her the knowledge of the names of her tormentors, and places in which they lived. . . .

After this Bargarran made diligent search for James Lindsay, elder brother to Thomas, having been all along accused by the afflicted damsel as one of her troublers, whom she called the gley'd or squint-eyed elf (as he was indeed) for that was the name the crew about her gave him, who, when he was brought upon the place, though he did at first most obstinately deny his guilt, yet at length, through the endeavors of Mr. Patrick Simpson, a neighbour minister, ingeniously confessed the guilt he was charged with, and in his confession did agree in every material circumstance with the other two, though he knew not what they had confessed, he having not seen them before his confession, nor had he any occasion of information in conference with the others thereanent. Being immediately brought to the place from the tolbooth of Glasgow, where he had been some weeks before that time in prison as a vagabond beggar, upon a design to have sent him to foreign plantations. . . .

Thursday, being March 23rd, the damsel being asleep in the bed with her mother, about three o'clock in the morning, was on a sudden awakened (having for some time struggled in her sleep) in great fear and consternation, and being seized with her blind and deaf fits, took fast hold of her mother, declaring to her father and her, that the devil was standing near to the bed assaulting her, upon which she cried suddenly, "God almighty keep me from thy meetings. I will die rather than go to them. I will never, through the grace of God, renounce my baptism; for I will certainly go to hell if I do it. Thou says I will go to hell, however, because I am a great sinner; but I believe what the word of God saith: though I have many sins, yet the blood of Christ cleanseth from all sin; and I will not add that great wickedness to my other sins, while thou art tempting me to do. It is no wonder thou lie to me, seeing thou wast bold to lie in God's face. I know thou art a liar from the beginning, and the red coat thou promises me, I know thou canst not perform it. And although I should never recover, I am resolved never to renounce my baptism. It is God that hath all this time kept me from being a witch, and I trust he will yet by his grace keep me, not because of anything in me but of his own mercy; and that he who hath kept me hitherto from being devoured by thee I hope will yet keep me." This conference continued near the space of an hour, her father, mother and others being ear witnesses to the same. And after recovery the damsel declared that it was the devil, who (in the shape of a naked man with a shirt, having much hair upon his hands and his face like swine's bristles), had appeared to her tempting her as aforesaid.

Part VII

THE SKEPTICAL
TRADITION

The beliefs which formed the cumulative concept of witchcraft never commanded universal agreement, and some demonologists and inquisitors were openly skeptical regarding the validity of charges brought against witches. Skepticism regarding witchcraft, just like belief, was rarely unqualified. There was a much greater tendency to doubt the reality of some aspects of the witch's alleged crime than to claim that witchcraft in its entirety was an impossible activity. Skepticism could also develop much more easily regarding the guilt of specific individuals than regarding the possibility of the crime itself.

The documents in this Part provide a range of skeptical sentiment and reveal the variety of contexts within which skepticism regarding witchcraft arose. One of the earliest and widely known skeptical voices raised regarding witchcraft, that of Johann Weyer (Chapter 51), reveals only a limited challenge to learned witch-beliefs. Weyer, like many skeptics, believed that the pact with the Devil was a compete delusion and that witches were not to be held responsible for confessing that they had concluded such deals, but he did not deny that the Devil could exercise great power in the world. Reginald Scot, inspired mainly by a radical Protestantism, made a much more emphatic denial of learned witch beliefs, although even he would not deny the effectiveness of certain forms of magic (Chapter 52). A very different skepticism found expression in the report written by the Spanish Inquisitor Alonso de Salazar Frias after investigating the validity of hundreds of confessions, many of them by children, during a large witch-hunt in the Basque country in 1609–1611. Salazar never even raised the question whether witches existed; his concern was only the validity of the confessions that had been made within his jurisdiction, and in that context he concluded that none of the activities to which the witches confessed had ever taken place (Chapter 53).

The concerns of two seventeenth-century philosophers, Thomas Hobbes and Baruch Spinoza, were very different from those of Weyer, Scot, and Salazar. Both of these men held, for somewhat different reasons, that demonic spirits did not exist (Chapters 54 and 55). The English physician John

Webster was much more involved than either Hobbes or Spinoza in the late seventeenth-century pamphlet wars regarding the reality of witchcraft. Like many skeptics Webster contended that the effects of witchcraft could be explained by natural causes. The world view which underlay this claim, however, was not one in which the universe obeyed natural laws but one charged with all sorts of occult forces that scientific research had not yet discovered (Chapter 56). The final selection (Chapter 57) comes from the work of the Dutch minister Balthasar Bekker, who used biblical scholarship to deny that the Devil exercised any power in the world and to conclude that witchcraft was an impossible crime.

51

JOHANN WEYER: WITCHES AS MELANCHOLICS, 1563

———⸻◦◦◦◦⸻———

Johann Weyer, the Dutch demonologist whose account of the possession of the nuns at Wertet appears in Chapter 44, was not the first writer of the early modern period to question the validity of the charges made against witches. Much of the demonological literature of the fifteenth and early sixteenth centuries gave voice to some elements of skepticism. *De praestigiis daemonum*, however, was the first sustained criticism of the theories that underlay the witchcraft prosecutions of the early modern period. In particular Weyer argued that the women who were being accused of making pacts with the Devil and performing maleficent deeds were afflicted by the disease of melancholy and not culpable of this crime. Weyer's book also became the target of many demonological treatises written in the late sixteenth century, especially that of Jean Bodin, who included a specific attack on Weyer's views. The first of the excerpts produced below comes from the section of Weyer's book that attacks practising magicians. Weyer argues that witches should not be confused with such magicians and that the biblical command not to allow witches to live (Exodus 22:18) refers to Hebrew magicians and poisoners, not the individuals being prosecuted for the crime in his day. In the chapters which follow Weyer makes further distinctions between magicians and so-called witches and argues that the Devil alone was responsible for the *maleficia* attributed to witches. He denies the reality of the pact with the Devil, attributing it to the Devil's deception of witches, whose imagination he was able to control. The witches themselves, whom he refers to as *lamiae*, were vulnerable to demonic deception because they were afflicted by melancholy or because they were of weak faith. Although Weyer is more sympathetic to accused women than more credulous texts, such as the *Malleus maleficarum*, he nonetheless has an equally contemptuous view of women, depicting them as morally weak and gullible. Unlike other demonologists, however, Weyer argues that women who were deceived by the Devil should not be classified as heretics. In this respect he took a position contrary even to the "skeptical" canon *Episcopi*, which assigned guilt to the women who, deceived by the Devil, believed they went out at night with Diana (Chapter 8).

Source: *Witches, Devils, and Doctors in the Renaissance: Johann Weyer, De praestigiis daemonum*, ed. George Mora (Binghamton, NY, 1991), pp. 93–94, 97–98, 165, 166, 173–4, 180–183, 498–499.

Book Two. Of Magicians of Ill Repute

Chapter 1. Old Testament names Denoting Magicians of Ill repute and Poisoners.

When a question is raised or a discussion begun about the activities of witches, men soon offer the testimony of scriptural passages containing the term "magician," or "evil-doer," or "enchanter" or "poisoner" or even "juggler" (as some translate). They then affirm that these terms denote, without distinction of meaning, the women who are commonly called "witches" or "wise women." I find, however, that these monstrous persons with their arts, their illusions, and their forbidden forms of divination are represented in differing ways by the Rabbis and the Hebrew interpreters, that our Latin translators use different names to describe them, and that the Greek translation does not agree precisely with the Hebrew or with the Latin translation. . . .

The first word, *Chasaph*, I see constantly translated in the Vulgate as signifying that evil-doing whereby men who are maddened by the demon do harm (or at least think they do), through the evil arts, to cattle, to crops and even to human beings. As a result of these misdeeds, they are called evildoers, and the law of Moses would have them banished from life, by the decree of Exodus 22:6. "Thou shalt not suffer an evil-doer [*malefica*, fem] to live." The word *Mechasesepha*, which the law employs here, is derived from *Chasaph*; and it is put into the feminine gender (as the interpreters say), not because the law wishes men to be unpunished, but because the female sex, on account of its innate simplicity, is more frequently susceptible to the demon's ambushes. Therefore, the Greek translation which we ascribe to the seventy elders [the Septuagint] translates this decree more freely: "You shall not allow poisoners to live" (by the Latin masculine I mean to include both masculine and feminine). I observe moreover that the word in question *Chasaph* and its derivatives are hardly ever used in the aforementioned Greek translation except to indicate poisoning – that is, by the Greek words *pharmakos*, *pharmakeus*, *pharmaka*, and other words of the same root. Even the common people (not to mention our authors, both Greek and Latin) believe that those whom we call "evil-doers" practice and accomplish their nefarious arts with the help of drugs, poisons, and medications. . . . If you wish my opinion as well, I should think that the word has broad application and that it refers to every sort of magical art, and I see that the majority of Hebrews are also of that opinion. . . .

Our fellow Germans use one and the same word *Zauberer* for the magician who is a professional deceiver and illusionist and often well educated, for the "wise woman" or witch who is deluded by the Devil because of her feeble-mindedness and corrupted imagination, and for the poisoner who makes studied use of his drugs or poisons. And so, when someone who mentions witches or poisoners, German speakers are deceived by the ambiguous German term, and soon bring up the subject of Pharoah's magicians, who are far removed from the activities of witches and poisoners. Accordingly I am not ashamed to proclaim publicly that all the German writers whom I have so far chanced to read in the vernacular have stumbled badly in this sort of argument, even if they have affixed pretentious titles to the covers of the books and even if they appear to have adduced the evidence of Sacred Scripture. I am especially ready to express my view because I see that they assign too much power to witches – power to disturb the atmosphere or cause disease; and thus unwittingly these writers provide drawn sword and kindling for the savage executioners, who lack judgment, discretion, and any trace of pity. . . .

Book Three: Of Lamiae

Chapter 1. A description of what a Lamia is.

I now turn to an account of the *Lamia*, commonly called *Striga* after the *strix* or screech-owl, an ill-omened night bird which is splendidly depicted by Ovid:

> They are greedy birds, not the ones who deprived Phineuus of his food, but trace their ancestry from them. The head is large, the eyes fixed, the beak suited for catching prey; there is a grayish whiteness on the wings and a hook on the talons. They fly by night and seek young children in want of a nurse; and they defile the bodies snatched from their cradles. They are said to pluck the milky intestines with their beaks, and their maw is full of the blood that they have drunk. Their name is *Striges* and the reason for the name is that they are wont to utter a shrill cry [*stridere*] in the fearsome night. [This is true] whether they are born as birds or whether they become so by a charm, when a false incantation changes old women into flying creatures. . . .

I use the term *Lamia* for a woman who, by virtue of a deceptive or imaginary pact that she has entered into with the demon, supposedly perpetrates all kinds of evil-doing, whether by curse or by glance or by some use of some ludicrous object unsuited for the purpose. For example, she can ignite the air with strange bolts of lightning, or shatter it with terrifying claps of thunder, beat [down upon the earth] with a damaging profusion of unexpected hail, rouse storms, ravage the fertile crops in the field or transfer them elsewhere, stir up unnatural diseases for men and beasts and then heal them again, travel great distances abroad within a few hours, dance with demons, hold banquets, play the role of succubus or have intercourse with demons, change herself or others into beasts, and display a thousand monstrous mockeries. From this, all would readily agree as to how far removed our *Lamia* is from the infamous magicians. . . .

Chapter III. The profession made by the Lamiae is refuted, and the pact is shown to be deceptive, foolish and of no weight.

Anyone who would not choose to be totally destitute of reason, and to be exposed as holding to an inflexibly conceived opinion, will readily judge how incoherent and dissonant those things are, and undeserving of the slightest belief. Moreover, we can clearly recognize that the pact is illusory and that it is fabricated and confirmed by the deceptive appearance of a phantasm, or a fancy of the mind or the phantastical body of a blinding spirit; it is therefore of no weight. The deception occurs ether when an apparition of Satan's choice is cunningly imposed on the optic or visual nerves by the disturbing of the appropriate humors and spirits, or when a whistling or whispering or murmuring, corresponding in form to the corrupt image, is aroused in the organs of hearing by the evil spirit's art. Especially will we recognize this to be true if we use the mind's keen eye to examine the disparate natures of the contracting parties, the form of the contract, the manner of procedure, and the circumstances, and if we weigh these factors quite accurately in the balance of reason and of our faith. It thus becomes obvious that virtually all of the actions hitherto attributed to the Lamia – actions to which the crazed woman even confesses, because her powers of imagination have been corrupted by the Deceiver – proceed not from the Lamia but from Satan himself. Satan needs the help of no second creature in displaying his power and declaring his actions, he who is constrained by the will or command of none but God and God's good ministers. The malicious rogue pursues evil not under compulsion but freely and willingly (with God's permission), although he feigns and pretends otherwise (as Porphyry attests) in order to trap us the more by his tricks. Nor is it necessary that this imaginary pact, entered into lyingly and with evil cunning by the one party, be concluded in strict form since things could scarcely be done otherwise by a blinding spirit in the presence of a dazed and mentally incompetent human. In fact, no one should doubt that the demon's receiving of the Lamia by means of outstretched hand and firm pledge is totally false, because a spirit does not have flesh and bone which compose a hand – as the Truth of Scripture attests. . . .

Chapter V. Which persons are more vulnerable to the demons' arts and illusions.

On this same subject, the sort of person most likely to be attacked is one who possesses such a temperament or who is so moved by external or internal causes (e.g., if he is attacked by a demon-specter or tempted by a demon's suggestions) that as a result of specious inducements he will readily present himself as a suitable instrument of the demon's will. Melancholics are of this sort, as are persons distressed because of loss or for any other reason, as Chrysostom says: "The magnitude of their grief is more potent for harm than all the activities of the Devil, because all whom a demon overcomes, he overcomes through grief." There are also the people without faith in God, the impious, the illicitly curious, the people wrongly trained in the Christian religion, the envious, those who cannot restrain their hatred, the malicious, old women not in possession of their faculties, and similarly foolish women of noted malice or slippery and wavering faith (for he who believes easily goes back on his belief easily).These persons (as being fitting instruments) the Devil waylays however he can, in his own time and place. He approaches, follows, and entices each in some special manner, since he knows from sure indications the interests and feelings of every heart. He may assume some attractive form, or variously agitate and corrupt the thoughts and the imagination, until finally these people agree to his proposals, give way to his persuasion, and believe whatever he puts in their minds, as though bound by treaty depending upon his will and obeying him. They think that everything that he suggests is true, and they are devoutly confident that all the forms imposed by him upon their powers of imagination and fantasy exist truly and "substantially" [in the theological sense] (if I may use this word). Indeed, they cannot do otherwise, since from the time of their first assent he has corrupted their mind with empty images, lulling or stirring to this task the bodily humors and spirits, so that in this way he introduces certain specious appearances into the appropriate organs, just as if they were occurring truly and externally; and he does this not only when people sleep but also when they are awake. In this manner, certain things are thought to exist or take place outside of the individual which in fact are not real and do not take place, and often do not even exist in the natural world. Such is the almost incomprehensible subtlety of these unclean spirits, and their indefatigable [pursuit of] fraud. Deceiving the senses of men. St Peter, in the writings of Clement, informs us that the demon also besieged the senses of the ancient Egyptians in this way.

Chapter VI. Concerning the credulity and frailty of the female sex.

Most often, however, that crafty schemer the Devil thus influences the female sex, that sex which by reason of temperament is inconstant, credulous, wicked, uncontrolled in spirit, and (because of its feelings and affections, which it governs only with difficulty) melancholic; he especially seduces stupid, worn out, unstable old women. Therefore, in the beginning when there were but two human beings, it was not Adam but Eve that he approached, as being an instrument more suitable for his persuasion; it was she that he overcame in argument with only a light skirmish. Hence, St Peter rightly calls woman the weaker vessel (1 Peter 3:7). And Chrysostom (if he is really the author), in the second part of his *Homilies on Matthew*, says, "The female sex is heedless and pliant: Heedless because it does not consider with wisdom and reason all that it sees or hears, pliant because it is easily bent from evil to good or from good to evil." In *Homily 23 on the Second letter to the Corinthians*, he says, "It is the special characteristic of women to be deceived." St Jerome, or (as it seems) some other author, in the *Letter to Eustochius on the Rule for Religious Women*, writes: the sex that you possess is surely weak and frail and fickle if it be left to its own judgment." . . .

Chapter VII. The distorted imagination of melancholics.

Now lest you regard it as quite absurd that the organs of the imaginative power should become corrupted in this manner in the case of these poor women, and that their eyes should be blinded (as I have shown above), consider the thoughts, words, sight, and actions of melancholics, and you will understand how in these persons all the senses are often distorted when the melancholic humor seizes control of the brain and alters the mind. Indeed, some of these melancholics think that they are dumb animals, and they imitate the cries and bodily movements of these animals. Some suppose that they are earthen vessels, and for that reason they yield to all who meet them, lest they be "broken." Others fear death, and yet sometimes they choose death by committing suicide. Many imagine that they are guilty of a crime, and they tremble and shudder when they see anyone approaching them, for fear that the person may lay hands upon them and lead them off as prisoners and haul them before the tribunals to be punished. A certain noble-born old man would sometimes suddenly leap from his chair thinking that he was being attacked by enemies; laying hold of them, he would at once stuff them into the oven (at least in his own mind). Another man used to be afraid that Atlas was growing tired of supporting the whole world on his shoulders, and that in his weariness he was going to shake off his burden, and everyone would be crushed by the great collapse. Also I have learned that three men in Friesland not far from Groningen were so carried away with religious enthusiasm that they believed they were God the Father, God the Son, and God the Holy Spirit, and that the barn in which they were standing was Noah's ark; and many similarly affected persons came streaming to this "ark" for safety. And I know of a melancholic Italian who believed that he was monarch and emperor of the whole world and that the title pertained to him alone.

Book Six. Of the Punishment of Notorious Magicians, Witches and Poisoners

Chapter VIII. Lamiae should not be classed among heretics. Also, some observations on the distinction between custody and imprisonment.

Since the so-called *Lamiae* are indeed poor women – usually old women – melancholic by nature, feeble-minded, easily given to despondency, and with little trust in God, the Devil all the more gladly attaches himself to them, as being suitable instruments for him, and he insinuates his way into their bodies all the more easily, in order to confound their minds with various images. Bewitched by these illusory images, they believe and confess that they have done that which it was quite impossible for them to have done – because if one assesses the whole matter with clearer mental vision, on the basis of what can be done and is done by the demon, and what is supposed to be done by men with the demon's help and with the instruments that he supplies, one will find that everything is really contrived and perpetuated by the demon. And so I would hardly dare to include those women among the heretics, since no one deserves the name of heretic unless he is warned once or twice and still constantly and stubbornly persists in his fanatical beliefs; heresy is not an error of the mind but a stubbornness of the will. Therefore, if these women – their minds totally corrupted by Satan and distracted by false imaginings – do nothing more in actual deed against another person, they should be examined and given a sounder instruction in the chief doctrines of our Christian faith, so that they might repent and – as a result of this saving instruction – strive with all their might to do (with God's grace) that which they promised to do when they first took up this religion [in baptism] and renounced Satan (although at his hidden and deceptive prompting they carelessly deviated from this promise, even as we know that our first parent Eve also went astray). . . .

Christians should not be so quick on the basis of false and malicious accusations to throw them into those noisome, filthy prisons, unfit for keeping men in custody – the horrid lodgings of evil demons who torment their captives. Christians should not strip themselves of every human emotion (as is done in many places, with less wisdom than severity) and hand these women over for the torture chamber (as though locking them up in the bull of Phalaris) where they will be tormented most cruelly by the executioner with the most savage tortures.

Apart from the pain of excessive torture unfairly afflicted, we should also note that the legal profession has established a great distinction between imprisonment and custody. In no way do the lawyers intend that the custody of a person who is later to be put to death should be a punishment; and yet they have perceived that a dreadful punishment *is* imposed by the horror of prison – even upon innocent persons who have sometimes been undeservedly thrown into jail. But just as considerations of fairness and compassion have fallen into neglect and contempt, so too the name and practice of custody has all but disappeared among many peoples. And so it happens that these poor creatures of God are frightened by long solitude, filthy cells, grim darkness, and various demonic specters. Already somewhat impaired of mind by the Devil's constant promptings, charms, and illusions, and now harassed anew by varied torments, they are cruelly subjected to questioning and they choose to exchange their wretched life for a swift death; they freely confess to any crime proposed to them rather than be thrust headlong back into the same dungeons and tortures within the stinking prisons.

52

REGINALD SCOT:
THE UNREALITY
OF WITCHCRAFT,
1584

Reginald Scot, the author of *The Discoverie of Witchcraft*, a massive treatise published in 1584, emerged as the most radical skeptic regarding witchcraft in the sixteenth century. An educated English layman of deep Calvinist convictions, his skepticism was in large part derived from his belief in the sovereignty of God and the absence of any biblical foundation for witch-hunting. Often linked with Johann Weyer, who wrote twenty years before him, Scot not only ridiculed the *Malleus maleficarum* and the works of other demonologists like Johannes Nider and Lambert Daneau but also responded to the attacks that were levelled against Weyer, especially by Jean Bodin in 1580. These selections present four different dimensions of Scot's skepticism. First, Scot provides a social analysis of witchcraft accusations, identifying poor women who begged for charity and who had been estranged from their neighbors as the most likely to be accused of having caused their misfortunes. Second, he argues not only that there was no biblical foundation to the belief in witchcraft but also that it was idolatrous to attribute power to witches. Third, he presents a devastating analysis of the different components of the crime of witchcraft enumerated by Bodin, showing that those components could be prosecuted on the basis of laws already in force. Finally, he uses philosophy and science to establish the impossibility of the deeds confessed by witches.

Source: Reginald Scot, *The Discoverie of Witchcraft* (London, 1584),
pp. 7–9. 11–12, 32–39, 49–51.

Book I

Chapter 3. Who they be that are called witches, with a manifest declaration of the cause that moveth men so commonly to think, and witches themselves to believe that they can hurt children, cattle, etc. with words and imaginations; and of cozening witches.

One sort of such as are said to be witches are women which be commonly old, lame, bleary-eyed, pale, foul, and full of wrinkles; poor, sullen, superstitious, and papists, or such as know no religion; in whose drowsy mind the devil hath gotten a fine seat; so as what mischief, mischance, calamity or slaughter is brought to pass, they are easily persuaded the same is done by themselves, imprinting in their minds an earnest and constant imagination hereof. They are lean and deformed, showing melancholy in their faces, to the horror of all that see them. They are doting scolds, mad, devilish, and not much differing from them that are thought to be possessed with spirits; so firm and steadfast in their opinions, as whosoever shall only have respect to the constancy of their words uttered, would easily believe they were true indeed.

These miserable creatures are so odious unto all their neighbors, and so feared, as few dare offend them, or deny them anything they ask, whereby they take upon them and sometimes think that they can do such things as are beyond the ability of human nature. These go from house to house and from door to door for a pot full of milk, yeast, drink, pottage or some such relief, without the which they could hardly live, neither obtaining for their service and pains, nor by their art, nor yet at the devil's hands (with whom they are said to make a perfect and visible bargain) either beauty, money, promotion, wealth, worship, pleasure, honor, knowledge, learning, or any other benefit whatsoever.

It falleth out many times that neither their necessities nor their expectation is answered or served in those places where they beg or borrow, but rather their lewdness is by their neighbors reproved. And further, in tract of time, the witch waxeth odious and tedious to her neighbors, and they are again despised and despited of her, so as sometimes she curseth one and sometimes another, and that from the master of the house, his wife, children, cattle, etc. to the little pig that lieth in the sty. Thus in process of time they have all displeased her, and she hath wished evil luck unto them all, perhaps with curses and imprecations made in form. Doubtless (at length) some of her neighbors die or fall sick, or some of their children are visited with diseases that vex them strangely, as apoplexies, epilepsies, convulsions, hot fevers, worms, etc. Which by ignorant parents are supposed to be the vengeance of witches. Yea, and their opinions and conceits are confirmed and maintained by unskillful physicians, according to the common saying, "Witchcraft and enchantment is the cloak of ignorance"; whereas indeed evil humors and not strange words, witches or spirits are the causes of such diseases. And some of their cattle perish, either by disease or mischance. Then they, upon whom such adversities fall, weighing the fame that goeth upon this woman (her words, displeasure and curses meeting so justly with their misfortune) do not only conceive, but also are resolved, that all their mishaps are brought to pass by her only means.

The witch on the other side expecting her neighbours' mischances, and seeing things sometimes come to pass according to her wishes, curses and incantations (for Bodin himself confesseth that not above two in a hundred of their witchings or wishings take effect), being called before a justice, by due examination of the circumstances is driven to see her imprecations and desires, and her neighbors' harms and losses to concur, and as it were to take effect, and so confesseth that she (as a goddess) hath brought such things to pass. Wherein not only she but the accuser and also the justice are foully deceived and abused, as being through her confession and other circumstances persuaded (to the injury of God's glory) that she hath done, or can do that which is proper only to God himself.

Another sort of witches there are which be absolutely cozeners. These take upon them, either for glory, fame or gain, to do anything which God or the devil can do, either for foretelling of things to come, betraying of secrets, curing of malefices, or working of miracles. . . .

Chapter 5. A confutation of the common conceived opinion of witches and witchcraft, and how detestable a sin it is to repair to them for counsel or help in time of affliction.

But whatsoever is reported or conceived of such manner of witchcrafts, I dare avow to be false and fabulous (cozenage, dotage and poisoning excepted). Neither is there any mention made of these kind of witches in the Bible. If Christ had known them, he would not have permitted to inveigh against their presumption, in taking upon them his office, as to heal and cure diseases and to work such miraculous and supernatural things as whereby he himself was especially known, believed, and published to be God, his actions and cures consisting (in order and effect) according to the power of our witch-mongers imputed to witches. Howbeit, if there be any in these days afflicted in such strange sort as Christ's cures and patients are described in the New Testament to have been, we fly from trusting in God to trusting in witches, who do not only in their cozening art take on them the office of Christ in this behalf, but use his very phrase of speech to such idolaters as come to seek divine assistance at their hands, saying, "Go thy ways, thy son or thy daughter, etc. shall do well and be whole."

It will not suffice to dissuade a witchmonger from his credulity, that he seeth the sequel and event to fall out many times contrary to their assertion; but in such case (to his greater condemnation) he seeketh further to witches of greater fame. If all fail, he will rather think he came an hour too late than that he went a mile too far. Truly I for my part cannot perceive what is to go a whoring after strange gods, if this be not. He that looketh upon his neighbour's wife, and lusteth after her, hath committed adultery. And truly, he that in heart and by argument maintaineth the sacrifice of the Mass to be propitiatory for the quick and the dead is an idolater; as also he that alloweth and commendeth creeping to the cross, and such like idolatrous actions, although he bend not his corporal knees.

In like manner I say he that attributeth to a witch such divine power as duly and only appertaineth unto GOD (which all witchmongers do) is in heart a blasphemer, an idolater, and full of gross impiety, although he neither go nor send to her for assistance.

Book II

Chapter 9. The fifteen crimes laid to the charge of witches, by witchmongers, especially by Bodin, in Daemonomania.

[1]   They deny God and all religion.

Answer: Then let them die therefore, or at the least be used like infidels or apostates.

[2]   They curse, blaspheme and provoke God with all despite.

Ans. Then let them have the law expressed in Levit. 24 and Deut. 13 and 17.

[3]   They give their faith to the devil, and they worship and offer sacrifice unto him

Ans. Let such also be judged by the same law.

[4]   They do solemnly vow and promise all their progeny unto the devil.

Ans. This promise proceedeth from an unsound mind and is not to be regarded because they cannot perform it; neither will it be proved true. Howbeit, if it be done by any that is sound of mind, let the curse of Jeremiah 32: 36, light upon them, to wit, the sword, famine and pestilence.

[5]   They sacrifice their own children to the devil before baptism, holding them up in the air unto him, and then thrust a needle unto their brains.

Ans. If this be true, I maintain them not herein, but there is a law to judge them by. Howbeit, it is so contrary to sense and nature that it were folly to believe it, either upon Bodin's bare word or else upon his presumptions, especially when so small commodity and so great danger and inconvenience ensueth to the witches thereby.

[6]   They burn their children when they have sacrificed them.

Ans. Then let them have such punishment as they that offered their children unto Moloch: *Levi.* 20. But these be mere devices of witchmongers and inquisitors that with extreme tortures have wrung such confessions from them; or promises have won it at their hands, at the length.

[7]   They swear to the devil to bring as many into that society as they can.

Ans. This false and so proved elsewhere.

[8] They swear by the name of the devil.

Ans. I never heard any such oath, neither have we warrant to kill them that so do swear, though indeed it be very lewd and impious.

[9] They use incestuous adultery with spirits.

Ans. This is a stale ridiculous lie, as is proved apparently hereafter.

[10] They boil infants (after they have murdered them unbaptised) until their flesh be made potable.

Ans. This is untrue, incredible, and impossible.

[11] They eat the flesh and drink the blood of men and children openly.

Ans. Then they are the kin to the Anthropothagi and Cannibals. But I believe never an honest man in England nor in France will affirm that he hath seen any of these persons that are said to be witches do so. If they should, I believe it would poison them.

[12] They kill men with poison.

Ans. Let them be hanged for their labour.

[13] They kill men's cattle.

Ans. Then let an action of trespass be brought against them for so doing.

[14] They bewitch men's corn and bring hunger and barrenness into the country; they ride and fly in the air, bring storms, male tempest, etc.

Ans. Then I will worship them as gods, for those be not the works of man nor yet of witch, as I have elsewhere proved at large.

[15] They use venery with a devil called incubus, even when they lie in bed with their husbands and have children by them, which become the best witches.

Ans. This is the last lie, very ridiculous, and confuted by me elsewhere.

Chapter 10. A refutation of the former surmised crimes patched together by Bodin, and the only way to escape the inquisitor's hands.

If more ridiculous or abominable crimes could have been invented, these poor women (whose chief fault is that they are scolds) should have been charged with them.

In this libel you do see is contained all that witches are charged with, and all that also which any witchmonger surmiseth, or in malice imputeth unto witches power and practice.

Some of these crimes may not only be in the power and will of a witch but may be accomplished by natural means; and therefore by them the matter in question is not decided, to wit; whether a witch can work wonders supernaturally? For many a knave and whore doth more commonly put in execution those lewd actions than such as are called witches, and are hanged for their labour.

Some of these crimes also laid unto witches' charge are by me denied and by them cannot be proved to be true or committed by any one witch. Othersome of these crimes likewise are so absurd, supernatural and impossible that they are derided almost of all men and as false, fond and fabulous reports condemned: insomuch as the very witchmongers themselves be ashamed to hear of them.

If part be untrue, may not the residue be thought false? For all these things are laid to the charge at one instant, even by the greatest doctors and patrons of the sect of witchmongers, producing as many proofs for witches' supernatural and impossible actions as for the others. So as, if one part of their accusation be false, the other part deserveth no credit. If all be true that is alleged of their doings, why should we believe in Christ, because of his miracles, when a witch doth great wonders as ever he did.

But it will be said by some, as for those absurd and popish writers, they are not in all their allegations touching these matters to be credited. But I assure you that even all sorts of writers herein (for the most part) the very doctors of the church to the schoolmen, protestants and papists, learned and unlearned, poets and historiographers, Jews, Christians, or Gentiles agree in these impossible and ridiculous matters. Yea, and these writers, out of whom I gather most absurdities, are of the best credit and authority of all writers in this matter. The reason is because it was never thoroughly looked into, but every fable credited, and the word (witch) named so often in Scripture.

They that have seen further of the inquisitors' orders and customs say also that there is no way in the world for these women to escape the inquisitors' hands, and so consequently burning, but to gild their hands with money, whereby oftentimes they take pity upon them and deliver them, as sufficiently purged. For they have authority to exchange the punishment of the body with the punishment of the purse, applying the same to the office of their inquisition; whereby they reap such profit as a number of these seely women pay them yearly pensions, to the end they may not be punished again.

Book III

Chapter 7. A confutation of the objection concerning witches' confessions.

It is confessed (say some by the way of objection) even of these women themselves, that they do these and such other horrible things as deserveth death with all extremity etc. Whereunto I answer that whosoever considerately beholdeth their confessions shall behold all to be vain, idle, false, inconstant and of no weight, except their contempt and ignorance in religion, which is rather the fault of their negligent pastor than of the simple woman.

First, if their confession be made by compulsion, of force or authority, or by persuasion or under the colour of friendship, it is not to be regarded because the extremity of threats and tortures provokes it or the quality of fair words and allurements constrains it. If it be voluntary, many circumstances must be considered, to wit: whether she impeach not herself to overthrow her neighbour, which many times happeneth through their cankered and malicious melancholic humour; then, whether in that same melancholic mood and frantic humour she desire not the abridgement of her own days. Which thing Aristotle saith doth oftentimes happen unto persons subject to melancholic passions and (as Bodin and Sprenger say) to these old women called witches, which many times (as they affirm) refuse to live, threatening the judges that if they may not be burned they will lay hands upon themselves and so make them guilty of their damnation.

I myself have known that where such a one could not prevail to be accepted as a sufficient witness against himself, he presently went and threw himself into a pond of water, where he was drowned. But the law sayeth . . . his word is not to be credited that is desirous to die. And sometimes (as elsewhere I have proved) they confess that whereof they were never guilty, supposing that they did that which they did not, by means of certain circumstances. And as they sometimes confess impossibilities, as that they fly in the air, transubstantiate themselves, raise tempests, transfer or remove corn, etc., so do they also (I say) confess voluntarily that which no man could prove and that which no man would guess, nor yet believe, except he were as mad as they, so as they bring death willfully upon themselves, which argueth an unsound mind.

If they confess that which hath been indeed committed by them, as poisoning or any other kind of murder, which falleth into the power of such persons to accomplish, I stand not to defend their cause. Howbeit, I would wish that even in that case there be not too rash credit given, nor too hasty proceedings used against them, but that the causes, properties, and circumstances of everything be duly considered and diligently examined. For you shall understand that as sometimes they confess they have murdered their neighbors with a wish, sometimes with a word, sometimes with a look, etc., so they confess that with the delivering of an apple or some such thing to a woman with child they have killed the child in the mother's womb, when nothing was added thereunto which naturally could be noisome or hurtfull.

In like manner they confess that with a touch of their bare hand they sometimes kill a man being in perfect health and strength of body when all his garments are betwixt their hand and his flesh.

But if this their confession be examined by divinity, philosophy, physic, law or conscience, it will be found false and insufficient. First, for that the working of miracles is ceased. Secondly, no reason can be yielded for a thing so far beyond all reason. Thirdly, no receipt can be of such efficacy as when the same is touched with a bare hand, from whence the veins have passage through the body into the heart, it should not annoy the poisoner and yet retain virtue and force enough to pierce through so many garments and the very flesh incurably to the place of death in another person. . . . Fourthly, no law will admit such a confession as yieldeth unto impossibilities, against the which there is never any law provided; otherwise it would not serve a man's turn to plead and prove that he was at Berwick that day that he is accused to have done a murder in Canterbury, for it might be said he was conveyed to Berwick and back again by enchantment. Fifthly, he is not by conscience to be executed which hath no sound mind nor perfect judgement. And yet forsooth we read that one mother *Stile* did kill *Saddocke* with a touch on the shoulder, for not keeping promise with her for an old cloak to make her a safeguard and that she was hanged for her labour.

53

ALONSO DE SALAZAR FRÍAS: THE UNRELIABILITY OF CONFESSIONS, 1612

Alonso de Salazar Frías, a university-educated canon lawyer in the service of the Spanish Inquisition, became deeply involved in the largest witch-hunt in Spanish history. The hunt took place between 1609 and 1614 in the northern Basque-speaking provinces of Spain. It originated as an extension of the hunt conducted by the French magistrate Pierre de Lancre in the neighbouring southwestern French province of Labourd (Chapter 20). The hunt that took place in the Basque country grew to enormous proportions when young children began to confess that they were being taken to the *aquelarre* or sabbath. Eleven of the witches were tried by the tribunal of the Spanish Inquisition at Logroño and executed at an *auto de fé* in 1611. Alarmed by the confessions to witchcraft, the officials of the Inquisition published an Edict of Grace, which allowed witches to come forward and confess their crime without penalty. Salazar was instructed by his superiors in Madrid to conduct a visitation of the region where most of the confessions had been recorded. Carrying with him the Edict of Grace, he interrogated those who confessed, most of whom were children. After conducting this painstaking work, Salazar reached the conclusion that there was no foundation in reality to the confessions. All in all, Salazar made nine reports to his superiors between 1612 and 1623. In the Second Report of 1612, written after the conclusion of his visitation, he exposes the inconsistencies in the testimony given by those who confessed. Salazar's report is particularly effective because it does not in any way deny the possibility of the crime of witchcraft or the existence of the Devil. His only concern is the validity of these particular confessions. In his final report he made a series of recommendations regarding the prosecution of witches that virtually ended executions for witchcraft by the Spanish Inquisition.

Source: the *Second Report of Alonso de Salazar to the Inquisitor General*
(Logroño, 24 March 1612), in Gustav Henningsen (ed.), *The Salazar
Documents: Inquisitor Alonso de Salazar Frías and Others on the Basque
Witch-Persecution (1609–1614)* (Leiden: Brill, 2003).

An account of the results of the whole visitation and publication of the Edict relating to the witches

Most Excellent Sir:

In a letter which I addressed to Your Eminence from Fuenterrabía, on September 4, I reported how, as a sequel to the Edict of Grace granted to those members of the witch sect, 1546 persons of all ranks and ages came forward to avail themselves of it, even though, when I left this city of Logroño, there were no more than 338 confessions laid before the tribunal from people in the mountains of Navarre and from the rest of the district.

I now report that – during the period from 22 May 1611 when I set forth on the visitation, to 10 January this year when I finished – a total of 1802 cases has been dispatched by all of us. The figure can be broken down into the following groups: 1384 children, of twelve or fourteen years and under, were absolved *ad cautelam*. Of those older than twelve or fourteen, 290 were reconciled; 41 absolved *ad cautelam* with abjuration *de levi*; 81 retracted the confessions which they had made to the Holy Office in order to be reconciled either before the commissioners, in [the tribunal at] Logroño or during the visitation; and, finally, 6 confessed to having relapsed by returning to the *aquelarres*. Among the 290 whom I reconciled there were a hundred persons over twenty, of all ages, many of them being sixty, seventy, eighty, or even ninety years old. A survey of the cases of each one of the said groups has been set down separately in special reports. . . .

First Article. Of the manner in which the witches set out to, are present at, and return from the aquelarres.

1. As to the manner of the setting forth to the reunion of the witches or *aquelarre*, they agree that it was always after they had fallen asleep in their beds. A hundred and two persons alleged that this was so. Although others say that they also used to go while awake and before they had gone to bed and fallen asleep, they are very few, less than ten. Yet the majority in both the categories answered that they woke up on the way and maintained that during the outward journey, their presence at the aquelarre, and on their return they were awake.

2. Most of the aforementioned also say that they usually went and came back flying through the air, although on a few occasions they used to go on foot or on the shoulders of their mistresses who had made them witches. Likewise one said that she was wont to go in the form of a housefly and another stated that she went in the form of a raven.

3. As to how they leave their bedchamber, almost all of those referred to in the first gloss say that they got out through some chink or hole, window or chimney through which naturally nobody could pass without danger. A number of the same (the minority) say that they went out through the doors and down the staircases of their houses, returning in the same fashion. . . .

5. Thus, by whatever means they left and returned to their houses, none of them confess that they have been seen or heard by anyone in their house or outside. This will be made clear later in the third article [of this report] which deals with the external proofs of these things. The only exception is one Juan de Saldías, a man of eighty years and of a very sound disposition and reason. He stated that his wife had heard him many times and had asked him whence he came so cold when he returned to his bed. Unfortunately, his wife has been dead a long time.

6. Indeed, it is remarkable that in a village where everybody is on the watch for this event, because of the general pain and grief which afflicts the community, they have never come across the witches, even though so numerous, nor seen what happens among them. Even those in the same house or in the very chamber from which they depart remain in ignorance. For until now I have never met with anyone who has seen what takes place. It is still more a cause for wonder that neither have two accomplices leaving the same bed felt the other getting out or coming back. The latter is implied by the seven mature and responsible persons referred to in the glosses.

7. Even if we leave aside this incongruity we are faced with another yet greater. Several people who had come to confess stated that while fully awake in the middle of the day, eating or talking to people in public, without turning aside one single moment from the people to whom they were speaking, they have been transported to their *aquelarre*. In this way they once departed from the public procession of litanies in which the whole village was taking part to hold another one simultaneously before the Devil at the sabbath. They tell of a similar departure when the whole village was present in church to hear fray Domingo de Sardo declaring the Edict of Grace during a sermon. A third translation took place, they say, when those to be reconciled during the visitation came to the towns of Santesteban and Elizondo. The actual transfer occurred in the latter town. These events always took place by day and always without anyone noticing that the participants were missing. Another said that she also set out by daylight, while awake, and flew through the air in front of her parents and others in the house without any of them noticing her. . . .

9. Let us suppose that one was willing to give credence to all this, and to believe that the Devil is able to make persons present when they are not and make others invisible when they pass before people who would certainly recognise them, with the result that nobody can be sure that he or she who is present is any more real than he or she who is with the witches. Surely one could conceive far more readily another explanation: the Devil only

deludes those "invisible" ones, or those who think that they have been absent, without this ever happening, in order that the deceived ones should speak in good faith and find acceptance for these and similar lies, and consequently also be believed when they say that they have seen at his *aquelarre* other people whom they subsequently denounce. Thus immediately and without any effort the Devil leaves the village in an uproar, and those unjustly incriminated exposed to condemnation and other afflictions to be described later in the fourth article.

Second Article. Of the things they do and experience as witches.

10. Some of the things that cause most surprise are those experiences they say they undergo as witches. Thus one man says that, while living in sin with a certain woman (whom he named) he used to attend the *aquelarres*, and although both partners saw each other in the crowd, they never spoke to one another nor exchanged a single word about their illicit relationship. Again, a man who at the sabbath used to have sexual intercourse with another woman, says that outside the meetings they never talked about it. Another, an older man of eminently sound reason, stated that the Devil had married him off to a certain female witch at the *aquelarre* and that for a long time he had had sexual intercourse with her there. On the death of this woman he married another (whom he also named) and had marital relations with her for some time. But this only took place at the *aquelarre*, for when they met outside the gatherings he never succumbed to temptation with either of those women, nor was the topic ever mentioned. . . .

12. Another three women stated that two hours after having had sexual intercourse with the Devil they gave birth to large toads. A fourth says that, feeling a heavy obstruction in her throat, she gave birth to another such toad through her mouth. Thus she alleviated her discomfort and was free to reveal things about witchcraft, having been previously prevented by the said toad in her throat. Notwithstanding, none of the four produced witnesses, either from inside or outside the coven, who could substantiate their stories.

Third Article. Of the actos positivos *or external proofs which we have endeavored to substantiate.*

25. . . . Maria de Echevarría, alias Zunda, resident of Oronóz and eighty years old, made a full confession, showing by her heartfelt contrition and unceasing tears her genuine desire to heal her soul, for which she turned to the Holy Office. She said that while asleep, not knowing how, and entirely against her consent, she was taken to the *aquelarre* every night, including the preceding one. She affirmed that she woke up on the way and returned awake, although nobody ever met or saw her leaving or returning, not even an elderly daughter who slept in the same bed and was a witch belonging to the same coven. And basing ourselves on the interview and lengthy debate held with her by all the friars in the chamber and in my presence, we all

concluded that what this good woman was confessing about her witchcraft was, without doubt, nothing but a dream; and consequently all that she now adds in the case of her relapse may be taken as such. Many others made the same phenomenon clear, namely that their witchcraft had taken place in their dreams, as will be seen from the tenor of their confessions. . . .

34. Catalina de Echeverría, an old women who was reconciled at the tribunal in Logroño, said in her confessions that when she became a witch the Devil removed three toes from her left foot. Yet witnesses and people from her house, on being examined, declared that she had lacked those toes since infancy. This she admitted herself afterwards on revoking her confessions, and went on to state that all had been an invention and falsehood on her part. . . .

50. Our investigations into the potions and powders of witchcraft, which many accomplices claim they have employed to inflict damages or to anoint themselves with before setting out to the *aquelarre*, have up to now on the basis of their testimony revealed nothing. Nor have we come across anything to convince us of the existence of these ointments, nor the remains of any such things, but rather the opposite. Every one of the twenty-two pots produced in the course of the visitation have been revealed as false, fake and fraudulent. They were only made by people who were forced to fabricate these things to avoid the troubles and vexations (just as the *revocantes* fabricated their confessions about their being witches, subsequently shown to be false) employing means so devious and ridiculous that they would seem to merit nothing more than mockery and laughter. . . .

Fourth article. Of the evidence which might result from the above and serve to convict the guilty.

56. . . . [I]t is not surprising that in our search for evidence from witnesses who are not witches themselves, we have found not a single one from among the cases included in the [general testimonies of the] visitation of sufficient weight to warrant an arrest, in spite of all our efforts to use the evidence produced by the witches themselves to discover [material] proof. Moreover, there is still a more incredible, indeed amazing, feature of the case: How is it that in an affair which is so widespread according to the witches themselves, and which under any circumstances would be impossible to conceal for one hour, it is nevertheless so difficult, or rather impossible as it would appear, to ascertain anything at all? . . .

58. The trustworthiness of witnesses is further weakened by the force, inducements, and sinister methods used to extort their declarations. For they were imprisoned, molested and violently threatened. . . . Thus one woman stated that they burned her with a live coal and while torturing her in this manner they kept telling her that at that very moment she was with the witches at their evil work. All this is enough to fill one with horror, making one realize how by these means the truth was inevitably distorted. . . .

66. All the suspicions about the damage [caused by false denunciations] have been confirmed by those who revoked their confessions, as well as by others who, without revoking, asked to have removed from their confessions the names of several persons whom they had cited as accomplices. From both categories there are 1672 individuals against whom they admit that they bore false witness declaring them to be witches when, in fact, they were not. Thus with 1672 false statements from those who admitted to perjury one can hardly expect the truth from the remainder or give credence to their denunciations.

67. The trustworthiness of the witnesses is not enhanced by the widely believed rumours. The witchcraft stories are not merely vague and nebulous, but at times they actually name individuals. When, however, their origins and authors are duly investigated, these accounts turn out to be even more defective than the above-mentioned evidence of the witnesses. The only basis for this rumour-mongering appears to be the punishment of witches at the *auto-de-fé* celebrated in Logroño, the Edict of Grace, and the fact that an inquisitor has set out to visit so many places. All of which apparently provides a reason for everything to be immediately thought of as witchcraft. This grows at every telling, and today in fact there is no fainting-fit, illness, death or accident that is not attributed to witches. And there is no lack of people who believe in it and exaggerate every detail. . . .

69. After having duly studied the above with all the Christian attention of which I am capable, and after having investigated all these matters both in the chamber and outside, I have not found a single proof, not even the slightest indications, from which to infer that an act of witchcraft has actually taken place, whether it comes to sabbath journeys, participation in the *aquelarre,* damages or any other of the referred effects. Rather I have found what I had already begun to suspect in these cases before my experience during the visitation: that the testimony of accomplices alone – even if they had not been submitted to violence and compulsion – without further support from external facts substantiated by persons who are not witches, is insufficient to warrant even an arrest. For each and every one of these testimonies contain the two notable defects demonstrated by all the above: firstly, they contain the very confusion inherent in all matters of witchcraft.

70. And secondly (in the light of the first point and particularly what I have been led to suspect in the same persons discharged by the Edict of Grace) I am firmly convinced that at least three-quarters of them, if not more, have falsely accused themselves and their accomplices, contrary to the truth. They were impelled to do so by a mixture of good and bad motives, and by use of the unlawful methods. Consequently on account of the harm they have caused to third parties, their souls remain in grave danger of damnation until they make amends. . . .

54

THOMAS HOBBES:
THE NATURE OF DEMONS,
1651

―――――◉◉◉◉◉――――――

Thomas Hobbes (1588–1679), an English mathematician and philosopher, owes his fame mainly to his works of political theory, especially *Leviathan*, published both in England and France in 1651, during the period of the English Republic (1649–1660). Hobbes argued that the only way to avoid a continual state of war was for members of society to agree to surrender the independent power that they possessed in the state of nature to a sovereign who would possess absolute power and would legislate on their behalf and maintain order. The bearer of this sovereign power would also determine the religious life of the people. Hobbes's theory of government was secular in the sense that government was instituted by men, not by God. Hobbes, a royalist, was hostile to the members of the clergy who had exercised influence within the English government at the time of the revolution. His philosophy of nature was that all reality was material; there were no incorporeal spirits. Hobbes was no atheist, but he believed that God was himself corporeal, an unusual but not heretical position in Christian theology. His attitude towards spirits, and his belief that nature operated in a mechanical way, led him to dismiss the powers of witches and demons. In *Leviathan* Hobbes discusses witchcraft and demonology in three separate contexts. In Chapter 2, which is a discussion of human imagination, Hobbes classifies the belief in witchcraft as a mere fancy to which the vulgar sort of people subscribe. He denies that witches have any power but that they should nonetheless be punished because of the threat they pose to the order of society. In Chapter 34, he discusses whether the demons referred to in the Bible were incorporeal, as contemporary theologians argued. Hobbes, consistent to his materialist philosophy, argues that the spirits (angels and demons) created by God and referred to in the Bible were substances and thus possessed bodies. For Hobbes, an incorporeal body was a contradiction in terms. Finally, in Chapter 45 Hobbes attacks the entire study of demons by Greek philosophers and Christian theologians, denying once again that there are any incorporeal spirits. For Hobbes, demons either have bodies or they are the product of human imagination. He concludes by interpreting the words of Scripture to support his argument.

Source: Thomas Hobbes, *Leviathan* (London, 1651), pp. 7–8, 209–210, 352–366.

Chapter 2. Of Imagination.

From this ignorance of how to distinguish dreams and strong fancies from vision and sense did arise the greatest part of the religion of the gentiles in time past that worshipped satyrs, fauns, nymphs, and the like; and nowadays the opinion that rude people have of fairies, ghosts, and goblins, and of the power of witches. For, as for witches, I think not that their witchcraft is any real power, but yet that they are justly punished for the false belief they have that they can do much mischief, joined with their purpose to do it if they can, their trade being nearer to a new religion than to a craft or a science. And for fairies and walking ghosts, the opinion of them has, I think, been on purpose either taught or not confuted to keep in credit the use of exorcism, of crosses, of holy water, and other such inventions of ghostly men. Nevertheless, there is no doubt but God can make unnatural apparitions. But that he does it so often as men need to fear such things more than they fear the stay or change of the course of nature, which he can also stay and change, is no point of Christian faith. But evil men, under pretext that God can do anything, are so bold as to say anything when it serves their turn, though they think it untrue. It is the part of a wise man to believe them no further than right reason makes that which they say appear credible. If this superstitious fear of spirits were taken away and with it prognostics from dreams, false prophecies, and many other things depending thereon, by which crafty ambitious persons abuse the simple people, men would be much more fitted than they are for civil obedience. . . .

Chapter 34. Of the Signification of Spirit, Angel, and Inspiration in the Books of Holy Scripture.

The disciples of Christ, seeing him walking upon the sea (Matt. 14:26 and Mark 6:49) supposed him to be a spirit, meaning thereby an aerial *body*, and not a phantasm; for it is said they all saw him; which cannot be understood of the delusions of the brain (which are not common to many at once, as visible bodies are, because of the differences of fancies), but of bodies only. In like manner, where he was taken for a *spirit* by the same apostles (Luke 24:3, 24:7), so also when St Peter was delivered out of prison, it would not be believed; but when the maid said he was at the door, they said it was his *angel* (Acts 12; 15) by which must be meant a corporeal substance, or we must say the disciples themselves did not follow the common opinion of both Jews and gentiles that some apparitions were not imaginary, but real, and such as needed not the fancy of man for their existence; these the Jews called *spirits* and *angels*, good or bad, as the Greeks called the same by the name of *demons*. And some such apparitions may be real and substantial, that is to say, subtle bodies, which God can form by the same power by which he formed all things and make use of as ministers and messengers (that is to say, angels) to declare his will and execute the same when he pleaseth in extraordinary and supernatural manner. But when he hath so formed them they are substances, endured with dimensions, and take up room and can be moved from place to place, which is peculiar to bodies; and therefore are not ghosts *incorporeal*, that is to say ghosts that are in *no place*, that is to say, that are *nowhere*, that is to say, that, seeming to be *somewhat*, are *nothing*. But if incorporeal be taken in the next vulgar manner, for such substances as are perceptible by our external senses, then is substance incorporeal a thing not imaginary, but real, namely, a thin substance invisible, but that hath the same dimensions that are in grosser bodies. . . . .

And as the Gentiles did vulgarly conceive the imagery of the brain for things really subsistent without them and not dependent on the fancy, and out of them framed their opinions of *demons*, good and evil, which because they seemed to subsist really, they called substances, and because they could not feel them with their hands, incorporeal; so also the Jews upon the same ground without anything in the Old Testament that constrained them thereunto, had generally an opinion (except the sect of the Sadducees) that those apparitions, which it pleased God sometimes to produce in the fancy of men for his own service and therefore called them his *angels*, were substances, not dependent upon the fancy, but permanent creatures of God, whereof those which they thought were good to them, they esteemed *angels of God*, and those they thought would hurt them, they called *evil angels* or evil spirits; such as was the spirit of Python, and the spirits of madmen, of lunatics and epileptics; for they esteemed such as were troubled with such diseases, *demoniacs*. . . .

Chapter 45. Of Demonology and Other Relics of the Religion of the Gentiles.
. . . This nature of sight having never been discovered by the ancient pretenders to natural knowledge, much less by those that consider not things so remote (as that knowledge is) from their present use, it was hard for men to conceive of those images in the fancy and in the sense otherwise than of things really without us; which some, because they vanish away, they know not whither nor how, will have to be absolutely incorporeal, that is to say, immaterial, or forms without matter (colour and figure without any coloured or figured body), and that they can put on airy bodies, as a garment; and others say [they] are bodies and living creatures, but made of air or more subtle and ethereal matter, which is, then, when they will be seen, condensed. But both of them agree on one general appellation of them, DEMONS. As if

the dead of whom they dreamed were not inhabitants of their own brain, but of the air or of heaven or of hell, not phantasms, but ghosts, with just as much reason as if one should say he saw his own ghost in a looking glass or the ghosts of the stars in a river, or call the ordinary apparition of the sun of the quantity of about a foot, the demon or ghost of that great sun that enlighteneth the whole visible world; and by that means [they] have feared them, as things of an unknown, that is, of an unlimited power to do them good or harm; and consequently [they have] given occasion to the governors of the heathen commonwealths to regulate this their fear by establishing that DEMONOLOGY (in which the poets, as principal priests of the heathen religion, were specially employed or reverenced) to the public peace and to the obedience of subjects necessary thereunto, and to make some of them good demons and others evil; the one as a spur to the observance, the other, as reins to withhold them from violation of the laws.

What kind of things they were to whom they attributed the name of *demons* appeareth partly in the genealogy of their gods, written by Hesiod, one of the most ancient poets of the Grecians, and partly in other histories, of which I have observed some few before, in the twelfth chapter of this discourse.

The Grecians, by their colonies and conquests communicated their language and writings into Asia, Egypt, and Italy; and therein, by necessary consequence, their *demonology*, or, as St Paul calls it, *their doctrines of devils*. And by that means the contagion was derived also to the Jews, both of Judaea and Alexandria, and other parts, whereinto they were dispersed, and the name of *demon* they did not, as the Grecians, attribute to spirits both good and evil but to the evil only. And to the good demons they gave the name of the spirit of God, and esteemed those into whose bodies they entered to be prophets. In sum, all singularity, if good, they attributed to the Spirit of God, and if evil, to some demon, but a *kakodaimon*, an evil *demon*, that is a *devil*. And therefore they called demoniacs, that is, possessed by the devil, such as we call madmen or lunatics, or such as had the falling sickness, or that spoke anything which they, for want of understanding, thought absurd. As also of an unclean person in a notorious degree, they used to say he had an unclean spirit; of a dumb man, that he had a dumb devil; and of *John the Baptist* (Matt. 11:18), for the singularity of his fasting, that he had a devil; and of our Saviour, because he said, he that keepeth his sayings should not see death *in aeternum, Now we know thou hast a devil; Abraham is dead, and the prophets are dead.* And again, because he said *they went about to kill him*, the people answered, *Thou hast a devil: who goeth about to kill thee?* (John 7:20) Whereby it is manifest that the Jews had the same opinions concerning phantasms, namely, that they were not phantasms, that is, idols of the brain, but things real and independent on the fancy.

Which doctrine if it be not true, why (some may say) did not our Saviour contradict it and teach the contrary? Nay, why does he use on divers occasions such forms of speech as seem to confirm it? To this answer that, first, Christ saith *A spirit hath not flesh and bone* (Luke 24:39), although he show that there be spirits: yet he denies not that they are bodies. And whereas St Paul says, *We shall rise spiritual bodies* [I Cor 15:44], he acknowledgeth the nature of spirits, but that they are bodily spirits, which is not difficult to understand. For air and many other things are bodies, though not flesh and bone, or any other gross body to be discerned by the eyes. But when our Saviour speaketh to the devil and commandeth him to go out of a man, if by the devil be meant a disease, as frenzy or lunacy or a corporeal spirit, is not the speech improper? Can diseases hear? Or can there be a corporeal spirit in a body of flesh and bone, full already of vital and animal spirits? Are there not, therefore, spirits that neither have bodies nor are mere imaginations? To the first I answer that the addressing of our Saviour's command to the madness or lunacy he cureth is no more improper than was his rebuking of the fever or of the wind and sea, for neither do these hear. Or [no more improper] than was the command of God to the light, to the firmament, to the sun, and stars, when he commanded them to be; for they could not hear before they had a being. But those speeches are not improper, because they signify the power of God's word; no more is it improper to command madness or lunacy (under the appellation of devils by which they were then commonly understood) to depart out of a man's body. To the second, concerning their being incorporeal, I have not yet observed any place of Scripture from whence it can be gathered that any man was ever possessed with any other corporeal spirit but that of his own by which his body is naturally moved. . . .

But if there be no immaterial spirit nor any possession of men's bodies by any spirit corporeal, it may again be asked why our Saviour and his Apostles did not teach the people so and in such clear words as they might no more doubt thereof. But such questions as these are more curious than necessary for a Christian man's salvation. If we require of the Scripture an account of all questions which may be raised to trouble us in the performance of God's commands, we may as well complain of Moses for not having set down the time of the creation of such spirits as well as of the creation of the earth and sea, and of men and beasts. To conclude, I find in Scripture that there be angels and spirits, good and evil, but not that they are incorporeal, as are the apparitions men see in the dark or in a dream or vision, which the Latins call spectra and took for demons. And I find that there are spirits corporeal, though subtle and invisible, but not that any man's body was possessed or inhabited by them and that the bodies of the saints shall be such, namely, spiritual bodies, as St Paul calls them.

Figure 11 Credulity, Superstition, and Fanaticism (1762). Long after the last witchcraft executions in western Europe, the English engraver William Hogarth satirized the effects of fanatical religion, witchcraft, and superstition. The sermon has whipped the entire congregation into a highly emotional state. The woman in the foreground is Mary Tofts, who was believed to have given birth to rabbits. The boy next to her, allegedly possessed by the Devil, vomits pins. (See above, Part VI). The Protestant preacher's wig falls off, exposing the shaven head of a Roman Catholic monk. He is holding a witch on a broomstick, who is nursing a familiar spirit. An unemotional Turk observes this scene from outside the window. From *The Works of William Hogarth*, ed. Thomas Clerk, (London, 1812).

55

BARUCH SPINOZA: THE NON-EXISTENCE OF THE DEVIL, 1661, 1675

———⇒◦◦◦⇐———

Baruch Spinoza (1632–1677) an excommunicated Dutch Jew, was one of the most radical philosophers of the seventeenth century. Unlike the materialist Hobbes, his English contemporary, Spinoza believed that all reality was a manifestation of the divine. This pantheism, however, was no more conducive to the existence of demons than Hobbes's materialism. In these two excerpts from his works, Spinoza denies the existence of the Devil. In his treatise *God, Man, and His Well-Being*, written in the early 1660s, Spinoza argues that the Devil could find no place in a pantheistic universe, since he is the antithesis of a God who comprises all of reality. In the second excerpt, a letter to a nobleman who had accused him of being ensnared by the Devil, Spinoza argues that such a claim is incompatible with the belief in an infinite and eternal God. This view represents an extension of the argument presented by some theologians, especially Protestants, that attributing power to the Devil denies the sovereignty of God. Unlike those theologians, Spinoza would deny the Devil even the power to deceive.

Sources: The first excerpt comes from *The Collected Works of Spinoza*, ed. and trans. Edwin Curley (Princeton, 1985), vol. I, p. 145. The second excerpt, comes from *Spinoza: The Letters*, trans. Samuel Shirley (Indianapolis, 1995).

God, Man, and His Well-Being

Part II

Chapter XXV: Of Devils.

[1] We shall now say something briefly about whether or not there are Devils:

If the Devil is a thing that is completely contrary to God and has nothing from God, then he agrees completely with Nothing, of which we have already spoken previously.

[2] If, as some do, we maintain that he is a thinking thing that neither wills nor does anything at all that is good, and so completely opposes himself to God, then certainly he is quite miserable, and if prayers could help, we should pray for his conversion.

[3] But let us just see whether such a miserable thing could exist for even a single moment. If we consider this, we shall immediately find that it cannot. For all the duration of a thing arises from its perfection, and the more essence and divinity they have in them, the more constant they are. Since the Devil has the least perfection in himself, how, I wonder, could he exist? Moreover, constancy or duration in the mode of the thinking thing only arise through the union which such a mode has with God, a union produced by love. Since the exact opposite of this is posited in Devils, they cannot possibly exist.

[4] But because there is no necessity to posit Devils, why should they be posited? "For we have no need, as others do, to posit Devils in order to find causes of hate, envy, anger, and such passions. We have come to know them sufficiently without the aid of such fictions."

Letter 76. Greetings to the noble young man, Alfred Burgh, from Spinoza. Dec, 1675.

... But I return to your letter, in which first of all you lament that I allow myself to be ensnared by the prince of evil spirits. But please be of good cheer and come to yourself again. When you were in your senses, if I am not mistaken, you used to worship an infinite God by whose efficacy all things absolutely come into being and are preserved, but now you dream of Prince, God's enemy who against God's will ensnares most men (for the good are few) and deceives them, whom God therefore delivers over to this master of wickedness for everlasting torture. So divine justice permits the Devil to deceive men with impunity, but does not permit men, haplessly deceived and ensnared by the Devil, to go unpunished.

Now these absurdities might so far be tolerated if you worshipped a God infinite and eternal, nor one whom Chastillon, in a town the Dutch called Tienen, gave to horses to eat and was not punished.* And do you bewail me, wretched man? And do you call my philosophy, which you have never beheld, a chimera? O youth deprived of understanding, who has bewitched you into believing that you eat, and hold in your intestines, that which is supreme and eternal?

*In 1635 a French Huguenot general, after sacking this Catholic town, gave eucharistic hosts to horses as an expression of his disgust with Catholic idolatry.

56

JOHN WEBSTER:
WITCHCRAFT AND THE
OCCULT, 1677

John Webster's *The Displaying of Supposed Witchcraft* (1677) which was the first salvo in a heated debate with Webster's fellow countryman Joseph Glanvill, reveals some interesting aspects of the skeptical tradition in England, where it exhibited exceptional strength in the late seventeenth century. First, Webster's skepticism drew to a great extent on radical Protestant ideas, just as did that of Reginald Scot almost one hundred years earlier. The religious orientation of Webster's work also linked him with two later skeptics on the Continent: Balthasar Bekker (Chapter 57) and Christian Thomasius, the author of *The Crime of Magic* (1701). Webster repeats the argument of many other commentators, including Scot, that witchcraft was the product of ignorance of the Gospel and that it flourished mainly in those regions where the Gospel was not being preached. Second, Webster admits the existence of magicians, who he claims are deceivers and cheats, as well as those witches who are deluded into thinking they have special powers. His criticism is directed against those who believe that witches make pacts and copulate with the Devil and use demonic power to raise storms. Webster attacks these witch-beliefs as foolish and impious, and he bases his opinion on the claim that all the marvelous effects attributed to witches have natural causes. This position was not unlike that taken by Michel Marescot in explaining the symptoms of demonic possession in Marthe Brossier in 1599 (see Chapter 46). Webster appeals to natural causes not as a scientist committed to the belief that the world operates like a machine, but as a neo-Platonist who believes that nature is full of occult forces that will ultimately explain all natural phenomena. Glanvill, on the other hand, a member of the Royal Society, defended the belief in witchcraft on the grounds that the Devil worked through the forces of nature.

Source: John Webster, Practitioner in Physic, *The Displaying of Supposed Witchcraft; Wherein is affirmed that there are many sorts of deceivers and imposters and divers persons under a passive delusion of melancholy and fancy, but that there is a corporal league made betwixt the devil and the witch, or that she sucks on the witches body, has carnal copulation, or that witches are turned into cats, dogs, raise tempests, or the like is utterly denied and disproved* (London, 1677), pp. 25–36, 267–268.

Chapter 2. Of the Notion, Conception, and Description of Witches and Witchcraft, according to divers authors, and in what sense they may be granted, and in what sense and respect they are denied.

Those that were and are active deceivers, and are both by active practice and purpose notorious imposters, though they shadow their delusive and cheating knaveries under divers and various pretences, some pretending to do their feats by astrology (which is a general cheat as it is commonly used) some by a pretended gift from God, when they are notoriously drunken, debauched, and blasphemous persons, such as of very late years was the cobbler that lived upon Ellill Moor, named Richmond, and divers others that I could name, but that in modesty I would spare their reputations; some by pretending skill in natural magic, when indeed they can hardly read English truly; some by pretending a familiar spirit, as once Thomas Bolton near Knaresborough in Yorkshire, when indeed and in truth they have no other familiar but their own spirit of lying and deceiving; some by pretending to reveal things in crystal glasses or beryls, as was well known to be pretended by Doctor Lamb, and divers others I have known. And some by pretending to conjure and call up devils, or the spirits of men departed; and some by many other ways and means that are not necessary to be named here; for error and deceit have a numerous train of followers and disciples. And the existence of such kind of witches as these (if you will needs call them by that name, and not by their proper titles, which are, that they truly are Deceivers, Cheaters, Couseners, and Imposters) I willingly acknowledge, as having been, and are to be found in all ages, and these sorts are also acknowledged by Wierus, Mr. Scot, Johannes Lazarus Gutierius, Tobias Tandlerus, Hieronymous Nymannus, Martinius Biermannus, and all the rest, that notwithstanding did with might and main oppose the gross tenet of the common witchmongers. . . .

And as there are a numerous crew of active witches, whose existence we freely acknowledge, so there are another sort, that are under a passive delusion, and know not, or at least do not observe or understand that they are deluded or imposed upon. These are those who confidently believe that they see, do, and suffer many strange, odd, and wonderful things, which indeed have no existence at all in them, but only in their depraved fancies, and are utterly *melancholia figmenta*. And yet the confessions of these, though absurd, idle, foolish, false and impossible, are without all ground and reason by the common witchmongers taken to be truths and falsely ascribed unto demons, and that they are sufficient grounds to proceed upon to condemn the confessors to death, when all is but passive delusion, intrinsically wrought in the depraved imaginative faculty by these three ways or means.

1. One of the causes that produceth this depraved and passive delusion is evil education; they being bred up in ignorance, either of God, the Scriptures, or the true grounds of Christian religion, nay not being taught by the common rules of morality, or of other humane literature; but only imbibing and sucking in with their mother's and nurses' milk the common and gross and erroneous opinions that the blockish vulgar people do hold, who are all generally inchanted and bewitched with the belief of the strange things related of devils, apparitions, fairies, hobgoblins, ghosts, spirits and the like; so that thereby a most deep impression of the verity of the most gross and impossible things is instamped in their fancies, hardly ever after in their whole life time to be obliterated or washed out; so prevalent a thing is custom and intuition from young years though the things thus received, and pertinaciously believed and adhered unto are most abominable falsities and impossibilities, having no other existence but in the brains and phantasies of old, ignorant, and doting persons, and are merely *muliercularum et nutricum tericulamenta et figmenta*, and therefore did Seneca say: *gravissimum est consuetudinis imperium*. And that this one main cause of this delusion is manifest from all the best historians, that where the light of the gospel hath least appeared, and where there is the greatest brutish ignorance and heathenish barbarism, there the greatest store of these deluded witches or melancholists are to be found, as in the north of Scotland, Norway, Lapland and the like, as may be seen at large in *Saxo Grammaticus, Olaus Magnus, Hector Boetius*, and the like.

2. But when an atrabilarious temperament or a melancholic complexion and constitution doth happen to those people bred in such ignorance, and that they have sucked in all the fond opinions that custom and tradition could teach them, then what thing can be imagined that is strange, wonderful or incredible but these people do pertinaciously believe it, and as confidently relate it to others? Nay even things that are absolutely impossible, as that they are really changed into wolves, hares, dogs, cats, squirrels, and the like; and that they fly in the air, are present at great feats and meetings, and do strange and incredible things, when all these are but the mere effects of the imaginative function depraved by the fumes of the melancholic humour, as we might show from the writings of the most grave and learned physicians, . . .

3. And as ignorance and irreligion meeting with a melancholic constitution doth frame many persons to strange fancies both of fear and credulity; so when to these is added the teachings of those that are themselves under a most strong passive delusion, then of all others these become most strongly confident that they can perform admirable things. And when a person hath by education sucked in all the grossest fables and lies of the power of witches

and familiar devils, and therein becometh extremely confident, heightened with the fumes of black choler, and so thinks, meditates, and dreameth of devils, spirits, and all the strange stories that have been related of them, and becometh maliciously stirred up against some neighbour or other, and so in that malicious and revengeful mind seeketh unto, and inquireth for some famed and notorious witch, of whom they believe they may learn such craft and cunning, that thereby they may be able to kill or destroy the persons or goods of those that they suppose have done them injuries, then meeting with some that are strongly deluded, and consistently persuaded, that they have the company and assistance of a familiar spirit, by whose help they believe they can do (most) anything, especially in destroying men or cattle, they are presently instructed what vain and abominable ceremonies, observances, unguents, charms, making of pictures, and a thousand such fond, odd flopperies they are to use, by which they believe they can do strange feats. . . .

Besides these two sorts of witches, whose existence we deny not, there is an acceptation of the word witch in another sense, the existence of which I absolutely deny, and that is this according to Mr. Perkins: "A witch is a magician who either by open or secret league wittingly and willingly consenteth to use the aid and assistance of the devil in the working of wonders." . . .

Chapter XIII. That the ignorance of the power of art and nature and such like things hath much advanced these foolish and impious opinions.

The opinions we reject as foolish and impious are those we have often named before, to wit, that those that are vulgarly accounted witches, make a visible and corporeal contract with the devil, that he sucks upon their bodies, that he hath carnal copulation with them, and that they are transubstantiated into cats, dogs, squirrels and the like or that they raise tempests and fly in the air. Other powers we grant unto them to operate and effect whatsoever the force of imagination joined with envy, malice, and vehement desire of revenge, can perform or penetrate, or whatsoever hurt can be done by secret poisons and such like ways that work by mere natural means.

And here we are to show the chief causes that do and have advanced these opinions and this principally we ascribe to men's ignorance of the power of nature and art, as we shall manifest in the following particulars:

1. There is nothing more certain that, that how great soever the knowledge of men be taken to be, yet the ultimate sphere of nature's activity or ability is not perfectly known, which is made most manifest in this, that every day there are made new discoveries of her secrets, which prove plainly that her store is not yet totally exhausted, nor her utmost efficiency known. And therefore those men must needs be precipicious and build upon a sandy foundation that will ascribe corporeal effects unto devils and yet know not the extent of nature, for no man can rationally assign a beginning for supernatural agents and actions that does not certainly know where the power and operation of nature ends.

2. And as it is thus in general, so in many particulars, as especially in being ignorant of many natural agents that do work at a great distance, and very occultly, both to help, and to hurt, as in the weapon salve, the sympathetic powder, the curing of diseases by mumial applications, by amulets, appensions, and transplantions, which all have been, and commonly are ascribed unto Satan, when they are truly wrought by natural operations. And so (as we have sufficiently manifested before) by many strange and secret poisons both natural and artificial, that have no bewitching power in them at all, but work naturally and only may be hurtful in their use through the devilishness of some persons that use them to diverse evil ends.

3. There is nothing that doth more clearly manifest our scanted knowledge in the secret operations of nature and the effects that she produceth, than in the late discoveries of the workings of nature, both in the vegetable, animal and mineral kingdoms, brought daily to light by the pains and labours of industrious persons: As is well evident in those many elucubrations, and continued discoveries of those learned and indefatigable persons that are of the Royal Society, which do plainly evince that hitherto we have been ignorant of almost all the true causes of things, and therefore through blindness have usually attributed those things to the operation of Cacodemons that were truly wrought by nature, and thereby not smally augmented and advanced this gross and absurd opinion of the power of witches.

Figure 12 A satirical depiction of the witches' sabbath. In the early eighteenth century some educated people ridiculed witch beliefs. This satirical engraving of the witches' sabbath in Laurent Bordelon, *L'Histoire des imaginations extravagantes de Monsieur Oufle* (Paris, 1711) depicts male witches performing backwards somersaults, mocking the belief that witches showed reverence to the Devil by bowing down backwards. The scenes of dancing in the upper left, eating dismembered infants in the lower left, witches standing over and kneeling under the cauldron to the right, and the flight of witches are parodies of Jan Ziarnkov's credulous engraving produced a century earlier (see Figure 6).

57

BALTHASAR BEKKER:
THE DISENCHANTMENT
OF THE WORLD,
1695

Between 1691 and 1693 Balthasar Bekker, a Dutch Calvinist pastor and biblical scholar, published a massive, four-volume demonological treatise, *The Bewitched World*. The book, which was translated into English, German, and French and widely circulated throughout Europe, mounted a sustained attack on learned witch-beliefs. Bekker denied the pact with the Devil, the sabbath, metamorphosis, flight, conception by a demon, demonic possession and the very practice of harmful magic itself. Bekker's skepticism regarding witchcraft was far more systematic and consistent than that of Johann Weyer and even that of Reginald Scot, both of whom had written in the late sixteenth century (Chapters 51 and 52). Whereas Weyer could not bring himself to abandon the belief in a powerful, knowledgeable and deceptive Devil, Bekker denied that the Devil even possessed knowledge, much less a capacity to intervene in the operation of the material world. In Bekker the Calvinist insistence on God's sovereignty is carried to the point that the Devil is rendered completely powerless. Bekker writes mainly as a Biblical scholar. He was, to be sure, a follower of the philosopher and scientist René Descartes, subscribing both to Descartes' rigid distinction between body and soul and also to his mechanistic view of the natural world. But as these selections from *The World Bewitched* make clear, Bekker's denial of demonic power is for the most part based on Scripture. Bekker still believed in the Devil, but for him the Devil was nothing more than a symbol of evil. Once the Devil was reduced to this status, the possibility that a human being could commit the crime of witchcraft vanished. Indeed, Bekker suggested that when accusations of witchcraft are made, the state should prosecute the accusers, not the accused, a course of action that was becoming common at precisely the time he wrote.

Source: Balthazar Bekker, D.D. and Pastor at Amsterdam, *The World Bewitched; or, An Examination of the Common Opinion concerning Spirits: Their Nature, Power, Administration and Operations*, translated from a French copy, approved of and subscribed by the author's own hand (London, 1695), vol. I.

An Abridgement of the Whole Work

An Abridgement of the First Book.

... After the Pagans, which know neither the true God nor religion, I treat of those which have the Scripture among them, of whom the first are the Jews, having known God a long time before all the others and received his word in the writings of the Old Testament, where they have learned that in truth the souls of men are immortal, but that there are no demons, or inferior gods, such as the pagans fancy. That God alone by himself rules the universe, and that none can have knowledge or produce effects beyond the strength of nature, for that belongs to God only. I observe further that Judaism in the state into which it is insensibly fallen since the coming of Christ, and as it is at this day, is very much mixed with paganism, or at least very much infected with it; whence proceeds the practices of divinations and sorcery, that are in fashion among the Jews ...

After that I represent that the Mahometans, who acknowledge but one God and created angels good and bad, and the Devil as chief of them. That the Mahometans, I say, who have admitted the books of the New Testament, and reverence Jesus Christ as a great prophet, have nevertheless mixed in all their opinions a great many of those of the pagans, which they have for the most part received, and that they are no less inclined to divinations and witchcraft. Chapter the 14th.

After the Jews and the Mahometans who keep a kind of mean between the Pagans and the Christians, I pass to these last and distinguish them according to the time, before popery, under popery, and since popery. By this means I show that the primitive Christians since the Apostles have insensibly introduced amongst them many opinions of Paganism and Judaism, which have been increasing under popery till they attained to the highest pitch, and that they have ascribed to the angels the souls of the deceased, especially to the Devil, all the miracles which the pagans attributed to the demons, the Devils, and inferior gods ...

In the meanwhile, I take notice that among the ancient Christians there arose a sect called *Manichees* which had admitted in particular a great many pagan opinions and made the devil almost equal to God. And I show that their opinions have insensibly been propagated in Christianity, even to our times. After that I come to these last ages, and to the doctrines of the Protestant churches, among which I rank all those that are called *The Reformed*, that is, all those that are separated from Popery, upon which I remark that the more we are remote from paganism, either for time or place, there's the less credit given to all those things which respect the Devil and his power. Nevertheless I show that part of our people, not having comprehended enough what are the foundations of the Protestant doctrine, nor in what it differs from popery, are taken with the common opinion of Devils, to whom as well as to men that have communication with him they attribute more easily so many marvelous effects, and so much above the power of nature, than others do who have more meditated and reflected upon those doctrines and variations. . . .

An Abridgement of the Second Book.

As to what concerns my Second Book, see the method I have taken. I begin with the distinction [of] names, in fixing at first what must be understood by a body and a spirit, to avoid all equivocations: which I have done in the first chapter. I speak of God in the second, proving not only that the supreme being which I denote by that word is only one but also that there is not the least communion between it and created things; directly confuting the opinion of Spinoza upon this subject; which I pretend to do with more force and evidence than any hitherto, because ordinarily they undertake to demonstrate by the most perfect and incomprehensible essence of God the manner and virtue of the operations of created spirits, which I absolutely reject as a way which is used to lead us into error. By consequence I cannot admit the arguments which are taken from the sovereign perfection of God that there are none of those sorts of spirits that the pagans esteem to be gods and mediators of men towards the supreme divinity; because the reasons of those that ground that belief upon the perfection of God are directly opposite to this perfection.

We then having taken off the imaginary spirits, I come to those which we certainly know to exist, that is, our souls that are a part of ourselves and which by consequence are better known to us by our own experience. . . .

But as the possessed are universally alleged for a certain proof of the great power of the Devil, and that we read so many times in Scripture that the evil spirits have been cast out by our Saviour Jesus Christ, I bestow five chapters upon examining what is in it. I see that the term of *Diabolus*, which we translate Devil, is not found in any of the passages in which those relations are contained; but only that of daemon, which I illustrate in the 26th chapter. In the 27th I show that the most dangerous diseases, especially those of the head, were usually ascribed to demons; and in the 28th that our Saviour Jesus Christ has not changed the usual way of speaking but made use of them according to the custom of that time; neither did he always immediately confute all the errors in the 29th and 30th chapters; so that the cure of *Demonia* was not properly an expulsion of devils but a miraculous cure of incurable diseases.

I come after to other passages of Scripture where neither the names of Devils, Satan, or Demon are made use of, but those of *the Prince of the World,*

Prince of the power of the air, Prince of this age, of Lordships, Powers, Dominions. and the like; and I show that there is not the least cause to apply them to the Devil, but that the style of Scripture leads us of itself to understand by all these names a certain order of persons. . . .

Afterwards, in the 33rd Chapter, I show that the knowledge that the Devil may have, as well of things natural as civil, and above all of things spiritual, which concerns our salvation, is nothing of what is believed. I rest upon the same foundation of Scripture and reason to prove the empire of the Devil is but a chimera, and that he has neither such a power nor such an administration as is ordinarily ascribed to him.

An Abridgement of the Third Book.

I propose at first the true state of the question showing that the query is not whether magic is possible, for I grant it, but whether there is a magic, which by virtue of agreement made between men and the Devil, may discover hidden things, predict those that are to come, and to produce effects above the course of nature . . .

In the first [part] I examine whether it be possible to conceive that men have any commerce with Spirits; that the one and the other may rely upon mutual help, or that the one may act one upon another. In the second part I examine whether it be possible to believe that there may be express compacts between them, and that they may mutually contract and reciprocally perform the conditions of their Covenants. I expressly deny the first of these, founded upon the reasons alleged Book 2, Chap. 2. And I unfold a little more precisely in the second Chap. of this what is contained in the first, which I defend against the argument of Glanvil, an English author. I bestow the third chapter upon confuting those compacts of the magicians with the Devil as ridiculous and altogether incredible, and I answer at the same time several objections and shifts of Glanvil, convincing him by his own reasons that are sufficient for that purpose. . . .

In the 12th [chapter] I run over again the whole Scripture from the beginning to the end, from the Covenant of God with Abraham to our Savior and examining whether from whatever has been said upon that subject, there is any occasion to infer that the Devil may likewise on his part make his detestable compacts. I demonstrate that the opinion which supposes such contracts between the Devil and men by virtue of which they are said to have performed all their witchcrafts, can by no means consist with what is contained in the doctrine of the Holy Scripture, nor with the dispensation of God's covenant as well before the Law as under the Law, and much less under the Gospel.

An Abridgement of the Fourth Book.

. . . These proofs show that there are no natural reasons, nor revelations in the Holy Writ, no certain experiments that give us cause to ascribe to wicked spirits all the operations and effects that are generally supposed to proceed from the Devil or from men, his confederates. This is contained in the 33rd chapter, whereupon it must be remembered that what I say concerns only the common doctrine and opinion. Afterwards 'tis not difficult to show how wrongfully such a superstition is cherished and increased, instead of moderating it or even rooting it out, if possible.

Part VIII

DRAMATIC REPRESENTATIONS OF WITCHCRAFT

Ever since classical antiquity, dramatists have used the theme of witchcraft in their literary work. The human exercise of mysterious or supernatural evil has always appealed to audiences and offers the dramatist numerous possibilities for character and plot development. The value of such literary works to historians of witchcraft, however, is highly problematic. The main problem is that dramatists generally have little need (and certainly no requirement) to present an accurate depiction of historical reality. A strict adherence to the historical record could easily deprive their work of its literary appeal. Only occasionally, therefore, have dramas about witchcraft revealed much concern for historical accuracy. Thomas Dekker's seventeenth-century drama, *The Witch of Edmonton*, which drew upon contemporary narrative accounts of Elizabeth Sawyer's trial, is one of the few exceptions. Shakespeare, Marlowe, and other dramatists who exploited the theme of witchcraft in the late sixteenth and early seventeenth centuries were far more indiscriminate than Dekker in selecting their sources. They drew on any materials available, including earlier literary depictions of witchcraft in classical literature, in writing their plays. Dramas set in the period of witch-hunting are no more helpful in clarifying the historical record than most dramas written about witchcraft in the twentieth century. Thomas Middleton's *The Witch*, for example, tells us no more about witchcraft in seventeenth-century England than Arthur Miller's play, *The Crucible* (1953) tells us about the Salem witchcraft trials.

Dramatic representations of witchcraft can nonetheless serve as useful sources for understanding witchcraft in earlier periods. Because they reached large and diverse audiences, they could actually help to shape contemporary perceptions of witchcraft. Dramas produced before the age of the witch-hunts, like Seneca's image of Medea (Chapter 58), contributed to the formation of the image of the witch in both learned and popular culture. Fernando de Rojas's development of the character of the witch Celestina in his play *The Tragick-Comedy of Calisto and Melibea*, which was written at the beginning of the period of witch-hunting, not only drew on that of Medea, but also influencd his readers' image of the urban sorceress (Chapter 59). Thomas Middleton's *The Witch* (Chapter 60), produced during the period of witch-hunting, might also have contributed to a heightened awareness of witchcraft in England during the early seventeenth century.

Dramatic representations of the witch in the twentieth century, long after the end of the trials, serve different functions in the study of witchcraft. The early twentieth-century representation of the trial of Anne Pedersdotter in Bergen, Norway, in 1590 (Chapter 61) does not add anything to the historical record and in many respects misrepresents it, but it does suggest ways in which family tensions could lead to witchcraft accusations. It also presents a plausible though historically unverifiable account of how a person might be persuaded that she is in fact a witch and thus make a genuinely free confession.

58

SENECA:
THE WITCH IN
CLASSICAL DRAMA

Lucius Annaeus Seneca, known usually as Seneca (5 BCE–65 CE), a Roman philosopher, dramatist and statesman, wrote about Medea, one of the most important witch figures in the ancient world. Medea was one of the main characters in the epic *Argonautica* by Apollonius of Rhodes in the third century BCE. In that play she fell in love with Jason, the leader of the Argonauts, betrayed her own people and helped the Greeks obtain the Golden Fleece. Medea also used her maleficent powers to destroy the bronze monster, Talos, and she employed the power of the evil eye to work counter-magic at a distance. Later ages labeled her a witch, but she may be a minor goddess or the priestess of a goddess from a distant age. Ovid (43 BCE–18 CE) writes about her in a tragedy that is no longer extant and also in *Metamorphoses*. In Seneca's play, which may have been performed on stage, Medea is a professional witch, determined to harm the man whom she had loved but who had betrayed and abandoned her. She is possessed of frightening powers and even claims to be able to bring down the constellation of the snake. The play has been compared to a contemporary horror movie, and it helps to establish the archetypical witch figure. In this passage Medea invokes the powers of the underworld as she brews magical herbs in her cauldron.

Source: Seneca, *Medea* vv. 670–843 in Georg Luck (ed.), *Arcana Mundi* (Baltimore, 1985) pp. 86–89.

MEDEA'S OLD NURSE [*observing Medea*]: I am frightened, horrified. Something terrible is going to happen. It is amazing how her anger grows, inflames itself and renews its former strength. Often have I seen her mad, assailing the gods, pulling down the sky, but now Medea plans something more monstrous, yes, more monstrous than ever before. As soon as she hurried away, out of her mind, and entered her cabinet of horrors, she spread all her materials, even those she had long been afraid to use, and unfolded a host of terrors, secret, occult. She touched with her left hand magic utensil and invoked all the plagues which the hot sands of Libya produce and which the Taurus, covered with arctic snow, imprisons; she invoked every monstrosity on earth. Drawn by her magic incantations, a whole army of reptiles appears from their hiding places. A fierce dragon hauls its enormous body, darts its triple tongue, and looks around for victims to kill. It hears the magic song and stops and wraps its bloated, knotty rump in spirals around itself. Medea cries: "Small are the evils, weak the weapons that hell can produce: I shall claim my poison from heaven. It is time, high time, to carry out a most unusual scheme. I want the Snake that lies up there to come down here like a gigantic torrent. I want the two Bears – the big one, useful to Greek ships, and the small one, useful to Phoenician ships – to feel the Snake's enormous coils. Let the Snake-Keeper at long last relax the tight grips of his hands, and let the poison pour out. I want Python, who dared to challenge the Twins, to obey my song and appear! I want Hydra and all the snakes that Hercules killed to come back, renewed from their death. Leave Colchis and come here, watchful snake, put to sleep for the first time from my songs." After she had summoned up all kinds of snakes, she stirred together poisonous herbs: whatever impassable Eryx produces on its rocks; what the Caucasus, sprinkled with Prometheus' blood, grows on peaks covered with eternal snow; the poisons that the warlike Medes and the fast Parthians carry in their quivers; the poisons that the rich Arabs smear on their arrows; the juices that Suebian noblewomen gather in the Hyrcanian forest under a cold sky; whatever the earth sprouts in the spring, when birds build their nests, or later, when the numbing winter solstice has destroyed the beauty of the landscape and shackled everything with icy frost; every kind of plant that blooms with deadly flowers; every virulent juice in twisted roots that causes harm. All this she takes, Mount Athos in Thessaly has contributed some poisonous herbs, huge Pindus others; some tender leaves were cut on the peaks of Pangaeum with a bloody sickle; some grew near the Tigris, lord over deep currents; some near the Danube; some near the Hydaspes, which runs lukewarm water and carries many gems; some near the Baetis, which gives its name to a country and sluggishly joins the Hesperian Sea. This plant was cut as Phoebus started the day; that stalk was lopped off deep in the night; this crop was mown with a magic fingernail. She plucks the deadly herbs and squeezes out the poison of the snakes and mixes them with hideous birds: the heart of the night owl, which brings sorrow, and the vitals of hoarse screech owls, cut out alive. The mistress of crime sorts out other ingredients and arranges them: this one has the ravening power of fire, that one the paralyzing cold of icy frost. The words she speaks over her poisons are not less frightening. Listen: her frenzied step has sounded. She sings. The whole world trembles at her first words.

MEDEA: I pray to the silent crowd, to the gods of doom, the dark Chaos, the shadowy house of gloomy Dis, the caves of horrible Death circled by the banks of Tartarus. Shades, your torments have ceased; hurry to this new kind of wedding! The wheel that tortures Ixion's limbs must stop and let him touch the ground; Tantalus must drink undisturbed the water of Pirene. A heavier punishment should weigh on my husband's father-in-law alone. Let the slippery stone make Sisyphus roll backwards over the rocks. You, too, Danaids, whose wasted efforts are mocked by your pitchers full of holes, assemble! You are needed today.

Come now, star of nights! My offerings call you. Come, wearing your most sinister expression, threatening with all your faces.

For you have I loosened my hair from its band, according to the custom of my people. On bare feet have I wandered through remote groves and conjured water from dry clouds. I have pushed the seas down to the bottom. I have conquered the tides, and the Ocean has sent its heavy waves farther into the land. I have upset the cosmic laws, and the world has seen at the same time the sun and the stars. The bears have touched the sea, which was forbidden to them. I have changed the order of the seasons: my magic chant made the summer earth bloom, and compelled by me, Ceres saw a winter harvest. Phasis has turned its rushing streams back to its source, and the Danube, split into so many mouths, has checked its currents and become a sluggish river in all its beds. The waves have roared, the sea swelled madly, but there has been no wind. The framework of an ancient grove lost its shadows at the command of my voice. The day was over, yet Phoebus still stood in the middle of the sky. Moved by my magic songs, the Hyades are falling. Phoebe, it is time to present at your sacred rites.

For you my bloody hands are wreathing these garlands, each entwined with nine serpents; to you I present these limbs which rebellious Tiphys had when he shook the throne of Jupiter. This contains the blood of Nessus, the treacherous ferryman: he offered it as he died. These are the ashes left from the pyre on Mount Oeta: it drank the poisoned blood of Hercules. Here you see the torch of Althaea, the avengeress: she was a good sister, but a bad mother. These are the feathers that the Harpy left in her unapproachable lair after she had fled from Zetes. And finally you have the quill of the Stymphalian bird after it has been wounded by the arrows of Lerna.

Altars, you made a sound. The goddess is favorable. I can see how her approach moves my tripods.

I see the fast chariot of Trivia. It is not the chariot that she drives at night when her face is full and shining. It is the one that she drives when she stays closer to the earth, troubled by the threats of Thessalian witches, her face sad and pale. Yes! Out from your torch a gloomy, pallid light through the air! Frighten the peoples with a new kind of horror. Let precious Corinthian bronze gongs sound to help you, Dictynna! On the bloody turf I bring you a solemn offering. A torch snatched from the middle of a funeral pyre illuminates the night for you. For you I toss my head, bend my neck, speak my words. For you I have tied loosely, as is the custom at a funeral, a fillet round my flowing locks. For you I wave the branch of sorrow from the Stygian stream. For you I will bare my breasts and, like a Maenad, slash my arms with the sacrificial knife. Let my blood flow to the altar. My hand must learn to draw the sword, and I must learn to endure the sight of my own blood. There! I have cut myself and given my sacred blood.

If you resent the fact that I call on you too often in my prayers, please forgive me, daughter of Perses: the reason why I call on your bow again and again is always the same: Jason.

Poison now the robes of Creusa! As soon as she puts them on, let a hidden flame burn her marrow deep inside. Within this dark-golden box lurks an invisible fire. Prometheus gave it to me: he stole the fire from heaven and pays for this with his ever-growing liver. He taught me by his art to store magic powers. Hephaestus gave me fires covered by a thin layer of sulphur, and from my cousin Phaethon I received powerful shafts of lightning. I hold contributions from the middle part of Chimaera; I have flames that were snatched from the parched throat of the bull; those I mixed thoroughly with Medusa's gall, and I told them to preserve secretly their deadly effect.

Add your string to these poisons, Hecate, and preserve in my gift the seeds of fire that are in it! Let them deceive the sight and endure the touch; let the heat penetrate Creusa's heart and veins; let her limbs melt and her bones go up in smoke, and let the bride, her hair on fire, shine brighter than the wedding torches!

My prayers have been heard: three times has fearless Hecate barked, and she has sent out the fire of damnation from the torch that brings sorrow.

59

FERNANDO DE ROJAS: THE WITCH FIGURE IN THE RENAISSANCE, 1499

The Tragick-Comedy of Calisto and Melibea, written by the Spanish dramatist Fernando de Rojas, was first published in 1499, at a time when prosecutions for witchcraft in the Mediterranean world had begun but had not yet reached the intense levels of the late sixteenth century. De Rojas was a man of the Renaissance, steeped in classical culture, and his play was inspired to a large extent by his knowledge of witchcraft as depicted in Greek and Latin literature. The main protagonist in the play, the witch Celestina, is modelled upon that of Medea and Canidia, the witch figures in the work of Ovid, Horace, and Seneca. Celestina is a woman of ill repute and a professional who traffics in love magic and charms. As a sorcerer she has a clientele among prostitutes and other denizens of the urban Renaissance underworld. Many of the spells she uses are those described in classical texts, and she conjures up the classical gods, in imitation of Medea. Although Celestina derives from the literary classical world, she also had her counterparts in Spanish and Italian society at the beginning of the sixteenth century. De Rojas may have been drawing on his knowledge of these sorcerers, not just his classical learning, in writing the play. The play in turn contributed to the perpetuation of this image of the witch, and it is possible that some sorcerers modelled their own behavior upon that of Celestina.

Source: Fernando de Rojas, *The Tragick-Comedy of Calisto and Melibea*, trans. James Mabbe, 1631 (London, 1894), pp. 39–43, 76–77.

325

Act I

PARMENO, *servant of Calisto*: I shall tell you Sir, how I know her. It is a great while ago since my mother dwelt in her parish, who being entreated by this Celestina, gave me unto her to wait upon her, though now she knows me not, grown out perhaps of her rememberance, as well by reason of the short time I abode with her, as also through the alteration which age hath wrought upon me.

    CALISTO: What service didst thou do her?

    PARMENO: I went into the market place, and fetched her vitals; I waited on her in the streets, and supplied her wants in other the like services, as far as my poor sufficiency and slender strength was able to perform. So that though I continued but a little with her, yet I remember everything as fresh as if it were but yesterday, in so much that old age hath not been able to wear it out. This good honest whore, this grave matron, forsooth, had at the very end of the City, there where your tanners dwell, close by the waterside a lone house, somewhat far from neighbors, half of it fallen down, ill contrived, and worse furnished. Now, for to get her living, yee must understand, she had six several trades: she was a laundress, a perfumeress, a former of faces, a mender of cracked maidenheads, a bawd, and had some smatch of a witch. Her first trade was a cloak to all the rest; under color whereof, being withal a piece of a sempstress, many young wenches that were of your ordinary sort of servants came to her house to work: some on smocks, some on gorgets, and many other things; but not one of them that came thither but brought with her either bacon, wheat, flour, or a jar of wine, or some other the like provision, which they could conveniently steal from their mistress, and some other thefts of greater quality, making her house (for she was the receiver, and kept all things close) the rendezvous of all their roguery. She was a great friend to your students, noblemen's caterers, and pages. To these she sold the innocent blood of these poor miserable souls, who did easily adventure their virginities, drawn on by fair promises, and the restitution and reparation which she would make them of their lost maidenheads. . . . She professed herself a kind of physici'n, and fained that she had good skill in curing of little children. . . . One would cry, "Here mother" and another "There mother." "Look," says the third, where the old woman comes: "Yonder comes that old beldame so well known to all." . . . For the mending of lost maidenheads, some she help with little bladders, and other some she stitched up with the needle. She had in a little cabinet, or painted workbox, certain fine small needles, such as your glovers sew withal, and threads of the slenderest and smallest silk, rubbed over with wax. She also had roots hanging there of folia-plasm, fust-sanguinio, squill or sea-onion, and ground thistle. With these she did work wonders, and when the French ambassador came thither, she made sale of one of her wenches, three several times for a virgin.

    C: So she might a hundred as well.

P: Believe me (Sir), it is true as I tell you. Besides, out of charity forsooth, she relieved many orphans, and many straggling wenches, which recommended themselves unto her. In another partition she had her knacks for to help those that were lovesick, and to make them to be beloved again, and obtain their desires. And for this purpose, she had the bones that are bred in a stag's heart, the tongue of a viper, the heads of quails, the brains of an ass, the kalls of young colts when they are new foaled, the bearing cloth of a new-born babe, Barbary beans, a sey-compass, a horn-fish, the halter of a man that hath been hanged, ivy berries, the prickles of a hedgehog, the foot of a badger, fern seed, the stone of an eagle's nest, and a thousand other things. Many both men and women came unto her. Of some she would demand a piece of that bread where they had bit it; of others, some part of their apparel. Of some she would crave to have of their hair; others, she would draw characters in the palms of their hands with saffron; with othersome she would do the same with a kind of colour, which you call vermilion; to others she would give hearts made of wax and stuck full of broken needles; and many other the like things, made in clay, and some in lead, very fearful, and ghastly to behold. She would draw circles, portrait forth figures, and mumble many strange words to herself, having her eyes still fixed on the ground. But who is able to deliver unto you those things that she hath done? And all these were mere mockeries and lies.

Act II

CELESTINA: I conjure thee (thou sad god Pluto), lord of the infernal deep, emperor of the damned court, captain general and proud commander of the wicked spirits, Grand Signor of those sulphurous fires, which the flaming hills of Aetna flash forth in most fearful and most hideous manner; governor and supervisor both of the torments and tormentors of those sinful souls that lie howling in Phlegeton; prince and chief ruler of those three hellish furies, Tesiphone, Meghera, and Alecto; administrator of all the black things belonging to the kingdom of Stix and Dis, with all their pitchy lakes, infernal shades, and litigious chaos; maintainer of the flying harpies, with all the whole rabblement of frightful hydras. I Celestine, thy best known and most noted client, conjure thee by the virtue and force of these red letters, by the blood of this bird of the night wherewith they are charactered, by the power and weight of these names and signs which are contained in this paper, by the fell and bitter poison of those vipers, whence this oil was extracted, wherwith I anoint this clew of yarn, thou come presently without delay to obey my will, to envelop and wrap thyself therein, and there to abide and never depart thence, no, not the least moment of time, until that Melibea, with that prepared opportunity, which shall be offered unto her, shall buy it of me, and with it, in such sort be entangled and taken, that the more she shall behold it, the more may her heart be mollified, and the sooner wrought to yield unto my request: That thou will open her heart to my desire and wound her very soul with the love of Calisto; and in that extreme and violent manner, that despising and casting off all shame, she may discover herself unto me and reward both my message and my pains. Do this, and I am at thy command to do what thou will have me. But if thou do not it, thou shall forthwith have me thy capital foe and professed enemy. I shall strike with light thy sad and darksome dungeons; I shall cruelly accuse thy continual lyings and daily falsehoods. And lastly, with my charming words, and enchanting terms, I will chain and constrict thy most horrible name. Wherefore again and again; once, twice, and thrice, I conjure thee to fulfill my command. And so presuming on thy great power, I depart hence, that I may goe to her with my clew of yarn, wherein I verily believe I carry thyself enwrapped.

60

THOMAS MIDDLETON: THE WITCH IN ENGLISH DRAMA, 1613

Thomas Middleton wrote *The Witch* between 1613 and 1616, at a time when the theme of witchcraft had become increasingly popular on the London stage, especially in the plays of Shakespeare and the masques of Ben Jonson. Like those other dramatists, Middleton drew upon a wide variety of contemporary beliefs about witchcraft, most of which he found in literary sources. Many of the activities of witches that his characters engage in, such as flying through the air and meeting at nocturnal sabbaths, are based mainly on Continental demonology. Middleton in fact reveals little apparent concern for contemporary English witch beliefs. The play is set in Ravenna, and the chief witch in the play is named Hecate, after the witch of classical mythology. Hecate's powers resemble those of urban sorcerers who flourished in the Mediterranean region and who conformed to the archetype of Seneca's Medea and de Rojas's Celestina. Like those witches, Hecate specialized in love magic, and in the second scene of Act I she helps Sebastian, a soldier returning from the war, impede the sexual powers of his rival Antonio, who is married to the woman to whom he had been betrothed. Hecate's powers, however, were not restricted to love magic. She was capable of brewing all sorts of concoctions to perform *maleficia*, and in that respect she could just as easily have represented a typical English witch. One of the sources that Middleton drew upon was Reginald Scot's *Discoverie of Witchcraft* (1584), from which Middleton extracted names of demons, invocations, and the ingredients in a cauldron. Scot was highly skeptical of contemporary witch beliefs, especially those that flourished on the Continent, but Middleton reflected none of Scot's satire. As a dramatist he looked wherever he could for material that would have popular appeal. To this extent he was successful in familiarizing his literate audience with contemporary Continental witch beliefs.

Source: Thomas Middleton, *A Tragicomedy Called The Witch* in Peter
Corbin and Douglas Sedge (eds.), *Three Jacobean Witchcraft Plays*
(Manchester, 1986) pp. 92–96, 119–120.

Act I, Scene 2

[*Enter Stadlin wuith a brazen dish*]

STADLIN: Here's Stadlin and the dish.

HECATE: There, take this unbaptised brat [*giving the dead body of a baby*]
    Boil it well; preserve the fat.
    You know 'tis precious to transfer
    Our 'nointed flesh into the air,
    In moonlight nights o'er steeple tops
    Mountains and pine trees, that like pricks or stops
    Seem to our height; high towers and roofs of princes
    Like wrinkles in the earth. Whole provinces
    Appear to our sight then even leek
    A russet mole upon some lady's cheek,
    When hundred leagues in air we feast and sing,
    Dance, kiss and coll, use everything.
    What young man can we wish to pleasure us. But we enjoy him in an
        incubus?
    Thou knowst it, Stadlin?

S: Usually that's done.

H: Last night thou got'st the Mayor of Whelplie's son.
    I knew him by his black coat lined with yellow;
    I think thou'st spoiled the youth – he's but seventeen.
    I'll have him the next mounting. Away, in!
    Go feed the vessel for the second hour.

S: Where be the magical herbs?

H: They're down his throat;
    His mouth crammed full; his ears and nostrils stuffed.
    I thrust in eleoselinum lately,
    Aconitum, frondes populeus, and soot –
    You may see that, he looks so black i'th' mouth –
    Then sium, acarum vulgaro too,
    Pentaphyllon, the blood of a flitter-mouse
    Solanum somnificum et oleum.

S: Then there's all, Hecate?

H: Is the heart of wax stuck full of magic needles?

S: 'Tis done, Hecate

H: And is the farmer's picture and his wife's
    Laid down to th' fire yet?
    Stadlin. They're a roasting both too.

H: Good. [*Exit Stadlin*]
    Then their marrows are a-melting subtly
    And three months'sickness sucks up life in 'em.
    They denied me often flour, barm and milk,
    Goose grease and tar, when I ne'er hurt their charmings,
    Their brew locks, nor their batches, nor forspoke
    Any of their breedings. Now I'll be meet with 'em.
    Seven of their young pigs I have bewitched already
    Of the last litter, nine ducklings, thirteen goslings,
    And a hog fell lame last Sunday after evensong too;
    And mark how their sheep prosper, or what sop
    Each milch-kine give to th' pail. I'll send
    Those snakes shall milk 'em all beforehand.
    The dew-skirted dairy wenches shall stroke
    Dry dugs for this and go home cursing.
    I'll mar their syllabubs and frothy feastings
    Under cows' bellies with the parish youths.
    Where's Firestone? Our son, Firestone!
    [*Enter Firestone*]
FIRESTONE: Here am I, mother.
H: Take in this brazen dish full of dear ware. [*Gives dish*]
    Thou shalt have all when I die; and that will be
    Even just at twelve o'clock at night come three year.
F: And may you not have one o'clock in to th' dozen, mother?
H: No.
F: Your spirits are then more unconscionable than bakers; you'll have lived then, mother, six score year to the hundred, and methinks after six-score years the devil might give you a cast, for he's a fruiterer too, and has been from the beginning. The first apple that e'er was eaten came through his fingers. The costermonger's then, I hold to be the ancientest trade, though some would have the tailor pricked down before him.
H: Go and take heed you shed not by the way.
    The hour must have her potion, 'tis dear syrup;
    Each charmed drop is able to confound
    A family consisting of nineteen or one-and twenty feeder.
F: [*Aside*] Marry, here's stuff indeed!
    Dear syrup you call it? A little thing
    Would make me give you a dram on't in a posset.
    And cut you three years' shorter.
H: Thou'rt now
    About some villany.
F: Not I, forsooth.
    [*Aside*]. Truly, the devil's in her, I think.
    How one villain smells out another straight! There's no

knavery but is nosed like a dog and can smell out a dog's meaning. [*To Hecate*] Mother, I pray give me leave to ramble abroad tonight with the Nightmare, for I have a great mind to overlay a fat parson's daughter.

H: You're a kind son!
But 'tis the nature of you all, I see that.
You had rather hunt after strange women still
Than lie with your own mothers. Get thee gone;
Sweat they six ounces out about the vessel
And thou shalt play at midnight. The Nightmare
Shall call thee when it walks.

F: Thanks, most sweet mother. [*Exit*] . . .

SEBASTIAN: [*Aside*] Heaven knows with what unwillingness and hate
I enter this damned place; but such extremes
Of wrongs in lovefight 'gainst religious knowledge,
That were I led by this disease to deaths
As numberless as creatures that must die,
I could not shun the way. I know what 'tis
To pity madmen now; they're wretched things
That ever were created, if they be
Of woman's making and her faithless vows.
I fear they're now a-kising. What's o'clock?
'Tis now but supper-time, but night will come
And all new-married couples make short suppers.
[*To Hecate*] Whate'er thou art, I have no spare time to feare thee,
My horrors are so strong and great already
That thou seemst nothing. Up and laze not.
Had'st thou my business thou could'st ne'er sit so;
'Twould firk thee into air a thousand mile
Beyond thy ointments. I would I were read
So much in the black power as mine own griefs!
I'm in great need of help; wilt give me any?

H: Thy boldness takes me bravely. We're all sworn
To swear for such a spirit. See, I regard thee;
I rise and bid thee welcome. What's thy wish now?

S: O my heart swells with't! I must take breath first.

H: It's to confound some enemy on the seas?
It may be done tonight. Stadlin's within;
She raises all your sudden ruinous storms
That shipwreck barks and tears up growing oaks;
Flies over houses and takes *Anno Domini*
Out of a rich man's chimney – a sweet place for't!
He would be hanged ere he would set his own years there;
They must be chambered in a five-pound picture,
A green silk curtain drawn before the eyes on't –

His rotten diseased years! Or dost thou envy
The fat prosperity of any neighbour?
I'll call forth Hoppo, and her incantation
Can straight destroy the young of all his cattle,
Blast vineyards, orchards, meadows, or in one night
Transport his dung, hay, corn, by ricks, whole stacks
Into thine own ground.

S: This would come most richly now
To many a country grazier; but my envy
Lies not so low as cattle, corn or vines.
'Twill trouble your best powers to give me ease.

H: Is it to starve our generation?
To strike a barrenness in man or woman?

S: Ha!

H: Ha? Did you feel me there? I knew your grief.

S: Can there be such things done?

H: Are these the skins
Of serpents? These of snakes?

S: I see they are.

H: So sure into what house they are conveyed,
[*giving skins to Sebastian*]
Knit with these charmed and retentive knots,
Neither the man begets nor woman breeds;
No, nor performs the least desires of wedlock,
Being then a mutual duty. I could give thee
Chiroconita, adincadtida,
Archimadon, marmaritin, calicia,
Which I could sort to villainous barren ends;
But this leads the same way. More I could instance:
As the same needles thrust into their pillows
That sews and socks up dead men in their sheets;
A privy gristle of a man that hangs
After sunset – good, excellent! Yet all's there, sir.

S: You could not do a man that special kindness
To part 'em utterly now? Could you do that?

H: No, time must do't. We cannot disjoin wedlock.
'Tis of heaven's fastening. Well may we raise jars,
Jealousies, strifes and heart-burning disagreements,
Like a thick scurf o'er life, as did our master
Upon that patient miracle, but the work itself
Our power cannot disjoint.

S: I depart happy
In what I have then, being constrained to this.

[*Aside*] And grant, you greater powers that dispose men,
That I may never need this hag again.
H: I know he loves me not, nor there's no hope on't;
'Tis for the love of mischief I do this,
And that we're sworn to – the first oath we take. . . .

Act III, Scene 3

*Enter Hecate, {Stadlin, Hoppo and three other} witches and Firestone {carrying eggs,
herbs, etc.}*

HECATE: The moon's a gallant; see how brisk she rides.
S: Here's a rich evening, Hecate.
HECATE: Ay, is't not, wenches,
   To take a journey of five thousand miles.
HOPPO: Ours will be more tonight.
HECATE: O 'twill be precious!
   Heard you the owl yet?
S: Briefly in the copse
   As we came through now.
HECATE: 'Tis high time for us then.
S: There was a bat hung at my hips three times
   As we came through the woods and drank her fill.
   Old Puckle saw her.
   Hecate. You are fortunate still;
   The every screech-owl lights upon your shoulder
   And woos you like a pigeon. Are you finished?
   Have you ointments?
S: All.
HECATE: Prepare to flight then.
   I'll overtake you swiftly.

61

HANS WIERS-JENSSEN: A NORWEGIAN WITCHCRAFT DRAMA, 1917

The play *Anne Pedersdotter* by the Norwegian writer Hans Wiers-Jenssen is based on one of the most famous cases in the history of Norwegian witchcraft. Anne Pedersdotter, the wife of the Lutheran theologian Absolon Pedersen Beyer, was originally charged with witchcraft and tried in 1575, the year after her husband's death. The charges against her grew out of opposition in the city of Bergen to the efforts of the clergy to destroy the images of Roman Catholicism. Although acquitted, Anne's neighbors kept alive the accusations, which led to a second trial and her execution in 1590. The play, and a Danish film based upon it, *Day of Wrath* (1943), directed by Carl Theodore Dreyer, take numerous artistic liberties with the historical record. Among these is the introduction of a second witchcraft prosecution, that of Herlof's Marthe, who is identified as a friend and fellow witch of Anne's mother. The search for Herlof's Marthe and her execution form the centerpiece of the first two acts. In the third and fourth acts attention shifts to Anne and the process by which she incurs suspicion of witchcraft. In so doing the play explores the ways in which tensions within families, in particular relations between mothers and daughters-in-law, could result in witchcraft accusations. In the play Absolon's mother, Merete Beyer, had never approved of her son's second marriage to the young and beautiful Anne. When Anne falls in love with Martin, Absolon's son by his first marriage, the relationship between Anne and Merete deteriorates. When Absolon dies suddenly upon discovering that his wife and son are having an affair, Merete charges Anne with having caused Absolon's death by witchcraft. Second, the play explores the way in which Anne gradually comes to the realization that she is a witch. Having learned from her husband that her own mother had been accused of witchcraft and spared by Absolon's intervention, she begins to believe that she had acquired her mother's powers. Her success in winning Martin's affection and in wishing her husband's death reinforce this realization, leading her to confess at the end of the play.

Source: H. Wiers-Jenssen, *Anne Pedersdotter: A Drama in Four Acts*, English version by J. Masefield (Boston, 1917), pp. 9–17, 32–33, 39–42, 48–50, 89–93.

Act I, Scene 2

[Bente and Jorund are maid servants in Absolon Pedersson's house. David is the choirmaster. Masters Klaus (Claus in script), Laurentius, Johannes and Jorgen are priests. Anne is 25, Martin, son by former marriage, 25; Absolon 60, Merete, 80. Scene: Absolon Beyer's house.]

JORUND: (*rushing from the house, before Anne has finished speaking, wailing*). Lord have mercy on us! Satan is loose.

OTHERS: (*hurrying towards her*) What is it?

J: I went to the door to hear what all the noise and running meant. Then Kristense, the tanner's —

O: Yes? Well?

J: They're going to take a witch on the common.

O: Lord a mercy!

J: The guards are there, oh, and crowds. Khris said they could see the witch. She were out on the roof, calling the Devil. He may blast the guards with fire and brimstone. And us, too, God help us.

MERETE: (*folding up the clothes*) Shall we ever be rid of witches? We burnt six at the stake only two years back.

BENTE: God spare us. The Devil begets new ones. All round us.

M: Let's lock ourselves in and read the Bible. God'll guard us until Absolon comes back. [*David, Choirmaster enters, running into the garden from the back.*]

DAVID: The blessing of God on you. Is Master Absolon back yet?

M: The blessing of God on you, David Choirmaster. No, Master Absolon is still at the castle with Sir Rosenkrantz.

D: When'll he be back?

M: Not before six. And we women are alone here with the Devil of hell not a hundred yards away.

D: (*coming to chair C.*) Gird up thy loins, Merete Beyer. The Devil will be beaten in the fight. Oh, my feet have been swift upon the mountains! [*Bente comes to L right of seat. Merete to above seat. Bente pushes beer-jug respectfully towards him*]

D: Ah, no. Great things are happening here. Strange things to the glory of God. (*takes a deep draught of ale*) Thanks for God's good gifts. Well, they're arresting Herlofs–Marte.

ANNE: (*advancing*) Herlofs-Marte? I know Herlofs-Marte. She lived on the common. Mother and I lodged with her. [*The others look anxiously at her.*]

D: I advise you not to say much about that just now, Anne Pedersdotter. The city guard and half the town are surrounding that house on the common. They're going to take it by storm. She'll be tried for the witch she is.

B: So that's what it's come to Jesus, Mary, and all the saints! (*sits chair R*)

D: (*starts up*). Pah! Fie! Popish blasphemy. You may come to suffer in the cellar of the Council House for idolatrous talk like that.

B: Ah! God forgive me, David. It's old habits. I am Lutheran at heart, but the tongue is wickedly popish, without God bridles it.

M: What about Herlofs-Marte?

D: She was formally accused this morning by three honourable women. And their husbands were present and swore to what was said. God be praised and glorified that we can rid the town of them that hate Him.

M: Amen. Amen Praise Him and magnify Him for ever.

A: (*affected like the rest*). What has she done?

D: Well! What has she not done? Blasted Tolmer Piper's eldest; milked blood from Skriver's cow, and given a hard birth to two women in childbed. All because they wouldn't lend her butter, or something.

M: (*with great seriousness*) That the Devil can have such power!

D: And us with the true doctrines.

B: He goes about like a roaring lion (*folds her hands and sings with strong but trembling voice*)
"But he that doth exalt the Lord
The Lord shall save alway-a
The moon by night him shall not smite
Nor yet the sun by day-a."

M: (*before Bente has finished singing*). The Council lost no time.

D: No. Thank God (*rises*) that they are prompt, those gentlemen, when it concerns God's kingdom. When they had heard the evidence, they ordered the guards to Marte's house at the double.

B: Yes, You must pounce to catch fleas.

D: Ah! He might have taken her confession. That man of Glad always had great power with witches. Can't we send for him?

M: Disturb Sir Rosenkrantz at his prayers? No, David.

[*Distant cries and heavy blows. Cries have always been heard during the foregoing conversation. The speakers have then paused in their speeches, the tone of the whole being affected by their interruptions*]

D: (*turns and goes upstage*). There! Hark! They're storming her house.

J: *(at gate)*. And the witch. She's up by the skylight, calling fire out of the air.

B: *(up)* And a south wind blowing.

M: Is there no one there from the church to pray against her?

D: Only Lucas, the organist. But the priest of St Martin's has been sent for, and ought to be bringing Master Absolon. I mustn't wait longer. Tell master Absolon the instant he comes from the castle. I must run. God save us all! [*Goes out of the gate to L. and is heard going to the right*]

M: *(calling after him)* Wait David. I'm coming. We can see her taken. There'll be no fire out of the air. [*Throws a shawl around her*]

B: *(hastily folding up her work)* Beelzebub has power in the air.

M: Are you coming too, Anne Pedersdotter?

A: No. I'm not

B: No. Anne Pedersdotter has probably no great wish to see Herlofs-Marte caught.

A: Some one must be here to tell Absolon when he comes. [*Merete and Bente hasten out through the gate, and are heard going to the R*)

J: *(can only stand still from fear and curiosity)*. May I go too, Anne?

A: Yes, go.

J: Oh what times we live in! Well, thank God, she'll be burned to a cinder.
. . .

Scene 3

A: [*in a low voice*] Burn Herlofs-Marte! Burn Herlofs-Marte!

[*Herlofs-Marte appears in the passage between the house and outbuilding. A little women, old and wrinkled, about 78 years old. Face wild and white with terror; clothes in rags; hands bloody. She glides a few steps silently forward, and then speaks in a low voice.*]

MARTE: Anne!

A: *(turning, looks in silent horror at Marte, and says half aloud)* Herlofs-Marte!

M: *(at L. of wall; beckons her nearer)*. Help me, can you?

A: I don't know.

M: *(coming nearer)*You must. You can't drive me straight to death. Anne. Help me. You must!

A: How can I?

M: Oh, you can. It's only just to show me a place. When they broke in, I went straight through the cellar and hid in the passage. They passed close to me when I was in the ditch. Then I got through the hedge. Look at my hands, Anne. *(Stretching out her hands, from which blood is dripping)* Then I came here. I've been here ever since David came. God in heaven, have mercy! God sent them away. Anne, you must help me.

I helped your mother. It's only just to hide me till dark. Anne! Anne! They'll burn me on North Point if you don't.

A: Marte, I daren't. There's Absolon, my husband. Remember him.

M: For the sake of Christ's dear wounds, Anne. Hark! They're shouting again. Anne! It's death. It's death. They'll burn me if they catch me. (*Almost kneeling, she entreats catching hold of Anne's dress*)

A: Will you swear by God's blessed death and Word that you're not a witch?

M: Not a witch? (*A short pause; she glances from side to side in terror*). I don't know.

A: (*tearing herself free*) God save us all!

M: (*rising*) You hold your tongue. Do you know when the Devil may come to you? Do you know how he tempts? Do you know how he had your mother in your power? do you know how he may get you.

A: Get out of here, Marte. Or I'll call at the gate that you're here.

M: You wouldn't? Anne, you can't. You do it, and I'll accuse you. Your mother got off because you were her child. But you shall burn too, if you give me up. Oh, no, no, don't listen to me. I'm mad with terror. I'm old. I've palsy. If they torture and burn me! [*Sinks on steps, staring with chattering teeth, hands clasped round her knees.*]

A: (*slowly*) You said that my mother –

M: (*rousing herself*). No, no. Don't listen to me. I'm mad. Let me hide. Don't call them. For God's sake! For God's precious blood and wounds! Have mercy, Anne. You may need mercy some day.

A: (*turned away*) Hide, then. Get up the loft. It's dark there. They won't look here. God forgive my sin. But you were a true friend to my mother.

M: God reward you. . . . Satan blast the hounds for all they do to a poor old woman. I'm so afraid of death, Anne. I was by when they burned Maren Gjeit. . . .

Scene 7 [After Herlofs-Marte has been captured in Absolon's house]

MARTE (*rushes up to Absolon, and falls on knees*) Ah, Master Absolon, save me! For God's sake. For Christ's sake. I am innocent. I won't be burned. Anne! Beg for me. God blast you all! God blot you out! Absolon! Absolon! (*Absolon does not answer. Guard grabs her. Marte starts up hissing and spitting like a cat*). Fie! Get out. Out you drunken dog! Satan take you! The Devil take you all! (*In despair*) Let me go. I won't be tortured. I'll confess. You needn't torture me. Yes. Yes. I've been with Satan. Oh, let me go! I won't be tortured. I'll tell everything, everything. . . . You are all the Devil's. You're all the Devil's black dogs. I know you. Curse you, Absolon, for kicking me out. Curse you, Anne Pedersdotter. You'll come to what I've come to. Curse you all! . . .

Act II, Scene 1 [Absolon Beyer's house]

. . .

CLAUS: *(quickly)* And then the witch who was burnt to-day. Perhaps that was the most edifying of all. Only once before has God allowed me to see a witch being burnt. Yes, yes. It was a special providence that it happened now, with all the clergy in the town come up for the Synod.

LAURENTIUS: And then the Lord letting the rains stop directly the faggots were lit, that was beautiful. It showed that He was pleased.

JOHANNES: It went hard with the old beast.

L: So it did in Gospel days. When devils were cast out, they struggled. They didn't go easily.

C: Did she denounce anyone?

ABSOLON: *(painfully affected by the conversation)*. No, no one.

L: Not even when tortured?

A: She was not tortured, She confessed as soon as the pincers were shown her. She said she had know Satan and borne devils to him. But that she had been alone in it.

L: If she'd been tortured, she'd have accused her accomplices.

A: The Lord will reveal them in His good time.

L: Yes, but He employs men a means thereto. I heard from Peter Espikom, who is just back from Hamburg, that in Germany they've made some grand invention for torturing witches. There's a wheel with ropes for stretching their limbs. It brought out the truth almost every time.

C: That's very clever, now.

L: *(to Martin)* You must be able to tell us about that, Mr. Martin. You're just back from the Holy Roman Empire. But there you sit without a word.

A: He hasn't quite got over this morning, seeing Herlofs-Marte burnt.

L: That ought to have been a joy to a devout young priest.

A: Well, he rejoiced. But still, it is painful for flesh and blood. Isn't that so, *mi fili* ?

MARTIN: *(rising)* I'm not used to such things. I never before saw a person burnt. Though my heart rejoices over the defeat of Satan, her screams ring in my head.

L: It's the Devil tempting you. You must pray against it, Dr. Martin.

C: Have you really never seen a witch burnt? Can it be that faith is getting lukewarm in Denmark and Germany?

M: While I was in Copenhagen a lot of witches were burnt in Jutland. But none in Zealand. Nor were any burnt in Wittenberg while I was there. Some people there even doubt Satanic possession altogether.

L: Just what I expected. Those damned followers of Melanchthon. *(To Absolon)* You must look well after your son, Mr. Absolon, lest he bring in those false doctrines here.

A: Well, bodily possession is not the corner stone of Lutheran teaching.

L: Not the corner stone, no. But a battering ram that can destroy the whole building. You don't see it, Mr. Absolon, because you won't see it. You've fallen away from your first zeal. (*All excited*) Oh, yes, you have. Did you proceed properly against that Herlofs-Marte? Did you force confession from her? Did you bid her denounce any one while she was burning? No. You drowned her words with prayers and psalm-singing. And instead of rejoicing at God's victory, you grieved all day, as though you pitied the Devil because his prey was taken from him. [*All rise, much excited*]

A: Mind what you say, Master Lars. I don't want to quarrel. My zeal is well known.

J: (*stands; he is now quite drunk*) Master Lars, if you don't shut your dirty mouth, may the Devil fly away with you.

L: Shut my mouth? When I see God's agents halting? We should be like a storm beating down Satan under our feet, and here we are like hirelings that flee.

J: Shut up, Master Lars. Let Mr. Absolon alone. He'll manage God and Satan in his own way. Only shut your mouth.

L: It's not for you to talk, Mr. Johannes. You've got two or three in your parish ripe for burning. But in your heart you're a papist. That's one for you. . . .

Scene 3

ABSOLON: (*stands now near window*) You weren't in bed, Anne?

ANNE: (*with guarded smile*). No. You made such a noise, it was no good. You wished to say something to me, Absolon.

ABSOLON: My son and my wife, it'll seem strange, what I have to say, and that I say it. But it has tortured me long, and today worse than ever. I ask your foregiveness. I never cease to ask God's forgiveness . . . It is now seven years since – No, I'll begin at the beginning. Your father was an old friend of mine; we were students together. When he was ordained, he married your mother. But he died soon afterwards. Before you were born, your mother was left a poor widow. She found a good friend in her trouble with another widow, Marte Herlofs.

MERETE: Herlofs-Marte?

ABSOLON: Herlofs-Marte, yes. They lived for some years up in Selje, and then came here. Marte proposed the change. She had relations here; she thought they could help them. Times were bad in Bergen then. The two women only had what people gave them; I gave what I could. It wasn't much. I wasn't so well off in those days. If I had been – There! Well, seven years ago Bishop Schelderup told me privately that the word went about that the two widows kept themselves by Satan's help. They weren't accused, but the word was going about. Would I look into the case?

(*Anne and Martin listen with increasing horror*) I was zealous then. (*With a smile*) Even Mr. Laurentius would hardly have complained of me in those days. I went to Marte Herlofs and your mother, talked to them as God inspired me, and the two women confessed. Yes, (*goes over to L.*) they confessed. Without torture and to me alone. They had been there, hungry and forsaken. They had been starving on charity. So they fell into temptation and invoked the Devil. Marte had learned bad arts from the Finns. Satan came when they called. He came in the form of a young lord. They signed a compact with him for body and soul, and he taught them how to make a living.

ANNE: And my mother?

ABSOLON: I fear she was the stronger of the two. For she could summon the quick and the dead. She could bind the wills of others. She could strike people sick. She told me herself she could do all these things, and more. Satan gives his servants the power. I know what I *should* have done. God's word is plain. "Thou shalt not suffer a witch to live." But Satan came to me, too. Do you know what bait he used? He used you, Anne. You were barely sixteen then, but you were a woman. I had had no delight in women. Your mother (forgive me, my son) never moved me like that. But *you* were young and beautiful. I was not a young man. But my blood boiled in my veins each time I saw you. Had your mother been burnt, you would have gone the same road. The two women begged in the terror of death for pity. They swore on the Gospels to reform. I went to the Bishop and lied to him. I acted against my Christian duty and my oath as a priest. He knew I was zealous against God's enemies, and believed me. Then, six months later, your mother died. If she killed herself, or if Satan took her because she had cheated him, I don't know I do know that I could have saved her soul. I could have made her burning her salvation. (*A pause. He goes from window to table, leaning on the back of a chair at the end of table. He continues*) And now she burns in hell forever. My fault! But if I had burned her, you would never have been my wife. I've suffered tortures of conscience for this. Not so much of late years. No. My mind's been quieter. You made me happy, Anne. I thought that a sign that God had forgiven me. But it all came back when Herlofs-Marte was taken. All the old terror. For when she was in prison, she begged me to help her, as I helped your mother, and when I refused, she cursed me. While she stood at the stake today, she accused your mother as a witch and you as the witch's daughter. I drowned her words in loud praying and psalm-singing. The congregation did not hear them; but I heard them. I could bear it no longer after that. (*sinks down into chair to L. of table*) Now I've confessed. I've told my son that I've been false to my priestly oath. I've told my wife that I've thrust her mother's soul into hell. For ever! . . .

Act IV, Scene 4 [The choir in Bergen's Cathedral.]

MARTIN: (*at his father's bier*). He died suddenly – his heart failed – in the presence of his wife, Anne Pedersdotter. His mother, Merete Beyer, and I were with him before his eyes closed. I have said it once. I now repeat it. He died peacefully. And a third time. I ask you all to bear witness. He died peacefully. May he rest in peace. (*Comes down to L.C*)

BISHOPS ETC: Amen

MERETE: (*stops him with a wave of the hand*). Bishop Jens. You must wait a moment. I'll speak now. (*All rise in astonishment*) If the son won't defend the father, the mother shall. (*Under increasing horror on the part of all present, she goes to the bier, up the steps, and standing near the head, she says*) What Martin has said here is a lie. It's a lie. My son did not die peacefully. My dead son here was murdered. Murdered by a witch and the Devil's help. (*Horror and alarm. Solemnly*) I declare before heaven and earth that this dead man was cut off in the midst of his days. I say it once, twice, three times. He was murdered. Murdered by witchcraft. Murdered by his wife, Anne Pedersdotter. Murdered by her there. (*Bishop comes down L. of bier*) I ask life for life, death for death, blood for blood. Death and the stake for the witch there. [*sensation. The women go forward round her. All is now confusion. Martin has drawn near Anne. Anne seizes his right hand.*]

BISHOP: (*voice heard over the noise*). Peace in God's House.

MARTIN: Don't listen to her. She's mad. (*Continues with loud voice*) I will ask for Anne Pedersdotter. She had no part in Father's death.

B: (*coming forward*) You ought to be ashamed, Merete Beyer, for acting like this. Hate and sorrow have driven you mad. But to lie like that in God's House, by your own son's coffin!

MERETE: (*freeing herself from the women*) I'm not lying, Bishop Jens. God strike me dead if I am lying.

MARTIN: Don't listen to her. Is it likely that I'd leave my father unavenged in order to defend my stepmother?

MERETE: Yes, very likely. For you're in her power too. (*To the others*) I'll tell you why he defends her. She has bewitched him too. I denounce her as a witch. She killed the father. She has seduced the son. Let her deny it if she dare.

B: Lord, Lord!

MARTIN: (*draws back slowly, says in a low tone, in horror*). By witchcraft! by witchcraft!

ANNE: (*cries out*) Martin! [*Martin drawing near the foot of the bier. Anne stands quite alone on R. side; all have unconsciously drawn away from her*)

B: (*forward to L. side of bier*) Anne Pedersdotter. What do you say to this, Anne Pedersdotter?

A: (*looking not at the Bishop but at Martin; in a dull voice*). It – is – all a, lie. I haven't. No, I haven't.

343

B: This is an unusual case. We may go unusual ways. And expect a sign from God. You have heard the accusation, Anne Pedersdotter. The dead man is lying here in his coffin. All the power and dominion of this diocese is present here. I pronounce that you prove your guilt or innocence by the test of touching the dead. We will pray to God to bring us to the truth (*all indicate approval*). . . . Anne Pedersdotter, are you ready and willing to be tried by such a test.

ANNE: {*still looking at Martin*} Yes. . . .

ANNE: Absolon, my husband and master. I have – I have – you know it (*With her hand on the forehead of the corpse*). I bear witness. I bear witness. (*Sits and talks to the corpse, quite mad*) So you get your revenge, Absolon. Now I've no one. Yes. I murdered you by witchcraft. And I bewitched your son. I got your son into my power. By witchcraft – Now you know it. Now you know it.

INDEX